The Orvis
Fly-Tying
Guide

OTHER BOOKS BY TOM ROSENBAUER

The Orvis Fly-Fishing Guide
The Orvis Guide to Reading Trout Streams
The Orvis Streamside Guide to Approach and Presentation
The Orvis Streamside Guide to Leaders, Knots, and Tippets
The Orvis Streamside Guide to Trout Foods and Their Imitations
The Orvis Fly-Tying Manual
The Orvis Guide to Prospecting for Trout
Casting Illusions

The Orvis
Fly-Tying
Guide

TOM ROSENBAUER

ILLUSTRATIONS BY ROD WALINCHUS
TYING PHOTOGRAPHS BY TOM ROSENBAUER
FLY PATTERN PHOTOGRAPHS BY HENRY AMBROSE

THE LYONS PRESS
Guilford, CT
An Imprint of Globe Pequot Press

The Lyons Press is an imprint of The Globe Pequot Press.

10 9 8 7 6 5 4

Printed in the United States of America

ISBN 1-59228-121-4

Library of Congress Cataloging-in-Publication Data is available on file.

Contents

Acknowledgments

To all the fishing buddies who have generously shared ideas and patterns over the years: Luca Adelfio, Bill Bullock, Tony Biski, Sean Brillon, Monroe Coleman, Rick Eck, Kevin Gregory, Steve Herter, Jim Lepage, Del Mazza, Jim McFadyean, Galen Mercer, Dave Perkins, Perk Perkins, Ed Schroeder, John Shaner, Tony Stetzko, Tim Sullivan, Wayne Walts, and Rick Wollum. To the people in the business who have patiently answered my questions about patterns and materials: Otto Beck, Bill Black, Lee Christianson, Joe Dion, John Harder, John Juracek, Steve Kenerk, T.L. Lauerman, Craig Matthews, Tom McMillen, Angelo Musiani, Art Scheck, Tom Schmeucker, Kevin Sloan, Barry Unwin, Frank Vadala, and Tom Whiting. Special thanks to Carl Coleman for giving me a start in commercial tying and putting his trust in a fourteen-year-old tier. I still use many of the techniques that Carl taught me thirty years ago. Greg Nesbit was a wizard in getting digital images of materials from the Orvis catalog—and also one of my star fly-tying pupils. Pat Neuner spent many bleary-eyed nights assembling the Orvis pattern descriptions. Tom Miller of the Minolta Corporation helped me with much needed technical advice on the photography in this book. Thanks to the crew at Photographer's Eye for being friendly, helpful, and quick: Carol Accetta, Andy Fields, Mike Gadway, Martin Kalish, and Julie Watson. Finally, I couldn't ask for a warmer, more supportive, and understanding editor/publisher team: J. McCullough, Jay Cassell, Nick Lyons, and Tony Lyons.

Part I

The Basics

I'd be willing to bet my first attempt at fly tying 35 years ago was more pathetic than yours was or will be. I had sent away for a kit from Herter's. The only instructions in the kit were for the Fanwing Royal Coachman, one of the most difficult patterns to tie in the history of fly tying. I hacked my way through the fly and, having read somewhere that dry flies had to be dipped in some kind of potion to make them float, promptly dipped the entire fly in head cement. This should have made the fly immortal, like an ancient insect preserved in amber, but I was so frustrated I threw it in the trash.

I have tried to remember what those early days were like so you don't begin in the same fashion. I don't think I've ever forgotten what it's like to be faced with a pile of strange materials and unusual tools, because I've taught fly tying all my adult life—at Trout Unlimited meetings, impromptu neighborhood "tie and lie sessions," and to coworkers at Orvis on lunch hours. One of my favorite classes was during my college years at SUNY Syracuse Environmental Science and Forestry School, where I'd spend Saturday mornings at Vad's Sport Shop, earning beer and textbook money teaching classic Catskill dry flies to a bunch of guys three times my age.

There were only two or three fly-tying instruction books available when I first started tying. At any one time, they might all be out of print, and if the local library didn't have one you were out of luck. No Lyons Press to keep them in print. No Amazon.com to find them. Now there are hundreds of fly-tying books in print.

Why do we need another one? This is the one I would have wanted when I started. I don't believe there is a tying book available that goes into the basic detail that this one does, with every step examined and explained.

There is also not a pattern here that I don't carry in my fly box all the time. Most fly-tying books show patterns like winged wet flies, elegant patterns with historic pedigrees, but not flies that anglers carry in their boxes. Instead of winged wet flies, I have chosen a couple of emergers—which are far more effective at catching fish. In case you did not buy this book along with an Orvis kit, all the materials listed for these patterns can be found at any fly shop that carries basic fly-tying tools and materials. Many of them can even be found at craft shops or obtained from local hunters.

What about videos? I don't feel videos can replace books for fly tying, because they can't be used easily at the tying bench, plus they can't be taken into the bathroom. Still, they are an excellent supplement, and you'll learn techniques that may be difficult to understand in print. Most videos cover a group of patterns, and they're wonderful once you have mastered the basics and want to concentrate on a specific kind of fly. You can find videos on anything from tying with glue guns to tying flies for fishing over open-ocean wrecks. The last time I looked, Amazon.com offered 71 different titles.

This book is divided into three parts: The first part teaches you the basics of tying flies, assuming you have never faced a fly-tying vise and the only tying you've done is lacing your shoes or attaching a fly to your leader. The second part shows how to tie the most popular and effective flies available. The third part of the book offers the recipes for every fly in the 2001 Orvis Fishing catalog, plus many others. Once you master the basic patterns in Part II of this book, you can move on to the world of fly tying by finding the ones in the pattern index you want to try. I've marked each fly in the pattern index with a difficulty level so you don't get frustrated attempting patterns that are beyond your skill.

If you are just starting out, I recommend you read the chapters on Getting Started, Materials, and Hooks, Threads, and Cements. Then skim over all the step-by-step patterns so you see what's involved. Make a note on patterns you want to tie or things that aren't clear—another pattern might present the technique in a slightly different manner. Then start with one of the basic patterns, such as the Woolly Bugger, Bead Head Soft Hackle, or Clouser Minnow. Tie one pattern until you feel comfortable with the techniques; only then should you move on to another.

How fast should you progress, and how much time should you devote to tying? Some people pick up fly tying instantly, and others struggle. It has little to do with patience or finger dexterity. Del Mazza, perhaps one of the best dry-fly tiers I've ever met, has fingers like spare ribs and the patience of a Labrador retriever.

Your first flies will catch fish, because fish are far less picky about style than fishing buddies. Try to plan at least 30 minutes for each tying session. It might be 30 minutes a night, 30 minutes a week, or 30 minutes a month. These will be some of the most relaxing, therapeutic half-hours you'll ever spend, and they'll add a new dimension to your fishing. One of my greatest pleasures is to start a fishing trip with a small box of new patterns I've created, just waiting to be sampled by a rising trout. I hope my book will bring some of this satisfaction into your life.

CHAPTER 1

Getting Started

A Place To Park It

The ideal place to tie flies is a room of your own, an office or a spare bedroom, with plenty of shelf space for books and materials. Natural light is wonderful for fly tying, so having a big window either next to you or behind you is ideal. Make sure there is a door that can be closed tightly. Sharp dubbing needles and scissors are attractive to small children, and both cats and dogs seem to prefer chewing on expensive hackle capes to anything else in your possession. You should have a broad, clean worktable and a chair that lets you sit hunched over a vise without back pain.

Barring this ideal location, you can use a temporary spot on a kitchen or dining-room table if you are well organized and all of your gear is portable. In this case, get a pedestal vise and store all of your materials and tools in boxes that can be moved easily from one room to another.

There is no right height for a fly-tying vise. Some people like to look down on the fly and therefore set the vise so that it is at chest level. I like mine higher, about chin level, but you should experiment to find the height that works best for your vision problems, if any, and to prevent strain on your muscles. Adjusting the height is easier with a clamp vise, as the jaws can be moved up or down on the stem. If you have a pedestal vise, you'll have to find a table that brings the vise to a comfortable height. Your chair should be centered on the vise and it should be close enough to let you see every turn of thread in detail.

Storage

The best primary storage contains for all fly-tying materials are Ziploc bags. They are perfect for any material that contains feathers, skin, or hair, because carpet beetles and moths can't get inside sealed bags. Carpet beetles are the biggest destroyer of fly-tying materials. Learn to recognize these small insects by the red band in the middle of their bodies. If you find any in your fly-tying area, inspect anything that they might be into. If you find them (look also for sawdust-like material in the bottom of a bag, which means larvae have been chewing there), remove any bags that may have been infested. Throw them outside in the trash or open the bags, insert some mothballs or crystals, re-seal the bags tightly, and put them in the garage for a few months. Some of the materials may have been ruined already, but if the larvae hatch they might be killed before they get a chance to ruin anything else. The material might still have eggs in it, though, and should remain suspect as long as you keep it. Keeping the door to your tying room closed and making sure the window screens are tight will eliminate most problems before they start. However, sometimes bugs come in with materials you have purchased. Tanned hides don't have bugs, but other materials like wing quills and feathers and bucktails can't be tanned.

Even though bugs are not a problem with synthetics, tinsels, and other man-made materials, Ziploc bags still make great organizers because loose stuff stays put. Most materials already come in these bags; you can then put smaller bagged materials inside bigger bags.

Plastic shoe boxes with tight lids make perfect storage devices. They stack, are usually clear, and keep bugs and pets out of your stuff. Label each box on three sides and on top with a waterproof marker—even when the boxes are stacked in a closet, you'll always know where to find a white bucktail when you need it. Drawers made for nails and screws are great for storing hooks, threads, tinsels, and other man-made materials, but they are not so good for animal products because they aren't airtight. Big tackle boxes are also useful, but they don't stack.

There is a portable tying bench on the market that opens up into a big storage area underneath. If you tie in various rooms in your house, you can move your materials and work surface in a single trip.

Eventually you might want to invest in a big roll-top desk. These are great for fly tying, especially if you tie in an area that is used by the rest of the family. The top can be rolled down to keep your messy work area away from prying hands and paws, and you can stop in the middle of a bunch of flies and walk away without worrying.

Lighting

You need a lot of light to tie flies, and the older you get the more light you need. Trust me—strong lighting makes a huge difference in the quality of your flies. The best indoor setup is to have natural light from a window coming from one side and light from a strong lamp on the other. Of course this only works during the day, and you will probably do a lot of your tying in the evening.

Your working light should come from overhead, but be angled slightly so the shadow from your hands working on the fly does not fall directly onto the hook. The best lights available are ones with special bulbs that simulate the natural spectrum. You will be able to see the true outdoor colors of your flies, and the lights are easier on your eyes. They are also supposed to improve your mood and combat Seasonal Affective Disorder—not uncommon when you're tying flies in the middle of February and get a nasty case of spring fever. You can buy lights with adjustable necks from fly shops and catalogs.

The next best light is a draftsman's lamp that combines a fluorescent tube with an incandescent bulb. These also provide a pretty close approximation of the natural spectrum.

Cheaper but not as good are high-intensity desk lamps. They don't give you the full spectrum of light, but can be focused on the fly to give you good visibility.

Whatever lamp you buy, consider portability. If you don't have a fly-tying room,

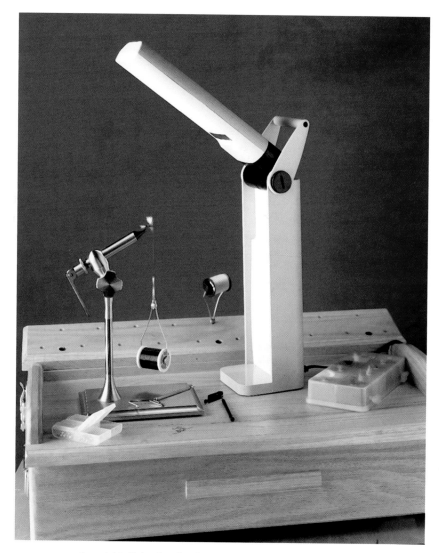

A portable light that duplicates the spectrum of natural light.

chances are the light where you tie won't be right. And if you travel with your kit, count on motel rooms to have the worst fly-tying light imaginable.

Magnification

About ten years ago, the quality of my flies started slipping and I figured I had lost my touch or my concentration. I didn't realize I was losing my near vision with age, and it took me a couple of years to figure it out, because I could read just fine. Fly tying requires top-notch close focusing, and if you can't manage naturally you'll need mechanical aids.

If you are under thirty-five years old you can probably skip this section. But for most of us, magnification of some type is as critical as good light. Even if you wear bifocals, the magnifiers in your glasses were designed for reading, not for attaching a Size 24 hackle to a light-wire hook with 10/0 thread. The maximum magnification you can get in standard reading glasses is about three diopters. Going to glasses with a four- or even five-diopter magnification improves the quality of your flies and lowers the frustration level.

You can get half-glasses in this range in some fly shops and catalogs. You can also buy clip-on magnifiers that attach to regular prescription glasses. One of the best devices for improving your close-up vision is a visor that has magnifiers you can flip out of the way when not needed. The one I like has two levels of flip-down magnification plus a loupe for very close work. It even has tiny flashlights on each side of the head for directing a portable light source.

You may also see big magnifying loupes mounted on a flexible gooseneck. Adjusting to these can be difficult, though, and they tend to get in the way when you're winding materials around the hook.

There is another answer for those of you who are extremely nearsighted. I have been cursed with poor vision from birth, and can barely negotiate my own living room without glasses or contact lenses. However, years ago I heard someone with the same vision problem talk about being blessed for fly tying. People who are nearsighted can focus at a very close distance, and this guy said he could tie the most incredible flies by taking off his contacts or glasses. I tried it. Without corrective lenses I focus at between three and four inches, like having built-in magnifiers. I don't tie like this in public because it looks pretty stupid, but when I'm home alone it looks like I am kissing an Elk Hair Caddis.

These flip-down magnifying visors offer three levels of magnification

Clamping the Hook

For most patterns, you should place the hook in the vise by clamping it at the bottom of the bend. This gives you more working room. With a spring-tension vise, merely pull on the clamp until the jaws open up enough to accept the hook. Release the clamp and the hook will be secure. With a screw-adjustment vise, open the jaws enough to accept the hook and tighten the knurled knob firmly until it is hand-tight. With a cam-operated vise, it's a little trickier. Somewhere on the vise, either a knurled knob or a set screw on the stem pre-adjusts the jaw opening. With the cam lever up, open the jaws enough to about one and a half times the diameter of the hook wire, and then depress the cam lever. The cam should move to a fully closed position with some resistance and not snap back. If it won't close fully under hand pressure, remove the hook and open the jaws a small amount. If the cam closes fully but the hook wiggles up and down in the vise when you pull on it, remove the hook and tighten the jaws a hair. A well-designed vise will hold a hook so well that you can bend the hook without moving it.

It's important to place the hook properly in the jaws. If the hook is too far back into the jaws, you will have trouble closing them, and the jaws can even snap under pressure. If the hook is too close to the narrow end of the jaws it can be shot out of the jaws like a bullet, with dangerous consequences. With most vises, the hook should be set about one quarter inch into the jaws for hooks bigger than Size 6 and half that for hooks down to Size 16. For the smallest hooks, it's safe to place them almost to the end of the jaws, and you'll get more working room.

Threading the Bobbin

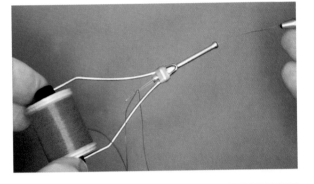

1. Run a bobbin threader through the tube until the wire loop pokes out of the end of the tube closest to the spool of thread. If the thread is frayed, snip it clean with scissors so it is easier the thread. Pull about six inches of thread from the spool and poke the end through the bobbin-threader loop.

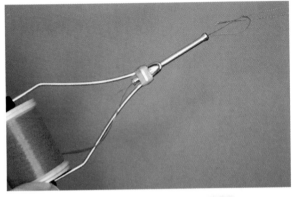

2. Pull the bobbin threader back through the tube. If your bobbin tube is not coated with wax, you can also just poke the thread into the tube and suck it back through.

Check the tension on the legs of the bobbin. You should be able to feed thread from the spool by just pulling on the bobbin as you wind around the hook. It should be tight enough to provide moderate tension, but not so much that you twist materials around to the far side of the hook.

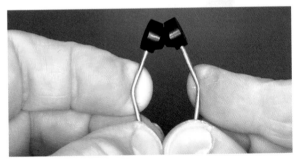

3. If the tension is too loose, remove the thread spool from the bobbin and bend the legs of the bobbin inward.

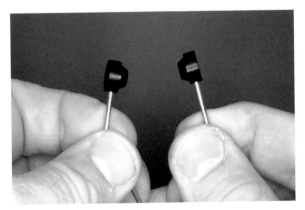

4. If it's too tight, spread the legs.

Attaching Thread to a Hook

1. Assuming you are right handed, pull six inches of thread from the bobbin and cross the thread in front of the near side of the hook, holding the bobbin in your right hand above the hook and holding the tag end of the thread in your left hand. Bring the bobbin over the top of the hook and around the far side to the bottom of the hook.

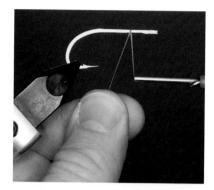

2. By pushing the bobbin to the left and the thread in your left hand to the right, wind the thread from the bobbin one wrap over the tag end of the thread.

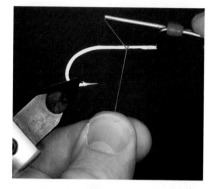

3. Make four more wraps over the tag end of the thread. Keep pushing your left hand to the right and your right hand to the left. Keep tension on both ends and work the thread coming from the bobbin to the left with each turn of thread. You should now be able to release the loose thread in your left hand and put pressure on the thread coming from the bobbin without the thread slipping off the hook. If it slips, start over with more tension and make a few more wraps.

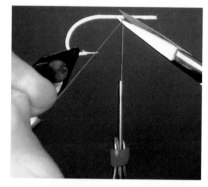

4. Using the loose thread and the shank of the hook as a guide, snip the loose end of the thread close to the hook. If you use both of these as guides, you won't accidentally cut the thread going to the bobbin. Pull on the bobbin enough to feed thread from the spool. The thread should be secure and not unwind or spin around the hook. If it does, unwrap and start again.

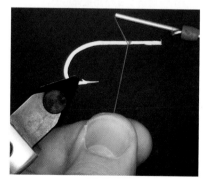

Winding the Thread

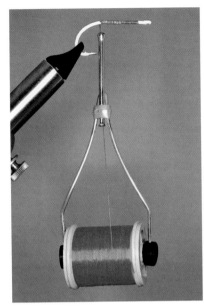

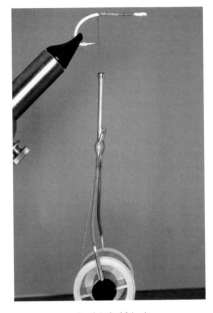

For most operations, this bobbin is too far from the hook, and you'll lose control.

This bobbin is too close to the hook. The tube will get caught against the hook shank.

For most work, this bobbin is the correct distance from the hook.

You should always wind away from you, as you did when starting the thread. Experiment with winding thread along the hook shank. Cradle the bobbin in your right hand, with your index finger just below the tube and your thumb on the spool. The bobbin tube merely rotates around the shank as you wind. For almost all tying, you should keep about one inch of distance between the end of the bobbin tube and the hook. When the tube gets too close, spin the spool with your thumb to release more thread. If you have to back up, just wind thread back onto the spool by rolling your thumb in the opposite direction. If the bobbin tube is too close to the hook, you'll have trouble maneuvering the bobbin; if it's too far away, you'll lose control.

When you get close to the point of the hook, you'll have to weave in and out to keep the thread from catching on the point and getting nicked. Even though you are weaving, still guide the thread in one direction only—either toward or away from the bend.

Thread Tension

Every turn of thread should be made under tension. Think about each turn as you make

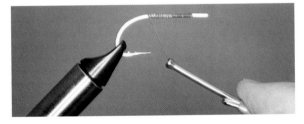

Weave the thread away from the hook point when winding close to the bend.

it. Haphazard winds make sloppy flies that fall apart. When you are advancing the thread from one part of the shank to another, you should be pulling at about half the breaking strength of the thread. When tying in materials, you may need to put almost eighty percent of the breaking strength into your winds. You get extra tension by locking your thumb on the spool.

A great exercise is to attach the thread to a hook, make a few winds, and pull on the bobbin, locking the spool with your thumb, until the thread breaks. Clean the thread off the hook and try it again. After repeating this a few times you'll know how much tension you can use.

Twisting and Flattening Thread

Most fly-tying thread comes wrapped around the spool with a moderate twist. To be honest with you, for most tying I never worry about the twist in the thread, perhaps because I use the finest thread I can get away with. However, the twists in the thread can be manipulated for certain steps.

When you don't want any bulk on the hook shank, such as when binding down materials that will be covered by tinsel or floss, you can unwind or flatten the thread by giving your bobbin a good counterclockwise spin (looking down on the bobbin from above). You'll see the twists go out of the thread and it will flatten close to the hook shank. Flatten thread for smooth underbodies, for binding down bulky materials, and for a smooth head on a streamer or saltwater fly. You may have to untwist thread in several steps if you are winding over a large hook.

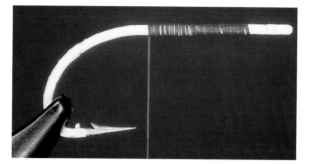

The thread at the front of this hook (closest to the eye) has been flattened. It does not add as much bulk to the shank. The thread wraps closest to the bend have been twisted, which gives more precise placement of materials.

Twisted thread adds bulk and gives you very precise placement of materials. Spin the bobbin in a clockwise direction (as viewed from above) until the thread twists into a tiny rope. Use twisted thread for building up bulk when raising dry-fly wings upright, when tying in loose materials like hair, or when placing tails at the bend of the hook.

Attaching Materials to the Hook

Attaching materials to the hook requires precise tension. More than anything else, thread tension distinguishes an experienced from an advanced tier, and like all things that are worth the trouble, it takes practice. You may watch a professional tier wind around the hook so fast that the bobbin blurs, but you can bet that each turn of thread he or she is taking has carefully controlled tension.

Almost all materials are attached to the upper side of the hook shank, so most techniques work to force the material to stay on top of the hook. This is not easy when your thread is rolling around to the far side. Don't ever just "tie something to the hook." It will end up everyplace except where you want it.

The Finger on Far Side

This technique is the easiest. It is used for materials that are not stiff and do not consist of a loose bundle of material. Tying yarn, chenille, floss, tinsel, and other body materials to the hook are typical uses for this technique.

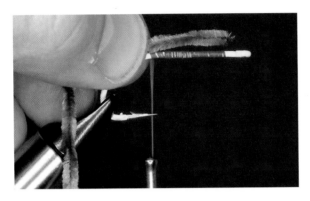

1. Start by placing the material you want to attach directly on top of the shank, or perhaps just slightly on the near upper side. Both ends of the material should lie parallel to the shank. Your thumb and forefinger should be holding the material right at the tie-in point, with your forefinger rolled slightly to the far side of the hook.

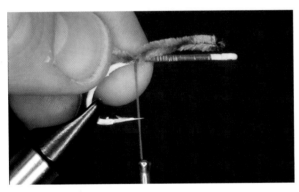

2. Loosen your thumb and forefinger and bring a loose loop of thread over the top of the material and around the hook. When the bobbin is below the hook, pull straight down while pinching your forefinger to the far side of the hook. Loosen up tension slightly and repeat the process three times, putting more tension on each successive wrap. In general, when attaching materials, you apply little tension on three-quarters of each wrap and only apply firm tension in one direction. For placing materials on top of the hook, the normal scenario, pressure can be applied either straight up or down. When you want materials to lie along either side of the shank, as when making split tails, pressure horizontally.

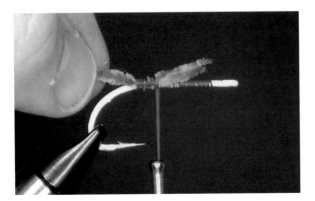

3. After three wraps in the same spot, advance the thread along the shank of the hook, always working away from the tie-in point. If you wrap back over the tie-in point, you add sloppy bulk and take the chance of moving the material you so carefully placed on top of the hook. After the initial wraps, you should not put any turn of thread directly on top of another. This is a critical process in fly tying, and one of the most difficult concepts for beginners to grasp.

The Forty-five-Degree Roll

This is the best way to attach stiffer materials like hackle stems, tails, and synthetic materials such as vinyl ribbing.

1. Start with the material on top of the hook shank, with the material to be bound in at a 45-degree horizontal angle. The end of the material to be bound under should be pointing toward you and to the right. The end of the material that will not be bound under should face away from you.

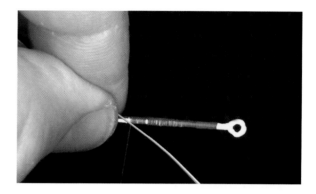

2. Bring the thread loosely over the top of the material, gradually rotating it so that it is parallel to the shank of the hook. Put some moderate tension on the material in a downward direction after the bobbin is under the hook.

3. In subsequent turns, advance the thread toward the right with each wrap. Unlike the last method, no wraps should overlap so the foundation formed by the bound-in material is very smooth.

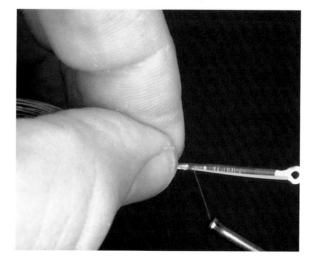

The Pinch

This is the best way to attach materials that consist of a bundle of fibers—hair, feather fibers, or wing quills.

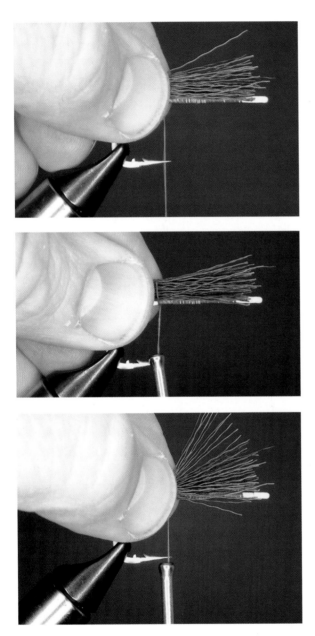

1. Place the material directly on top of the shank, pinching it with the tips of your thumb and forefinger directly over the tie-in spot. It's usually best to spin the thread into a tight rope for the first part of this method, to ensure that you get precise placement of the thread.

2. Rock your thumb and forefinger slightly so that pressure is on the first knuckle. This opens up a spot over the tie-in place but still keeps the material in place. Keep pressure on the sides of the hook shank.

3. Take one loose turn of thread over the tie-in spot, and work the thread back into the space between your thumb and forefinger. Bring the thread all the way around the hook to a point underneath the tie-in spot. Rock your fingers back over the tie-in spot so that the thread you have just wound is covered up and pinched between your fingertips. Pinch the thread and the material together, keeping pressure on the sides of the shank. Pull the thread straight down with firm tension, about 80 percent of its breaking strength. You can also experiment with bringing the thread over the top of the material, under the hook, and back up again, tightening with an upward instead of downward pull. Don't tighten horizontally unless you want the material bound to the sides of the shank.

Open up your fingers and take another wrap, pulling straight down in the same manner. Repeat once or twice more for a total of three to four wraps. Ensure that the material has not rolled to the far side. If it has, try to roll it back in place with your fingers, or unwrap and start over.

Now untwist the thread and bind the butts of the material under with smooth wraps, moving away from the part of the material that you do not want bound to the hook. If you have to start over, it's best to cut a new piece or bundle of material, as you will have already put a permanent crimp in the first clump.

The Gravity Drop with Upward Pull

This method is mainly used to attach wide, flat, delicate materials on top of the hook: wing cases and shellbacks on nymphs, and grasshopper and caddis quill wings. It keeps them flat on top of the hook without crushing the fibers together.

1. Place the flat material directly on top of the shank. Push your index finger down on the material at the tie-in point.

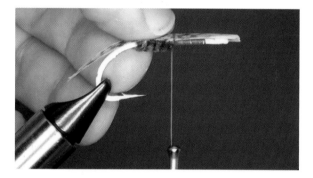

2. Rock back slightly on your index finger and place a loose loop of thread over the material. Bring the bobbin around and back down below the shank, and just let it drop of its own accord while pushing your index finger down at the tie-in point. Make another wrap in the same fashion. Make a third wrap, then pull the bobbin straight up above the tie-in point.

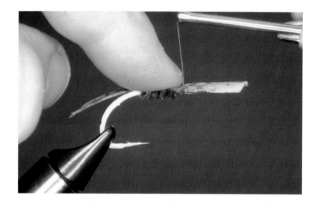

3. (Top view). Start advancing the thread down over the part of the material you will be binding under, using an upward pull for the next couple of turns and then returning to a standard downward pull as you get farther away from the tie-in point.

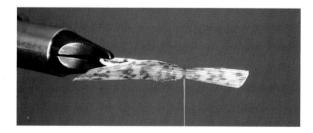

Winding Materials and Tying Off

Winding materials around a hook comes almost instinctively, and I'm always surprised how quickly most beginners grasp the concept of switching the material from one hand to the other. In contrast, many people have trouble tying off a material under the thread; instead, they merely wrap thread up against the material to be secured rather than crossing it with the thread. Here are the basics:

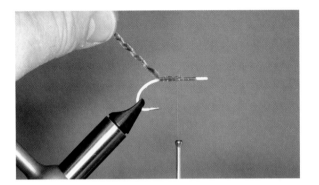

1. Begin by holding the material to be wrapped with your right hand. Wind it away from you, around the back side of the shank.

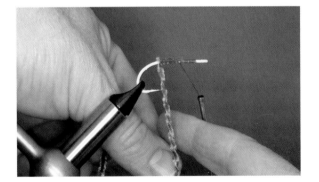

2. Underneath the hook, switch the material to your left hand while your right hand passes around the bobbin. Otherwise, you'll be knocking the bobbin out of control with every revolution.

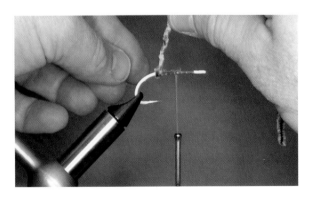

3. Switch back quickly to your right hand and make another three-quarters of a wrap before using the left hand again.

4. After you have made enough wraps and want to secure the material to the hook, hold the material above the hook with your right hand.

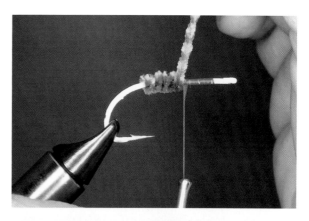

5. Use your left hand to push the bobbin over the top of the hook, making sure you cross over the material to be bound under.

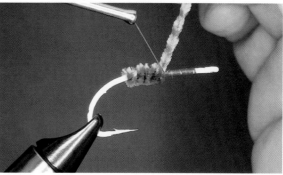

6. After the bobbin is three-quarters of the way around the shank, release it and let it fall under the shank so it hangs suspended by its weight. Now bring your left hand back to the near side to put downward pressure on the bobbin to help secure the material. Repeat the process at least three times or until the material is secure.

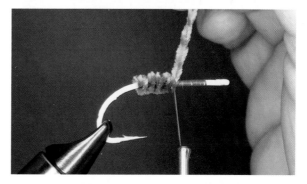

7. Let the bobbin hang below the shank and trim the material above the shank. This keeps you from accidentally cutting the thread.

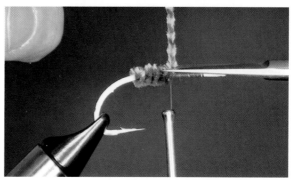

The Whip Finish

Half hitches are useful on occasion, both in the middle of a pattern if you have to remove the hook from the vise to trim a hair body, or at the end of a fly when finishing the head. But I don't recommend them. You can just as easily whip finish in the middle of a fly as you can tie half hitches, and a whip finish is neater and more secure.

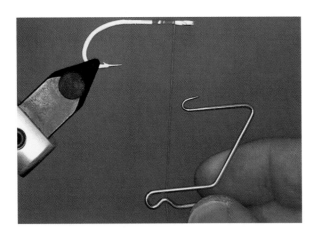

1. Start with three inches of thread between the hook and bobbin. Hold the whip-finish tool in your right hand with your thumb on the near side of the handle, the lower loop of wire (the one with the notch) off to the left, and the open end of the hook at the top, pointing to the right. Brace your index finger against the far side of the open loop, and brace your last three fingers on the far side of the handle. Hold the tool parallel to the thread, and raise the bobbin to a horizontal position, pressing the notch of the lower loop against the thread. Do not let the tool rotate.

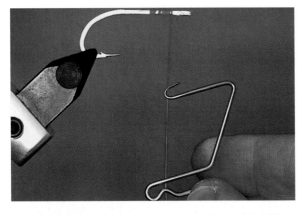

2. Catch the thread in the hook at the top by swiveling the top of the tool slightly to the left and then back. Keep tension on the bobbin so the thread does not slip out of the lower notch. Keep your fingers in place so the tool does not rotate.

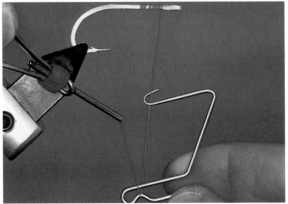

3. Move the bobbin up and toward the hook while releasing your forefinger. The upper end of the tool will rotate and flip sides. The most common problem at this point is keeping the thread securely on the hook and in the notch. If you wait until the bobbin is higher than the tool to release your forefinger, you can keep better control.

4. Keep moving the bobbin up and toward the hook while pulling the handle toward you.

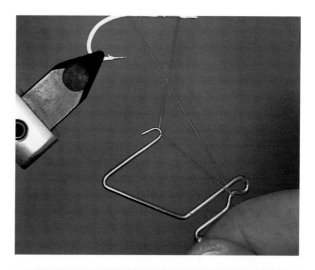

5. Bring the tool above the hook while letting it rotate freely. You'll notice there is now a place where the thread crosses itself on the far side, making a triangle.

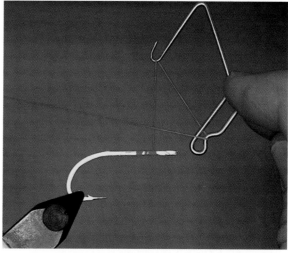

6. Move the lower left point of the triangle down to the tie-in point by keeping the tool stationary and moving the bobbin down and parallel to the hook shank. The point of the triangle should now be touching the fly at the point you want your whip finish to be placed.

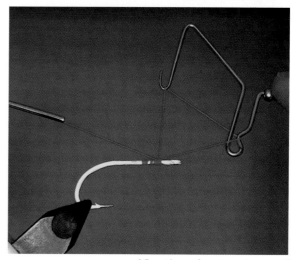

(Continued on next spread)

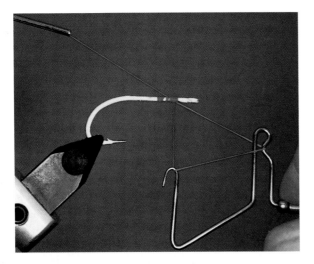

7. Hold the bobbin steady and rotate the tool smoothly around the eye of the hook. Make sure you clear the eye as the thread goes around. Repeat for five complete revolutions. Finish your last wrap under the hook.

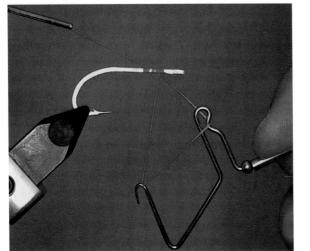

8. Push the tool down and to the left while tilting the handle up.

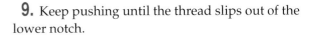

9. Keep pushing until the thread slips out of the lower notch.

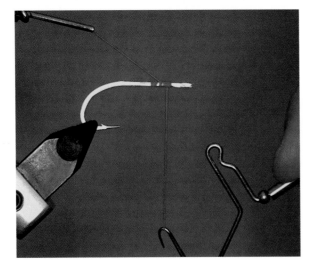

10. Pull up with the bobbin. Follow the thread up with the hook of the whip-finish tool.

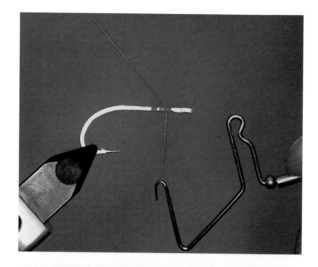

11. Keep pulling until the tool's hook is trapped against the shank.

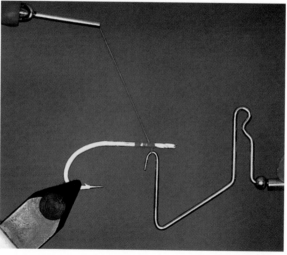

12. Slip the hook out of the loop and give a couple of short, firm pulls on your bobbin to secure the knot. Trim the thread carefully and your whip finish is complete.

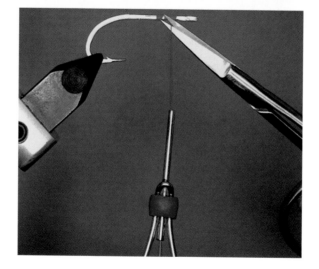

What to Do if the Thread Breaks

Breaking thread in the middle of a fly, or cutting it on the hook point, is part of the game.

Everybody does it. It's wise to have a pair of hackle pliers within reach even if you aren't winding hackle, because they're an important part of reattaching thread.

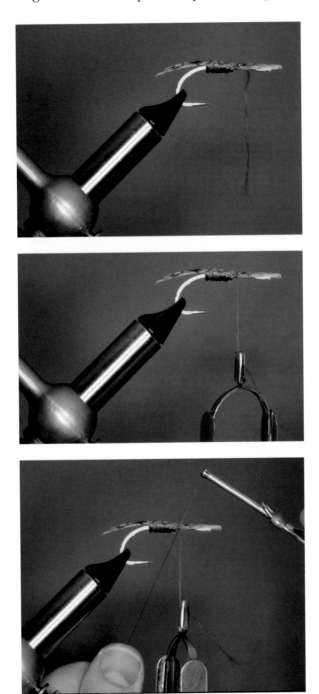

1. If pre-waxed thread breaks, it won't unwind too fast, so you have time to react.

2. Catch the loose end of thread still attached to the fly, clamp a pair of hackle pliers to it, and let the pliers hang below the hook just like a bobbin. The weight of the hackle pliers will keep the thread in place while you get your bobbin re-threaded if necessary, as the thread often slips out of the bobbin tube when it breaks.

3. Re-thread your bobbin if necessary. Pull six inches of thread from the bobbin tube. Push the hackle pliers slightly to one side and start the new thread right on top of the broken thread, as if you were beginning on a bare shank.

4. Wrap the thread over itself five times. It should now be secure.

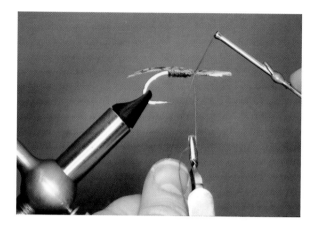

5. Pull both the broken thread and the tag end of the new wrap together on top of the shank. Carefully trim both. It's a good idea to put a small drop of head cement at this point before you continue the fly. You're back in business.

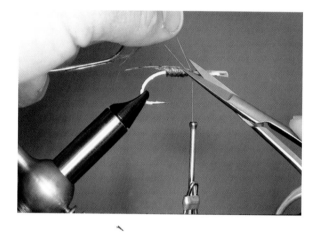

CHAPTER 2

Tools

It's possible to tie a fly without tools. It is also possible to ride a bicycle from Maine to California or climb Mount Everest without oxygen. I wouldn't advise taking on any of these for fun. I once tied a bunch of hairwing salmon flies in a dingy Nova Scotia motel room without a vise or bobbin. I held the hook in my left hand and manipulated materials with the thumb and forefinger of my right hand, while the other three fingers kept tension on the thread. The flies looked terrible and didn't catch any salmon. Good tools are not very expensive, and most will last for decades.

Vise

The vise holds the hook securely so that you can use both hands to manipulate thread and materials. Some will hold everything from a Size 28 midge to a Size 4/0 tarpon hook. Others specialize in either large or small hooks; some have removable jaws for different size ranges of hooks. Most advertising literature will tell you what size range a vise holds, but if it doesn't, assume the vise will hold at least Sizes 4 through 20 hooks, which is the range of most trout flies.

Jaw Systems

The most common fly-tying vises use a lever-and-cam system, whereby depressing a lever jams the jaws together around the hook. They all have adjustments so you can change the opening between the jaws and vary the pressure applied when the cam is engaged. You should adjust the jaws so that when the cam is fully engaged the hook is held so firmly that it will bend before it will move in the jaws. If the hook slides up and down in the jaws, open the cam, tighten the jaws slightly, and try again. If you have tightened the jaws so much that you have to force the cam, open the space between the jaws slightly. Forcing jaws, especially over a big saltwater hook, can snap them.

Screw-tightened jaws are also available. With these, you simply tighten a big knob on the end of the jaws until it is hand-tight and the hook is held securely. The disadvantage with this type of vise is that you have to tighten and loosen the screw every time you change hooks, even if they are all the same size.

A third vise design uses an ingenious spring clamp that needs no adjustment, ever. You pull a lever to open the jaws against the spring tension enough to place the hook between the jaws, and when you release the lever the jaws spring closed around the hook. This vise is fast when tying lots of flies in different sizes, and is popular with commercial tiers.

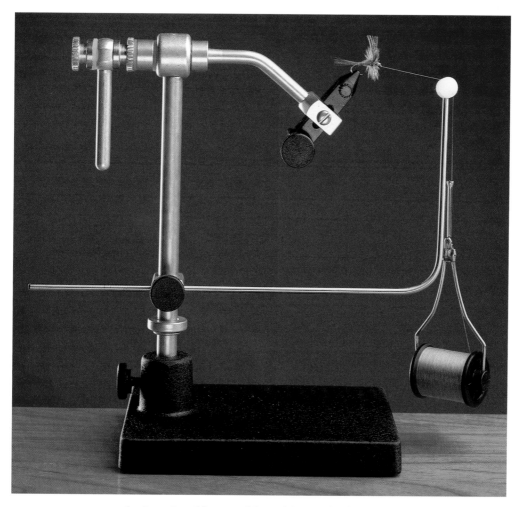

A rotary vise with screw-tightened jaws and pedestal base.

Clamp or Pedestal?

Vises must be secured to a table or other firm surface. One travel vise is built onto a metal ring that goes around a couple of fingers, allowing you to tie anywhere. Another actually comes with a special clamp for attachment to a car steering wheel. Neither of these is particularly handy, but if you are about to start on your coast-to-coast bicycle trip. . . .

Most vises are made to attach to a table with either a C-clamp or a movable but weighty pedestal. Many vise designs can be attached either way, and you can usually buy the vise with one type of attachment and purchase the other later. C-clamps are very sturdy and are great if you tie fast or if you're tying a lot of big saltwater flies or are working with deer hair where a lot of pressure is put on the fly. However, if not used carefully, they can mar the surface of a nice dining room table, and it is sometimes difficult to find a table with the right thickness at the

A vise with a spring-clamp jaw system.

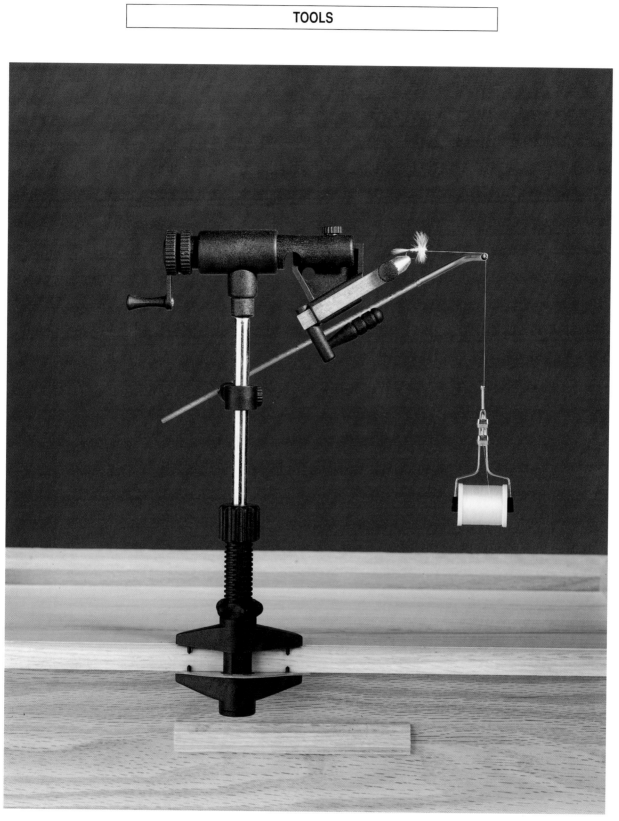

A cam-operated rotary vise with C-clamp attachment.

edge for the clamp. Motel nightstands are notorious for not having a wide enough lip for a fly-tying vise.

With a pedestal, you can move your vise from one table to another in seconds, and you can tie on any surface, regardless of whether it has a lip or not. You can tie on a picnic bench, in your den, or on the kitchen table. The disadvantage of pedestal bases is that they are heavy if you take your stuff on a trip, and you are stuck with one jaw height above the table because the stem of the vise does not raise and lower as it does with a C-clamp vise.

Rotary or Not?

Vises can be made with stationary or rotary jaws. There is no advantage to stationary

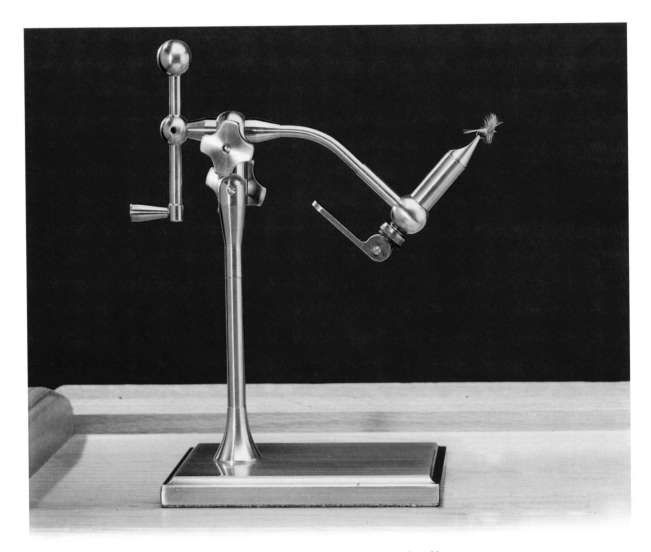

Another type of cam-operated vise with a pedestal base.

jaws other than cost, because a rotary vise can be made stationary simply by tightening the rotating feature until it does not move. With a stationary vise, if you want to look at the bottom or far side of the fly, you must either remove the fly from the jaws and remount it upside down, loosen the stem and flip the vise from right-handed to left-handed, or crane your neck around the far side of the vise. With a rotary vise, the jaws can rotate 360 degrees without removing the hook from the jaws. A set screw controlled by a knob or Allen wrench tightens or loosens the rotation of the jaws. By experimenting with this adjustment, you can come up with an amount of tension that keeps the vise stationary throughout most tying operations yet allows you to rotate the jaws and look at the far side or bottom of the fly (or to actually place materials at these hard-to-reach points).

There are certain operations in fly tying that lend themselves to true rotary tying as well. In rotary tying, the bobbin is placed out of the way, in a thread cradle. You grab the material you want to wind and rotate the jaws while feeding the material to the proper place on the hook. Not only is this faster, it

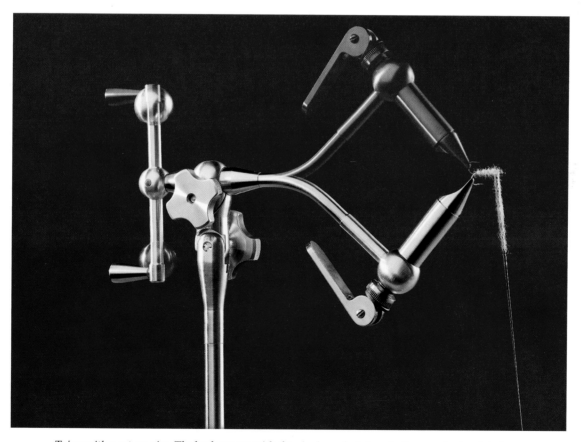

Tying with a rotary vise. The hook rotates with the vise jaws, but stays in the same horizontal plane.

lets you see where the material is going at every angle.

Let's say you are tying a fly on which the entire hook shank needs to be covered with two layers of tinsel. In traditional winding, you bind one end of the tinsel in place, then wrap it around the hook by reaching over to the far side of the hook with one hand, picking it up with the other hand, and then catching it again with the first hand. You can't just wrap the material around the hook with one hand because the bobbin gets in the way. Nor can you see how the material is lying on the far side of the hook or underneath it.

In rotary tying, the bobbin is placed out of the way in a bobbin cradle and the tinsel is held in one hand while the other hand rotates the vise jaws. You can see exactly where each turn of tinsel is placed, eliminating any sloppy gaps or overlaps. When winding hackle, you also get smooth, even wraps. Some people find it an annoyance to switch from stationary to rotary tying, but if you tie lots of flies on which much wrapping is necessary, rotary tying can be a fun and productive option.

Vise Recommendations

My recommendation is to get a C-clamp, stationary vise for your first vise. They are inexpensive, durable, and simple. You can get a decent one for under $50 and a great one around $100. If you want to upgrade, then advance to a pedestal, rotary vise. For this one you should expect to pay a minimum of $150, and as much as $400 for a beautifully machined tool with lots of adjustments, ma-

terial clips, parachute tools, and other bells and whistles.

Scissors

Your scissors should be fine and sharp enough to cut a single hackle fiber or a few strands of marabou without pulling the fibers. Fine points are essential for precision work, such as when you need to clip off a hackle tip without cutting your thread or leaving too much waste material sticking in the hook eye. You'll find straight blades more useful than curved. Finger handles should be wide and comfortable. Some tiers, particularly professionals, tie with the scissors around their fingers all the time, slipping the scissors up and down their fingers as needed. Don't feel bad if you can't get used to doing this—I have been tying for thirty-five years, and I have never gotten used to keeping scissors on my fingers.

Most tiers like at least two pairs of scissors: one fine pair for delicate work and a heavier pair for cutting hair, tinsel, and large clumps of feathers like marabou. If you stick to one pair, get fine-tipped scissors and use the heavier inside edge for cutting hair and wire.

Tiny serrations on scissors help the blades grab materials. They are an advantage even on fine-tipped scissors, and are essential on heavier hair scissors.

The best scissors are those sold by fly-tying shops and catalogs. I am a scissors freak and own more than twenty pairs. I've bought expensive manicure scissors that cost three times as much as fly-tying scissors, and they don't work as well. Fly-tying scissors

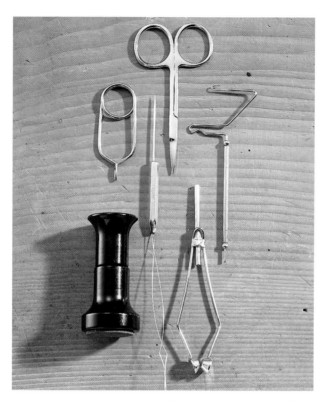

Basic fly-tying tools: hackle pliers, stacker, bobbin threader, scissors, bobbin, whip finisher.

come from surgical-supply manufacturers, but suppliers modify these tools specifically for tying.

Bobbins and Bobbin Threaders

The best modern bobbins consist of a narrow tube attached to a set of wire legs, which hold the spool of thread or other material in place with plastic or metal balls or discs. The tube helps you place thread where stubby fingers won't go. The bobbin holds the spool and keeps tension on the thread while you tie, so that your hands are free to prepare materials. Some of the tubes are polished metal, others are ceramic or metal lined with ceramic in-

sert, which will last a lifetime of tying. Tying thread is often coated with wax, and bobbins with flared ends don't plug up with wax as easily.

If you get a bobbin that has rough edges on the tube that cuts your thread, send it back for a refund immediately. This never happens with the more expensive models, but will occasionally happen with budget-priced bobbins that cost only a few bucks.

Because most of the threads we use today are pre-waxed, the bobbin tube gets plugged, and you cannot always suck the thread through the tube. Get a bobbin threader, which is a simple piece of bent wire soldered to a handle. The wire is soft enough not to score the inside of the bobbin tube. If you're on a budget, floss threaders work, too.

Hackle Pliers

Hackle pliers are used to hold hackles and other delicate materials, and to position them with an exactness not easily obtained with stubby fingers. They can also be used to spin dubbing in a loop or to temporarily hold thread if it breaks in the middle of a fly.

Hackle pliers are simple positive-locking clamps. Squeezing the sides opens the jaws and releasing them tightens the jaws on the material. They should hold a material firmly enough so that it does not slip out under tension, and must not have sharp edges that might cut the material.

Basic hackle pliers, sometimes known as "English style," are the best all-around choice. The best ones have wide side plates that make the pliers easy to squeeze, and one side of the jaws is covered with soft plastic or rubber. This helps the pliers to grip delicate feathers without cutting or breaking them.

A smaller pair of hackle pliers is handy for winding hackles smaller than Size 20, or for winding delicate feathers such as peacock herl, single strands of ostrich, or pheasant-tail fibers.

Most pliers have a wide loop at one end for slipping around your finger. This way, a hackle can be wound smoothly around the hook without having to let go of the pliers, except for a brief moment when you pass the pliers around the bobbin. Some tiers say you get better control by just holding the pliers by your thumb and forefinger and switching

Rotary hackle pliers.

hands when winding around the hook, but I think you can get equal control by placing the loop over a finger.

One special design consists of a tiny pair of hackle pliers attached to a stem that allows the pliers to rotate freely, both horizontally and vertically. They are great for all-purpose work and especially handy for tricky procedures like winding parachute hackles.

Large or long hackles can also be wound with your fingers. Big saltwater hackles and dry-fly saddle hackles longer than three inches can be handled nicely without pliers, but this may be limited by the dexterity of your fingers.

Dubbing Needle

A dubbing needle is simply a needle attached to a handle. Avoid dubbing needles with round handles because they can roll off the tying table. I have a habit of involuntarily catching materials that fall off the table between my thighs, and have impaled myself more than once on a sharp dubbing needle! A dubbing needle is used to pick out dubbing to make it look fuzzier, and for folding wing cases on nymphs. It is also the way you apply head cement to the fly, either in the middle of the fly or after you have whip finished the head. You can also use this tool to pick stray fibers out of the hook eye or to make minute adjustments to materials. Some people use the sharp point of their scissors for these procedures, but scissors aren't as precise, and sometimes the thread gets cut involuntarily.

Whip Finisher

A knot must be used to finish the fly so the head does not unwind. Some flies also require that you tie off the thread in the middle of a pattern; for example, when you're putting epoxy on the body of a fly before you put it back in the vise to attach a wing. Several half hitches are sometimes recommended, but don't use them. They are bulky and nowhere near as secure as a whip finish. The whip finish is a knot that winds the thread over itself about five turns—like the nail knot used to attach a leader to a fly line, or when you pull the thread under the wrap when winding a guide onto a rod.

Whip finishes can be done by hand or with a handy tool invented by Frank Matarelli. The tool makes a tighter, neater knot, and it can place the knot in tricky places, such as at the head of a tiny midge or under a parachute hackle. It is by far the hardest tool to use in fly tying; even so, it can be mastered in a half-hour of diligent practice. Nothing seems to be more satisfying to a novice fly tier than to learn to use this tool, and once mastered, it's a crowd-pleaser for non-tiers to watch.

Stacker

This tool is used to even the ends of many kinds of hairs, so the fine tips line up flush before the bunch is tied in. You can do this by hand by pulling small bunches out and repositioning them, but it takes a long time and the results are never as neat as with a stacker. The basic type consists of a brass tube with a stainless-steel or aluminum base. You place a bunch of hair in the end of the tube, fine ends first, and tap the stacker on the table. When you slide the tube out of the base, the ends of the hairs will be perfectly even. Really clever stackers have clear or open bases so you can see exactly when the hairs are lined up. For most flies the medium size is fine, but if you do a lot of work with big streamers you may want to get a large size to accommodate wide bunches of hair.

Other Tools

Dubbing Spinner

You can use your hackle pliers to spin fur in a loop, but a dubbing spinner is faster and more fun. The basic type consists of a pair of small hooks to catch the loop, plus a heavy brass weight that you start spinning with your fingers and allow to continue spinning by its momentum. Another model mounts

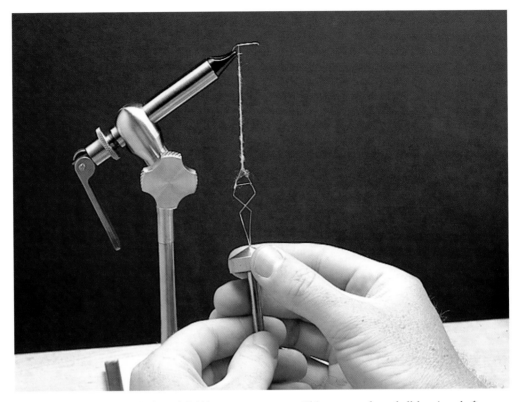

Dubbing spinners make looped dubbing an easy process. This one even has a ball-bearing shaft.

the weight on a shaft with ball bearings, and once the loop is spun you can use the shaft to wind the spun fur around the hook.

Rotating Drier

If you tie epoxy flies or big streamers with glossy heads, this motorized tool gives the finished product a perfectly smooth finish. You place the flies in a piece of foam attached to a battery-operated motorized shaft on a slow governor, and let them rotate from a few minutes to overnight, depending on how long it takes the finish to cure. Without this tool, you have to rotate the flies by hand or in a rotary vise as they dry to keep the epoxy from running to one side.

Hackle Gauge

This is a tool with a small post that you fan a hackle around. It is marked with the correct hackle size for each hook size. I don't use this tool because I fan hackles around the hook as I am tying, but these gauges are very popular. Later in the book I'll show you how to gauge hackles without a tool.

Hackle Guards

This is another tool I don't use, but which is popular nonetheless. Hackle guards are cone-shaped pieces of metal or plastic that keep you from catching hackles in the thread when you finish the head of a fly. I think you can do

This rotating drier is battery-operated and portable.

just as good a job with your fingers, even on tiny flies.

Tweezers

These are almost essential, but not quite. Tweezers or fine-tipped forceps should be fine enough to pluck a single hackle fiber that has gone astray. They are useful for picking up hooks or small materials. Mine are usually downstairs in the kitchen, where they are used to remove ticks from pets, and I don't miss them very much.

Dubbing Teaser

This can be anything from a piece of male Velcro glued onto a pencil to a fine wire brush to a miniature plastic rake. It is used to brush dubbing under the thorax of a nymph or between the ribs on the abdomen of a fly. Slightly handier than a dubbing needle and fun to use, it is not essential.

Wing Burners

Elegant wings for dry flies can be made by placing a hackle feather inside a brass tool that is cut to the shape of a mayfly, caddisfly, or stonefly wing, then burning the outside of the feather away with a butane lighter. This can also be done with certain synthetic materials. The practice is not as common today as it was ten years ago, but these tools do make gorgeous realistic wings.

Tools from the Hardware Store

Double-Edge Razor Blades

Use these to trim deer-hair bodies. Carefully break a blade in half and put some electrician's tape on the broken end to make it easier to hold. It's also handy for scraping head cement off your dubbing needle. Single-edge blades are fine for scraping the dubbing needle, but not sharp enough for trimming deer hair.

Needle-Nose Pliers

Pliers are useful if you like barbless hooks, as you can debarb each fly as you tie it. They also come in handy for opening stuck bottles of head cement or caps on tubes of superglue.

Post-Its and Pencil

Keep a Post-It pad handy for writing down materials you realize you need as you are tying. They are also great as disposable mixing areas for epoxy.

Trash Can

Make sure you have one unless you live alone. You can buy handy wire trash-bag frames that fit on the edge of a table right under your work area. I just use a plastic trash can on one side or the other, and sometimes I actually hit it. Needless to say, I keep a small vacuum cleaner close at hand.

Plastic, Stackable Boxes

Plastic shoe boxes or the bigger styles are wonderful for storing materials. They are airtight enough to keep out beetles and moths and can be stacked in the corner of a room or in a closet. They keep out most cats and dogs, but not ferrets. A heavy rubber band around the outside will discourage even ferrets, though.

Lighter

A lighter is essential if you burn wings or tie extended bodies with Vernille or Ultra Chenille, as you taper this material by singeing the ends.

Tippet Material

You can make weed guards with heavier monofilament, and I like to use 4X tippet when I need a strong, clear rib on a fly.

CHAPTER 3

Materials

Just about anything you find in a craft or fabric store, dead alongside the road, growing on your pet, or pulled from the lint screen of your drier can be used to tie flies. (I am not kidding; when I was a teenager an older guy I fished with had a fantastic nymph pattern dubbed from drier-screen lint). If you stick with this hobby, you will own the most eclectic closet in the neighborhood.

Here are the basic materials sold in fly shops and catalogs today, with which you can tie ninety percent of all the flies you see. Which ones do you need? Only the materials for the patterns you want to tie right now. A material that might be unusual on most tier's tables could be the most essential one in your collection if the recipe for your favorite pattern calls for it.

Feathers

Wing Quills

Wing quills are used for many parts of flies, mostly trout and salmon flies. Sections of wing quills make durable and lifelike wing cases on nymphs. Traditional wet-fly wings have been made from duck and goose wing quill sections for centuries. Delicate and effective (but not very durable) wings on dry flies have been made from duck quills for more than 100 years. More durable materials like hair, synthetics, and turkey flats (body

feathers) have replaced duck wing quills on most flies these days.

Duck

Duck wing quills are usually light gray, almost translucent, and fragile once sections are removed from the center stem. These days they are used most often for wing cases on nymphs, but twenty years ago half the wings on the dry and wet flies in your box would have been made from duck quills. The ones you see most often for sale are mallard wings, which have the biggest and best quills. Don't pass up other duck wings if you see them for sale or shoot your own. Black-duck wings have nice dark gray quills, and smaller ducks like wood duck and teal have light, almost transparent quills.

Buy a pair of wings, because if you tie wet- or dry-fly wings from these you will need to match a primary quills from the right and left wings to get the curve of the quill sections to oppose each other.

Turkey

Two kinds of turkey wing quills are sold for fly tying: domestic white ones, which are usually dyed bright colors for salmon flies, and speckled or oak mottled turkey. The speckled feather is one of the most useful feathers in fly tying, and an essential ingredient in many nymph patterns, the March Brown wet fly, many grasshopper patterns, and the famous Muddler Minnow streamer. Wild-turkey secondary feathers are almost as good. If you have a hunter save you some, make sure you ask for the secondary feathers, the ones behind the primary flight feathers on the front of the wing. The primary feathers are too stiff to be useful in fly tying. If you are making Muddler Minnows or wet flies, you'll need matched pairs of quills; if you're tying nymphs or grasshoppers, pairs aren't necessary.

Goose

Domestic white-goose secondary wing feathers, dyed bright colors, can be used interchangeably with dyed turkey. Wild Canada-goose wing quills, medium to dark gray in color, make nice wing cases and bodies on nymphs.

Biots

Biots are stiff fibers from the short side of a primary feather. The ones you see most often are from goose or turkey wing quills, but any large feather will have biots long enough to make a quill body on a fly. Many modern midge and emerger patterns call for bodies wound with a single biot, which gives the fly a segmented look with fuzzy "gills" at each segment. Biots are also used for tails on some nymphs, and white ones are an essential part of the famous Prince Nymph.

Duck Flank Feathers

Duck flank feathers are used for the wings on famous wet and dry flies such as the Light Cahill. These "Catskill style" flies, once the mainstay of a dry-fly angler's fly box, are not as commonly used today, as duck feathers have been replaced by hair and synthetics in most patterns. But many anglers (myself in-

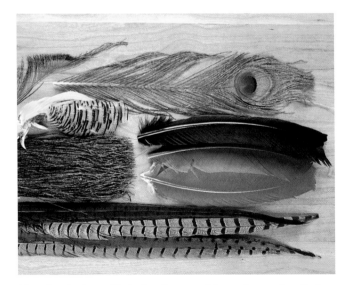

Fly-tying feathers. Clockwise, from top left: eyed peacock tail, three colors of dyed turkey wing quills, ring-necked pheasant tails, strung peacock herl, golden pheasant crest and tippets, peacock sword.

cluded) still love to tie and fish these tiny bits of fly-fishing history, and consider wood duck a staple on the fly-tying bench. The delicate speckles on wood duck, mallard, teal, and merganser feathers also make prefect legs and tails on nymphs. Commonly, you will see mallard for sale, and also mallard feathers dyed a dark yellow to imitate wood duck, which is more expensive and harder to find. If you do see natural wood duck flank for sale, snap it up: No other duck feather has such insect-like markings.

Fly-tying feathers. Clockwise, from upper left: various colors of dyed ostrich plumes, wood-duck flank, Hungarian partridge skin, dark and light mottled turkey secondary quills, CDC feathers.

CDC

CDC stands for *cul de canard,* which in French means something like "butt of the duck." The feathers actually come from the dorsal part of a duck's hind end, and surround the oily preen-gland feathers. These wispy feathers have become extremely popular in the past ten years, after American and British tiers discovered French patterns that had been used with deadly success on continental chalk streams for decades.

It is commonly thought that the feathers are prized because they will float a dry fly without needing treatment with fly dressing. However, European anglers credit the feather's lifelike behavior on the water with its killing properties—the feather is so delicate that a fly tied with CDC seems to develop a life of its own on the current. The great floating properties of flies tied with CDC are probably due more to the feather's ability to hold

tiny pockets of air than to its oil content, as most feathers we buy for tying have already been washed and processed. CDC can be bought in bigger feathers for flies Size 8 to 16, or in what is called "oiler puffs" for tiny patterns. It is most useful in natural gray, but some tiers like to use white ones because they show up better on the water. You can also get it dyed in many different shades. It is a wonderfully easy feather to use, even for a novice.

Pheasant Tail

Cock ringneck pheasant tail feathers are one of the four basic food groups on my fly-tying bench. There is something about this feather, when wound as a body on small dries and nymphs, that fools trout time after time. Pheasant tail is also used for tails and wing cases on many other nymph patterns. Make sure you get cock, not hen, tail feathers, if you are asking a hunter friend for them, and the bigger the feather, the wider the rusty brown edges. The plain, undyed feather is most commonly used, but you can also buy them dyed olive, brown, black, and other insect-like colors.

Soft Gamebird Feathers

The most common gamebird feathers for sale are Hungarian partridge feathers, which is fortunate because they are also the most useful. One small Hungarian partridge skin will give you hundreds of feathers for hackles on wet flies, and legs and wing cases on nymphs. It is one of the most useful feathers in fly tying. If you hunt or know a bird hunter, breast feathers from quail, pheasant, ruffed grouse, snipe, woodcock, and nearly every other gamebird will also give you beautifully speckled hackles.

Peacock

Peacock is a staple fly-tying material. Bodies on dry flies and nymphs are made from strands of the tail feather. Strands can be stripped of their flue to make the most buggy quill bodies you will ever see. Peacock herl is used on salmon and steelhead flies, and even to create a dark median or dorsal stripe on saltwater patterns. Most commonly, you will use the eyed tail feathers, and the best ones are tails whose individual herls are covered with heavy, dense flue. You can also buy strung herl, which is fine for winding bodies, but does not include the eyed strands that are used for quill bodies. A few patterns call for peacock sword feathers, which are from the side of the tail and don't have the distinctive eye.

Marabou

Marabou is a soft, downy feather from under the wing of a domestic white turkey. You can buy this feather dyed nearly every color imaginable, in the plain-vanilla variety or with black bars across the feather to imitate baitfish with vertical stripes. Besides being an essential item in the costume of every Las Vegas showgirl, these feathers make lifelike wings on everything from trout streamers to bass bugs. The feather, like CDC except much bigger and coarser, wiggles when pulled through the water with a movement that looks just like a minnow, or a pork rind. The deadly Woolly Bugger is tied with marabou, although the original pattern used ostrich herl for its wiggle.

Turkey Flats

Turkey flats are breast feathers from a domestic white turkey. They are usually dyed muted colors like tan or dun gray. These feathers are used primarily for wings on parachute and thorax dry flies. Wings made from turkey flats are durable and are lighter than hair wings, so they are great for delicate or small patterns.

Ostrich

Bunches of ostrich herl can be used as a tail to tie the original Woolly Bugger, but most often individual herls are wound around the hook to simulate the feathery gills of aquatic larvae. Ostrich is also used on a few bonefish flies, and as a long, lifelike tail on Lou Tabory's famous Snake Fly striper pattern. It has an action similar to that of marabou in the water.

Hair

When I first started tying, hair was used infrequently on dry fly patterns. It was pretty much restricted to Wulffs or big Western stonefly patterns like the Sofa Pillow. Now, we use as much hair as we do hackle on our dry flies, even the tiny ones. It pays to have a number of different types of hair on your tying table, as size and texture of hair can be critical to the way your fly looks and acts on the water.

White-Tailed Deer Belly Hair

Hair from the belly of larger deer flares dramatically when thread is tightened over it. Many bunches are lashed to the hook and then trimmed with scissors or a razor blade to sculpt the fly. This hair is long, coarse, and hollow, which makes it flare and holds air to keep the fly afloat. You can buy this hair in natural gray/brown or dyed just about any color you can find in a box of Crayolas—after all, it is used for bass flies as well.

White-Tailed Deer Back and Face Hair

This hair is harder to find, but if you tie small hairwing caddis flies or Comparaduns, the finer deer hair will work better than elk. It is sometimes sold as "Comparadun Hair." It is finer and shorter than deer belly hair and flares about half as much, so you can tie in a wing that will keep its shape yet still flare enough to give the fly a robust profile. If you deer hunt or know someone who does, the best hair is from Southern climates or from bow-killed deer earlier in the season. As the season progresses, deer hair in Northern animals develops long, crinkly black tips that act as solar collectors for the heat stored farther down the hollow chamber of the hair. These black tips make the hair harder to even up in a stacker, and the finished fly does not have as clean a profile.

Coastal Deer

Coastal deer is a fly-tying name for black-tailed or mule deer that live in the more moderate climate of the Pacific Northwest. Because of milder winters, this fine-textured deer hair does not develop the long, black tips of animals from colder regions, so it stacks and ties very well. Coastal deer can be used interchangeably with white-tailed deer back or face hair, and is often more easily obtained.

Bucktail

These are tails from white-tailed deer. Bucktail is used for streamer wings, saltwater flies, dry-fly wings and tails, bass-fly wings, steelhead-fly wings, and salmon-fly wings. Unlike deer body hair, bucktail flares little, so it is used in places where you want the durability of deer but a narrower profile. Most of the usable part of a bucktail is on the half of the tail toward the tip. As you get near the base of the tail, the hair flares when you tie it in. The best bucktails are those with fine, crinkly hair. The bigger the tail the better, especially if you tie saltwater flies. A natural bucktail will give you both brown and white hair. Bucktails can be purchased in many dyed colors as well.

Elk

Elk body hair flares less than deer hair of a similar diameter, but is coarser and stiffer. It is used most often for wings of caddis and stonefly dry flies. Bull elk is dark and coarse, and works well on large flies; cow elk is finer and lighter; and calf or yearling elk is almost as fine as deer hair. Because elk body hair gives just a slight flare when compressed with thread, it forms a neat caddis-like wing profile without getting out of control. Sometimes you will see elk hocks or mane for sale. These hairs do not flare at all and are used for tails and antennae.

Some hairs used for fly tying. Clockwise from upper left: gray squirrel, fox squirrel, dyed white-tailed deer belly hair, antelope, elk.

Antelope

Antelope have coarse but very hollow hair that is used only for spinning bodies, as the ends are usually broken. It is soft and does not hold up as well as deer hair, but it is easy to flare for spun-hair bodies or heads on sculpin imitations.

Caribou

Caribou hair is also soft and hollow, but much finer than antelope. If you can find caribou with clean, unbroken tips, it makes superb tiny parachute and Comparadun wings. Because this hair compresses well, there is no bulk where the wing is bound to the shank, and small patterns tied with it look as slim as natural insects. Caribou comes in natural dark gray, light gray, and almost pure white—great for tiny parachutes that you can see in broken water.

Moose

Moose hair is strong and coarse, and does not flare. It is sometimes used for wings, but is more often used for tails on large dry flies. Moose mane is usually used only for tails; because moose body hair comes in both dark brown and white, you can tie on one of each and wind them together to get a realistic, segmented body.

Squirrel Tail

Squirrel tail is a soft, barred hair that is used for streamers, salmon flies, and saltwater flies. It's an easy material to use and has nice action in the water. Spiky dubbing that looks like rough hare's ear can also be obtained from the base of the tail. Look for clean, straight, fluffy tails. Both gray and fox squirrels are used, and tails from the little red squirrel are sometimes used for Canadian salmon patterns.

Arctic Fox

Arctic fox is a relatively new material, mainly used for streamer flies, saltwater patterns, and mixed hairwing Atlantic-salmon patterns. If you substitute Arctic fox tail for bucktail, your fly will "breathe" in the water much like one tied with marabou. Dubbing obtained from the base of the tail or in packages is one of the softest and easiest furs to use, and makes very tight, slim bodies. Tails and fur can be purchased in natural white or many dyed colors.

Calf Body

Calf body hair is short, fine, and solid, and does not flare at all. Its main use is in Wulff and parachute wings, because very neat, well defined wings can be made from it. Calf body hair is extremely durable and stacks instantly. It is most commonly used in pure white, but natural black and brown are also available. It is sometimes dyed, most often to a blue-dun color to imitate mayfly wings.

Calf Tail

Calf tail can be used for wings on parachutes and other dry flies, and some tiers think this crinkly hair is better because it does not hold water as easily as calf body, so water absorbed by the wing is easily flicked off with a single false cast. The downside of using calf tail is that it does not stack as easily, and the resulting wing is not as clearly defined, which might look more like an insect wing but is not as appealing to fly tiers. Take your pick. Calf tails make wonderful streamer wings, are especially easy to use on smaller patterns, and are essential to many bonefish flies. They come in natural white, tan, and brown, and the white ones are easily dyed. When picking calf tails, try to find those with long, relatively straight hair all the way to the tip of the tail. Calf tail with a natural curve is almost impossible to use.

Hackles

The world of fly-tying hackles has changed dramatically since I first started tying. Then, you had two choices: You either bought small necks from India—free-range, semi-wild chickens used for household food, which were imported in huge quantities—or, if you were lucky, you found a domestic chicken neck that was raised especially for fly tying, usually by a famous tier who only grew fifty to 100 capes a year. Now, most hackles you see are domestic capes raised especially for fly tying, and the quality is nothing short of a revelation to older tiers. Thirty years ago, a tier would have given his best bamboo rod for a run-of-the-mill cape from the rack of a contemporary fly shop. It's ironic that as the supply of quality hackle has increased in the past couple of decades, a great many highly effective dry flies that use no hackle at all have been developed. Nearly half the dry flies in my box have no hackle.

Neck Hackles

Inexpensive, imported (Indian) capes are still available, but they are virtually useless for fly tying. As the demand for capes from India decreased, Americans stopped going to India in search of the best quality, and importers no longer grade them. If you dress poppers, small streamers, or smaller saltwater flies, you might find a use for Indian capes, but the same feathers can be obtained from the top of a domestic cape. The lowest-grade domestic cape is still far better for tying dry flies than the best imported one, and will have three times as many usable feathers. I would urge you not to buy imported capes when you first start tying, as they are harder to wind, and you'll only get discouraged about tying dry flies.

A decent domestic hackle cape will tie from fifty to several hundred flies in each size, depending on the size and quality of the cape. They are usually graded 1, 2, or 3; sometimes gold, silver, and bronze. The more expensive capes will have better feathers overall and a complete range of sizes, for flies from Size 10 down to Size 28. Most of the grade 4 capes, called "rejects," are sold to commercial fly-tying operations, but if you ever see any for sale, snap them up. These capes are usually just smaller than average or are missing a size, but they are well worth their price.

All hackles contain some web. You'll most often see it at the bottom of a feather, and it will extend up the center of the feather in a triangle. Unlike the shiny, translucent hackle fibers at the top of the feather, webby fibers are fuzzy and opaque and will not support a dry fly on the surface because they are too weak. Hen hackles are all web; good dry-fly hackles will show web only at the base of the feather and next to the stem in the lower quarter of the feather. Hackles with web that tapers to less than one-sixth of the length of the individual fibers can be used for dry flies.

When buying neck hackle, look for shiny, fluffy capes, as the shine indicates stiff hackles and the fluff indicates a high quantity of feathers. Look for hackles that have barbs or fibers the same length all the way up the stem. Feathers that have a smaller amount of web along the center stem will have more usable hackle. Not all capes have an equal distribution in hackle sizes. If you tie mainly Sizes 14 and 16 flies, pick a cape that seems to have a higher density in the bigger sizes. You usually pay more for a cape that has many tiny feathers that will tie Sizes 24 and 26 flies, but most of us don't use those sizes often.

Hackle capes come in many natural and dyed colors, but for 95 percent of all dry-fly patterns you will need only a brown, grizzly (barred black-and-white), cream or light ginger, and blue dun. Get a medium blue dun to start; eventually you will want to buy a dark and light dun, as most insect wings and legs are some shade of gray. Natural blue dun has a special mystique, supposedly due to minute flecks of different colors in the hackle, but it is an unusual color in chickens, and the quality of the hackle is typically not as good as brown, grizzly, or cream. Dyed dun necks start as cream, and the hackles are much denser and stiffer.

Natural colors used in fly tying include the following shades. (White, cream, or grizzly hackles can be dyed any shade, from bright red to chartreuse to purple. The most brightly dyed feathers are most often used for streamers and saltwater flies.)

White: Pure white with no tinge of brown. Very few dry flies call for pure white, so most of these end up dyed to other colors.

Cream: White with a slight yellowish-tan tinge.

Light ginger: Slightly more of a golden cast than cream.

Dark ginger: Also called light brown, it is a golden-brown shade.

Brown: Medium brown.

Coachman brown: A deep, dark brown. It's a hard color to obtain naturally in good quality, and cream capes are often dyed to get this color.

Furnace: A dark-brown hackle with a black center along the stem.

Badger: A cream to light ginger hackle with a black center along the stem.

Grizzly: A white feather with black bars, also known as Plymouth Rock. Those with heavy dark barring are most desirable.

Ginger Grizzly: A cream or light ginger hackle with black bars.

Dun grizzly: A blue dun color with black or brown bars. Can be used anywhere a pattern calls for blue dun, and the speckling gives the resulting fly a most insect-like appearance.

Cree: A hackle with black, brown, and white bars. Quite rare, but good ones allow you to tie a fly like the Adams, which requires both brown and grizzly hackle, with one type of feather.

Light blue dun: A pale, almost transparent gray. Blue dun hackles of any shade in natural colors are hard to obtain, so most you find will be cream capes dyed gray.

Medium blue dun: A medium-flat gray shade.

Dark blue dun: A dark-gray, almost black color. Highly prized is the bronze blue dun, a dark dun hackle with tints of brown.

Black: Hard to obtain by breeding, so most are brown capes dyed black.

Hackle capes have uses other than to provide dry-fly hackles. At the side of each cape are short feathers with very stiff fibers. Called spade hackles, these are used to get the stiff tails needed for dry flies. The bigger hackles at the top of a cape can be stripped of all their fibers and wound around hooks to make durable and lifelike bodies on dry flies and nymphs. The bigger hackles about halfway up the cape make great streamer wings, and the biggest hackles at the top of the cape can be used for large saltwater flies.

One type of hackle cape, usually called a saltwater/streamer cape, is used for just that.

Hackles. Clockwise from upper left: blue-dun dry-fly cape; dyed-olive grizzly saddle hackle; brown saddle hackle; white, green, and orange saltwater capes; blue-dun dry-fly saddle hackles; badger dry-fly saddle hackles; grizzly dry-fly saddle hackle; blue-dun hen-hackle cape.

These are capes from our domestic food industry, usually white or grizzly capes dyed to any color desired. We used to call them "junk" capes, but with the explosion in saltwater fly tying, a cape with really big feathers for tarpon flies can be as hard to find as a Grade 1 dry-fly cape. These big feathers can also be purchased packaged, usually sold as "strung neck hackle" because the feathers are tied together at the base on a long string to keep them together in a package, and for ease of use at the tying bench.

Hen Hackles

Hen capes and saddles (from the back of a chicken rather than the neck) are used for wet flies, streamers, and saltwater patterns. Small hen feathers also make superb wings for dry flies. They are almost 100 percent web, so a wet fly or nymph hackled with a hen feather will have lifelike action in the water. Hen hackles dyed bright colors are also used as substitutes for exotic feathers such as Indian crow or blue chatterer on full-dress Atlantic-salmon flies.

Saddle Hackles

Saddle hackles from a rooster, taken from the upper back of the bird, can either be purchased loose in packages or on the skin. They once were used only for streamer, bass, and saltwater patterns. Thanks to recent advances in the genetics of fly-tying hackle, you can buy superb dry-fly saddles as well. The advantage of using saddles for dry flies is that they wind easier, and you can tie a fly with a single hackle because the feathers are so much longer than neck hackles. Actually, you can tie up to a half-dozen dry flies with a single feather if it is a good one. When you buy a dry-fly saddle, you usually get only two sizes of feathers—in other words, some saddles will tie Size 10 and 12 flies, another might tie 14s and 16s. This is fine if you can pick out the saddles in a fly shop, but if you buy them through the mail, you cannot specify the size you want. However, saddles can also be purchased already sized and packaged in packs of about fifteen feathers (which will tie 100 flies). So far, saddles have been bred for feathers as small as Size 20, but the 18s and 20s are hard to find. I have no doubt we will eventually be able to buy either full saddles or loose hackles down to Size 26. Get these in the same colors I recommended for neck hackles.

Saddles for saltwater flies and streamers come either on the skin or strung and packaged. These are wider feathers with heavier stems and more web than the dry-fly variety, and are less expensive. You want a wider profile for baitfish imitations, and the heavier, stiffer stem keeps the wing from fouling around the bend of the hook when cast. These feathers can be bought in a wide range of natural and dyed colors.

Schlappen and Cocktails

These are wide, webby feathers from the rear end of a chicken. They are used when a long, wide profile is needed, usually for imitations of the bigger species of saltwater baitfish. They come in natural white or dyed colors.

Floss

Floss is a smooth, shiny, threadlike material, wound around the hook to make a glossy body. Although salmon-fly tiers like to use traditional silk floss, most tiers these days use the more durable and inexpensive rayon variety. Floss absorbs water quickly and is best used on wet-fly and streamer bodies. The famous Royal Wulff, though, calls for a floss body, and we defer to tradition on that pattern and a few others. You could just as easily get the red band in the middle of a Royal Wulff with dubbed red fur or some more durable plastic material, but most tiers don't. Some patterns just shouldn't be messed with.

Chenille

Chenille is a soft rayon wound around a thread core. It is durable and easy to work with, especially for the beginner. Two kinds are available: traditional chenille, which is fairly loose in texture, and Ultra Chenille or Vernille, a tight, fuzzy, finer variety. Both can be used for bodies on streamers and wet flies, but the traditional kind is used most often. Vernille is an essential component of the deadly San Juan Worm, and is also used for extended bodies on caddis and midge imitations. When it is used for these types of flies, the rough end of the material is singed with a butane lighter to give it a realistic taper. Chenille can also be made incorporating strands of tinsel or strands of colored Mylar; these are sold under such names as Cactus Chenille or Estaz.

Tinsel and Wire

Metallic Tinsel
Metallic or "French" tinsel is a thin metal tape coated with silver or gold. When wound around a hook, it forms a shiny, even body. It is used for wet, streamer, salmon, steelhead, and saltwater flies, and can be used to make a whole body or as a rib to give the fly a segmented look. It can be purchased in various sizes.

Mylar Tinsel
Mylar tinsel is a modern development. It typically is gold on one side and silver on the other, so you don't have to worry about buying more than one color. Mylar stretches slightly, so it is easier to use than metallic tinsel, and it won't tarnish with age. The one disadvantage of Mylar is that it can be cut easily by sharp fish teeth, but you can overcome this by applying head cement or epoxy to the finished body, before tying on the wings and hackle. Pearlescent and holographic Mylar is also available, which gives the finished fly the appearance of air bubbles or the translucence of a baitfish.

Mylar Tubing
Mylar tubing is tinsel woven into a round cord, usually over a thread core. You cut the tubing to length, slip the thread out of the

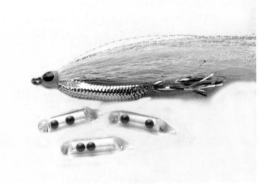

The body on this rattle fly is made from Mylar tubing.

center, and slip the tubing over the hook. This produces an outrageously realistic imitation of a baitfish, and a durable fly to boot. The tubing comes in gold, silver, black, and in various pearlescent shades.

Oval and Embossed Tinsels

Oval tinsel is fine tinsel wound around a thread core to produce an oval shape. It produces a softer, more subtle glitter when used as a rib on trout flies, and is used over almost any type of body material, including flat tinsel. It can be wound all by itself as a body, although few patterns call for this technique.

Embossed tinsel is flat tinsel with a pattern embossed onto its surface. When wound as a body, the effect is a shiny body with many facets. Some traditional Atlantic salmon patterns still call for it.

Ribbing Wire

Fine metallic wire is often used on small nymphs as a rib to give the fly segmentation and flash, and to reinforce delicate materials such as pheasant tail and peacock herl. It can also be wound just by itself to form a thin, segmented body. A few nymphs are actually tied by using very fine wire in a bobbin, which weights the fly slightly and gives the finished product a sparkly, translucent effect. Copper wire is most commonly used, but silver, gold, red, and green wire are also available.

Weighting Wire

To lead or not to lead? Nymphs and streamers often need additional weight to get them down to the fish. Traditionally, soft lead wire was wound over the hook before the thread was started, and the fly was then tied over the wire. Using lead weight to flies is still legal in this country. It is not in the U. K. I don't use lead on my flies anymore, because I don't want even the remote chance of one of my flies ending up in the stomach of a loon or merganser. There are non-toxic alternatives to lead wire that are better for weighting flies: using unweighted flies and putting tungsten putty on the leader, using tungsten or brass beads in the dressing of the fly, or winding an underbody of flexible tungsten sheet. Orvis does not sell lead wire for fly tying, nor do we sell any finished flies tied with lead.

Soft tin wire is sold as an underbody material, and as I write this tungsten wire that is soft enough to use on flies is being developed by Orvis product developers. Tin is only about two-thirds the weight of lead, but it's inexpensive. Tungsten wire is heavier than lead, but it will be quite expensive.

Yarns

Natural Yarns

Yarn is almost always used for bodies, although the tails on a few wet flies and streamers call for short stubs of yarn. Wool yarn is inexpensive and can be purchased on cards at tackle shops or in bulk at stores that sell knitting supplies. Wool yarn is monochromatic and thus not very effective in imitating the subtle colors of insects, but it forms a quick and durable body on many colorful streamer patterns. Another natural yarn you'll see is angora yarn, often sold as "leech yarn." It is very fuzzy, with many long fibers sticking out, and is used for leech patterns and some saltwater flies. Yarn is typically made up of several strands. It can be used as is for bigger flies, or the single strands can be unwound for smaller flies.

Synthetic Yarns

The most common and useful types of synthetic yarns are used for wings and trailing shucks on trout flies rather than for bodies. Antron yarn and Z-Lon are the most common types. These fibers hold tiny air bubbles to their surfaces (they were developed for stain-resistant carpets), and imitate a hatching insect well. They can be obtained in many colors; the most useful are gray, white, tan, and brown. Bodies can be wound with these yarns, but the effect is not particularly useful or interesting.

Another type, sparkle yarn, is used for bodies on large nymphs, streamers, and saltwater flies. It is also known as Antron yarn or Aunt Lydia's rug yarn. Del Brown's deadly Permit Fly uses segments of sparkle yarn tied across the hook, which are then combed and trimmed to a flat, crab-like shape.

Dubbing Brushes

A dubbing brush, or Magic Dub, is yarn made by twisting soft copper wire around fur, peacock herl, CDC, and other materials. The resulting strand has an interesting sparkle and is easy to wind for a body. You can purchase pre-made dubbing brushes, or you can buy a kit to make your own.

Flocked Dubbing

Flocked dubbing or Microchenille is a very fine, fuzzy chenille-like material. The fibers

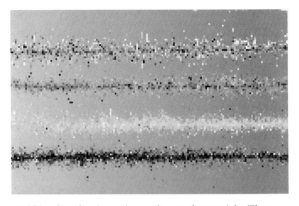

Dubbing brushes in various colors and materials. These make dubbed bodies quickly and easily, but because the cores are made from copper wire, they are not used for dry flies.

and resulting strand are much slimmer than any other type of yarn or chenille, and a body wound with this material seems to sprout tiny gills like those of a natural mayfly nymph. It is the closest synthetic substitute for pheasant-tail fibers, and is far more durable.

Beads and Eyes

Brass vs. Tungsten

Nymphs and streamers tied with brass beads are some of the most effective subsurface flies ever developed. Beads add more weight to a fly than is possible with a lead underbody, and they add a sparkle to the head that may imitate the air bubble around an emerging nymph. All of the popular nymph, streamer, and even wet-fly patterns are now tied with bead heads. The bead is simply slipped onto the hook before attaching the thread, and the fly is either whip-finished just behind the bead, or the thread is carried forward and a hackle or wing case is applied over the bead. The first beads used in fly tying were brass with non-tapered holes drilled in the middle;

Beads and cones in brass and tungsten can be plated various colors.

now most beads made for fly tying have holes with wide and narrow ends. The wide end threads easier over the point of the hook, and the narrow end keeps the bead from slipping over the hook eye.

Brass beads should be used when a fly is to be fished in relatively shallow water. Tungsten beads, which are heavier than lead, can add a massive amount of weight to a tiny fly and can get a caddis pupa to the bottom of a deep, fast run in a hurry. Some tiers tie double-bead flies, and if you do this with tungsten flies, make sure you wear a hat, as a tungsten fly on a forward cast can sting harder than a shot from a pellet gun.

The most common beads are brass, but both brass and tungsten beads can be purchased silver, black, or copper plated, or in bright painted colors. They come in various diameters for different hook sizes.

Cones

Cones, made from either brass or tungsten, are made for use on streamers and saltwater flies. Like beads, they pack a lot of weight onto a fly and add sparkle.

Glass Beads

Glass beads from the craft industry are mainly used for tying nymphs. They don't add as much weight as brass or tungsten, but they give flies a deep, transparent sparkle. Make bodies by threading a series of glass beads onto the hook, or use a single bead for a head. All sizes are available, from tiny sizes that don't crowd a Size 24 midge larva, to beads large enough to use on large streamers. You can buy them in craft stores or packaged for fly tiers.

Bead-Chain Eyes

Bead chain can be cut into pairs and attached to the head of a fly with a figure-eight wrap. This gives a lifelike effect to flies, and adds just a moderate amount of weight. Bead chain is the essential ingredient on most popular bonefish flies. You can get it at a hardware store or buy it from a tackle shop. Before you go off and save yourself a few bucks, you should know the stuff you buy for fly tying is sometimes pre-cut into pairs, saving you a lot of time, and is made from stainless steel. Most hardware-store bead chain is not stainless, and it rusts and corrodes easily.

Dumbbell Eyes

This is the main ingredient of the deadly Clouser Deep Minnow and its variations, without question the most useful saltwater fly ever developed. Dumbbell eyes are attached to the front of the hook with a figure-eight wrap and sink a fly quickly, giving it a jigging action when retrieved. Some are made of plated lead, but you already know my feelings about lead. The best ones are made from plated brass and don't tarnish in salt water.

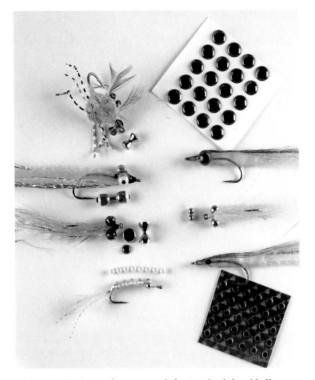

Fly eyes. Clockwise from upper left: standard dumbbell eyes, stick-on glass eyes, bead-chain eyes, holographic stick-on eyes, plastic eyes, dumbbell eyes with recessed ends to hold glass eyes, pre-painted dumbbell eyes.

Plastic Eyes

When you want a pair of bug eyes on a fly but don't want weight, plastic eyes are useful. They are used for everything from adult damselfly imitations to crab flies to slow-sinking bonefish flies. They can be purchased as plastic dumbbell shapes or as plastic bead chain.

Glass Eyes

These look like doll or taxidermist's eyes—which they are. The best ones for tying flies come on an adhesive-backed strip. You simply pluck them off the paper and stick them on the head of your fly with epoxy or head cement. Some brass dumbbells are recessed so that you can stick a glass eye on each end for a fly that looks real enough to swim in your goldfish bowl.

Furs and Dubbings

Pre-Blended Furs

The pleasure of mixing furs to make dubbing blends is becoming a lost art. Being privy to the sale of fly-tying materials for the past twenty-five years, I have seen sales of such items as muskrat and mink fur dwindle to a trickle. In contrast, sales of pre-mixed dubbing blends, with their convenience and easy storage, have taken over. You can buy anything from authentic hare's ear to combinations of synthetics like Antron with a binder of rabbit fur, perhaps with some Lite Brite mixed in for extra sparkle. It's handy to buy a set of dubbing blends because you always have the perfect shade of fur for a Pale Morning Dun Spinner on hand, in just the right color, with no added labor. The natural fur blends like beaver and possum are easier to dub and are better, I feel, for dry flies, because the fibers are finer and easily hold air bubbles and fly flotant. Most synthetic dubbings are coarser, but have more sparkle, and are better, I feel, for nymphs. Some dubbing blends combine both natural furs and synthetics, which are great for any kind of fly.

You can make your own pre-blended fur in custom colors by taking any number of colors or types of furs and synthetics and mixing them in a coffee grinder. This mixes and chops all the fibers so they are easier to dub. You can also "felt" your dubbing blends by adding the blend to a bowl of soapy water,

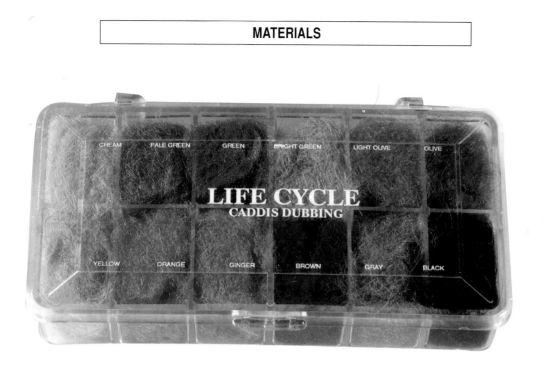

Pre-blended dubbings are convenient and are blended to match aquatic-insect colors.

draining and rinsing the fur in a colander, and letting it dry on a piece of paper. The idea is to get all the fibers going in different directions, as unidirectional fibers don't hold well to waxed thread when spun between your fingers.

I still feel compelled to mention some furs, in case you decide to mix your own dubbings. I still do, and find it one of the most satisfying aspects of fly tying. It's a creative process that takes absolutely no skill, yet the finished product is exactly what you want. How many elements of our lives are so simple and satisfying?

You can tie with fur from any animal, from a road-killed woodchuck to a snippet from the household cat. When I was a kid, I trapped and skinned a mole because there was a pattern I wanted to tie that called for

mole fur. It had the most disgusting smell, and I still cringe when I think about it.

Hare's-Ear Fur

You cannot replace fur from the ears of an English hare with any synthetic, and even the hare's-ear blends on the market don't have enough of the short, spiky hairs for my taste. Hare's ear is one of those magical fly-tying materials that seems to make any fly pattern better. It may be the earthy, impressionistic colors you blend together, or it may be that the resulting fuzzy body imitates the tiny struggles of an emerging fly. I would advise you to mix all your hare's-ear fur at once, because it takes a few minutes and is quite messy. You can put the fur from a pair of ears into a Ziploc bag and use it whenever you tie. You can buy natural hare's ears in natural gray/brown or dyed to insect-like colors. The most useful dyed color is olive.

Muskrat Fur

The Adams is the most popular dry fly ever invented and, in my opinion, it should only be tied with muskrat fur. Muskrat is a silky, translucent fur rich in natural oils that keep muskrats warm and dry—and your Adams floating high! It's inexpensive, especially if you know a local trapper. One skin will last a lifetime.

Fox Fur

It's not easy to find red fox fur these days, but well worth the effort. Nothing dubs as nicely as fox fur, and the cream belly fur is the preferred body material for the famous Light Cahill dry fly. If you can find a moth-eaten old fur stole at a garage sale, you'll be in heaven. The fur from an Arctic fox is almost as fine, with the advantage that the white fur can be dyed any color.

Rabbit

Rabbit fur is almost as fine and easy to work with as fox. You can often find entire hides at a very reasonable price, or you can just snip some fur off the Zonker strips you use for streamers.

Zonker Strips

These are narrow strips of rabbit hide, cut with the grain of the fur, still on the tanned skin. Zonker strips are lashed down over the top of a hook to create the famous streamer pattern known as—you guessed it—the Zonker. There are also sculpin imitations and saltwater flies that use the same technique.

Another type of strip, called crosscut rabbit, is cut across the grain of the fur and is wound like hackle to produce the wiggliest fly you have ever seen. The Tarpon Bunny is one pattern that uses this technique.

Australian Possum

Australian possum is a wonderful fur that comes in an dizzying array of natural colors, everything from light cream to rust to dark gray. It dubs nicely and has a natural translucence. Many pre-blended dubbings use Australian possum as a binder.

Nylon Hair

Nylon hair is used on many saltwater flies for two reasons. One is because it is often impossible to find feathers or natural hairs long enough to tie an eight-inch fly. The other reason is that nylon hair is more durable and holds up to the sharp teeth of bluefish and barracuda far better than bucktail or hackles. There are scores of brands and types available today, with names like FisHair, Super Hair, and Diamond Hair. You can buy it in fine and coarse deniers, straight and crinkly, in every color known to baitfish and some

Fly tied with nylon hair. The material is easy to use and very durable.

This steelhead fly was tied entirely out of Krystal Flash.

that aren't, and even with strands of tinsel mixed in. It's easy to use, can be cut to length, and does not require the preparation and grading that bucktail and feathers require.

Flashy Synthetic Wing Materials

This is a category of fly-tying materials that has boomed along with saltwater fly tying. They are simply various kinds of Mylar tinsel cut very fine and sold in packaged hanks. Flashabou is one type that is straight and very shiny. Krystal Flash is a twisted fiber that reflects tiny points of light, which change as the fibers change position, thus creating an impression of fish scales and movement. Lite Brite gives off a translucent, prismatic effect, and holographic tinsel creates a rainbow of depth and colors you wouldn't think possible of something not plugged into a light socket. Besides using these materials "straight" as wings, you can mix them with bucktail or synthetic hairs. They are also very useful on trout flies. Tiny midge-pupa bodies, for example, can be wound with a single strand, and legs, wings, and tails on nymphs take on a whole new sparkle. A few fibers can even be used in dry fly wings or as legs on beetle imitations.

Miscellaneous Synthetic Materials

Popper Bodies
Most tiers don't get into making their own popper bodies, which involves shaping a piece of cork, gluing it onto a special hook, priming the body, and then painting it. Luckily, you can buy pre-made popper blanks, painted and unpainted, made from either cork or molded urethane. Then it's a simple matter of painting if necessary, adding rubber legs through the body with a heavy needle, and tying hackles or bucktail behind the body.

Foam
Special fly-tying foam is dense, closed-cell foam that compresses without tearing when wound with tying thread. It is used mainly for terrestrial imitations and large dry flies. You can buy it in flat sheets for tying beetles or grasshopper and stonefly bodies, or in round cylinders in various sizes for making extended bodies on damselfly imitations, to

Foam is especially handy for making imitations of terrestrial insects like beetles.

55

mention just a few uses. A wing case on an emerger tied with a slip of foam will keep just the head of the fly above water—a very realistic attitude. Foam comes in all different colors, and can be cut to shape with your scissors.

Rubber Legs

Rubber legs are used as nymph legs, on saltwater crab and shrimp imitations, and on bass flies. Some big Rocky Mountain attractor dries even use them. You can buy rubber legs in the standard opaque variety, or in translucent rubber mixed with metallic flakes, which gives flies an even buggier look.

Nylon and Vinyl Tubing and Strips

These synthetics are used for bodies on nymphs and saltwater flies. They are stretchy and translucent, and come in a wide variety of colors and sizes. One type, known as Larva Lace, is round and hollow and can either be slipped over the shank of the hook or wound like tinsel. Another, known as Swannundaze, is flat and solid. The third most common type, V-Rib, is flat on one side with a rounded hump on the other, so the segmented effect of the body is accentuated. Bodies with a lot of depth can be formed by winding clear or translucent V-Rib over tinsel; a bonus is that bodies made from these materials are nearly indestructible.

Synthetic Wings

Very realistic imitations of insect wings can be made from light, woven materials or

A mayfly spinner tied with synthetic wings.

polypropylene, which is lighter than water. They sometimes come pre-cut, or you can cut or burn your own to shape. You may even see artificial wings printed with veins to imitate the naturals. These are typically fad materials that never seem to catch on, possibly because the stiffer wings made from these have to be perfectly matched or they will twist your leader into a Slinky.

Fibetts

Fibetts are a nylon material, very fine and tapered, used to make tails on dry flies. They are much easier to prepare than spade hackle fibers for tails. However, they are more slippery than hackle when you tie them in, and are thus a bit trickier to use. They are not as stiff as real hackle fibers, but they are handy, and not all hackle capes have decent spade hackles. Fibetts come in clear, gray, and tan—all the colors you need for tails.

CHAPTER 4

Hooks, Threads, and Cements

Hooks

Some fly-tying hooks are still made by hand in England. A craftsman files a point on a piece of wire, cuts a barb, bends the wire around a jig to make the bend, and then puts a sharp loop at the end of the wire to form the eye. I have never seen this process, but I have seen relatively modern hook factories in Japan and Singapore. Even though machines form the point, barb, bend, and eye in one long assembly line, hook making is still almost a cottage industry that entails a lot of attention and labor, especially in the tempering and sharpening processes. Hooks made for fly tying are of the highest quality, and are as carefully made as giant tuna hooks, where thousands of dollars can be riding on a single piece of wire.

Yes, you can tie flies on plain old bait hooks, and you can tie materials on a hook with sewing thread. But you can spend a little more and get superb hooks designed especially for fly tying, properly tempered and needle-sharp right from the box. Unless you make a careless cast and knick the point of a hook or a fly rusts in your book, you may never have to sharpen a trout fly tied on a premium hook. (This is not the case with saltwater hooks. The best ones are ready to fish right from the box, but most of us take a stone to them anyway and check them frequently. Saltwater hooks, because of their bigger wire diameter, must be razor sharp to penetrate the tough mouth of a tarpon or bluefish.)

Parts of a Hook

Hooks start at the point, the part a fish likes least. The barb is a tiny, raised part of the wire that prevents a hook from slipping back out of the fish's mouth. The bend is the place where the wire is bent to create the shape of—well, a hook. The shank is the long, straight segment of the hook where you place materials when tying a fly. The eye is the little ring at the front end of the hook where you tie your tippet.

Buying Hooks

The hook is the most expensive part of a fly, unless you are tying full-dress Atlantic-salmon flies. At around 20 cents each for the best quality trout hooks and twice that for chemically sharpened saltwater hooks, a little thought should go into the hooks you buy. Fortunately, it's easy, and most packaging or catalogs will tell you the best uses for each style of hook.

If you don't know brands, how can you tell a high-quality hook? Look at the eye first. It should be fully closed, and the place where the final end of the wire was cut should blend into the shank with no sharp edges to cut your leader. The well-finished hook will be a light bronze color. If it's too dark, the hook has probably been coated with too much bronzing, which makes the point dull. The best hooks have needle points and are sharp 360 degrees around. Needle-points are chemically sharpened, which means the entire hook is dipped in a corrosive bath. The material removed from the point makes it sharper all around. Less expensive hooks have points that are machine-cut, and cannot be chemically sharpened. Also, some of their strength is sacrificed because material is removed at the sides of the point in the process.

Look for short points rather than long, thin ones, because thin points aren't as strong. Finally, a small, low barb is generally thought to be better because it not only penetrates easier but allows you to release your catch easier. Low barbs also mean that there has been less cutting into the wire behind the point: the deeper the cut when the barb is made, the weaker the point.

Hooks can be made barbless before tying materials to them by pinching the barb with a pair of flat-jawed (not serrated) forceps or pliers. Forceps made especially for fly tying have this feature, and you can even buy a special de-barbing tool for fly tying. Sometimes you break a hook pinching the barb—better to do it before you tie a fly than after you develop an emotional attachment to the finished product.

Hook Terminology

Hook terminology is not standardized, although it is consistent enough for fly tying—after all, it's only a hobby. Hooks are sized ac-cording to their gap or gape, the shortest distance between the point and the shank. This is pretty consistent. The smaller the hook size, the bigger the fly until you get to Size 1; then the hooks progress through 1/0, 2/0, 3/0, 4/0, and 5/0 in increasing order of size. A 4/0 hook is about the largest size used in tying flies; 28 is the smallest.

However, shank length can vary, and it is this variation as much as anything that can give a fly pattern its character and personality. A 1X-long Size 10 hook means a hook with the shank length of a Size 9. (Although we use mainly even-sized hooks, odd sizes do exist.) A 3X-long Size 10 would have the shank length of a Size 7 hook. A stonefly nymph on a regular-shank Size 10 hook looks foreshortened and cramped; the same fly on a 3X-long Size 10 looks perfect. 1X- and 2X-short hooks do exist, but they are not used as often, except for specialized nymphs.

Wire diameter is treated in a similar fashion, but here is where differences among manufacturers vary greatly. Hypothetically, a 1X-fine Size 10 hook has the wire diameter of a Size 11 standard hook. But wire standardization is supposed to come along the same year as campaign-finance reform, so I'd advise you to look for dry-fly hooks that say "extra-fine wire" or are just labeled as dry-fly hooks. If a hook is labeled as a nymph or streamer hook and the package doesn't say anything else, it is probably regular-weight wire, which is fine. Nymph or streamer hooks labeled "heavy" or "2X stout" are advised if you fish for Atlantic salmon or steelhead with small wets and nymphs, or if you expect to be fishing for trout over twenty inches long with heavy tippets. A regular or fine-wire hook fished on a 2X tippet might bend into an arrow when attached to a heavy trout in fast water.

Hooks can be made with straight or "ring" eyes, turned-up eyes, or turned-down eyes. Because eyes on fly-tying hooks are almost always tapered, you'll see designations like "TUTE" for "turned-up tapered eye." Turned-down eyes are more traditional for trout flies, and about three-quarters of the hooks used for trout flies have them. Flies tied with parachute hackle are difficult to finish when tied on up-eye or ring-eye hooks, so use down-eye hooks when tying these patterns.

Turned-up eyes are seen on salmon flies because they accept the Turle knot better (an older knot that always gives a perfectly straight pull, which makes a wet fly swim straighter but is not as strong as a clinch knot, Orvis Knot, or non-slip mono loop). We used to believe the hooks with turned-up eyes gave a bigger "bite" when using small flies, but this is just not the case. The best small hooks for hooking fish I have ever used are the Bigeye Hooks tied on ring eyes. Weighted nymphs tied on down-eye hooks ride upside down in the water. It's harder to hook a trout that spits out a fly quickly with a hook showing this attitude, and if you hook a small trout in the upper jaw the point sometimes penetrates their eyes or brain. I believe that weighted nymphs tied on up-eye hooks lessen these problems.

I like ring-eyed hooks and think they give a finished fly a classy look. I also believe they are better at hooking and holding fish, and studies done on the physics of fish hooks seem to support this. Saltwater flies are always tied on ring-eye hooks, which may be due to habit and tradition, but perhaps also because of their strength.

Other than these guidelines, choose a hook that looks good to you, or is recommended in the pattern description. All of them will do a fine job of hooking and holding fish if they are sharp.

Some Basic Hook Recommendations

Dry-Fly Hooks
You can get by most of the time with a standard dry-fly hook, with extra-fine wire and a regular-length shank. The sizes you will use most often are 12, 14, 16, 18, and 20. In sizes smaller than 16, you may want to try the Bigeye hook style. They are made with an oversized eye that adds insignificant weight to the fly but allows easy threading of tiny tippets. One other style that comes in handy is a 2X-long dry fly. The proportions of spent spinners look better on this length, and they are perfect for tying smaller grasshopper and adult stonefly imitations.

Wet-Fly and Nymph Hooks
Here, your options are wider. Traditionally, wet flies are tied on standard-length or 1X-short hooks, while nymphs are tied on 1X-, 2X-, and 3X-long styles. Additionally, nymph hooks come as curved styles, where you can tie a little farther down the bend and get a fly that looks naturally curled while drifting in the currents. Or you can tie nymphs on what is called a swimming nymph hook, which has

a double curl and makes a fly look as if it is wiggling in the water. Shrimp/caddis or worm/caddis hooks have short shanks, and help get the proportions of a freshwater scud or caddis pupa right. You can also buy a special Bead-Head hook, with an oversized eye to keep the bead from slipping off the hook, and a slightly curled bend.

If you want to limit your styles, I'd get some 2X-long nymph hooks in Sizes 8 through 18 and some shrimp/caddis hooks in Sizes 12 through 16. These two will get you through most nymph patterns with the right look. Most tiers just use dry-fly hooks, especially Bigeye hooks, when tying nymphs smaller than Size 18.

Streamer Hooks
Unless you tie long-shanked flies for trolling or want to tie presentation patterns for framing, just buy 4X-long streamer hooks in Sizes 4, 6, 8, and 10. These will tie perfect Muddlers, Zonkers, traditional streamers and bucktails, and Woolly Buggers.

Salmon and Steelhead Hooks
These hooks are traditionally made from heavy wire, japanned (a process that blackens the wire), with looped, turned-up eyes. Supposedly, the turned-up eye makes a salmon fly swim more provocatively in the water. Double hooks are used in very fast water to help stabilize the fly and show the salmon the fly's side profile. (If you went through all the trouble of tying a full-dress salmon fly, you wouldn't want a fish looking at its *bottom*, would you?) Regular bronzed trout-fly hooks work great for catching Atlantic salmon, and steelhead can be caught on stainless saltwater

hooks. But if you are going to tie flies for these species, with their rich history, at least make a salute to tradition with some flies you've tied yourself on traditional up-eye hooks.

Bass-Fly Hooks
Subsurface bass flies are usually tied on large streamer hooks with 3X- or 4X-long shanks. Poppers are tied on a special kink-shank hook to keep the cork or plastic bodies from twisting on the hook once they are glued. Deer-hair bugs can be tied on large wet-fly hooks (but never dry-fly hooks, as they aren't strong enough to pull a largemouth out of the weeds!). However, most are tied on special "stinger" hooks, which are strong and light and have a wide gape so the deer-hair body does not get in the way when a bass inhales it.

Saltwater Hooks
Saltwater flies should all be tied on stainless hooks. Plated hooks can rust, ruining a fly, and perhaps sending you off for a tetanus shot if you hook yourself. For a while, plated hooks were the rage because they are stronger, and it was believed that a plated hook would rust out of a fish's jaw if the fish broke the tippet. However, hook wounds fester, and the hook slips out on its own. Barbless hooks slip out even easier. If you pinch the barb on all of your saltwater flies, you will never have to struggle removing a hook from a fish or from your ear.

The following is a chart showing most basic fly-tying hooks and their uses. I have referenced the four top hook brands so you can substitute where a dressing calls for a particular brand and model of hook.

Type	Descriptions	Uses	Orvis Model #	Daiichi Model #	Tiemco Model #	Mustad Model #	Hook shape
Dry	Extra-fine dry fly	Sparse dry flies and emergers.	1523	1180	5210	94833	
Dry	Barbless dry fly	All dry flies.	1877	1190	900BL	94845	
Dry	2X-long dry	Terrestrial dry flies, spent spinners, stonefly dries.	1638	1280	5212	94831	
Dry	Bigeye dry fly, straight eye	Size 16–26 dry flies; oversize eye allows easy threading to tippet.	4641	1110			
Dry	Bigeye dry fly, down eye	Size 16–26 dry flies; oversize eye allows easy threading to tippet. Down-eye makes finishing parachute flies easier.	4864	1100			
Wet/Nymph	Traditional 2X-long nymph hook	Standard mayfly nymphs.	1524	1710	5262	9671	
Wet/Nymph	Short-shank curved nymph	Caddis nymphs, midge larvae and pupae, worm flies, freshwater shrimp imitations.	1639; 8891	J220	2457	37140	
Wet/Nymph	Curved nymph	Long-shank nymphs and big stonefly dries. Gives the finished fly a more lifelike, curled shape.	1510	1270	200R	80050BR	
Wet/Nymph	Swimming nymph	For imitating nymphs that wiggle when hatching.	1512	1770	400T	80150BR	
Wet/Nymph	Heavy wet/nymph hook	Traditional wet flies and shorter-bodied nymphs. Sinks fly well and will hold up to very large fish without bending.	1641	1530	3761	3906	
Wet/Nymph	Up-eye nymph	Weighted nymphs. Fly rides hook-down in water so hooking qualities are better. Fish are more likely to be hooked in lower jaw, so less damage to eyes and head.	594F	1740			

(continued)

Type	Descriptions	Uses	Orvis Model #	Daiichi Model #	Tiemco Model #	Mustad Model #	Hook shape
Wet/Nymph	Bead-head hook	Bead-head flies. Beads slip easily over bend and are held in place by oversize eye.	122J				
Nymph/Streamer	3X-long nymph/streamer	Muddler Minnows, smaller streamers, stonefly nymphs.	1526	1720	947BL	9672	
Streamer	4X-long streamer	Bulkier, broader streamer patterns like sculpins, Zonkers, Matukas.	8808	2220	9395	79580	
Streamer	6X-long streamer	Slimmer, skinny streamer patterns like Gray Ghost and other traditional northeastern streamers. Trolling streamers.	1511	2340	300	3665A	
Bass	Bass bug	Deer-hair bass bugs.	8810	2720	8089	37187	
Salmon	Salmon dry-fly hook	Steelhead and Atlantic salmon dry flies.	1644	2421	7989	90240	
Salmon	Salmon wet-fly hook	Steelhead and Atlantic salmon wet flies.	1645	2441	7999	36890	
Salmon	Double salmon wet-fly hook	Atlantic salmon double-hook wet flies.	0528	7131		3582F	
Saltwater	Pre-sharpened stainless hook	Tough-mouthed saltwater species; less likely to need sharpening out of the box.	9034	2546	800S		
Saltwater	Standard stainless hook	All saltwater flies; will need to be sharpened before use. Less expensive than above.	0549–00			34007	
Saltwater	3X-long stainless hook	Longer, skinnier saltwater flies like sand-eel imitations.	0549–60		911S (4XL)	34011	

Threads

Until the middle of the twentieth century, all fly-tying thread was silk. Silk fibers were twisted into a thread, and it was great stuff because it is much stronger than cotton. However, silk rots and loses its strength quickly. In the 1960s, flat nylon thread for fly tying was developed, and fly tying has been better and easier since. Up until five years ago, I still used silk thread for tiny dry flies because it was smaller in diameter than nylon. But in the past few years polyester threads have been offered that are as small as the finest silk, many times as strong, and they never rot.

Thread Sizes

Thread is measured on a scale based on diameter that dates back to silk days, and the scale is only useful on a relative basis. The sizes used in fly tying are A, G, 3/0, 6/0, 8/0, and 10/0, with A the heaviest. Size A is hardly ever used today because the smaller threads are so strong that 3/0 is acceptable for the biggest saltwater flies. Sizes 3/0 and G are used where the material being tied in needs to be under a lot of pressure, as when you're tying in large clumps of hair. It is also handy where you need to cover a long stretch of hook shank and don't care about bulk, as in tying saltwater and bass flies. Heavier thread also builds a big head more easily, again mainly in the construction of saltwater flies. You can use 6/0 for streamers, big nymphs, and for most saltwater flies as long as you aren't working with large bundles of hair. Size 8/0 is now the standard for trout flies in Sizes 8 to 16, and 10/0 is best for the smallest patterns. You should use the smallest diameter you can without breaking the thread, because six turns with 6/0 will hold materials on the hook far better than three turns of 3/0.

Thread Materials

Fly-tying threads are made from many tiny filaments that are given only a light twist, and not twisted into a rope as in sewing thread. This is a huge advantage in fly tying, because by spinning your bobbin you can either flatten the thread for ultra-smooth wraps, or introduce a twist for precise placement of materials.

Always buy pre-waxed thread. It will keep the thread from fraying, and it won't go spiraling out of control if you loosen up accidentally on your tension. You can even dub softer materials to pre-waxed thread without adding additional wax.

Nylon or polyester? Nylon stretches, which some feel squeezes materials onto the hook better. Polyester does not stretch as much, and usually pops without warning if you push it too far. But polyester is marginally stronger and lasts longer than nylon. Polyester also has a slightly rougher finish, which aids in gripping materials to the hook. Polyester is also much better in the smaller sizes. Both are very good threads, but you have probably guessed my preference.

Kevlar thread, available only in a large diameter in yellow, is sometimes used where you have to put great amounts of pressure on the thread, as when tying large deer-hair bugs. It is difficult to use and frays easily, but is incredibly strong. I have it on my fly-tying bench but haven't used my one spool in about ten years.

One other thread, monofilament thread, looks just like fine tippet material. It is tough to control because the round, slippery thread goes all over the place. Its one use is with epoxy flies; in spots where materials are lashed to the hook before glue is added, the clear thread disappears after the epoxy is dry. Monofilament thread is also used in smaller trout nymphs tied with plastic tubing such as Larva Lace, as it blends well with these translucent materials.

Thread Colors

You can tie almost any fly with either of two thread colors, black and white. Tie dark flies with black thread and light flies with white. Most times the thread never shows at the tiny head of the fly, and it's doubtful it ever makes a difference on trout flies. When tying trout flies with thinly dubbed bodies, however, the thread *can* show through when the fly is wet. The same hue of thread as the body material blends with the dubbing, or a contrasting color can give the fly a lifelike translucence. The great fly tier and author Darrel Martin has an innovative approach: he ties all of his flies with white thread and tints the thread with a permanent marker to get the color he wants. This way, he can change thread colors several times in the same pattern.

Some saltwater flies call for heads of bright red or green thread; here the thread color does become an essential part of the pattern, because the heads on saltwater flies are so large.

Cements

Head Cement

Head cement is a clear lacquer placed at the head of a fly with the dubbing needle after the whip-finish knot is tied. Some tiers say a tight whip finish makes head cement unnecessary, but I have experimented with leaving it off, and my heads do fall apart easier if not coated with cement. Head cement also soaks into the hackles of a dry fly, and stiffens and

strengthens the exposed stems. You can also use head cement in the middle of a fly to strengthen places where certain slippery materials like hairs are tied in.

You can buy head cement in a thick consistency, called "high gloss cement," which makes a nice glossy head on saltwater flies and streamers. It is also available in a thinner, "deep-penetrating" formula. This is best for intermediate steps like strengthening quill bodies or protecting tinsel bodies, and for the heads of dry flies, where you don't want to add bulk to the fly. Both are usually just the same cement with different amounts of solvent or head-cement thinner. You can buy head cement thinner and cut the stuff to any consistency you want.

You can also find water-based head cements, which can be thinned with water but are waterproof once dry. They don't seem to be as strong as solvent-based cements, but are easier on your respiratory system in confined areas.

Flexible Cements

Standard head cement is hard and stiff once it dries. Certain materials, especially wing quills used for wing cases on nymphs or wings on grasshopper flies, tend to split when you tie them in, and are best reinforced with a flexible cement before you tie with them. Vinyl cement is also used for this purpose. You must treat the feather first and then let it dry, usually for thirty minutes, before using it.

Spray Fixative

I prefer treating fragile feathers with a spray fixative instead of brushing on flexible cement with a brush or dubbing needle, as the spray is quicker and gives a light but uniform coverage. This is sold in art-supply stores under names like Tuffilm or Krylon Krystal Clear, and is used to spray charcoal or chalk drawings to keep them from smearing. I have also found stuff called Clear Acrylic Sealer in discount stores in the craft section that works just as well. Spray this stuff outside, as it has a pretty strong solvent.

Hobby Paints

Model airplane paints in white, black, and yellow are handy for painting eyes on flies. Just make a big dot on each side of the head with yellow or white paint by dipping a nail head or the cut-off end of an old, fine paintbrush. Let it dry, and add a pupil of black with a smaller nail or with the shaft of a paintbrush cut at a narrower diameter. Make sure you put a coat of head cement or epoxy over the eyes after they've dried.

Thirty-Minute Epoxy

Clear thirty-minute epoxy is great for painting heads and bodies of saltwater flies. Five-minute epoxy usually sets up too quickly to be of any use, as it takes a few applications to cover the entire head of a fly, and by that time it might get too hard to apply. To get an evenly coated head you must rotate the fly

for ten minutes until the epoxy stops running. You can either hold it in your hand (not recommended), spin it slowly in a rotary vise (not much fun either unless you like watching glue dry), or you can buy a small rotisserie device made for fly tying or rod winding. With this little machine you can do dozens of flies at once, placing each one on the big block of foam as you paint the head.

Five-minute epoxy can be used for wing cases on nymphs because you only want it to stay in one place on top of the wing case.

When using epoxy, don't use toothpicks as color bleeds out of the wood and makes the finished result less than clear. Brushes leave bristles, which are messy to remove, even when the epoxy is wet. The best tool is your dubbing needle, which can be cleaned with acetone before the epoxy has completely hardened.

Superglue

Some tiers use quick-drying cyanoacrylate glues to reinforce tricky steps in flies. If you do, be careful where it goes and remember that these glues are stiff and might turn white when dry. The best ones to use are the more viscous types like Zap-A-Gap. I don't find much use for them, and have not really found a place where either head cement or epoxy won't do a better job.

Part II

Tying Instructions

Each of the flies in this section was chosen for two reasons: because it is one of the most popular flies in the world today, and because it illustrates specific tying operations. For instance, most beginning fly-tying guides show a traditional Catskill-style dry with divided wood-duck wings. Countrywide, these aren't as popular as they were ten years ago, so I showed an Adams and a Royal Wulff dry. These are far more popular patterns, and if you learn their steps a Catskill dry will be a snap; just follow the recipe and look at the photo in the Index later in this book. For the same reason, I left out a winged wet fly, instead showing you some nymphs and emergers. Winged wet flies are effective fish catchers, but aren't as popular as they used to be. I want to show you the stuff that fly fishers are using in the twenty-first century.

When photographing fly-tying sequences, there is always a temptation to tie them bigger than normal because the shots are easier. I did not shoot oversized flies for this book. Although proportions are the same, materials behave differently on oversized hooks and I did not want you to get frustrated because your flies didn't look like the ones in the book. Yours may not right away, but they *will* in time.

Speaking of sizes, are there any secrets to tying very small flies, Sizes 18 through 28? Sure. Keep patterns simple—you'll notice most midge patterns incorporate one or two materials and no tricky techniques. Use 10/0 thread or you'll crowd the hook, especially the eye. Take fewer turns of thread if you can. Use magnification, even if your near-vision is perfect. And develop a light touch so you don't bend the hook or break the thread.

The Game Plan

Don't skip right to the Royal Wulff because you need some for fishing a small stream in North Carolina this weekend. I don't care what kinds of flies you like to fish, start with the Woolly Bugger and don't move off to another pattern until yours look a little like the ones in the photos and you feel comfortable with the techniques. Then you can move off to the Bead-Head Soft Hackle in the "Nymphs" section, or the Clouser Minnow in the "Saltwater" section, because I've chosen the flies in each section in increasing order of skill. Tie one pattern at a time; in thirty years of teaching people to tie flies in person, in print, and on video, I've noticed that teaching by pattern is the best method, rather than teaching abstract skills before moving on to complete recipes.

The only time I'd advise you to skip ahead is if you're having problems with a particular technique. Maybe winding hackle on the Adams is driving you nuts, and you're just not getting it. Skip ahead to the hackle-winding steps on the Royal Wulff, as maybe the text and photos there will be just different enough that something will click. If you're still having trouble, examine your materials critically. Did you substitute red wool because you didn't have red floss? The wool is thicker and fuzzier, and that may be the problem. Or maybe the only piece of deer hair you own is belly hair, and when you tie it in for dry-fly tails it flares all over the place and doesn't look like the picture in the book. Then you go back and read the pattern description and discover that the pattern calls for bucktail—different part of the animal, and totally different behavior when wrapped with thread.

Realizing you may not have all the materials listed here and can't always run off to a neighborhood fly shop, I've listed the most common substitutes in each pattern description. All of the materials used in these patterns are commonly available, either in basic fly-tying kits or in mail-order catalogs and stores that sell fly-fishing gear. Some materials can also be found in craft stores and the hobby sections of department stores.

The Road Map

You never have to measure anything with a ruler when tying flies. All proportions are based on the hook, and all directions are relative to it. Here's the convention I'll use in the pattern descriptions:

Hooks

The **gape** or **gap** is the distance between the point of the hook and the shank.

The **shank** is the straight part of the hook where most of the tying goes on, between the eye and the bend. It's the most important measuring reference in fly tying, and we often divide it up into imaginary halves, thirds, and quarters. For very small distances, I like to use a subjective but useful measurement, the "thread width." Saying "one-thirty-second of a shank length" would have you going cross-eyed trying to divide a Size 14 hook into 32 pieces in your head; it's easier to estimate the distance three or four thread wraps would take.

Back or **back to** means toward the bend.

Forward or **up to** means toward the eye.

Feathers and Hairs

The **tip** of a feather of feather fiber or hair is always the finer end. These are usually not cut and are left with their natural taper, sticking out of the finished fly to form one of its features.

The **butt** of a feather or hair is the heavier end, the end you've probably just cut from a stem or hide. This is the end that usually gets trimmed and bound under in a finished fly.

Parts of a Fly

Some of the parts of flies, particularly nymphs and complicated salmon flies, are not intuitively understood. Here are a few basic fly types with their parts labeled.

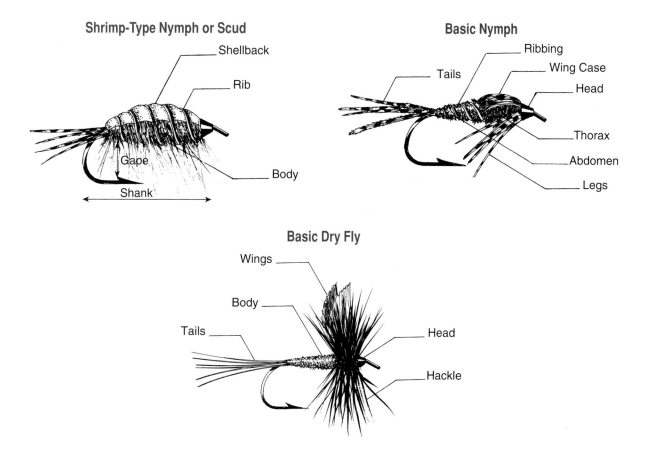

Shrimp-Type Nymph or Scud
Shellback
Rib
Gape
Shank
Body

Basic Nymph
Ribbing
Tails
Wing Case
Head
Thorax
Abdomen
Legs

Basic Dry Fly
Wings
Body
Tails
Head
Hackle

Salmon Wet Fly

Streamer

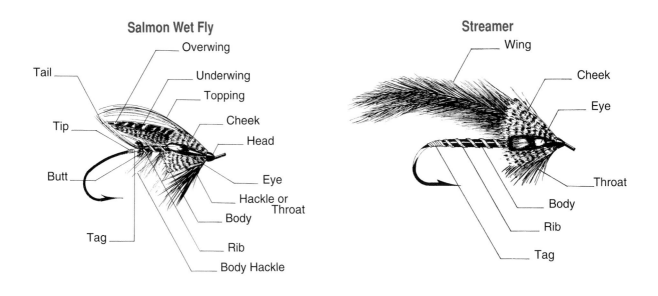

Saltwater Fly

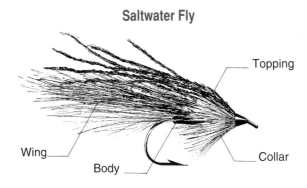

CHAPTER 5

Streamers

Woolly Bugger

This is most fly tiers' first attempt, and I'd advise you not to buck the trend. I can teach someone who has never held a hook in his or her hand to tie a fishable Woolly Bugger in forty-five minutes. Other than a somewhat sloppy head, it will look as good as one of mine. The other reason the Woolly Bugger is satisfying is that you can take one to your nearest bass lake, bluegill pond, trout stream, striper estuary, or bonefish flat, and be tight to a fish in short order—assuming some willing fish and a decent presentation. I've caught everything from steelhead to carp to

sunfish to tarpon on this fly; it's probably the most universal fly for both fresh and salt water known today.

The Woolly Bugger was first tied in 1967 by Russell Blessing of Lancaster, Pennsylvania, who added a marabou tail to a Woolly Worm in an attempt to imitate a hellgrammite, the big, mean larva of the dobsonfly. I saw the fly about five years later on the upper Beaverkill. I was sitting on the edge of a deep pool with Ron Kusse, a bamboo rod maker who was running the old Leonard Rod Company at the time. It was one of those midday breaks in August when you realize you won't catch a fish until the sun leaves the water in seven hours.

"Wanna see something amazing?" Ron asked. I cringed as he knotted this big ugly fly to his 38H Leonard bamboo and cast right across the pool. After letting the fly sink for a few seconds, he began stripping it back with about the same fast retrieve you'd use for barracuda. Four or five trout nailed that fly despite the bright sunlight and August heat, and I was hooked as firmly as they were.

The way we fish Woolly Buggers today has little in common with the behavior of hellgrammites, which are poor swimmers. Although the fly is deadly fished on a dead-drift like a nymph, most of the time it is stripped actively, and probably looks more like a sculpin or crayfish to a trout or bass.

You can tie this fly in any color you want. Blessing's original pattern had a peacock-herl body and black ostrich tail; the classic version today uses olive chenille and black marabou, which are cheaper and more durable. Saltwater angler Tom Piccolo's version for stripers, the Picabugger, is all chartreuse. Jim Finn of northern Virginia uses a color scheme for his "Golden Retriever," with a body of tan Estaz or Crystal Chenille and a tail of tan marabou. I've used a giant pink-and-white Bugger for salmon in Alaska, and steelhead in the lower forty-eight.

Whatever colors you try, it's best to weight these flies, at least slightly, because the palmered hackle and fluffy marabou can float a streamer hook for the first few casts, until the fly gets wet. A terrific variation is adding either a brass bead or cone to the head of the fly before tying; the bead adds some sparkle and gets the fly down quickly.

In a pinch you can even slide a bead down the tippet in front of an unweighted fly, but you didn't hear it from me.

Pattern Description

	MATERIAL	**SUBSTITUTE**
Hook	4X-long streamer, Sizes 2 through 12.	3X-long nymph.
Weight	Non-toxic wire.	Brass or tungsten bead or cone slipped over hook and pushed up to eye.
Thread	Black 6/0.	Red.
Tail	Tip of black marabou feather.	Bunch of black ostrich herls. Either feather may also be used in white, yellow, tan, or chartreuse.
Body	Olive chenille.	Peacock herl; or any other color of chenille to match tail.
Hackle	Black, palmered through the body.	Grizzly is most common alternate, but almost any color can be and has been used.

1. The non-toxic weighting wire should cover about one-half of the shank, leaving enough room to tie in materials at the tail and finishing the head without making a lump. Hold the end of a piece of wire with your left hand. Cross the wire behind the shank and wind it around the hook with your right.

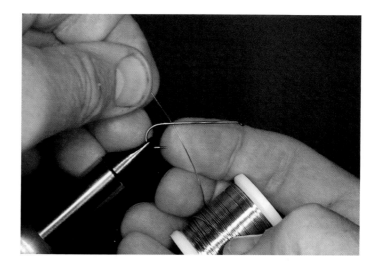

2. Feed wire from your palms as you wind the wire in even turns. Don't worry if they aren't adjacent to each other, as you can push the turns together with your fingernails as you wind.

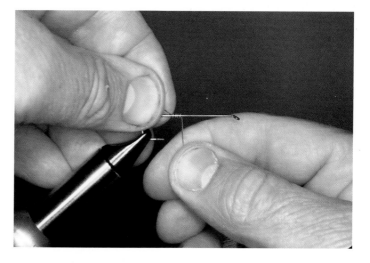

3. Stop the wire when it is about one-sixth shank length behind the eye. Start your thread in front of the wire.

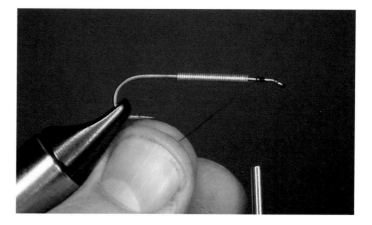

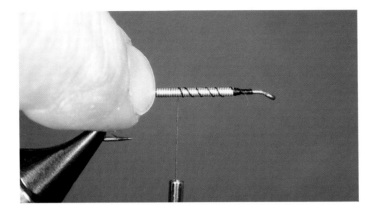

4. Wind back, building up thread in front of the wire until the thread bump is the same diameter as the wire. Keep the wire in place by holding the nail of your left index finger up against the rear portion of the wire.

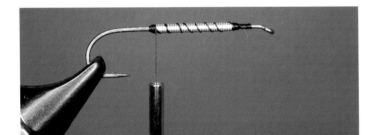

5. Spiral the thread back to the other end of the wire and build a bump there to hold it in place.

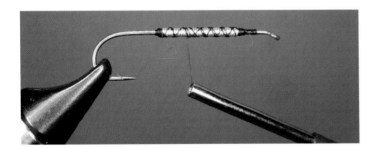

6. Spiral the thread back and forth over the wire several times. A light application of deep-penetrating head cement over the wire will keep the fly from twisting out of shape when a twenty-inch brown trout grabs it.

7. Select a marabou feather with even tips and lots of fuzz. For ease of handling, it should be at least twice the shank length.

8. Holding the marabou in your right fingertips, with the tip of the feather pointing toward the rear of the hook, hold it over the shank until about one shank length sticks out beyond your fingertips. Adjust your grip until the marabou is the right length.

9. Grab the marabou with your left fingertips at a spot even with the end of your right fingertips.

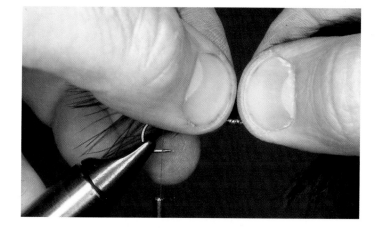

10. Trim the butt of the marabou feather, leaving at least half an inch sticking beyond the end of your fingertips. Wet the part of the feather beyond your fingers, as this makes it easier to handle. Bring the thread back to the point where the shank ends and the bend starts. Make sure you come back far enough; if you don't, the marabou will wrap around the bend when you cast and the fly won't swim properly. Don't wrap the thread back over the bend, because the marabou will be tied in pointing down—it should come straight off the shank.

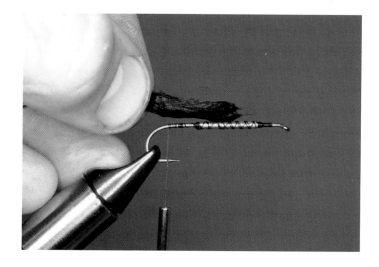

11. Attach the marabou to the spot where the thread was hanging with three Pinch Wraps. Hold it in place at the tie-in point with your left thumb and forefinger, bring the thread over the shank and around the far side while rocking your left thumb and forefinger back onto the first knuckle, slipping the thread in between them. Pinch them back over the marabou and tighten the thread by pulling down with the bobbin tube. The marabou should stay on top of the shank. If you pinch the sides of the hook, it should stay in place. Make two more tight Pinch Wraps.

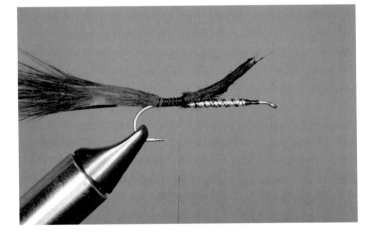

12. Wind the thread forward to the wire in smooth, tight, slightly overlapping wraps. Stop just short of the wire.

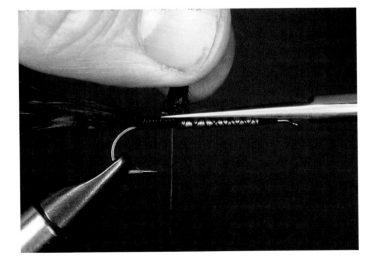

13. Trim the marabou by lifting the butts straight up and trimming with your scissors, using the shank as a guide. Wind a few turns of thread over the butts of the marabou, then wind the thread back to the bend, stopping right at the spot you made the first wrap over the marabou.

14. Select a saddle hackle with a wide center web. The fibers on each side of the stem can be anywhere from one to two hook gaps in length. Strip the fuzzy down at the base of the feather by pinching it with your thumb and forefinger and pulling straight down toward the butt of the feather.

15. Grasp the saddle hackle by its tip and stroke the fibers back toward the butt with the fingers of your other hand.

16. Hold the feather just below the tip and carefully snip the hackle fibers from each side of the stem for about the top half-inch of the feather. Stroke back any fibers that stick out over the tip and hide them under your fingertips.

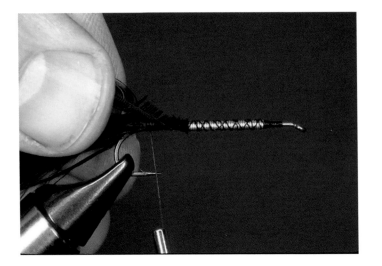

17. Without releasing your grip, hold the trimmed tip of the feather against the near side of the hook and tie it in place with a Forty-Five-Degree Roll. Make a half-dozen very tight turns over the tip so it does not pull out when you begin wrapping it.

18. Wind forward to the edge of the wire and back to the bend to further secure the feather.

19. Cut a five-inch piece of chenille. Grab one end and remove the cotton fuzz with your fingertips, leaving the black threads at its core exposed.

20. Tie the chenille in at the same spot you began wrapping the marabou and the hackle. Wind forward with tight wraps, binding down the thread core of the chenille.

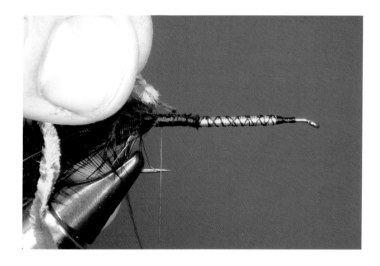

21. Advance the thread to a point just beyond the bump in front of the wire. Don't get too close to the eye; if you do, you'll end up with a bulky head and possibly waste material stuck in the eye. This is not good for tying on a fly when fish are feeding! Twist the chenille between your fingertips four or five times: this makes it look better when it's wound.

22. Wind the chenille away from you, over the top of the shank with your right fingertips.

23. Catch it under the shank with your left fingertips while you bring your right hand around the bobbin.

24. Catch the chenille again with your right hand.

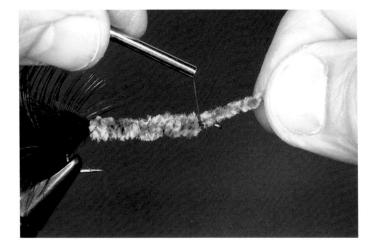

25. Continue wrapping the chenille forward in adjacent turns, so that each turn of chenille touches the preceding one but does not overlap. When you get to the spot where the thread is hanging, hold the chenille in your right hand while bringing the bobbin over the shank with your left. You'll have to let go of the bobbin on the far side, then grab the bobbin underneath the shank and pull down with firm pressure. Repeat the process to make four wraps.

26. Trim the chenille on top of the hook, close to the shank.

27. Make about half a dozen wraps over the trimmed end of the chenille.

28. Grasp the saddle hackle that was left hanging at the bend of the hook. Pull it gently, straight up, and stroke the hackle fibers back until they all sweep back toward the tail. It may help to wet your fingertips.

29. Grasp the butt of the hackle in your fingertips or in a pair of hackle pliers. Wind the hackle forward in even spirals. You may have to twist the hackle to keep all of the fibers pointing back toward the bend, and you should stroke them back after each turn.

30. When you get to the point where the chenille was tied off, secure the hackle in the same manner. Make sure you take at least a half-dozen turns—hackle is harder to secure than chenille.

31. Trim the remainder of the hackle feather on top of the hook, close to the shank.

32. Stroke any hackle fibers that are not sweeping back toward the bend with your left fingertips and hold them in place while you take another half-dozen wraps just in front of the hackle. If any of the hackle at the front of the fly is unruly, wind back onto it for just a thread width or two.

33. Flatten your thread and wrap until a smooth, neat head is formed, right up to the eye. Whip finish the thread. Apply a drop of head cement to the thread wraps.

34. The completed fly as it should look after a little practice.

35. If you own a rotary vise and want to try your hand at rotary tying, the Woolly Bugger is a perfect candidate. Both the chenille and hackle can be applied with the rotary technique. Weight the hook and tie on the tail as you did on the first Woolly Bugger, then bring the bobbin cradle around in front of the hook as shown. The hook should be placed in the vise so there is a minimum of up-and-down wobbling as you rotate the vise. Try to line up the shank with the axis of rotation. Place the bobbin in the cradle—no need to tie a knot to secure it.

36. Grab the chenille and begin rotating the vise away from you, counterclockwise if you were sighting down from the front of the hook. Guide the chenille with your hand as it rolls forward.

37. When you're ready to tie off the chenille, remove the bobbin from the cradle, swivel the cradle back out of the way, and tie off the chenille as above.

38. Wind the hackle in the same way. Rotary tying is especially useful when winding hackle because you can see how it looks from all sides as you wind, not just the near side.

Black-Nose Dace Bucktail

Although most of us carry more than a couple of minnow imitations in our fly boxes, you can probably cover most instances when a trout will grab a big fly with two patterns: a wide, wiggly, bushy pattern like the Woolly Bugger to imitate sculpins, crayfish, and hellgrammites; and a sparse, thin imitation of baitfish like dace, fallfish, young whitefish, or chubs. The Black-Nose Dace Bucktail is one of the best imitations of tiny baitfish ever developed. Twenty years ago, fly tiers made careful distinctions between "streamers" and "bucktails," the former used to describe a minnow imitation with feather wings and the latter for flies tied with hair. These days, we lump them all into the generic streamer designation because it's hard to categorize modern fly-rod lures like the Tequeely, Double Bunny, or Egg-Sucking Leech.

The Black-Nose Dace Bucktail was created by the legendary Catskill fly tier Art Flick

and described in his landmark book of fly patterns, *Art Flick's Streamside Guide*. In the late 1960s, when I began fly fishing, his book and Ernie Schwiebert's *Matching the Hatch* were the only books you could find on fly patterns, unless you came across a dusty copy of one of Ray Bergman's or Preston Jennings's 1930s-era books in the library or a used bookstore. The Black-Nose Dace was the only minnow imitation Flick used, and this venerable pattern still catches trout, bass, landlocked salmon, yellow perch, and any other freshwater fish that eats minnows, often far better than "modern" imitations.

I have a painful memory of a raw, windy day on a landlocked-salmon lake when my friend Jim Lepage was slamming one salmon after another and I couldn't buy a strike. I kept edging closer to him, but still didn't get a hit. I finally resorted to wading right alongside him, and mimicking his casts and retrieves, but by the time darkness fell and rain drove us from the lake I had not touched a fish. When I finally got a look at his fly, it was a tiny, sparse Black-Nose Dace in Size 12, far more subtle than any streamer I had in my box. Since that day the Dace has come through for me on rivers from Vermont to California, especially when trout weren't interested in the bulky streamers that everyone else was using. It's an especially good pattern in calm, shallow water, and when fished upstream in pocket water during the heat of summer.

I once had the honor of spending the afternoon with Flick, and he showed me some of his Black-Nose Dace patterns. The underwing was made of white polar-bear hair, the middle part was brown bucktail, and the upper wing was black bear hair. These days, polar-bear hair is illegal to sell, and black bear is hard to find, so most tiers use bucktail in three colors. It doesn't seem to change the effectiveness of the fly one bit.

Pattern Description

	MATERIAL	SUBSTITUTE
Hook	4X-long streamer.	3X-long nymph or 6X-long streamer.
Thread	Black 6/0.	Red or white.
Tail	Red wool yarn.	Red floss.
Rib	Oval silver tinsel.	Silver wire.
Body	Flat silver tinsel.	Silver Mylar tubing slipped over shank and lashed down at both ends.
Wing	White, brown, and black bucktail in three distinct sections.	Relatively straight calf-tail hair or arctic fox tail in white, dyed brown, and dyed black.

1. Attach the thread about one-third of the shank length behind the eye.

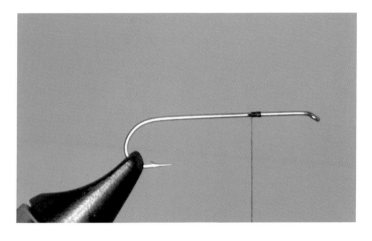

2. Wind thread back to the end of the shank, just before it starts to dip below the horizontal.

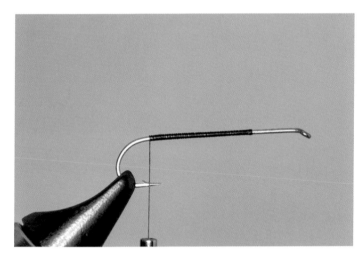

3. Cut a one-inch piece of red yarn. Yarn usually comes in three lightly twisted strands; gently unwind a single strand. Measure it with your right hand so that a short stub extends beyond the bend. (You can eliminate this step if you want; the red yarn can be trimmed later, as its blunt, cut end is part of the pattern.)

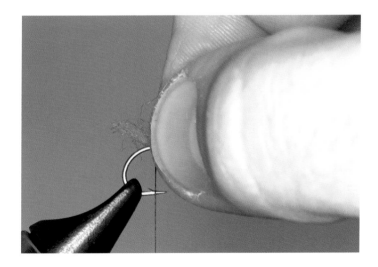

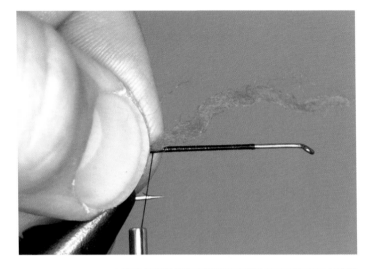

4. Switch the yarn to your left hand and tie it in, using the Pinch Method, with three firm wraps.

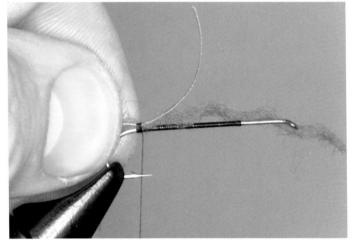

5. Using the Finger On Far Side Method, tie a five-inch piece of fine oval silver tinsel on top of the yarn with two wraps, moving toward the eye with the second wrap. Only a section of tinsel long enough to reach the initial tie-in point should lie along the shank. The rest of it should trail off behind the fly.

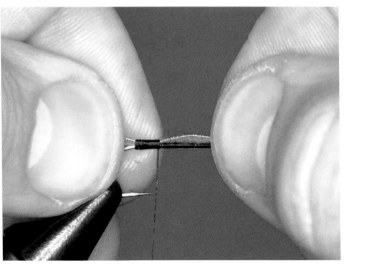

6. Flatten the thread and begin winding toward the eye. The underbody should be as smooth as you can make it. Keep the yarn and tinsel on top of the hook—keep rolling it back toward you, as it will slip over the far side if not kept in place with your fingers.

7. When you get to the initial tie-in point, hold the yarn and tinsel straight up and trim them as close as possible to the shank.

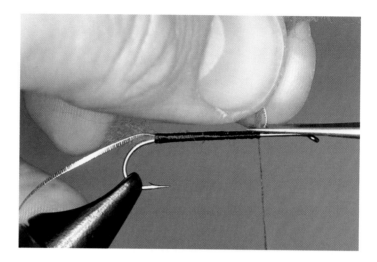

8. Cut a seven-inch piece of Mylar tinsel from the spool. Taper one end to a point with your scissors. Tie in about halfway down the taper with a Finger On Far Side wrap, then tighten with three firm wraps. Don't trim the end. The gold side of the tinsel should be facing you.

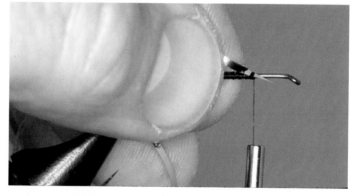

9. Lift the tinsel straight up and make a half-wrap around the shank. The tinsel should flip sides as you do this so the silver side shows. As it wraps over the top of the hook, smooth the bump with your fingertip.

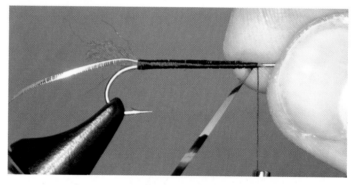

10. Wrap toward the bend, slightly overlapping each previous turn. As you begin each wrap, pull the tinsel toward the bend to slide it in place alongside the previous turn. You'll feel a little click in your fingertips as it slides into place. The idea is to cover the shank with a layer of tinsel with no bumps.

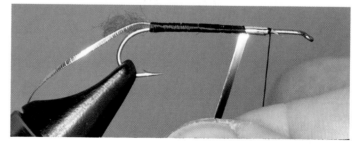

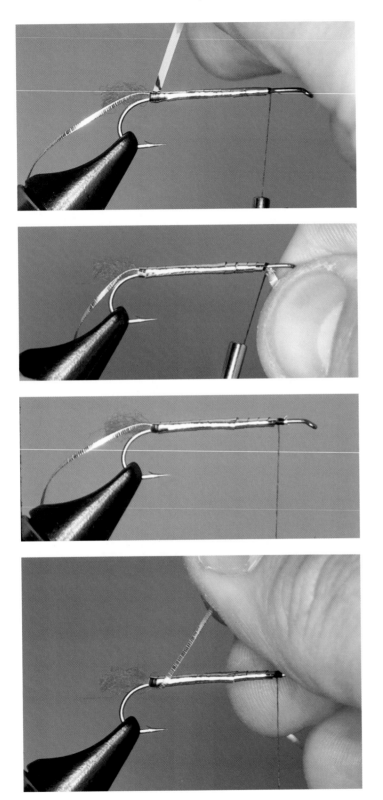

11. Wrap right down to the last turn of thread, then reverse direction and do the same back in the other direction. Don't leave a gap of thread at the bend, but don't tarry here too long with your wraps either. The fly in the photo appears to have a gap of thread, but it's just a slight bump in the tinsel that reflects the light differently than the rest of the body.

12. Wind forward to the eye, one wrap of tinsel beyond where you started. Hold the tinsel in your right hand and wind over it with three very tight wraps, pushing the bobbin over the top of the shank with your left hand, catching it down below the hook, and tightening with firm downward pressure.

13. Trim both ends of the tinsel—the one you just finished wrapping and the initial tapered end you tied in. Wrap two more turns of thread over the ends of the tinsel.

14. Grab the end of the oval tinsel and wrap toward the eye in an open, even spiral.

15. Tie off the oval tinsel the same way you did the flat tinsel, but make sure you tie it off *under* the shank. If you tie it off on top, the last wrap of tinsel creates a bump that makes it hard to set your wing in place. The flat tinsel doesn't matter as much because it's not as bulky.

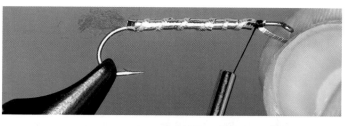

16. Flatten your thread and make a few wraps back and forth. There should be a smooth base for the wing without much difference in diameter between the thread and the end of the tinsel body.

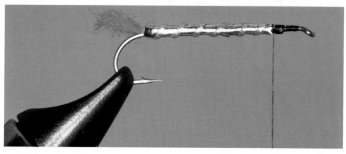

17. Cut a small bunch of white bucktail, holding the bunch at right angles to the tail until the ends are even. Pinch the ends together and cut the base of the bucktail. Don't even the hair in a stacker—it should have a slightly ragged, tapered look at the tip ends to imitate the body of a baitfish. The best hair for sparse flies like this comes from the upper half of the tail (toward the tip). The hair at the lower end of a bucktail, nearest the tail's junction with the body of the animal, is too coarse. The bucktail should be one-and-one-half to two times the length of the shank.

18. Make sure the thread is hanging just ahead of the tinsel. Bring the bobbin up over the shank and take one loose wrap around the bunch of bucktail but not around the shank. Don't put any tension on the thread.

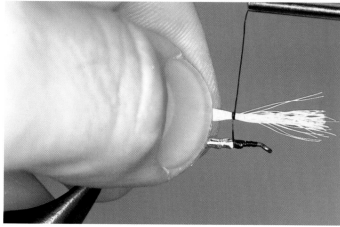

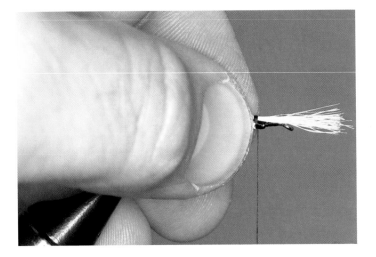

19. Bring the bobbin down below the shank. As you do, work the bucktail down onto the top of the shank, letting the loop of thread slip as you do. Once the bucktail is firmly on top of the shank (roll it back into place if it is not), secure it with three firm Pinch Wraps. Optionally, you could have merely tied the bucktail onto the shank without taking a loop of thread around it, but this method keeps the three colors of bucktail in distinct layers. The Pinch Wraps also make the bucktail less likely to pull out under pressure.

20. Trim the bucktail at an angle, as shown.

21. The head should now look like this.

22. Prepare a bunch of brown bucktail and tie it in, as you did the first bunch. Choose brown bucktail from as close to the tip of the tail as possible.

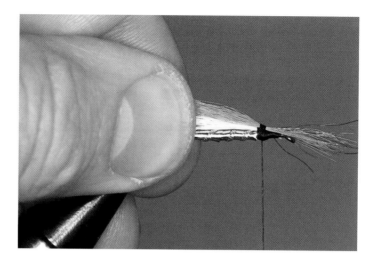

23. Trim the brown bucktail on an angle parallel to the first trim.

24. Tie in a bunch of black bucktail and trim in the same fashion. Flatten the thread and make firm wraps over all of the hair butts, holding them in place with your left hand as you do.

A

25. Whip finish. Apply one coat of deep-penetrating head cement, letting it soak back into the wing a tiny bit (A). After it dries, apply a coat of high-gloss head cement (or a little deep-penetrating cement that you let sit out for a few minutes to thicken). If your head does not look as neatly tapered as this (B), you probably used too much bucktail. The Black-Nose Dace is a sparse fly; don't overdo the wing.

B

CHAPTER 6

Nymphs

Bead-Head Soft Hackle

In 1995, Joe Bressler, legendary guide and home-town favorite, won the Jackson Hole One-Fly contest with this nymph. The One-Fly is a charity event where you are only allowed to use a single fly each day. Needless to say, the fly patterns are carefully chosen. Joe, who grew up on the banks of the Snake while his father, the late Vern Bressler, managed some of the finest fishing lodges in Wyoming, knew he would need a fly that would catch nearly any trout in the river. He needed a pattern that could be fished deep or shallow, in fast water or slow. The morning of the competition, Joe had enough presence of mind to pull this fly out of his box.

This nymph is a cross between a 100-year-old Yorkshire soft-hackle wet-fly pattern and the modern bead-head nymph. Beads, made from glass, brass, or tungsten, have been added to every popular nymph pattern over the past ten years. They let you add sparkle and weight without having to tie lead wire under the fly or use split-shot on the leader. Tungsten beads are the heaviest, brass beads are about fifty percent lighter, and glass beads are the lightest.

This is a pattern that works best when there are caddisflies around. If you see them in the air, on the water, or see their cases covering the bottom, a Bead-Head Soft Hackle should interest the fish. If you see no rises at all, fish it slow and deep, adding a pinch of soft weight to your leader. Fish upstream, dead drift, with a big, fuzzy yarn indicator. If you see caddis in the air and a few sporadic but splashy rises, take off the weight and indicator. Fish the fly just below the surface, across and downstream.

Using what you learn in the following fly, you can tie either regular soft-hackle wet flies or bead-head nymphs. Soft-hackle wets are usually tied with bodies of thin floss, very sparsely dubbed fur, or feather fibers such as pheasant. The hackle is sparse, typically three turns of a soft body feather. The most common feather used is the Hungarian par-tridge shown here, because it is widely available and has lifelike speckled markings. Hen chicken hackle can also be used. If you hunt, ruffed grouse, woodcock, quail, and dove feathers all make wonderful soft hackles.

Bead-head nymphs are among the easiest flies you can create. If you want to turn the fly in this section into a plain old bead-head nymph, merely leave off the hackle in front of the bead, finishing the fly with the first whip finish. Bead heads sometimes have tails and sometimes don't; the ones I use most often have merely a body with a bead. You can make the easiest bodies from pre-made materials like dubbing brushes, microchenille, or yarn. Fancier flies can be dubbed fur, peacock herl, pheasant tail, rubber bands, or nearly any material you can wind on a hook.

Pattern Description

	MATERIAL	**SUBSTITUTE**
Hook	Bead Head, Sizes 8 through 18.	2X-long nymph, or short-shanked curved nymph.
Thread	Tan 6/0.	Any pale 6/0 or 8/0 thread, depending on hook size.
Tail	Small bunch of brown Hungarian partridge hackle fibers.	Brown hackle fibers.
Body	Natural Hare's Ear Plus Dubbing Brush	Dubbed hare's-ear fur or other rough fur with short guard hairs mixed in.
Bead	Match to hook size. ⅛-inch Brass Bead for Size 12 fly shown here.	Tungsten bead for quicker sink rate.
Hackle	Hungarian-partridge body feather.	Any mottled gamebird feather or speckled hen chicken feather.

1. Slip a one-eighth-inch brass bead over the hook point. You'll notice the bead has a wide opening on one side and a narrow one on the other. Slip the point of the hook into the narrow end, as this makes it easier to thread the bead on the hook. Slip the bead about three-quarters of the way to the eye. Apply a drop of head cement onto the bead, letting the cement run into the hole inside the bead.

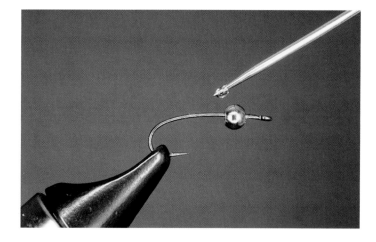

2. Start your thread immediately behind the bead.

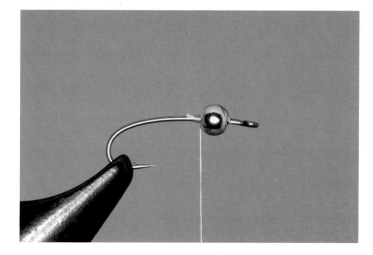

3. Wind the thread back to the end of the hook shank, to where the bend starts to angle down.

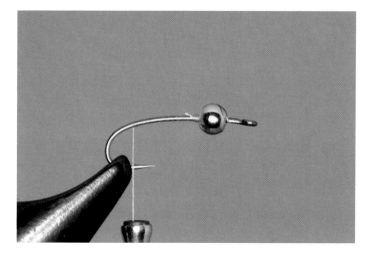

4. Strip the fuzzy down from the base of a well-mottled Hungarian partridge feather. Separate six to eight fibers and line them up by pulling them at right angles to the stem. Pluck them all at once from the feather.

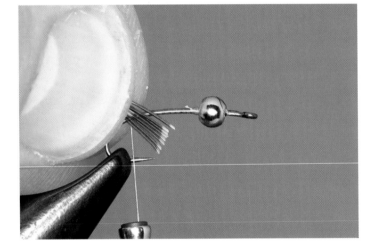

5. Measure the fibers against the shank. The fine ends should extend about one-half shank length beyond the bend. Place the fibers at a forty-five-degree horizontal angle to the shank, with the blunt, plucked ends facing toward you.

6. Take one soft turn of thread around the tail material without tightening.

7. Start working the thread toward the eye in non-overlapping turns, applying more tension with each wrap and guiding the tail fibers parallel to the shank. They should do this naturally as you wrap. Don't let the tail fibers slip around the far side of the hook; keep them right on top of the shank.

8. Wrap the thread back to the initial tie-in point. You can make smooth turns or just spiral the thread back quickly. There is no need to wrap a smooth foundation of thread at this point. Pull the fur off about one-eighth inch of a piece of dubbing brush. There will be twisted copper wires exposed. Tie the exposed wire in with about five non-overlapping tight turns of thread. Work toward the eye. Wind the tying thread up to the bead and let it hang.

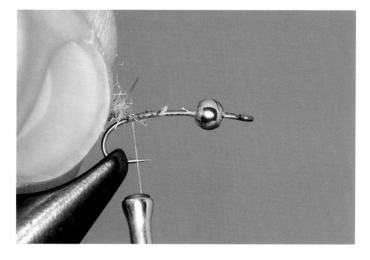

9. Wind the dubbing brush forward in turns that just touch each other. Start winding with your right hand over the top and around the far side. Transfer the material to your left hand while you bring your right hand around the bobbin. Catch the material again in your right hand.

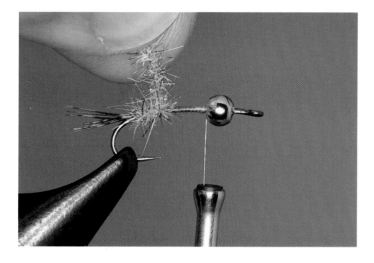

10. Wind the dubbing brush all the way up to the bead. Tie it off tightly by holding the end of the material in your right hand while bringing the thread and bobbin behind the material with your left hand. When the bobbin reaches the far side, let it drop gently. Bring your left hand around the vise and apply tension by pulling straight down on the bobbin with your fingers locked against the spool so it does not turn. Repeat this four times.

11. Trim the dubbing brush, using the lower inside of your scissors so you do not damage the fine points when cutting the wire. If a little wire sticks up after you trim, just push it down with your finger; it's already locked in place and won't unwind.

12. Whip finish behind the bead. Let the knot dig into the dubbing so it disappears. Apply a couple of drops of head cement.

13. Re-attach the thread just in front of the bead.

14. Pick a Hungarian-partridge feather with unbroken fibers. The fibers on each side of the stem should be about one hook shank long. Strip the fuzzy fibers from the base of both sides of the butt, or heavier end of the stem, by pulling down as shown.

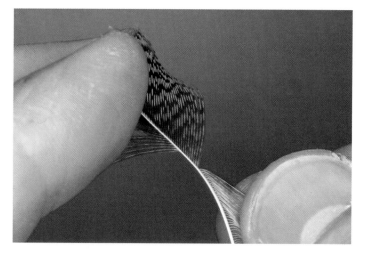

15. Grasp the feather by its very tip and stroke all of the fibers back toward the butt.

16. Trim the fibers very close to the stem, about one-eighth inch down from the tip. These stubby fibers will help hold the delicate feather in place.

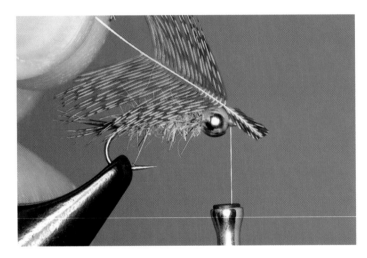

17. Tie the trimmed end of the feather just in front of the bead with five tight turns of thread. The concave or shiny side of the feather should be facing you. Work from the base of the bead toward the eye. You should not tie the feather all the way to the eye; leave a small space so you can finish with a neat head. Leave the thread hanging here.

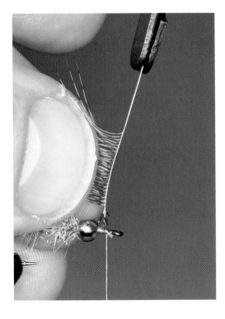

18. Grasp the heavy end of the feather with hackle pliers. Pull gently straight up and stroke all of the hackle fibers back toward the bend of the hook. Any manipulation of this delicate feather should be with a light touch, as partridge hackles break easily when winding.

19. With the hackle pliers in your right hand, begin winding the hackle away from you and around the far side. Transfer the pliers briefly to your left hand on the bottom to allow your right hand to clear the bobbin. Keep light but steady pressure on the hackle pliers. Wind slightly closer to the eye with each turn. Stroke the fibers back toward the bend with your left hand as you wind. Make about three complete turns of hackle or until there is a collar of hackle fibers encircling the fly equally, 360 degrees around the hook.

20. End with the feather straight up. Tie off using four tight turns, with the bobbin in your left hand. Trim the feather close to the hook. If you trim on top as shown, with your thread hanging underneath the hook, you won't cut the thread accidentally.

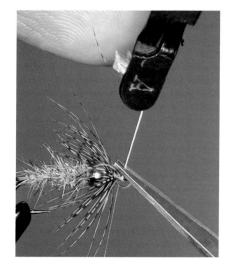

21. Wrap a single layer of thread over the head. If the hackle fibers don't slope back at about forty-five degrees from the vertical, wind the thread back onto the base of the hackle very slightly while pulling the fibers back toward the bend. Whip finish, and add a drop of head cement to the head.

Gold-Ribbed Hare's Ear Nymph

The Hare's Ear fly is at least 500 years old. Medieval flies were not dry flies or nymphs or wets—they were simply "flies," although they were fished under the surface. Sometime during the first half of the twentieth century, nymphs became the favored way of imitating subsurface insects because they are more exact replicas of subsurface life. Standard procedure was to take a wet fly and substitute a tied-down wing case for the wings, turning the old standard into a nymph. The pattern shown here is the most commonly used version. The tails, wing case, and rib might be made from other materials in some variations. A bead might be added to the head of the fly. The fly might be tied on a dry fly hook, or with a short wing of CDC to create an emerger. But all of them incorporate that magic fur blend.

It is not an accident that this material has stayed popular over the centuries. There is something about the mixed natural colors of fur from the face of a rabbit that synthetic materials have yet to duplicate, based on the statistic that the Hare's Ear Nymph, with its many variation, outsells the next most popular nymph two to one in fly shops all over the world.

Although we don't know why this nymph is so effective, the Hare's Ear, with spiky fibers that move in the water, looks like nothing specific but suggests many types of subsurface life. It can look like a mayfly nymph because the fibers sticking out between the gold ribs resemble gills between segments of a mayfly's abdomen. The fuzzy hairs under the wing case might appear to be the struggling legs of an emerging caddisfly or mayfly. They may also approximate the whirling legs of tiny crustaceans. Stripped through the water, the Hare's Ear might masquerade as a tiny minnow or crayfish. We hope trout pick out what they want to see, and it seems to work.

You can buy pre-packaged hare's ear blends, but I don't recommend them. By mixing the fur yourself, you'll obtain just the right color and texture and amount of guard hairs in the blend. Commercial blends are too soft, and they don't contain enough guard hairs because there aren't a lot of them on each ear and they are too tough for bulk suppliers to work with.

In the following pattern, I show you two ways to dub fur. The abdomen is made from fur dubbed directly onto the thread, the best method for making a slim or tapered body. The thorax fur is dubbed in a loop, which gives a fuzzier, wider profile. You can dub either part with either method, but this way seems to give nymphs the best profile. Besides, you get to learn two dubbing methods on one fly.

The Hare's Ear is such an effective fly that my best suggestion on fishing techniques is to warn you when and where it may *not* work. The Hare's Ear is not a productive spring-creek fly, although it is fair in smaller sizes, tied very sparse. If you're fishing weed-filled waters with slow, clear current, fish a spring-creek fly like the Pheasant Tail. It is also not the best pattern when skinny mayflies such as Blue Quills or Blue-Winged Olives are hatching. Otherwise—when meaty mayflies, caddisflies, and stoneflies are around—the Hare's Ear will catch trout. Fish it upstream, downstream, deep, or shallow. Like most nymphs, it is better fished dead-drift without added motion, but when trout are aggressive and you see splashy rises, an occasional twitch or downstream swing might get their attention.

Pattern Description

	MATERIAL	SUBSTITUTE
Hook	2XL nymph, Sizes 8 through 20.	Bead Head.
Thread	Black 6/0.	Any dark thread.
Weight	Non-Toxic Fly Wire, .014-inch diameter.	Brass or tungsten bead under the wing case instead of fur thorax.
Tail	Guard hairs from the face of a European hare. *Phesant tail few barbs*	Brown, webby hackle fibers.
Body	Dubbing mixed from fur and guard hairs of a European hare's mask, dubbed directly to waxed thread.	Dubbing from the back and belly of red or fox squirrel.
Ribbing	Fine oval gold tinsel. *→ gold wire*	Fine flat tinsel or gold wire.
Wing Case	Section from mottled turkey secondary feather.	Section from mallard primary wing quill or goose secondary wing quill.
Thorax	Same as body, dubbed in a loop.	Same as body, dubbed in a loop.

A

1. Pull about six inches of weighting wire from its spool (A). You can wind the wire with the spool cupped in the palm of your right hand or you can cut the wire from the spool first. Starting at about one quarter of the way from the bend to the eye, wind the wire in smooth, adjacent turns (B). Cover about the middle one-half of the shank.

B

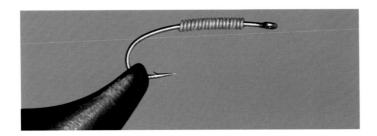

2. Don't get too close to the tail or your fly will look lumpy. And if you get too close to the eye, your materials will be crowded there when you finish. Snap or cut both ends of the wire and smooth the broken ends in place with your fingernail.

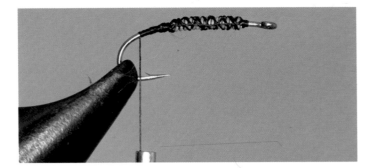

3. Start your thread in front of the wire. Wind back and forth over the wire three times with the thread. Add a few drops of head cement.

4. Gather a bunch of guard hairs and fur from the lower part of a hare's mask. The ends should be relatively even and the clump should be about the same diameter as the wire base on the hook. Cut the hair from the mask. Tie these in using either the Finger-on-Far-Side or Pinch technique. Wind over the guard hairs, toward the eye, in smooth, non-overlapping wraps. Trim the butt end of the hairs where the wire underbody stops, creating a smooth transition. Return the tying thread to the initial tie-in point.

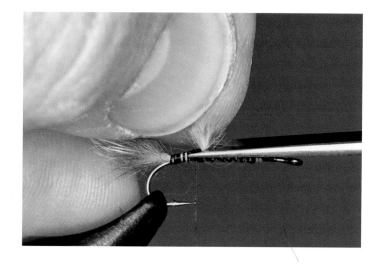

5. Pull four inches of fine oval gold tinsel from the spool (A). With the Finger-on-Far-Side technique, wind over one end of the tinsel toward the eye, halfway from the bend to the eye. Most of the tinsel should be hanging off the end of the fly, out of the way. Bind down the tinsel to the middle of the shank, and let the thread hang (B).

A

B

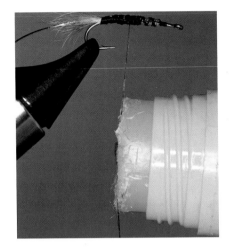

6. Pull about four inches of thread from your bobbin and coat it with wax. With practice you'll be able to dub even rough hare's ear onto the pre-waxed thread as it comes from the spool, but at the beginning I think you'll find it easier with extra wax.

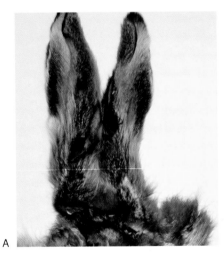

A

7. (This step is often done with large quantities before tying a number of flies.) Take one hare mask (A), and snip equal amounts of fur from the soft, bottom part and from the middle of the mask. Next, carefully skim the short, speckled hairs off the ears. Cut fur and guard hairs together, and only remove very large hairs or clumped bits of fur (B). Mix the three bits together in a coffee grinder, with soapy water, or by teasing and mixing back and forth with your fingers

B

7. (*Continued*) (C) until the whole thing is a scrambled mess. Take small amounts of fur (D) and, starting close to the hook, squeeze wisps of fur tightly around the thread, twisting in one direction only (E). Do about one finger width at a time. You will use too much and you won't squeeze with enough pressure on your first attempt—guaranteed. Your first bunch, close to the hook, should be about half as big around as the underbody. The next two bunches should be even tighter and smaller in diameter, and the final bunch or two should be as wide as the first one. The whole thing should vaguely resemble a greatly exaggerated, stretched hourglass.

C

D

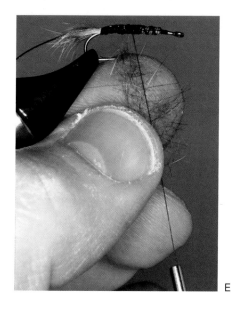

E

8. The reason for the hourglass shape is that I prefer to double-wind my dubbed bodies. This is not a conventional technique, but it makes it easier to get a tapered body, and the result is more durable.

9. Start winding the dubbed thread back toward the bend in even wraps that just touch each other. If your dubbing looks any thicker than what you see in the accompanying photo, start over. Pluck all of the dubbing off the thread and start from the beginning.

10. As you wind toward the tail, you should be winding that finer middle section. A well-tied nymph has a distinct taper from tail to thorax. If the dubbing is too thick at this point, back up, pluck some of the fur from the thread, and resume winding.

11. As soon as you reach the tail, wind back toward the eye. Try to keep that smooth taper. By controlling the thread tension and allowing the second wrap to bury into the first you can create a smooth, lifelike taper. If you don't have enough dubbing left on your thread, back up and add a pinch. If you are left with too much, back up and pluck some off. If you do add or subtract, make sure you twist the last part of the dubbing tightly to get a clean finish.

12. Spiral the tinsel through the body by wrapping mainly with your right hand, using the left hand to transfer the rib as your right goes around the bobbin. Tie off the rib with four very tight winds, and snip the end close to the hook.

A

13. Take the top portion of the shorter side of a mottled turkey secondary quill (A), and separate a section of quill that is about one hook gape in width. Cut it from the quill (B). Tie this in on top of the hook, right where the body ended, with the Gravity Drop with Upward Pull technique (C). The tip ends of the section should be pointing back toward the bend, and the shiny side should be facing up.

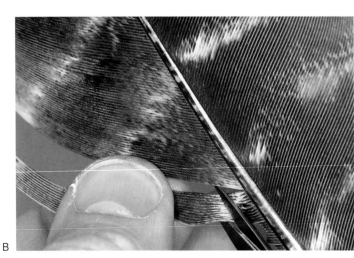

B

C

14. The quill section should stay flat on top of the hook. Avoid tying in the part of the section that was closest to the quill, as that part of the feather will split easily when you tie it in. If the piece slips to the far side, try to roll it back to the top; otherwise, cut a new section of feather and try again.

15. Bind the ends of the quill section under, winding about halfway to the eye. Snip the excess.

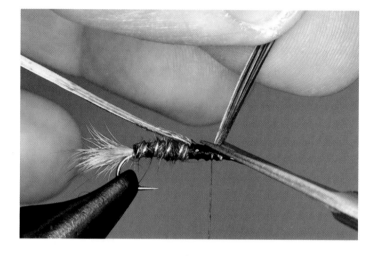

16. Pull eight inches of thread from your bobbin, loop it around your finger, and return the bobbin to the hook. Make a couple of winds around the hook to secure the loop. Wind the thread forward to a point that is about four turns of thread from the eye.

17. Place the ends of the loop in the hooks of a dubbing twister, or hang a pair of hackle pliers on the closed end of the loop. Wax both sides of the loop.

18. Push up slightly with the dubbing twister or hackle pliers to open the loop. Place a fairly large, loose clump of hare's ear fur inside the loop, as close to the hook as possible.

19. Close the loop by letting the tool or the hackle pliers drop.

20. Spin the tool or hackle pliers in a counterclockwise direction (looking at it from above the hook). Keep spinning until all of the fur is trapped between the thread and a fuzzy chenille is formed.

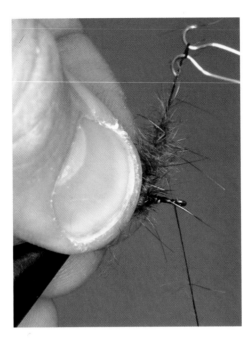

21. Wind the fur chenille forward to the eye with your right hand, stroking the long fibers back at each wrap with your left hand.

22. At a point that is well clear of the eye (between one-sixteenth and one-eighth inch behind the eye), tie off the fur chenille with your tying thread, using about five very tight wraps. Trim the ends very close to the shank.

23. Wind back over the fur a bit to allow plenty of room to tie in the wing case without crowding the eye.

24. At this point, I like to pull fibers straight out from the thorax with my fingers to get an impression of legs under the wing case.

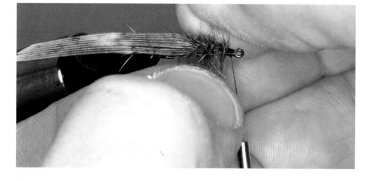

25. Pull the wing case straight over the eye and tie it in with the Gravity Drop with Upward Pull. After the first wrap, pull up and back slightly on the wing case to make sure it has not gotten too close to the eye.

26. Make four very tight turns over the wing case. While pulling up and back, trim the ends of the wing case very close to the hook. Flatten your thread and wrap over the head until the wing-case fibers are completely covered (A). Whip finish. At this point inspect your fly (B) to make sure there is enough fur sticking out from the thorax. If it doesn't look like this (C), gently pick out some fur with your dubbing needle. Add a drop of cement to the head windings.

A

B

C

Pheasant Tail Flashback

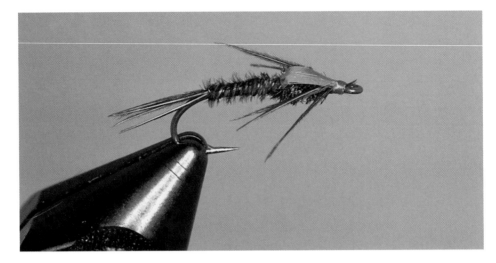

If the Hare's Ear Nymph is the meat-and-potato fly in a nymph fisherman's box, the Pheasant Tail is the bread and butter. It's a close second to the Hare's Ear in sales and popularity, and with the increase in tailwater and spring-creek fishing interest, the more subtle Pheasant Tail may soon become number one. Like hare's-ear fur, pheasant-tail fibers have a magical quality that seems to signal to a trout that the thing in front of its nose is alive and good to eat. This is probably a combination of its rusty color, a shade very common in aquatic invertebrates, and the hundreds of tiny fibers that may suggest the pulsating gills of mayfly larvae.

Frank Sawyer, a riverkeeper on the River Avon in England, developed the original Pheasant Tail in the middle of the twentieth century. He designed the fly for casting to trout that were visibly feeding just below the surface. The original pattern was tied by lashing the pheasant-tail fibers to the hook with fine copper wire. The wire acted as thread, rib, and weight, giving the fly glitter and just the right heft to sink below the surface. American tiers adapted the pattern for our faster waters and blind-fishing techniques. As a result, our Pheasant Tails are fatter and flashier. We put beads on the heads, make the wing case out of shimmering pearlescent tinsel, and make the thorax out of peacock herl.

When I'm fishing in spring creeks and clear tailwaters, where most of the insects are skinny and tiny, I still use Sawyer's original pattern, and feel it works better on picky trout. However, the original Pheasant Tail and the American version are both carried in the Orvis catalog; the domestic variation sells much better, so it's that fly I will show you here. Some Pheasant Tail Flashbacks carry the pearlescent tinsel all the way down the back, but this pattern just uses the tinsel over the wing case. Don't ignore the bead-head version, though. Some tiers make the tails and abdomen as shown here, substituting a copper-plated brass or tungsten bead for the entire thorax/wing-case arrangement. Others pull a wing case over the bead, which makes the fly trickier to tie but perhaps more realistic.

If you want to tie the original, use orange thread and merely rib the fly with copper wire, which makes it easier to tie. And leave off the legs: the tail, abdomen, thorax, and wing case are all simply pheasant-tail fibers. (If you tie this fly smaller than Size 18, you should tie the traditional variety because the American version gets too bulky and difficult to tie in the smaller sizes.) It's interesting that Sawyer also developed a companion nymph to the Pheasant Tail called the Grey Goose, which substituted silver wire and goose-wing fibers for the materials in the Pheasant Tail. It never caught on, either here or in the U.K., which says a lot about the special qualities that pheasant tail-fibers lend to a nymph.

Pheasant Tail nymphs work in both moving and still waters. The pattern is the best imitation of mayflies of the family Baetidae known, and these bugs are the most common insect in most trout streams.

The fly should be fished dead-drift, on a long, light tippet, with a small indicator. Although it catches trout in all waters, it is especially useful in productive streams such as tailwaters or spring creeks, and in rivers with fine gravel bottoms and lots of riffles. To give you an idea of the effectiveness of this fly around the world, a recent study of trout stomach contents in six South African trout streams discovered that 56.1 percent of their stomach contents were mayfly nymphs of the family Baetidae. Here's a pattern you can carry with confidence, anywhere!

Pattern Description

	MATERIAL	SUBSTITUTE
Hook	Bead Head, Sizes 12–24.	2XL nymph.
Tail	Three to six pheasant-tail fibers.	Hungarian-partridge fibers.
Thread	Orange, Size 8/0 or 10/0.	Brown or tan.
Body	Three to five ringneck pheasant-tail fibers.	There is no substitute. Without this stuff it wouldn't be a Pheasant Tail.
Rib	Fine copper wire.	Orange thread.
Wing Case	Pheasant-tail fibers, over which is a piece of pearlescent tinsel.	Just pheasant-tail fibers, or a half-dozen strands of Flashabou or Krystal Flash.
Throax	Two peacock-herl fibers.	Pheasant-tail fibers or a small brass or copper bead.
Legs	Pheasant-tail fibers from the wing case.	Just leave them off on smaller flies.

A

B

C

1. Attach the thread and wind it back to the point where the bend of the hook starts to angle down.

2. Find a center tail feather from a rooster ringneck pheasant that has a rusty color on the outside (A). Isolate three to six fibers in an area where the rusty part is longest. Trim them from the feather (B), make sure the tips are lined up, and tie them in (C) using the Finger on the Far Side or Pinch techniques. The uncut, tapered ends of the feather should point off the back of the hook and should extend only about one-half of the shank length beyond the hook.

3. Make three very tight turns in one spot to secure the tail fibers.

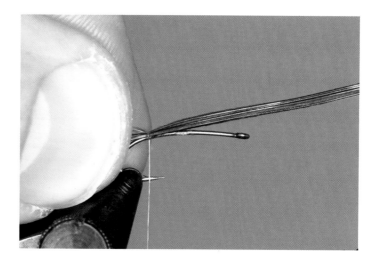

4. Pull about four inches of fine copper wire from the spool. (A) Pull the long pieces of pheasant tail back out of the way. Tie the wire in at the same spot with two very tight winds. There should be a short piece of wire lying on top of the shank, with the rest of the wire pointing off the end of the fly (B).

A

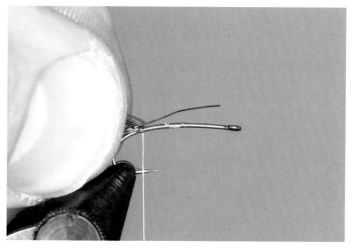

B

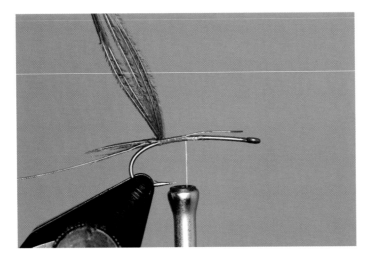

5. Wind the thread forward to the middle of the shank, binding the wire under with smooth, non-overlapping turns.

6. Trim the remaining wire using the heavier inside of your scissors, not the points as shown here! Your scissors will dull quickly if you persist in this habit.

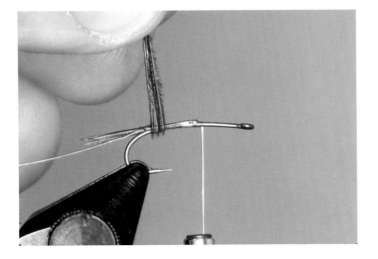

7. Grasp the pheasant-tail fibers left at the bend and wind them forward in smooth, adjacent turns. If the fibers spread and get out of control, twist them with your fingers. These fibers can also be tricky when transferring from your right to left hand, particularly if they are short. You may want to clamp a pair of hackle pliers on them to keep things under control.

8. When you get to the middle of the shank, tie the fibers off with four very tight turns of thread. Don't forget to hold the fibers with your right hand and tie off with your left; otherwise you won't cross the thread over the fibers and they won't get bound under. Trim the leftover fibers close to the hook.

9. Spiral the copper wire forward through the pheasant-tail body. The rib will hold the fibers in place when the tiny, sharp teeth of a twenty-inch brown trout cut them.

10. Tie off the copper wire in the same fashion as the feather fibers. Trim the copper wire. Watch those scissors—didn't I just tell you about using the points? Take about five tight turns of thread over the ends of the wire and feathers to secure them.

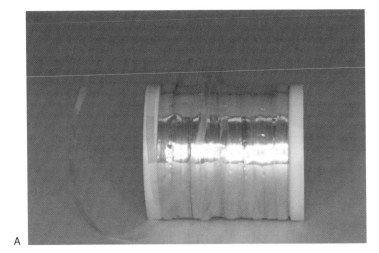

A

11. Cut a two-inch piece of pearlescent tinsel from a spool (A). Tie the tinsel using the Gravity Drop with Upward Pull so that most of it lies along the back of the fly and just about one-sixteenth inch lies toward the eye (B). Bind down this tinsel by winding a layer of thread forward and then back to the initial tie-in. Don't bind down the tinsel too close to the eye.

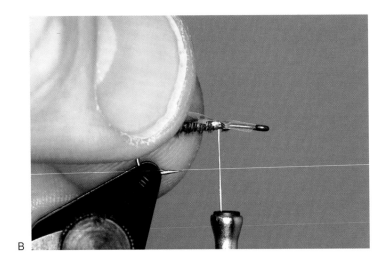

B

12. Tie in about six more fibers of pheasant tail over the top of the tinsel. The natural ends of the fibers should lie along the back of the fly, and they should extend just about a full shank length along the back.

13. Bind the ends under as you did with the tinsel and trim them. Again, don't venture too close to the eye.

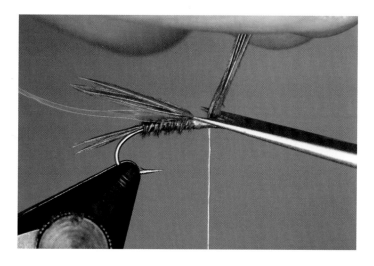

14. Select a pair of peacock herls from the bottom of an eyed tail feather (A). The feathers at the top are too thick for nymph thoraxes. Trim the very tips of these fibers (cut back about one-half inch) and tie them in by the thinner tips. Peacock herl is easy to tie in and three tight turns, working toward the eye, should suffice (B). Trim them about halfway to the eye and continue to wind the thread forward until you are about three to four thread widths from the eye. Let the thread hang here.

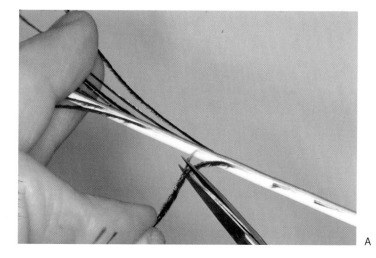

A

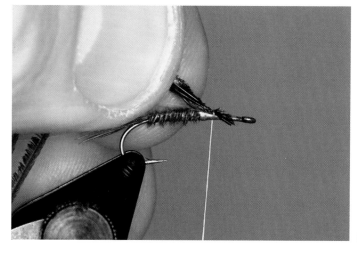

B

15. Lift the two peacock herls together in your right hand. You'll notice there is a side with short flue (the tiny green fibers) and a side with long flue. You'll want the long-flued side to point back toward the bend as you wind. If you have tied the herls in by the tip, this usually happens automatically; if not, twist the herls slightly until they behave.

16. Wind the herls forward to the place the thread was left hanging. Tie them off with three very tight wraps and trim. Wind back onto the herls a bit; about two turns of thread will do.

17. Pull the pheasant-tail fibers straight out over the eye and bind them in with the Gravity Drop with Upward Pull.

18. Don't use any more than three wraps. Make sure you are still about three or four turns of thread behind the eye. Don't trim the ends of the pheasant tail.

19. Split the pheasant tail fibers into two roughly equal bunches. Use a dubbing needle or your fingers to split them and pull each bunch straight out to the side.

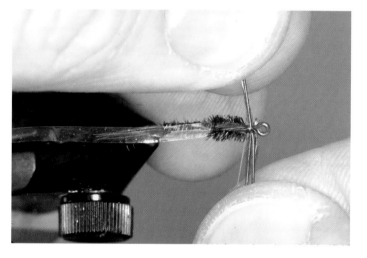

20. Wind the thread back toward the thorax and wing case, trapping the fibers on each side of the hook.

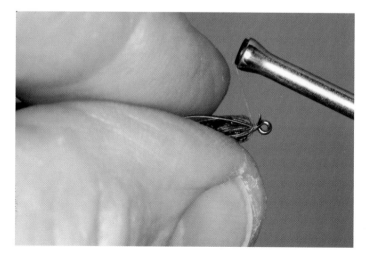

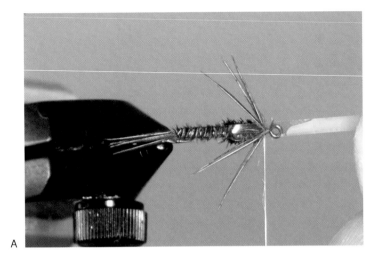

A

21. Pull the piece of tinsel straight over the eye (A) as you did with the pheasant fibers. Tie in with the Gravity Drop with Upward Pull (B), using about four wraps.

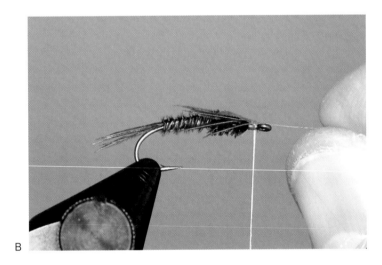

B

22. Pull the tinsel straight up to get it away from the eye. Trim carefully with the point of your scissors.

23. Flatten the thread and cover any material still visible just behind the eye. If you've been careful not to crowd the eye, the head should look like this.

24. Whip finish and apply a drop of head cement.

CHAPTER 7

Emergers

CDC Emerger

What is this fly, a nymph or a dry? Good question. It's whichever you want it to be, and it can be fished wherever trout are feeding. Add some sink putty to the leader and the CDC Emerger will dredge the bottom of deep riffles, holding air bubbles within the CDC and hare's-ear fibers, looking like a mayfly or caddisfly about to pop to the surface. Take off the weight, don't apply any fly dressing, and it drifts just under the surface like an insect trying to break through the film. Rub it in white powdered silica dressing and it floats like a dry, except the wings and

thorax ride above the surface and the tail and abdomen hang below the surface. It's deadly.

CDC comes from the French *cul de canard*, or "butt of the duck." The original French and Italian CDC flies I have seen were mostly just a dubbed body and a CDC feather wound like hackle at the front of the fly. CDC is difficult to wind but easy to tie in a bunch, so most of our American versions use CDC as a wing or wing case (or both, as in the following pattern). The pattern is a modern, generic emerger that can be tied in any color to match the emerging bug of the week. The dressing I show here is neutral and buggy, and dressed as shown this fly can imitate everything from a Size 10 caddisfly to a Size 22 mayfly.

Most tiers today use turkey or goose biots, fibers from the short side of a wing quill, for bodies. The material is inexpensive, strong, and easy to prepare. However, I like traditional peacock quill because I don't think any other quill does such a great job of imitating the segments of an insect's body. It's a pain to prepare, but sometimes you will see stripped peacock quills for sale. They're stripped with bleach and are often brittle, but easy to use if you soak them in water. A third alternative for a quill body is stripped hackle stems, which are also soaked in water prior to use so they don't split.

It's said that CDC flies should not be dressed with fly flotant because CDC has natural water-repellent oils from a duck's preen glands. This is true if you shoot your own CDC, and natural CDC might have marginally better floating qualities because of the oils, but the reason CDC floats so well has nothing to do with oil. The downy feather structure holds air and pinions the fly in the surface film. Any downy feather will float—have you ever tried to cast a weighted marabou streamer or Woolly Bugger without wetting the fly first? The downy marabou feathers will float even a weighted hook until soaked.

It's okay to treat CDC flies with fly flotant. Just make sure it's one of the dry types, not a silicone paste or liquid. The primary reason flies with CDC catch fish so well is because the hundreds of downy fibers move with each little gust of wind or twitch of current, so the fly looks alive.

Pattern Description

	MATERIAL	SUBSTITUTE
Hook	Short-shank curved nymph, Sizes 10 through 18.	Extra-fine dry-fly, especially in flies smaller than Size 16.
Tail	Three to five mottled Hungarian-partridge body feather fibers.	Wood-duck flank or Antron yarn.
Thread	Tan, Size 8/0.	White, yellow, or olive.
Body	Stripped peacock quill.	Goose or turkey biot in olive, tan, brown, or yellow.
Wing Case and Wing	Gray CDC feather.	Gray marabou or a tiny fluffy feather from the base of a pheasant or grouse feather (known as an "aftershaft" feather).
Thorax	Hare's-ear fur.	Any brown or olive dubbing.

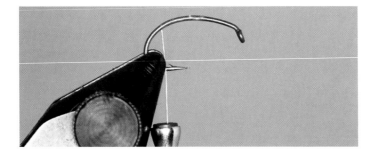

1. Attach the thread to the hook and wind it down about one-quarter of the way around the bend, farther than you would for most patterns. If the thread slips down, you can remove the hook from the vise and reposition the hook so the eye is tilted down.

2. Strip the down from the bottom of a Hungarian-partridge body feather. Isolate a few of the fibers and snip from the stem, keeping the ends even.

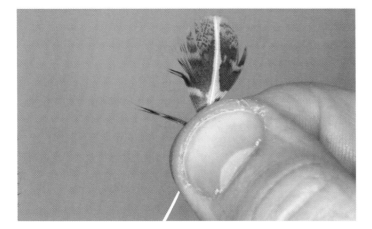

3. Measure the fibers against the hook so they extend about half a shank length beyond the hook, with the fine ends pointing back and the trimmed ends lying on top of the shank.

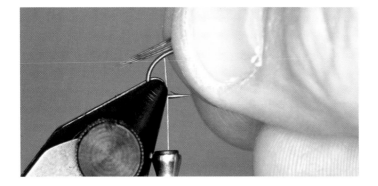

4. Tie the fibers in using either the Forty-five Degree Roll or Finger on Far Side technique. Three tight turns are sufficient.

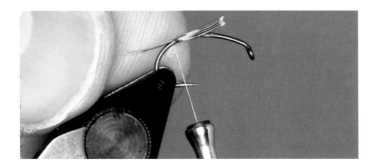

5. A smooth underbody is critical. Flatten the thread and continue to wrap over the ends of the partridge feather to the middle of the shank. It's hard to tell where the middle is on a curved hook, so let's say halfway between where you tied in the tails and the eye.

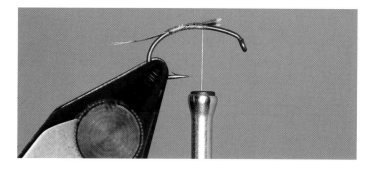

6. Still using flattened thread, return to where you tied the tails. Make smooth, non-overlapping wraps.

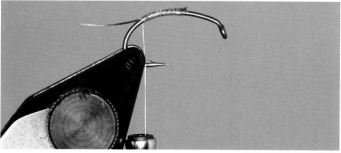

7. Snip one herl from just below the colored eye on a peacock feather. This is where you'll find the widest, most strongly marked quills.

8. Using an eraser or your fingernail, carefully remove the flue from the peacock quill. You'll have to work on one side, turn the feather over, and work on the other side. Peacock quill is fragile, so don't press too hard. You should strip the lower two and a half inches of the quill. The part closest to the tip is too fragile to wrap and too narrow to give any segmentation.

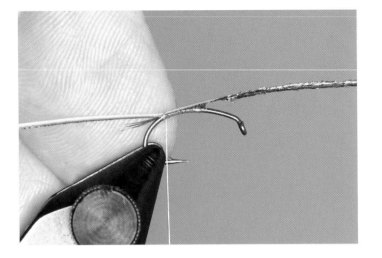

9. Lay the stripped peacock quill over the shank so that the fine stripped end just reaches the middle of the shank. Tie in the quill with three tight Finger on Far Side wraps.

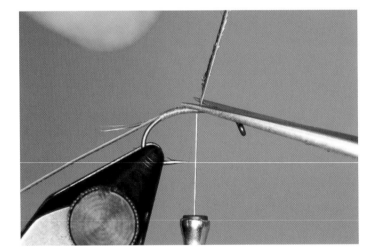

10. Make sure your thread is flattened. Wrap it forward to the middle of the shank, smoothing out any bumps as you go; quill bodies won't tolerate any bulges underneath. Trim the end of the herl flush with the hook.

11. Wind the quill forward in adjacent turns, with no overlap. It may be easier to hold the fragile quill with hackle pliers. You need a very easy touch with almost no tension. If the quill splits or breaks, you'll have to unwind and start over.

12. Tie off the quill where the thread has been hanging. Three tight turns will suffice. If you leave a small piece ahead of the tie-in point, it will be further bound under when you tie in the wing case.

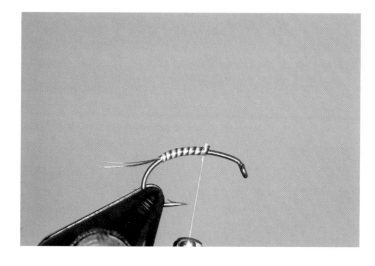

13. Apply a couple drops of deep-penetrating or thinned head cement to the quill body. Some tiers rib their quill bodies with fine wire for added strength; I don't like the looks of it, and take my chances with bare quill and one coat of cement.

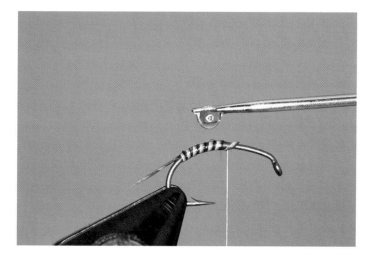

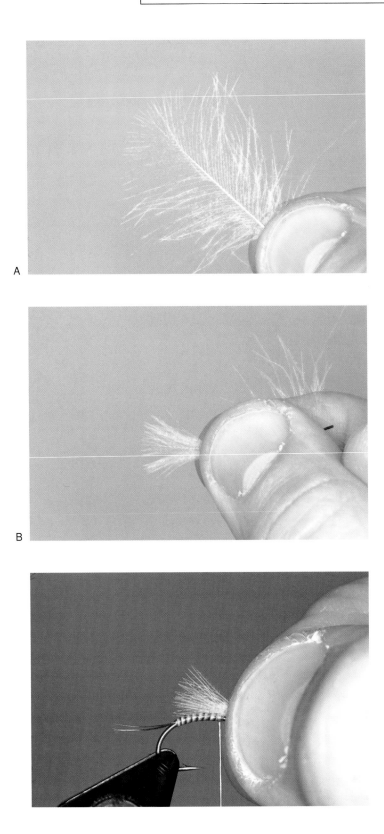

A

B

14. Select a gray CDC feather with dense fibers and even ends (A). Stroke the fibers toward the tip and pinch the feather in your right fingertips (B).

15. Measure the CDC at the point where the thread is hanging. The fine ends should extend just to the bend of the hook.

16. Transfer the feather to your left hand, placing the ends of your left fingertips where the ends of your right fingertips were. Tie in the CDC feather with the Pinch method, using about four wraps. Then take three very tight wraps at the same spot.

17. Pull the butt of the CDC feather back over the rear of the fly. Take a couple turns of thread up against it to hold it in place.

18. Dub a small amount of hare's-ear fur to the thread. You may want to wax the thread if you have trouble getting the fur to stick.

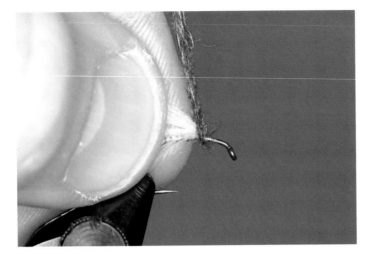

19. Pull the butt of the CDC feather back again and make a couple turns of dubbing up against the place where the feather was tied in.

20. Wrap the dubbing forward to within four thread turns of the eye.

21. Pull the butt of the CDC feather over the eye.

22. Tie in the CDC with the Gravity Drop with Upward Pull. After the first wrap, push back on the feather and lift it so it develops a slight bulge. This bulge holds air and also imitates the attitude of emerging wings.

23. Make four more tight wraps and trim the feather with the point of your scissors. Wrap a tight, neat head with flattened thread. Whip finish.

24. If the hare's-ear fur is not fuzzy enough (it should stick out the sides like tiny legs), pick some out with your dubbing needle.

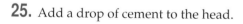

25. Add a drop of cement to the head.

Emerging Caddis

The original hairwing caddis imitations from the Rockies were tied with bucktail. Flies like the Bucktail Caddis were difficult to tie and didn't float well. Then, in the 1970s, brilliant fly tier and guide Al Troth, of Dillon, Montana, made some caddis imitations from elk hair, which flares a bit more than bucktail. This gave his flies a tent-shaped wing, better for imitating a caddis, and they floated better. His Elk Hair Caddis is still one of the most popular flies today. Craig Matthews of West Yellowstone, Montana, produced another elegant variation, the X-Caddis. This fly turned the hairwing caddis into an emerger with the addition of an Antron or Z-Lon tail. This tail imitates the pupal shuck, still clinging to a caddis attempting to escape its skin and the surface film for the freedom of flight.

Matthews' variation makes sense because trout eat caddisflies when they are emerging from the pupal stage far more often than they take fully emerged adults. His pattern calls for a wing of coastal deer hair, which floats well and gives a wonderful caddis-like profile. Coastal deer is harder to handle, though, so I have substituted more tractable elk hair. The fly is really just Matthews' X-Caddis with an elk hair wing, but for brevity and to avoid inventing a new pattern I have just called the fly a generic Emerging Caddis. You may want to experiment with coastal deer or hair from the mask or legs of a white-tailed deer after you have mastered the elk-hair version shown here. Stay away from deer belly hair on this one, because it is too coarse and flares too much for a decent caddis wing.

You can vary the body color on this fly to match the caddis you see emerging or those you expect to see after reading a book on caddis hatches. The color variation shown here matches many species of caddisflies with light green bodies, notably the apple caddis that hatches on Northeastern trout streams during apple-blossom season.

Fish this fly any time you see trout rising and caddis in the air. If you watch trout feeding during a caddis hatch, what you'll observe is most of the trout making splashy rises at nothing, ignoring the caddis adults twitching on the surface. These fish are actually taking caddis pupae just as they break the surface film. If you don't figure out what is going on, you can fish a high-floating dry fly over the fish for hours without a strike, or perhaps a couple of splashy refusals. Try this fly, which rides in the film just like the emerging naturals. Fish it without drag, just like a dry. If you have trouble seeing the fly, add a tiny piece of Strike Putty two feet up the leader above your fly. When the indicator moves, set the hook!

Pattern Description

	MATERIAL	SUBSTITUTE
Hook	Extra-fine dry fly, Sizes 10 through 14. Bigeye Dry on Size 16 through 20.	2X-long nymph.
Thread	Tan, 6/0 or 8/0.	Any color that matches the body.
Tail	Tan Antron yarn.	Z-Lon yarn.
Body	Dubbed Antron-Hare Blend. Light olive for this example.	Any natural or synthetic dubbing in olive, gray, black, tan, or brown.
Wing	Elk hair.	Coastal deer or fine-textured white-tail deer. CDC is also effective.

A

1. Pull a few inches of tan Antron yarn from the spool (A). Squeeze it tightly between the fingernails of your right and left thumb and index fingers (B) so that it gets kinky and "fuzzed out." The shuck should look contorted (C), rather than straight and neat.

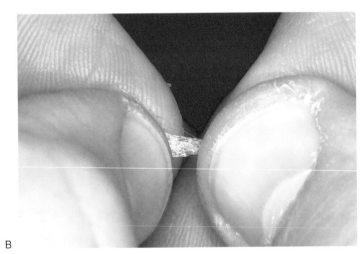

B

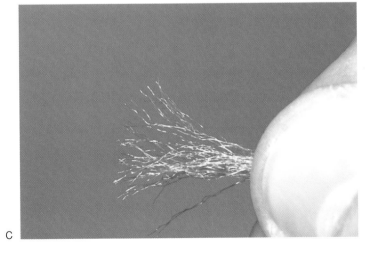

C

2. Attach your thread and bring it back to the point just ahead of where the shank of the hook ends and begins to drop below the horizontal. Measure the clump of Antron with your right hand: It should extend about one-half to one shank length beyond the end of the fly. It should also be about as wide as the hook gap when fuzzed out.

3. Transfer the yarn to your left hand, making sure you transfer it from your right thumb and forefinger directly to your left, pinching in the same spot so you don't lose your place. Angle the yarn at forty-five degrees on a horizontal plane even with the shank, with the butt end pointing toward you.

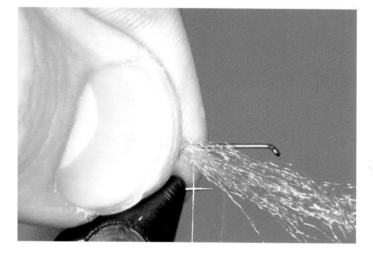

4. Take one wrap of thread around the yarn with light tension.

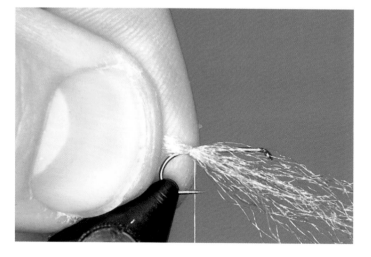

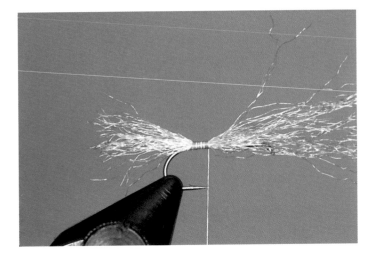

5. Take a second, third, and fourth wrap, each with increasing tension and each about one thread width closer to the eye. As you wrap, guide the butt ends of the yarn along the top of the hook shank. Don't let it roll around the far side.

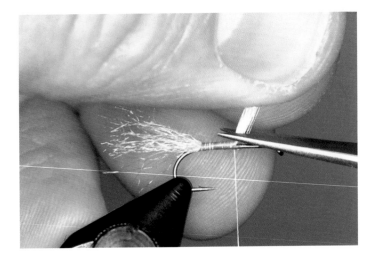

6. When you have wrapped the yarn halfway to the eye, stop wrapping, pull up on the rest of the yarn, and trim it close to the shank.

7. Wrap the thread about three-quarters of the way to the eye in smooth, non-overlapping wraps.

8. Dub light-olive Antron-Hare Blend on about four inches of the thread. Dub one finger width at a time by teasing a small amount of fluff from the dubbing and rolling it tightly onto the thread. Roll in one direction only. Use some wax on the thread if you have problems. Most dubbing problems stem from using too much fur and not enough pressure.

9. Begin to wind the dubbed thread back toward the tail. Don't overlap wraps unless you see a gap in the body as you wind.

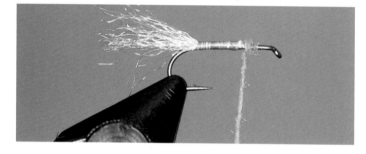

10. When you get to the tail, make one firm wrap at the base of the tail; hold the tail in your left hand so it does not roll to the far side of the hook.

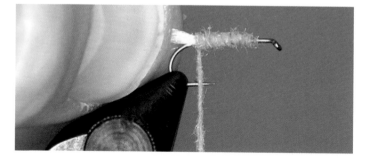

11. Finish off where you started. If you don't have enough dubbing left to finish, back off a couple of wraps and add a bit more. If you have too much, also back off a few wraps, pluck some of the dubbing from the bottom of the thread, and roll the material that is left on the thread hard between your fingers, as the plucking process will loosen all the fur not wrapped on the hook.

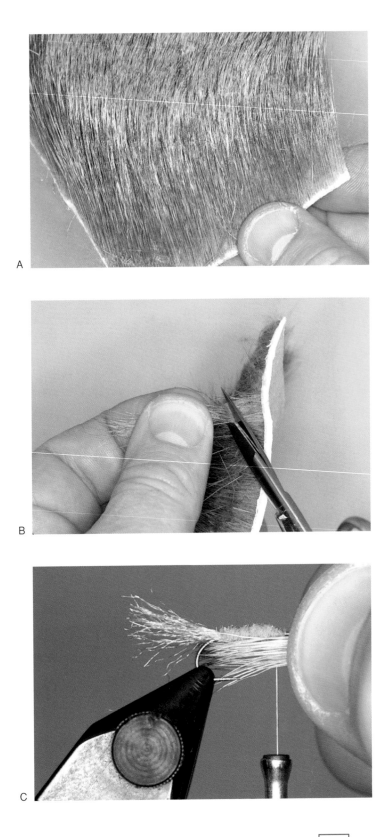

A

B

C

12. Take a piece of elk hair with fine, even ends (A), and cut a bunch (B) that is about one hook gap in diameter (C). If the bunch is too big, remove some hair. If it's too small, cut a bit more hair from the same area on the skin and add it to the bunch before stacking. Clean the fine hairs and fuzz out of the butt ends by holding the tips between the thumb and forefinger of one hand and pulling toward the butt with the thumb and forefinger of the other hand. Place the hair in a stacker, rap sharply three or four times, then remove the hair by its tips from the stacker.

13. Now measure the hair for length, using your right hand. It should extend just beyond the bend, as shown.

14. Transfer the hair carefully to your left hand and pinch the hair over the tie-in point, keeping the hair on top of the shank and your fingers pressed to the sides of the hook. Rock back onto your knuckles slightly to open up a spot to sneak the thread into.

15. Take a loose turn of thread around the bunch. As soon as the thread has passed over the hair, roll your fingertips back onto the hair and thread and pinch. Pull straight down on the bobbin, using firm pressure (the Pinch technique).

16. Repeat this wrap about five times, using the same Pinch technique. The hair will flare ahead of the tie-in point.

17. At this point, remove your fingers to make sure the clump of hair stayed on top of the shank. If not, unwrap and start over, or try to roll the hair upright. If you roll it back in place, secure it further with three more Pinch wraps.

18. Place the thumb and forefinger of your left hand back over the hair. Mentally divide the butt ends just in front of them into thirds. Pull the closest third upright by creeping your thumb and forefinger ahead and pulling back. Take four very tight turns of thread just ahead of the bunch.

19. Repeat for the second third. When you do the last third, lift all of it behind the eye and wrap ahead of it so nothing remains sticking over the eye.

20. The process you just completed, which gives the head of the fly a "Mohawk" appearance, locks the hair at ninety degrees. It will never pull out— often a problem with hair-wing flies.

21. Trim the butt ends of the hair (A) at a slight upward angle (B), using the hook eye as a guide.

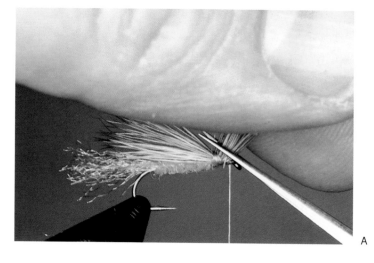

A

B

22. Whip finish by angling the tool slightly off to the right so the knot slips in under the head.

23. Apply Deep Penetrating Head Cement to the exposed winds behind the hair butts and to the whip-finish knot, and let a little cement slip into the hair butts.

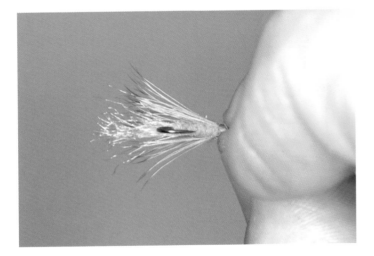

24. You now have a caddis pattern that will retain its tent-like shape even after being twisted around the jaws of a half-dozen big trout.

CHAPTER 8

Dry Flies

Adams

For as long as I have been with the Orvis Company, twenty-four years as I'm writing this, the Size 14 Adams has been the most popular fly, year after year. And it hasn't been just the most popular *dry* fly; in fact, more of these were sold than any pattern of any type, period! That's quite an accomplishment for a fly originally designed to imitate a pesky land-bred insect that hardly ever gets into the water.

The Adams was developed in the 1930s by Michigan angler Len Halliday as a deer-fly imitation for the Boardman River. I've never fished the Boardman, but unless it is unlike any other trout stream in the world, deer flies are probably not prime trout food. Deer flies hatch in dry soil in coniferous forests and mate over land, and the only deer flies I have ever seen in a trout stream are ones I swatted from around my head, gleefully crunched between my fingers, and tossed into the water.

I am having fun at the expense of one of the most devilishly productive dry flies ever invented. It is a traditional dry fly with classic lines, which means it does not look much like a mayfly. Yet during mayfly hatches, this gray-bodied, brown-and-black-and-white-winged fly catches trout even when pink-bodied, gray-winged Hendricksons are on the water. The Adams is known as a deadly fly during caddis hatches, yet it has upright wings and tails—appendages that adult caddis don't sprout. In smaller sizes, it fools trout during Blue-Winged Olive and midge hatches.

Why does it work? We don't know and probably never will. Trout may not see flies in their entirety, and may just pick out a certain pattern in the naturals and our imitations. Just use the Adams on faith, enjoy the fun of casting to rising trout, and delight in using a traditional pattern.

A few notes on tying this pattern: It's a traditional dry-fly pattern, and if you master this one, you'll also be able to tie the famous Catskill dries like the Hendrickson and Light Cahill. If you have trouble mixing the tails, don't. It's just as effective with either brown or grizzly tails. I prefer using natural muskrat because it's easy to dub, looks translucent, and floats well; you can use a gray packaged dubbing if you like. If you tie these smaller than Size 18 (the Adams makes a terrific adult midge imitation), just leave off the wings. Finally, try the Adams as a parachute, by substituting white calf-body hair for the grizzly hackle tips and winding the hackles around the base of the wing.

Pattern Description

	MATERIAL	SUBSTITUTE
Hook	Extra-Fine Dry Fly, Sizes 10 through 14. Bigeye Dry Sizes 16 to 24.	None.
Thread	Black, 8/0 or 10/0.	White.
Tails	Mixed brown and grizzly hackle fibers.	Just brown or just grizzly hackle fibers.
Body	Dubbed muskrat fur.	Medium-gray packaged dubbing.
Wings	Hen grizzly hackle tips.	Round hackle tips from grizzly rooster or saddle hackles.
Hackle	Mixed brown and grizzly.	Ginger grizzly or cree hackle.

1. Attach the thread in the middle of the shank and wind back to the bend in smooth wraps. Stop just before the bend starts to slope below the horizontal. Search the side of a grizzly hackle cape for a spade feather that has firm, glossy fibers. These will always be found about halfway up the cape on each side.

2. This step may sound silly, but it enables you to pluck tail fibers from a feather without removing the feather from the cape. Place the cape, skin side down, against your chest. Pull the selected feather out to the side with thumb and forefinger of your right hand. Brace the pinkie of your right hand at the bottom of the feather, at the far side of the stem. With thumb and middle finger of your left hand, find about a dozen stiff fibers, pull them together at right angles to the stem, and pluck them all at once.

3. You should have a nice bunch of tail fibers, all lined up. Set these down gently where they won't get knocked around.

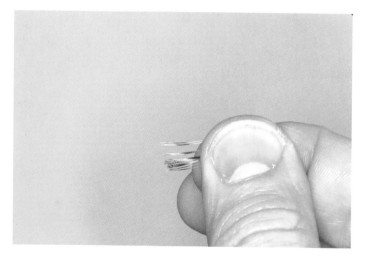

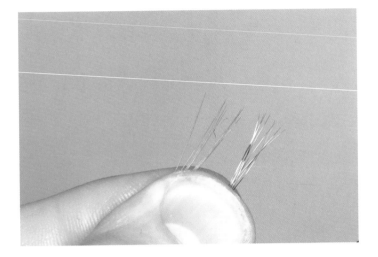

4. Repeat the procedure with a bunch of brown hackle fibers. Transfer these to your right hand so the tips are sticking out beyond the end of your thumb and forefinger. Now pick up the grizzly fibers and try to line up their ends with the brown ones. If you have trouble lining them up, place them in a small stacker and stack them as you would hair.

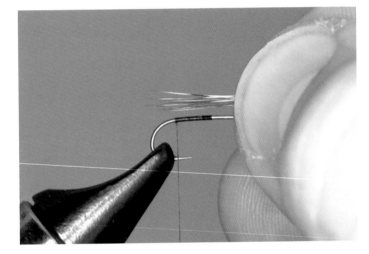

5. Measure the tails, using the shank as a guide. They should be about one shank length beyond the tips of your pinched fingers. If the length extending beyond them is too short, pull the fibers out. If they are too long, choke up a bit with your fingertips.

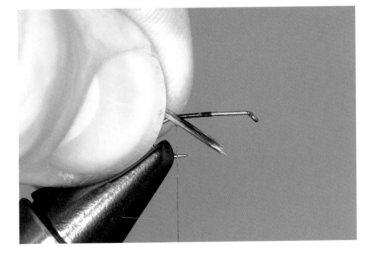

6. Carefully transfer the fibers to your left hand, pinching them at the same spot you just measured. Line them up at a forty-five-degree angle, horizontal with the shank, with the butts pointing toward you.

7. Make one fairly loose wrap as you start to angle the fibers so they line up with the shank.

8. Make three more wraps toward the eye with increasing tension until they line up perfectly. If they start to roll to the far side, roll them back.

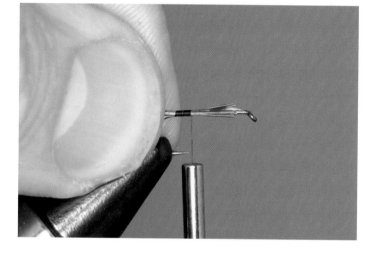

9. Wrap the thread in smooth wraps toward the eye until you get to the middle of the shank. Trim the butts of the tail fibers. Wrap the thread forward to about four thread widths short of the eye, then back toward the bend to a point that is one-quarter of the shank length behind the eye. This forms a thread foundation for the wings.

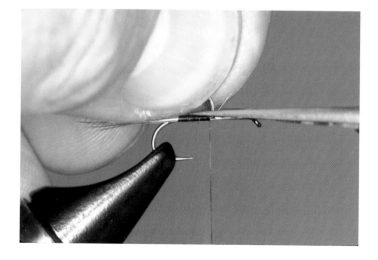

10. Select two hen grizzly hackles that are slightly less than one hook gap in width. They will be more evenly matched if you pluck them from the same place on the cape.

11. Place them along the shank and measure one shank length down from the feather's tips.

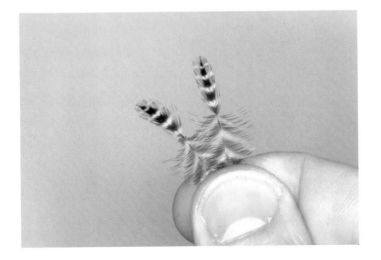

12. Beyond this point, stroke the fibers down toward the stems so they stand at right angles to them.

13. With the point of your scissors, trim the hackle fibers very close to both sides of the stems (A), leaving fine stubble on either side of them (B). Put the two hackles together, with their ties aligned as closely as possible. The concave side of each feather should face the other, so the feathers look like a single unit.

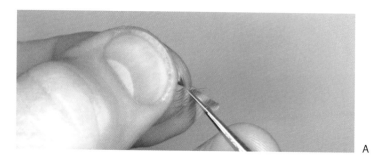

A

B

14. With your left hand, line up the point between the trimmed and untrimmed hackle stems right over the top of where the thread is hanging. The tips of the hackles should be pointing out over the eye.

15. Tie in the hackle tips with three wraps, using the Pinch technique.

16. Flatten the thread and wrap back toward the bend over the butts of the hackles until you meet the point where you trimmed the tails. Trim the butts here.

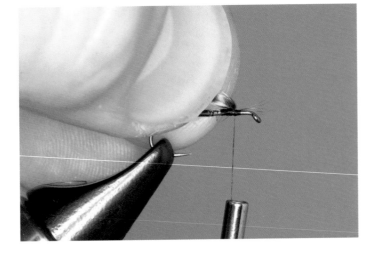

17. Wrap the thread forward. Pull the wings straight up with your left hand. Twist the thread, if it is not already twisted, and wind about four turns right up against the front side of the base of the wings.

18. The wings should now be sticking straight up. If not, make two more wraps in front of them, right against the base.

19. Push down gently on the wings to divide them.

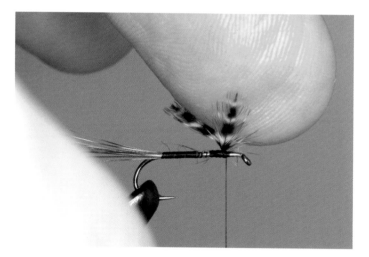

20. Grab the near wing with your left hand.

21. Bring the thread up and cross it between the wings on top of the shank.

22. Continue winding the thread on the far side and under the shank, directly behind the far wing. Grab the far wing with your left hand.

23. Bring the thread up behind the near wing and cross the shank between the wings, ending immediately in front of the far wing. These last four steps are called a figure-eight wind, and are essential steps in dividing upright dry-fly wings.

24. Repeat the figure-eight wind and make two more turns immediately in front of the wings. Trim any hackle fibers that might have gotten bound under.

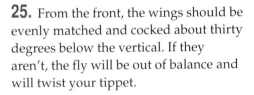

25. From the front, the wings should be evenly matched and cocked about thirty degrees below the vertical. If they aren't, the fly will be out of balance and will twist your tippet.

26. Prepare some muskrat dubbing (A). Pull a bunch of fur from the hide, about a pinkie width for each fly you plan to tie. Cut it as close to the hide as possible (B). Pinch the bunch of fur in the middle with one hand. Carefully pull the long brown guard hairs out of the bunch (C). You should be left with a soft, fuzzy pinch of fur. Tease the fur back and forth between your fingers until all the fibers are swirled around and confused (D).

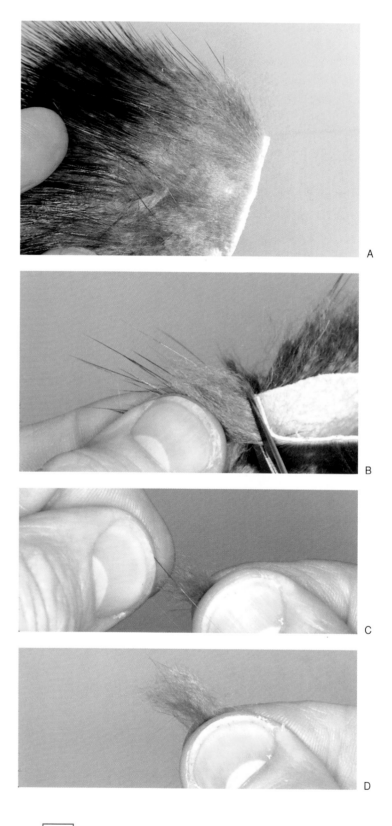

A

B

C

D

27. Tease a small bunch of fur from the ball. The fur should be as fine and loose as you see here.

28. Using small amounts of fur and lots of pressure, roll the fur onto the thread with your fingers. Roll in one direction only. Dub fur over about four inches of thread, in a very slight and elongated hourglass shape, with the thinnest diameter of dubbing in the middle.

29. You will have a short length of thread that is not dubbed. Use this to wrap back to a point just ahead of the midpoint of the hook. Wrap here until the dubbing first touches the shank.

30. Wrap back to the tail. If you've calculated correctly, the middle point of your dubbing, the thinnest place, will end up at the tail. If not, you can sometimes back up a bit or spiral forward, as the double layer of dubbing gives more margin for error. Wind the dubbing back toward the wings, striving for a slight taper. If you get a lump, either put more pressure on the thread or don't overlap so much. If you get a gap in the dubbing, make an extra wrap there or loosen up on your thread pressure to get a slightly bigger diameter.

31. Add a pinch of dubbing if needed, or pluck some off if you have too much. You should end up well behind the wings, just forward of the midpoint of the hook, so you have room to wind hackle behind the wings.

32. Select one brown and one grizzly hackle with fibers that are one and one-half to twice as long as the gap is deep. When tying a dry fly with two hackles from the same neck, take both hackles from the same spot on the cape so they are evenly matched. Because you must take hackles from two different capes, pay special attention to how close the fibers are in length; otherwise your fly will look sloppy. I like to fan them together around the hook before tying them in to make sure they match. Strip the bottoms of the hackles so any webby fibers are removed (A). Place them both together so the bottoms of their fibers line up and the shiny (convex) side of one is against the dull (concave) side of the other (B).

A

B

33. Tie the hackles in together, immediately in front of the dubbed body, with the dull sides facing up or toward you. Make sure you leave a bit of bare stem behind the tie-in point. The stems can extend between the wings if they are long. Wind the thread forward in smooth, very tight turns to just behind the wings.

34. Trim the stems in the middle of the wing crotch by lifting the stems gently and carefully placing the tips of your scissors between them.

35. Wind the thread forward to about four thread widths short of the eye.

36. Grab the top hackle, or the one facing you (could be either color, the order in which you tie them in is not important), with your right fingertips or hackle pliers. It should roll on its side so the dull side of the hackle is now facing forward. If not, twist it slightly or wrap backwards for one revolution until it behaves.

37. Wind this first hackle flush to the end of the dubbed body, but not on top of it. You should always be winding toward the eye. You'll probably make one revolution before the hackle fibers come into play; this is good, as it lets you line things up.

38. Wind up to the base of the wings with even wraps that don't quite touch. With some hackles this might be two turns, with others it could be three or four.

39. Grasp the wings in your left hand and pull them back slightly. Make a wind of hackle immediately in front of the wings.

40. Continue to wrap forward, about two more turns, until the hackle is where the thread was left hanging.

41. Hold the hackle on top of the shank and tie it in with three very tight wraps.

42. Trim the excess hackle carefully with the point of your scissors.

43. Go back to the other hackle and wind in the same manner. This one will have to wind its way between the wraps of the first, so try to place each wrap beside the stem of the first. You can also wiggle it back and forth a bit as you wind.

44. As you come in front of the wings, pull them back for a moment as you did with the first hackle.

45. On the very last wind, grasp all the other fibers by sweeping your left thumb and forefinger from the eye back until you capture them all. Make one final turn with the second hackle right in front of your fingers; this should help keep all of the other fibers out of the hook eye. Tie off this feather as you did the first, and trim the excess.

46. Flatten your thread, wrap until the ends of the hackle stems are covered (but no more than a half-dozen wraps), whip finish, and apply a drop of head cement.

Tan Comparadun

In 1971, Carl Richards and Doug Swisher introduced a revolutionary dry fly in their book *Selective Trout*. Even though it was designed to imitate a fully emerged mayfly dun, it had no hackle—almost heresy in the days when fully hackled dry flies were the only adult mayfly imitations sold in fly shops. The No-Hackle fly, with its delicate duck-quill wings, is still used by some anglers in tough situations, but it is hard to see and does not float well in riffles. The 1970s was the decade of innovative new dry-fly patterns, and in 1975 Bob Nastasi and Al Caucci introduced their own version of the No-Hackle, the Comparadun, through their book *Hatches*. This fly was based on a rough-water searching pattern called the Haystack, made with hair from a snowshoe hare and popularized by Adirondack tier Francis Betters, who learned the pattern from his father. Caucci and Nastasi

refined the Comparadun into a clean, precise mayfly imitation that is durable, floats well, and is easy to tie.

This is the pattern I use most often to imitate mayfly duns, as do many other serious tiers and fishermen. You can see it, even in the roughest white water. If the fly gets soggy or is mussed up by a trout, a quick pass through a bottle of white desiccant powder will spruce it up and keep it floating. Trout like it. They may take it for an emerger because the body sits in the water, but they'll also inhale it without hesitation when feeding selectively on duns. My only objection to the Comparadun is that it lands heavily on the water, without the drogue-chute effect of hackle, so it is sometimes a disadvantage when spooky trout are rising in flat water. I'd advise a parachute or standard hackled pattern in such a situation.

The version tied here is a standard tan Comparadun, a color scheme that can be used to imitate scores of adult mayflies. I like tying flies that imitate many species, and this one in Sizes 10 through 20 can imitate March Browns, gray foxes, Quill Gordons, Hendricksons, sulfurs, pale morning duns, and many other species. Sure, the wing and body are a shade too dark for Sulfurs, Hendricksons have more pink and olive in their bodies, and Quill Gordons are skinnier. At least that's what we think; the trout seem to find it close enough unless they've been pounded all season and are super-picky.

With some fine dubbing in a variety of shades and some light and dark deer hair, you can imitate any mayfly in the world with a Comparadun. Just change the body colors and use a light or dark deer-hair wing, whichever is closer to the bug you're trying to match. Hair for the wing should be chosen carefully, though. Fine hair with even ends,

in particular hair from coastal mule deer or from the face of a white-tailed deer, makes the best wings. If you can find a nice piece, reindeer or caribou is superb for smaller flies; better yet, it comes naturally in dark and light dun. Whitetail belly hair is too coarse and flares too much; elk is too coarse for flies smaller than Size 12.

A great variation of this fly, developed by Craig Matthews of West Yellowstone, Montana, is called the Sparkle Dun. Matthews substitutes a shuck of Antron yarn or Z-Lon for the split tails, which imitates the nymph's shuck trailing behind a just-emerged mayfly. This simple variation, easier to tie than a Comparadun because the split tails are the hardest part, turns it into a true emerger. I've chosen the tougher Comparadun to show you, because if you can tie this one, the Sparkle Dun is child's play. (See the tying instructions for the Emerging Caddis for adding the shuck.)

Pattern Description

	MATERIAL	SUBSTITUTE
Hook	Extra-Fine dry fly, Sizes 10 through 14. Bigeye Dry on Size 16 through 20.	2X-long dry fly
Thread	Tan Size 8/0.	White, olive, or yellow.
Tails	Stiff brown hackle fibers.	Microfibbetts.
Wing	Fine white-tailed deer face hair.	Fine coastal or mule deer, or gray caribou.
Body	Tan rabbit.	Any soft natural or synthetic dubbing in olive, yellow, cream, or brown.

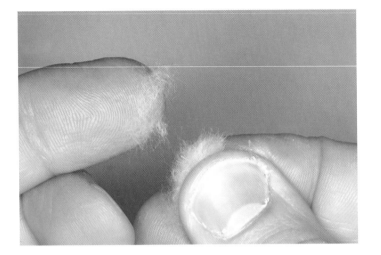

1. Attach the thread in the middle of the shank and wrap to the end of the shank. Tease a small amount of dubbing from a larger bunch onto your fingertip.

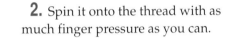

2. Spin it onto the thread with as much finger pressure as you can.

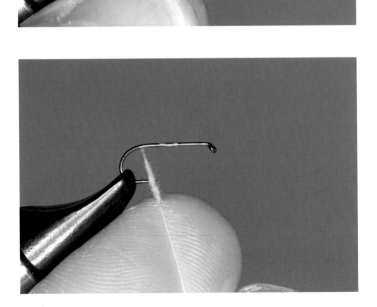

3. The dubbed part of the thread should be no longer than three-quarters of an inch for the Size 14 fly shown here, and very tight. If it's too long or loose, slide it up toward the hook.

4. Wrap the dubbing right at the end of the shank into a tight ball. Make one turn toward the bend, one just ahead of it toward the eye, and a third wrap in between and on top of the other two to create the ball.

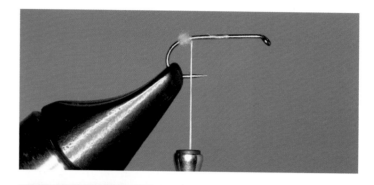

5. Find the spade hackles on a dry-fly cape. They are the wide, glossy feathers about halfway up the cape, on either edge. The long feathers at the top of the cape or saddle hackles won't give you fibers as stiff as these.

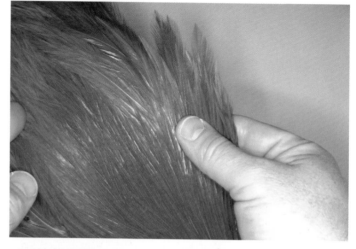

6. Isolate one feather (feathers are easier to handle if you don't pluck them from the cape) and pull it out to the side. Hold the base of the feather with the thumb and fourth finger of your right hand, the top of the feather with the index and third finger. Grab about six glossy, straight fibers from the middle of the feather, and pull them gently at ninety degrees to the stem. The fine ends should line up in your left fingertips when you do this.

7. Pull straight out with your left hand. The fibers should pluck neatly from the stem.

8. Transfer the fibers to your right hand. Make sure they are lined up at the fine ends. Adjust your grip until one shank length is beyond the end of your fingertips.

9. Switch the fibers to your left hand. Hold them at a forty-five-degree angle to the shank, with the butts pointing toward you and the fibers at the tie-in point touching the front of the far side of the dubbing ball. Spin your thread until it is twisted, to help get precise placement. Make one fairly loose wrap around the hackle fibers, pinning them against the dubbing ball. Make two more turns, tightening each turn by pulling the bobbin tube straight at your chest on a horizontal angle, rather than pulling straight up or down.

172

10. Do the same thing with another bunch of fibers against the front near side of the ball.

11. Tighten this bunch by pulling away from you on the horizontal.

12. The tails should now be split as you see them here. If not, wind back against the ball and take one tight turn only, pressing the fibers against the ball.

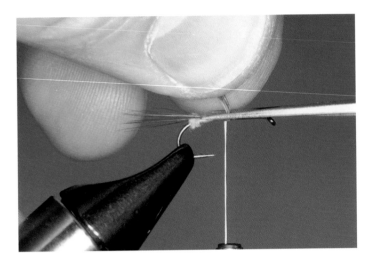

13. Wind the thread forward to the middle of the body, checking the tail position as you wind. The tails can still be knocked out of alignment until you bind down the butts of the the hackle fibers to the middle of the shank. Trim the remaining hackle fibers pointing toward the eye. Wind the thread forward almost to the eye, then back about one-third of the way from the eye to the bend.

14. Select a piece of fine deer hair with even ends. The hair on the left is too coarse and won't give the fly a strong wing profile. Hair that looks like the stuff on the right is perfect.

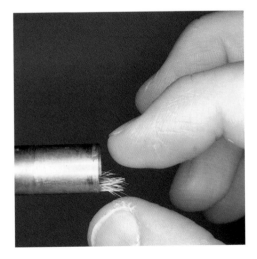

15. Place the hair in a stacker and rap several times. Carefully pull the hair out of the tube. It helps to keep the tube horizontal.

16. Measure the wing with your left hand. It should be one shank length high—that is, the hair should extend one shank length beyond the end of your fingertips.

17. Place your left fingertips directly over the place where you left the thread hanging. Work one loose wrap of thread inside your fingertips by rocking them backward slightly, then forward onto the thread (the Pinch Wrap).

18. Pull straight down with very firm pressure, making sure you pinch the sides of the shank so the hair stays on top of it.

19. Make at least four wraps in the same place, using even more pressure on each wrap. Release the wing—it should be partially flared and mostly on top of the shank, as shown here.

20. Trim the butts of the hair behind the wing on a slight angle.

21. The wing should now look like this.

22. Flatten your thread and wind over the hair butts to smooth and secure them.

23. Raise the wing upright with your left hand and bring the thread in front of the wing.

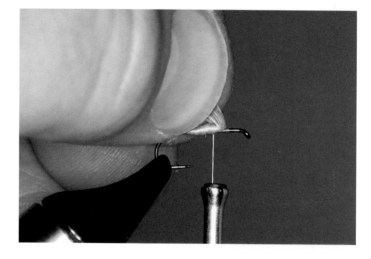

24. Twist the thread into a rope and build up a tapered hump of thread in front of the wing. Most of the thread should be right up against the base of the wing, but it should taper a little toward the eye so you don't develop an abrupt hump.

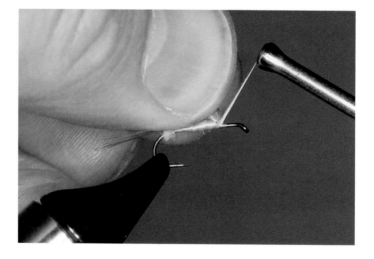

25. When you release the wing, it should stand up on its own. After a day in your fly box, improperly set wings will creep forward over the eye. Put a drop of head cement at the base of the wing, but don't rely on dubbing or head cement to keep the wing in place. Thread buildup in front of the wing is the key, and there should be almost as much thread and bulk in front of the wing as behind.

26. Dub tan fur onto the thread, making the dubbing tight and thin. Don't let it get any thicker than what you see here.

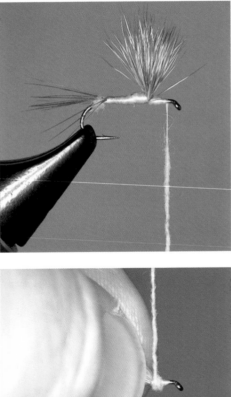

27. Pull the wing back out of the way and wind the dubbing back to the base of the wing in two wraps.

28. Now pull the wing forward over the eye and make a wrap of dubbing tight at the rear of the base of the wing. Leave the wing slanting over the eye—you'll fix it later.

29. Wind the dubbing back to the base of the tails. Start to space your wraps a little wider and put more tension on the thread as you get close to the tails. Make only one wrap close to the tails while holding them in place with your left hand, and then start wrapping forward.

30. Wrap up to the wing, then pull it upright and make one tight turn just in front of the wing. If there is any dubbing left on your thread, pick it off, spin the few remaining fibers to create a small taper, and wind about four turns of bare thread for the head.

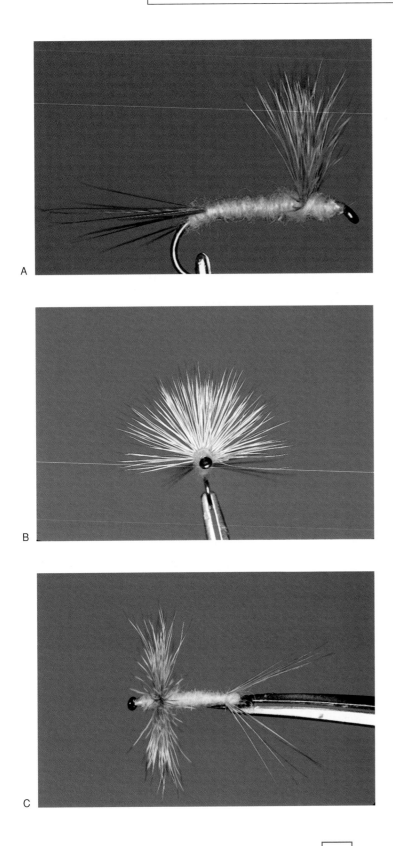

31. The finished fly (A). If the wing does not extend from one side of the hook to the other in a semicircle as shown here (B), preen it and pull both sides of the hair down until it does. The wing forms an outrigger, as do the tails (C), and keeps the fly floating and properly balanced.

Rusty Parachute

Parachutes are my favorite style for imitating adult mayflies. They look realistic in the eyes of a fisherman, apparently look good to the trout, float well, and land as softly as a natural. Parachutes give a delicate profile in slow water and fool even the most demanding brown trout, yet you can see them even in a fast run at dusk. If a parachute is the right size and close to the color of the naturals, trout eat it, whether they are feeding on an emerging dun, fluttering dun, or spent spinner.

This particular pattern, with its rusty body and gray wings and legs, is one of the most useful mayfly imitations. In Size 14, it emulates the famous Hendrickson mayfly and several other species of *Ephemerella* mayflies that hatch in the East in May and June. It looks like various species of *Paraleptoplebia* mayflies in Sizes 16 and 18. In a big Size 10 or 12 it works for the Leadwing Coachman (*Isonychia*) mayfly of June and September. And it seems to me that about 80 percent of the mayfly spinners I see on the water are some shade of brown, so this fly can become your jack-of-all-trades for spinner falls. Yes, I know it has upright wings, and many spinners fall to the water with their wings fully spent. But I can see this fly well after sunset, and trout eating spinners don't seem to mind. I carry this fly in Sizes 10 through 22 and would never be without it.

When tying flies bigger than Size 16, you can substitute fine elk or deer hair for the turkey body feathers I've used in this pattern. However, unless you can find some really nice gray caribou body hair, the smaller patterns will be easier to make using the turkey feathers. Some tiers also use synthetic yarns to make parachute wings. Although these materials are easy to work with, I don't think flies tied with yarn wings are as effective as those made with natural materials.

You can use any shade of blue dun (gray) for the hackle and wing. I like to use fairly

181

light dun because I can see it better—in fact, some times I'll tie this fly with a pure white wing. The body color is best as a deep rusty brown, and I have not found a natural fur with the right color, so I use packaged natural dyed fur like rabbit, a synthetic, or a blend of the two.

Why don't we fish parachutes all the time? Two reasons: They are less durable than tra-ditional dries and hairwings, and they're dif-ficult to tie. (If you have skipped ahead and are attempting to tie this as one of your first attempts at tying, slow down. Go back and tie a Caddis Emerger or Woolly Bugger. Mas-ter them before you attempt this one!) I have gotten over my fear of tying parachutes, and have learned a few tricks along the way. I hope you'll learn to enjoy tying them, too.

Pattern Description

	MATERIAL	SUBSTITUTE
Hook	Extra-fine dry fly, Sizes 10 through 14. Bigeye Dry Sizes 16 to 24.	2X-long dry fly.
Thread	Brown, Size 8/0 or 10/0.	Black or tan.
Tails	Blue-dun spade-hackle fibers.	Gray or clear Microfibbetts.
Body	Rusty brown pre-packaged dubbing.	Pheasant-tail fibers or stripped quill from a dark brown hackle feather with no black center.
Wing	Blue dun turkey-body feather.	Synthetic yarn or deer hair.
Hackle	Blue dun, parachute style.	Grizzly.

1. Attach the thread in the middle of the shank and wrap to the end of the shank.

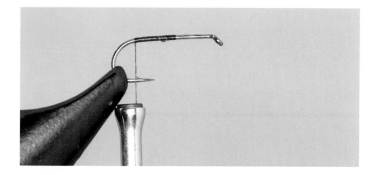

2. Dub a small amount of dubbing onto the thread with as much finger pressure as you can. The dubbed part should be no longer than three-quarters of an inch for the Size 14 hook shown here, and very tight.

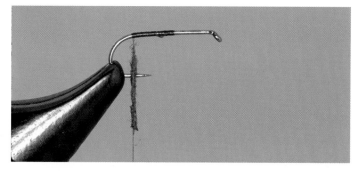

3. Wrap the dubbing right at the end of the shank into a tight ball. Make one turn toward the bend, one just ahead of it toward the eye, and a third wrap in between and on top of the other two to create the ball.

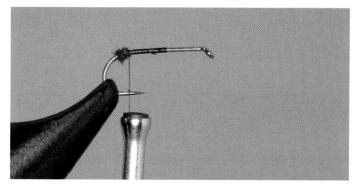

4. Pluck four to six stiff fibers from a blue-dun spade hackle, or grab three fibers from a package of Microfibbetts. Make sure they are lined up at the fine ends. Measure with your right hand until one shank length is beyond the end of your fingertips.

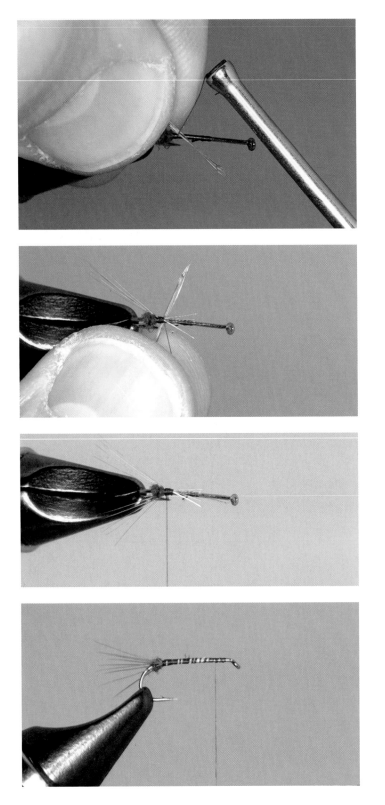

5. Switch the fibers to your left hand. Hold them at a forty-five-degree angle to the shank, with the butts pointing toward you and the fibers at the tie-in point touching the front far side of the dubbing ball. Spin your thread until it is twisted, to help get precise placement. Make one fairly loose wrap around the hackle fibers, pinning them against the dubbing ball. Make two more turns, tightening each turn by pulling the bobbin tube on a horizontal angle.

6. Do the same thing with another bunch against the front near side of the ball. Tighten this bunch by pulling straight away from you on the horizontal.

7. The tails should now be split as you see them here. If not, wind back against the ball and take one tight turn only, pressing the fibers against the ball. If you make too many turns, you'll end up with a lumpy body (and no one likes a lumpy body).

8. Spiral the thread forward to a point about four thread widths from the eye, then back about one-fifth of the shank length. You don't have to be too neat or even as long as you make thread base for the wings.

9. Select a gray turkey-body feather with even, unbroken tips. Snip the center stem about an inch from the tip. This is the part you'll use. Save the rest of the feather; you can use pieces on each side for smaller flies.

10. Gather all of the fibers (A) around the center stem so they line up at the tips (B). Some tiers don't like to include the center stem, but I feel it helps to give you a stiffer base for winding the parachute hackle.

A

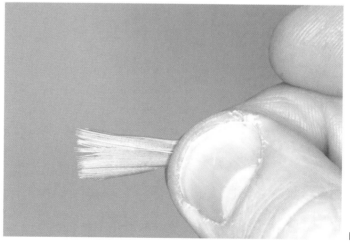

B

11. Measure the wing. It should be no longer than the shank.

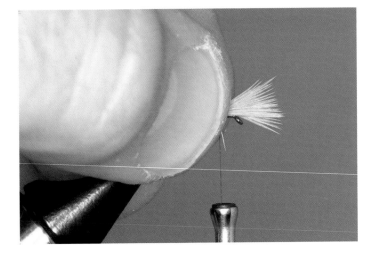

12. Lay the measuring point on the wings on top of the shank and pinch it in place, making sure you put finger pressure on the sides of the shank.

13. Using the Pinch Technique, tie in the wing with four very tight wraps.

14. Leaving a small stub beyond the tie-in point, trim the butt ends of the turkey feather.

15. Flatten your thread and make tight wraps over the wing butts until they are covered.

16. Lift the wing straight up with your left thumb and forefinger. Advance the thread to right in front of the wing. Spin the thread to twist it. Make four to five wraps right in front of the wing.

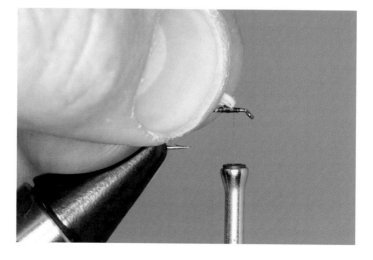

17. Release the wing. If it leans forward, lift up again and make two more wraps in front.

18. Lift the wing straight up again with your left thumb and forefinger. Bring the thread completely around the base of the wing just above the shank. You'll have to catch the bobbin with the last two fingers of your left hand as you pass the bobbin over the vise and bring your right hand back around.

19. Make three turns around the wing and tighten by pulling straight over the eye and then over the bend, on the horizontal. This will create more of a mayfly-shaped wing than a circular clump of fibers.

20. Select a blue-dun hackle with fibers no longer than one and one-half hook gaps. You can measure it as shown without even removing the feather from the cape—hold the cape between the third and fourth finger of your right hand, pull the feather away from the cape with your left hand, and flare it around the hook. This is easier and more accurate than using a hackle gauge. Just don't fan the hackle too hard or you'll crimp the stem.

21. Strip the lower stem of the hackle of all fuzz and webby fibers. Place the stem along the near side of the wing. The dull side should be facing you.

22. Tie the stem in front of the wing with four very tight turns of thread. There should be a fair amount of bare stem behind the tie-in point, as shown.

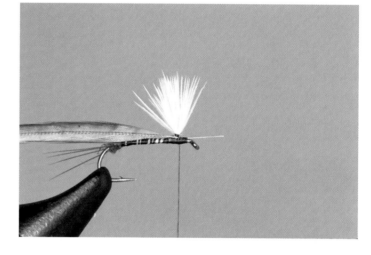

23. Pull the hackle straight up against the wing, with the dull side still facing you.

24. Wind up the wing about four turns, trapping the hackle stem against the wing, just as you did to gather the wing fibers a few steps ago.

25. Wind back to the front of the wing and snip the excess hackle stem. With the hackle tied in this way, it will be easier to wind and far less likely to pull out. Dub three to four inches of thread with a tight, thin layer of dubbing.

26. Make one or two turns of dubbing in front of the wing, holding the wing and hackle with your left hand to keep them out of the way.

27. Wind the dubbing in adjacent turns back to the tails. As you get close to the tails, make sure they are in place. Preen them if they are not splayed at 90 degrees to each other, then make one tight turn of dubbing against them to set them for good.

28. Dub back to the eye and hold the wing while passing the dubbing in front of it. End just a couple of thread widths behind the eye. Adjust your dubbing if necessary to get a slight taper toward the wing and a subtle thorax built up around it.

29. Grab the tip of the hackle with your right fingertips or with hackle pliers held in your right hand. Hold the wing tightly with your left fingers.

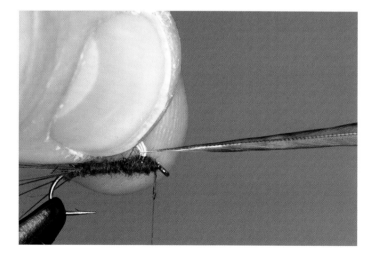

30. Pull the hackle in front of the wing until it is horizontal. Ideally, the dull side of the hackle will flip down as you pull the hackle horizontal. If not, try backing up a half-turn in a clockwise direction (looking down), or twisting the hackle until the dull side faces straight down and the shiny side faces up. With a long hackle, it might also help to choke up on it with your fingertips or pliers.

31. This is the hardest part. Wind the hackle around the base of the wing in a counterclockwise direction (looking down). The best way to do this is to hold the wing tightly with your left thumb and forefinger. Bring the hackle around the base of the wing about three-quarters of a turn, catching the pliers with the last two fingers of your left hand. Bring your right hand back in front of the fly and transfer the pliers back to your right hand, then continue the process.

32. Try to work down the wing, so that each wrap is below the previous one. You should expect to get anywhere from four to eight turns of hackle around the base of the wing, depending on the size of the fly and the thickness of the hackle stem. After the first two or three wraps of hackle have been established, you may be able to release the wing from your left fingers, which makes winding easier.

33. For your last turn of hackle, pull all the fibers you have wound so far up and out of the way with your left hand and make a turn of hackle around the very bottom of the wing base.

34. Let the hackle pliers hang over the far side of the shank, just behind the spot where the thread is hanging.

35. As the hackle hangs there, pull up all the parachute fibers once again with your left hand and tie off the hackle with four very tight wraps.

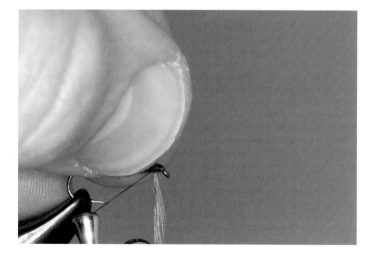

36. Pull your thread up and away from the underside of the hook with the bobbin in your left hand. Snip the hackle, and let the hackle pliers and hackle tip fall to the ground or onto the table.

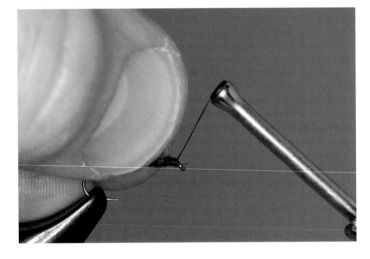

37. Again pull up all the parachute fibers with your left hand and make a few more tight winds over the hackle tip to secure it. Pulling the fibers out of the way will keep them from getting tied under.

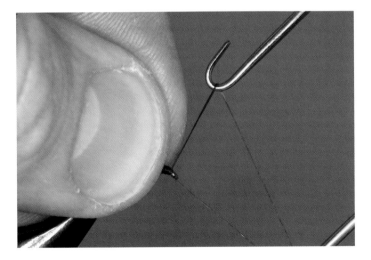

38. Pull four inches of thread from the bobbin. Begin a whip-finish knot. As you bring the point of the triangle of thread to the eye with your right hand, cradle the bobbin in your left palm and stroke all of the parachute fibers back with your left thumb and forefinger as you guide the whip-finish knot to the head. You can make the whole whip finish while holding the hackle out of the way with your left hand.

39. Once you make two wraps, you can remove your left hand and sneak the rest of the wraps under the hackle by tilting the tip of the whip-finish tool off to the right.

40. Trim the thread carefully. Apply Deep-Penetrating Head Cement to the underside of the head, letting it flow to the upper side.

41. Some tiers also like to place a very small drop of head cement at the upper part of the hackle junction with the wing.

Royal Wulff

Developed in the 1930s, the Royal Wulff is one of the early hairwing dry flies. Although it is named for Lee Wulff, who developed the Gray and White Wulffs, this is not a pattern he originated. Sometimes known as the Hairwing Royal Coachman, its color scheme is based on a Victorian wet fly, which at first seems too gaudy for an insect imitation. However, both the red floss and peacock herl change to shades of brown when wet, so the Royal Wulff could look like an ant or beetle to the trout. I hope we never know for sure. Its brilliant colors in an otherwise drab box of dries shout, "pick me," like the exuberant boy who wants to be chosen first in a sandlot baseball game.

This is a fast-water fly, its white wings allowing you to track the fly's progress through the heaviest pocket water. Still, the materials used in the patterns are not very buoyant, so it needs a lot of hackle. You might need three or even four hackles from a lower-grade hackle cape, though two might be sufficient with a premium dry-fly neck or decent saddle hackle. With the best dry-fly saddles, you may be able to pack in all the hackle you need with a single feather. Just make sure you cover at least one-third of the shank with hackle to support the heavy hair wings and tail.

You can make the wings out of calf tail or body hair. Calf tail does not hold as much water as body hair, so flies tied with it float marginally better, but it's harder to stack neatly and doesn't look as pretty on a finished fly. Some tiers use the same hair for the tail; I like brown bucktail because it matches the original Royal Coachman tails (golden pheasant tippets) better, is stiffer, and floats better.

Although the Royal Wulff is not a great pattern to use during hatches on most of our hard-fished trout streams, it's a terrific attractor pattern for small-stream fishing. In tiny waters, where trout don't see enough of any one bug to feed selectively, the Royal Wulff looks enough like an ant, beetle, caddisfly, or stonefly to draw rises from any fish remotely interested in surface food. In the United States, thirty-eight percent of our land surface is suitable for trout streams and eighty-five percent of these streams are less than twenty feet wide. There's a lot of water out there ready for your Royal Wulff!

Pattern Description

	MATERIAL	SUBSTITUTE
Hook	Extra-fine dry fly, Sizes 10 through 14. Bigeye Dry in Sizes 16 and 18.	None.
Thread	Black, Size 8/0.	White.
Tail	Brown bucktail.	Brown elk hocks or moose body hair. White calf is also used but does not float the fly as well.
Body	Peacock herl with a red floss band in the middle.	None for the peacock herl. Red thread or Flexi-Floss can be used for the center band.
Wings	White calf body hair.	Straight white calf tail.
Hackle	Brown, the darker the better.	Light ginger or furnace hackle.

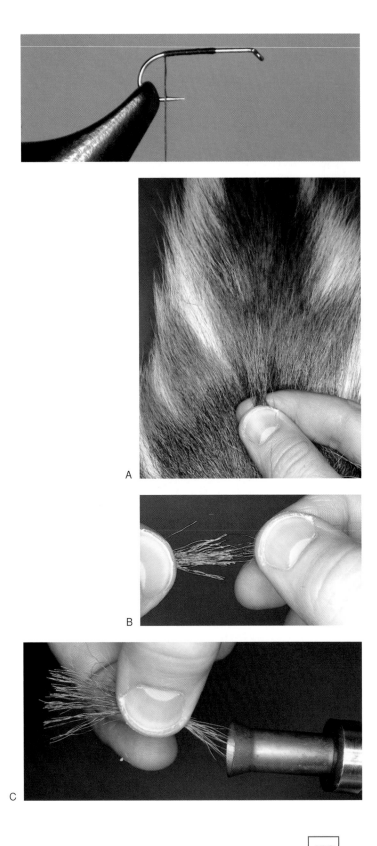

1. Attach black thread to the middle of the hook shank and wind back to the beginning of the bend.

2. Select a bunch of brown bucktail from the top half of the tail (A). (Bucktail from the lower half is not as stiff and flares too much.) It should be about one-half the hook gap in diameter. Hold the tips of the bucktail in your left fingertips and clean the fuzz and short hairs from the base of the hair (B). Place the hair inside a medium-sized stacker to even the ends (C).

A

B

C

3. Measure the bucktail. It should extend about one shank length beyond the bend.

4. Using the Forty-five-Degree Roll or the Pinch Method, attach the bucktail to the shank and wind toward the eye, binding it under halfway down the shank.

5. Trim the butts of the bucktail.

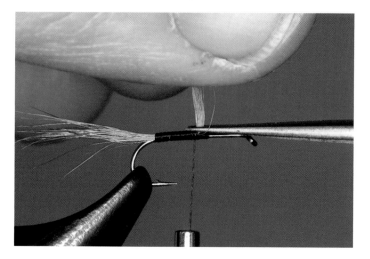

6. Wind a thread base forward to a point one-third of the shank length back from the eye, and let the thread hang. The thread base helps keep the wing on top of the shank when you tie it in. It doesn't matter whether your thread is flattened or not, as long as you cover the shank here with a single layer.

7. Select a bunch of long calf-body hair (A) or straight, fine calf tail, at least twice the shank length for easy handling, and as wide as the hook gap. Clean the calf hair as you did the bucktail and stack it. Calf body stacks with about two raps; calf tail requires a few more taps and perhaps a second round of stacking (B).

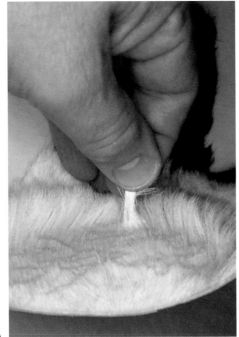

A

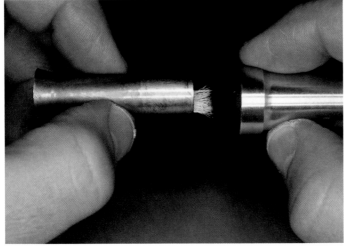

B

8. Measure the hair so the distance between where you are pinching the hair and its tip is one shank length. Tie it in where you left the thread hanging, using the Pinch Method, with lots of thread tension and a tight pinch. Calf hair will not flare. Make about a half-dozen tight, adjacent thread wraps back toward the bend, until the butts of the calf hair almost meet the trimmed butts of the bucktail in the middle of the shank.

9. Trim the butts of the calf hair so they meet the bucktail. Wind over them with a few turns. Pull the bunch of calf hair straight up with your left fingertips and advance the thread to just in front of the calf hair. Twist the thread into a rope. Wind tight turns in front of the wing, moving forward toward the eye every couple of turns so the hump of thread in front of the eye is tapered.

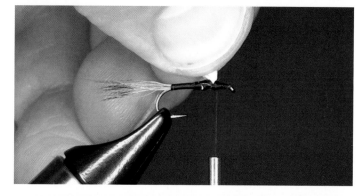

10. Looking down on the wing, separate the calf hair into two equal bunches with your dubbing needle. Pull the bunches apart with your fingertips and make one or two figure-eight wraps between the bunches to separate them. See sidebar on divided wings for details.

11. Holding the far wing firmly with your left fingertips, roll the bobbin around the base of the wing in a clockwise direction (looking down on the wing), close to the shank, two or three times. Keep your working thread short and the bobbin tube close to the wing, letting go of the wing with your left fingertips as you bring the bobbin around your left hand. Apply tension on the thread, pulling forward and then backward, parallel to the shank, while holding the wing in place with your left hand. Take one turn of thread around the shank in front of the wings.

12. Repeat the process with the near wing, going around its base two or three times in a counterclockwise direction. Take one turn of thread around the shank behind the wings.

A

13. Both wings should be positioned about thirty degrees below the vertical on each side. Check them from the top (A) and front (B) and work them into position with your fingers if they are not balanced properly. The hackle, applied later, will hold them in position, but you can also add one drop of Deep Penetrating Head Cement at each base now.

B

14. Select a peacock herl from the base of an eyed tail, below the eye (A). The herl should have short but dense flue. Bring the thread back to the tail. Snip about one-quarter inch of herl off the tip, as the herl is very brittle right at the tip and may break as you start to wind it. Tie the tip of the peacock herl right at the base of the tail with three tight turns. Advance the thread forward about four thread widths (B).

A

B

15. Wind the peacock herl toward the eye about four turns. The flue should point back toward the bend as you wind. If you examine the peacock herl, you'll see it has a concave and convex side. The concave side should point backward, and usually does so naturally if you tie it in by the tip. If it doesn't point back, the flue traps itself as you wind forward, giving the peacock a sloppy look. Tie off the peacock herl when it reaches the thread with another three turns and snip off the rest. Peacock needs few turns of thread to hold it in place, so don't overdo it.

16. Floss comes in either two- or four-strand varieties. Cut six inches of red floss from the spool and carefully separate the strands. Use only a single strand per fly; put the others aside for the next flies.

17. Starting right where the peacock herl was tied off, tie in the floss with a single very tight wrap of thread. Then untwist the thread and continue forward about six thread widths, binding the floss under and forming a smooth underbody. Snip off the end of the floss closest to the eye; don't worry about trimming it too close, because it will be hidden under the second band of peacock herl.

18. Wind the floss forward in smooth, slightly overlapping turns. The floss band should be as thin as you can manage, and should not be tapered. Tie off the floss when you get to where the thread is hanging. Tie in a second piece of peacock herl, advance the thread forward several wraps, and wind a second joint of peacock herl.

19. Trim the second joint of peacock herl. Make sure you leave space between the base of the wings and the herl for winding hackle—there should be as much space from the herl to the wings as there is from the wings to the eye.

20. Select two high-quality neck hackles or a single dry-fly saddle and strip the web from the base of the feathers. Tie them in, starting just in front of the peacock herl and winding forward in smooth, very tight turns. Leave some bare stem on the hackles between the fibers and the tie-in point, to make the initial turn of hackle easier to start.

21. The hackles should be tied in with their dull (concave) sides up, and the stems should lie between the wings. Snip off the butt ends of the hackles between the wings. Advance the thread to a point about three thread widths behind the eye.

A

B

C

22. Grasp the top hackle (A) with hackle pliers and make a single wrap, tight to the peacock herl (B). The first revolution will be with bare stem—which is fine, because it helps you get the stem winding properly before the hackle fibers sprout from it (C). After the first wrap, the hackle will start to form around the hook. Wind forward in even turns (D). If you're using two hackles, leave a tiny gap between each turn. With a single saddle hackle, make each turn tightly in front of the one behind it (if you wind back and forth with a hackle, it may float okay, but the fly will look horrible).

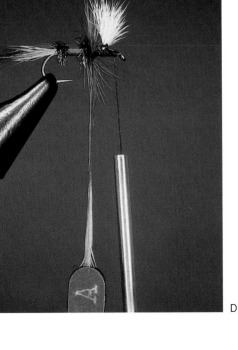

D

23. When you get to the wing base, make one turn immediately in back of the wings. Grasp the wings with your left fingertips and pull them back, and then wind the hackle in front of them.

24. Make two or three more turns of hackle in front of the wings and tie off the first hackle.

25. Wind the second hackle through the first hackle, weaving from side to side as you wind to keep from binding the first hackle under. Grasp the wing as you wind in front of it. Before your last turn, sweep all the other hackle back toward the bend with your left fingertips, making the final turn of hackle immediately forward of the rest of the hackle. This keeps most of the fibers perpendicular to the shank. Flatten the thread, form a neat head, whip finish, and apply a drop of Deep-Penetrating Head Cement.

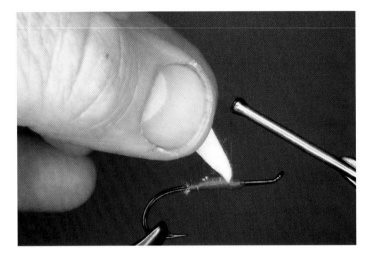

Divided Dry-Fly Wings in Detail

1. After you bind in the material (calf tail, calf body, duck-flank feathers), pull it straight up. Twist the thread into a rope and wind enough turns tight to the wing so that it stands upright by itself.

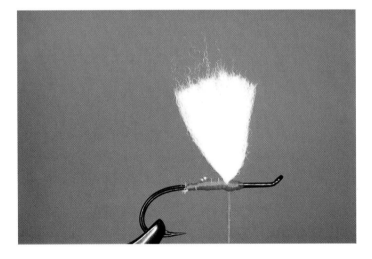

2. To get the wing to stay upright and not slant forward later, you'll have to wind enough thread in front of the wing to equal the bulk in back of it.

3. Looking at the fly head-on or from above, split the wing into two equal parts with the point of your scissors or a dubbing needle.

4. First figure-eight the wings. Grasp the far wing with your left hand and bring the thread between the wings on top of the shank (A). You'll have to release your grip on the wing briefly as the bobbin crosses over the wings. Let the bobbin hang just behind the wings (B).

A

B

5. Now bring the thread up and between the wings, again on top of the shank. As you bring the thread between the wings, grasp the near wing to hold it in place. Let the bobbin hang in front of the wings.

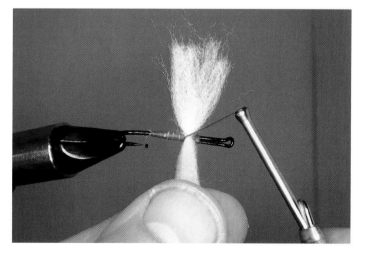

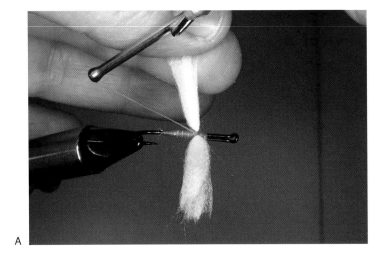

A

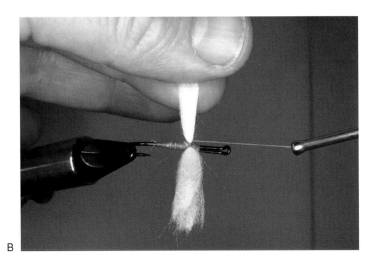

B

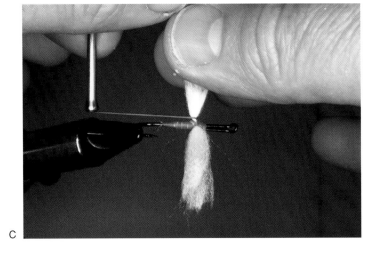

C

6. Hold the far wing with your left hand. Bring the thread back between the wings (A), then wind around the base of the far wing (B) two or three clockwise (as you look down on the wing) revolutions (C). Let go of the wing briefly as the bobbin comes around and ease up on thread tension as you do; pull tighter when you grab the wing again. Finish up behind the wings and let the thread hang.

7. Grab the near wing with your left hand (A), bring the thread forward between the wings on top of the shank, and make two or three clockwise wraps around the base of the near wing (B).

A

B

8. Check the alignment and angle of the wings. They should each be cocked about thirty degrees from the vertical. If one slants forward or you don't like the way they are lined up, take a couple more figure-eight turns between the wings, preening them into position.

Letort Hopper

Fishing in midsummer without a hopper pattern in your box is like playing cards without any aces. The combination of a trout stream, a grass meadow, and a gust of wind serves up the easiest dry-fly fishing (and sometimes the biggest trout) of the season. You'll be warned by the soft castanet crackling of grasshopper wings in the brush; the trout already know. Trout eat hopper artificials as eagerly as they do naturals because your fly does what a hopper is supposed to do—it plops onto the water with no semblance of grace, unlike the delicate aquatic insects that come from beneath the surface.

The best place to fish this hopper is right up against the bank—not a foot, but an inch from the bank, as large trout will lie in open, shallow water during hopper season, especially if there is deeper water or a big log nearby. Cast to a likely spot as close to the bank as you can, or actually up on the bank, twitching the fly into the water quickly be-

fore the current drags your line. If nothing happens, try casts increasingly farther from shore. If you still don't have any luck and you haven't disturbed the water with a clumsy cast, try twitching the fly a fraction every few inches as it drifts downstream. If all else fails, try a steady retrieve. Don't ignore tiny side channels, as trout will move into them to eat hoppers, and most are overlooked by fishermen and drift boats.

Complicated hopper patterns are fun to tie and look great in your box. However, I've had my best luck with an older, simpler pattern, developed by the great Pennsylvania limestone-stream expert Ed Shenk in the 1950s. The Letort Hopper is clean, straightforward, easy to tie, and easy to see on the water. In contrast, some of the fancier imitations float so low in the water that they are difficult to keep track of, an important consideration because, despite the size of a grasshopper, a large brown trout can eat one while barely wrinkling the surface. This pattern can also be tied down to a Size 14, great for the first part of hopper season when the tiny nymph hoppers are just emerging.

This pattern also teaches you an important tying technique, the deer-hair head. Put a collar on the bottom of the hook as well as on the top as you see here and you've mastered the head of the famous Muddler Minnow. Spin deer hair on the entire shank as you'll do for

the forward part of the head on this fly, and you'll be able to make a Bomber salmon dry or a bass bug.

After you've mastered this one, have some fun making hoppers with knotted legs, foam bodies, and golden pheasant tippet underwings. But keep those on the top layer of your fly box for show. Underneath, make sure you have Letort Hoppers in Sizes 6 through 14.

Pattern Description

	MATERIAL	SUBSTITUTE
Hook	2XL dry fly, Sizes 6 through 14.	Extra-fine dry fly.
Thread	White or yellow, Size 6/0.	
Body	Yellow fuzzy yarn or dubbed fur.	Tan or green yarn.
Wing	Mottled turkey secondary wing-quill section, strengthened with acrylic sealer and trimmed to shape.	Synthetic, imitation turkey feather.
Head and collar	Fine white-tailed deer.	Coastal deer.

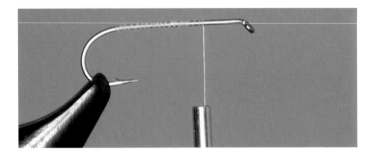

1. Attach the thread to the hook about one-third of the way back from the eye. Wrap back to where the bend starts, then forward to your starting point. The idea here is to get a thread base so that the dubbing has something to grip when you wind it. It doesn't matter if the thread is twisted or flat; in fact, don't even worry about neatness.

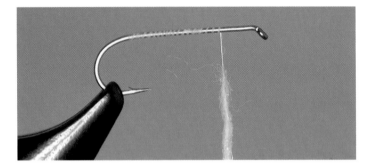

2. Dub any soft yellow fur or synthetic dubbing onto the thread. Taper is not as important in this pattern, but a slight "waist" in the middle of the dubbing helps prevent a lump at the bend. The dubbing applied can be thicker than for a mayfly imitation—even thicker than you see here.

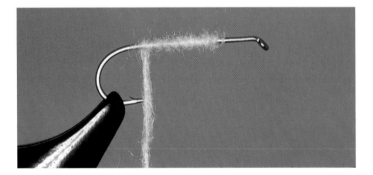

3. Wind dubbing back to the bend with slightly overlapping turns. To thicken the dubbing, overlap more and ease off on thread tension. To thin the dubbing, especially at the bend, space out the wraps a bit and put more tension on the thread.

4. Wind dubbing back to the starting point. Add or remove small amounts of dubbing as needed toward the end. Wind bare thread back onto the dubbing a few turns to form a base for the wing.

5. Snip a section from the middle of a mottled turkey secondary wing quill. It's easier if you spray the feather with fixative and let it dry first. The section should be about three-fourths as wide as the hook gap.

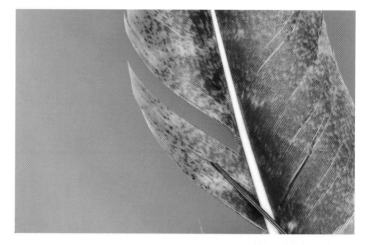

6. Round the tip end of the feather section with your scissors.

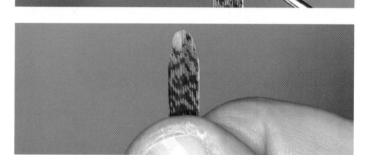

7. The trimmed section should look like this. Make sure the piece you started with was long enough so you won't be tying over the lower one-third of the section (the part that was closest to the quill), as it will split as soon as you put any tension on the thread.

8. Place the turkey section flat over the top of the shank, concave side down. It should extend about one-quarter shank length beyond the bend. Hold it in place with your left index finger.

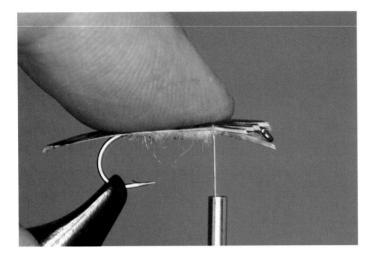

9. Bring one wrap of thread over the top of the feather with no tension—the Gravity Drop method. Lift your finger to let the thread in, but put it back in place as soon as the thread passes over the wing. Let the bobbin's weight apply the pressure. Make a second wrap the same way, then push down with your left fingertip while pulling down with the bobbin.

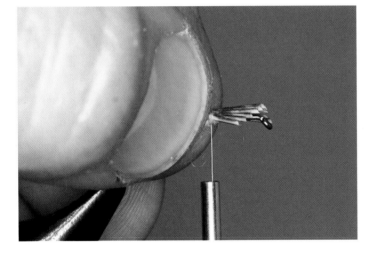

10. Now grasp the base of the wing with your left thumb and forefinger while making about six tight wraps, working slightly forward with each wrap.

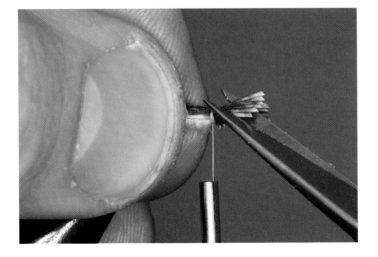

11. Trim the butt of the wing, leaving a short stub, but keeping it well clear of the eye. Wrap about six more turns over the wing butt. You should still be left with about one-eighth of the bare shank just behind the eye.

12. Snip a bunch of fine deer hair with even tips from a hide. It should be about one hook gap in diameter.

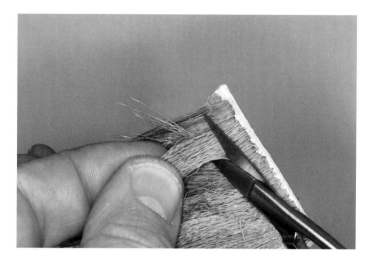

13. Clean the fuzz and short hairs from the butt ends of the hair by holding the fine, untrimmed ends in your left thumb and forefinger, and pulling the fuzz out with your right fingertips.

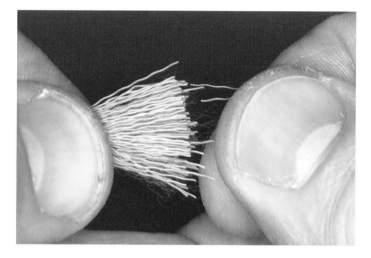

14. Place the hair in a stacker, fine ends down, and rap sharply about four times.

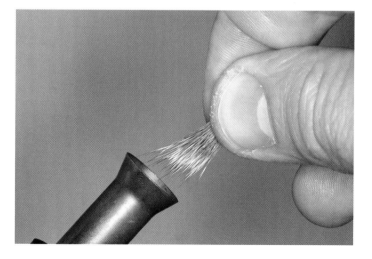

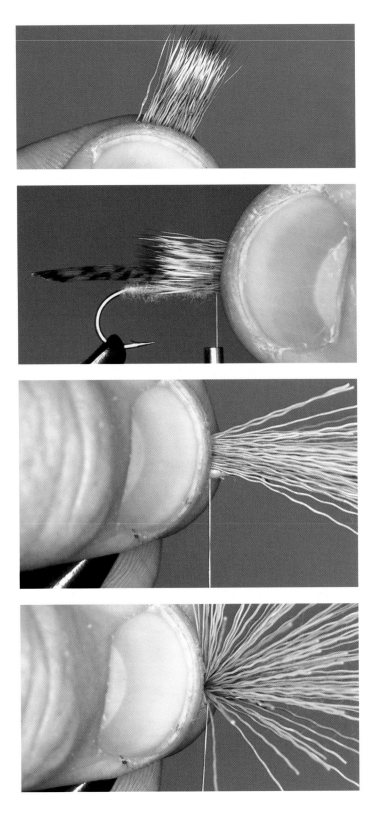

15. Hold the stacker horizontally, slowly remove the tube, and grab the bunch of hair carefully by its tips with your left hand. Transfer the hair to your right hand, so you are holding the butts of the hair between your right thumb and forefinger.

16. Hold the hair over the place where you tied in the wing. The tips should extend about halfway down the wing—just short of the hook bend.

17. Pinch the hair in the same spot with your left thumb and forefinger and remove your right hand.

18. Putting lateral pressure on the hair with your left fingertips, keep the hair on top of the shank while working a wrap of thread between your fingertips. Pull straight down with the thread while pinching the hair. Repeat the pinch method about six times, making firm wraps in the same place.

19. When you remove your fingers, the fly should look like this—a neat collar of fine hair pointing back, and a mess of flared hair in front. Check to make sure that the collar is mostly on top of the shank.

20. Reach in front of the tying thread. Place your thumb and forefinger against the shank and push the flared hair butts back toward the wing with your fingernails. Wiggle the hair around slightly, until it is fairly evenly distributed, 360 degrees around the shank.

21. Grab the hair butts with your left thumb and forefinger and pull them back over the wing, exposing the shank in front of the wing and collar. Wrap enough tight turns of thread immediately in front of the hair so the butts stand ninety degrees to the shank when you release them.

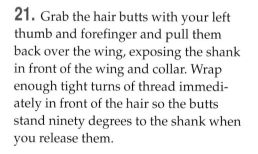

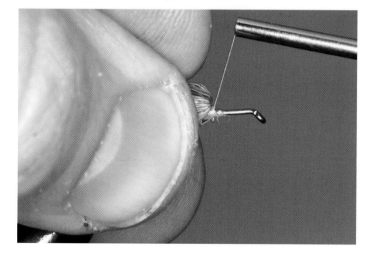

22. Cut another bunch of hair, slightly bigger than the first. Cut off the tips so that when you trim the head you can tell the collar from the rest of the deer-hair head and won't trim any of the collar by mistake.

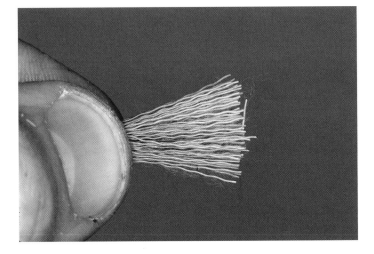

23. Hold this bunch of hair in the middle with your left fingertips. The length of this bunch does not matter.

24. Place the middle of this hair on top of the shank, right over the bare shank you have been saving. Deer hair spins nicely over a thread-covered shank, but better over a bare shank. Take one loose turn of thread over the hair. Don't put any tension on the thread; don't even let the bobbin drop out of your hand.

25. Take a second turn of thread in the exact same spot. This time, apply slight tension to the hair and begin releasing your grip on the hair.

26. Take a third wrap, this time applying full tension with the bobbin with your right hand and letting go of the hair with your left. The hair will flare and spin around the hook. Take about four more tight turns of thread in the same place, letting the hair spin all around the hook. If it doesn't cover the top, bottom, and both sides of the shank evenly, work it around with your fingers.

27. Push the deer hair back toward the wing by sliding your fingernails back along the shank.

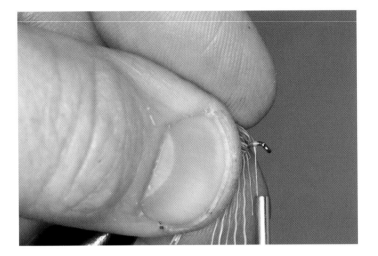

28. Pull all of the hair back out of the way. Make about six tight wraps immediately in front of the hair, then wrap a few more to form the head.

29. Whip finish, being careful not to catch any deer-hair fibers.

30. You can trim the deer-hair head in the vise or in your hand. A rotary vise makes trimming easy while still keeping the fly in the vise. Turn the fly upside-down and trim almost all of the hair from the bottom of the fly. If you keep the scissors parallel to the shank and use the body as a guide you won't cut into the thread wraps securing hair by mistake.

31. Turn the fly right side up and trim the top of the head. Cut upward at about a thirty-degree angle, using the eye and collar as guides.

32. The head should now look like this, ready to trim the sides.

33. Trim first one side, then the next. As on the bottom, trim fairly close to the hook, using the shank and body as guides.

34. You will probably be left with some long hairs still on top of the head. Trim these by placing your scissors sideways against the collar, sliding them down toward the head, and opening them at the same time. The long butt hairs should get caught in your scissors, where they can be snipped without cutting into the collar.

A

35. Inspect the head from all angles to make sure it is trimmed evenly (A). Neat deer-hair heads (B) don't matter to the fish, but you might care. Apply two drops of Deep-Penetrating Head Cement to the thread head, letting one drop seep back into the base of the deer hair.

B

CHAPTER 9

Saltwater Flies

Chartreuse Clouser Minnow

I'm showing this fly as a saltwater pattern, tied on a saltwater hook, but don't ignore it for freshwater fishing. Lefty Kreh has caught more than 70 different species of fish on this fly, from Alaska to Australia. The original pattern, developed by Bob Clouser for smallmouth bass in Pennsylvania's Susquehanna River, was designed to keep moving through the water no matter what the angler is doing. The rationale is that baitfish, when pursued by bigger fish, don't stop to look at the scenery. When this fly hits the water it sinks quickly. When you start a retrieve, it swims through the water, but if you stop moving the fly, it keeps moving as it sinks deeper. The only time it stops is when it's lying on the bottom or grabbed by a fish.

Although the Clouser Minnow is a superb baitfish imitation, I don't believe its usefulness stops there. Tied with sparse, translucent materials it becomes a credible facsimile of a shrimp. Tied shorter and fuller, it may remind gamefish of a crab, as stripers often inhale a Clouser lying motionless on the bottom.

I've been surprised by the number of salt-water fisheries where a chartreuse-and-white Clouser is the most popular fly. From New England stripers to North Carolina Spanish mackerel to Gulf Coast seatrout, the fly most anglers start with is a Chartreuse Clouser. In Sizes 4 and 6, it has even become a top bone-fish fly in the Florida Keys and the Bahamas.

In open water, particularly over breaking fish, just cast a Clouser as far as you can and strip it back with a steady retrieve. Often, a very fast retrieve will interest fish that ignore a slower-moving fly. It's smart to experiment with depths; probably the best line for fishing Clousers is an intermediate, but there will be times when the fly must run deeper, and fast-sinking lines might be needed. Although a floating line is not the best line to use with a Clouser, an advantage when using this fly is that you can switch from a popper to a Clouser and, letting the Clouser sink before you retrieve, get a wide range of depths without changing lines.

In currents, along jetties, or in water flowing swiftly through an estuary, a deadly technique is to cast up-current to let the fly sink, then pump the rod with six-inch twitches as the fly swings around, without retrieving any line. You can cover a lot of water this way, and your fly looks like a crippled baitfish tumbling in the current.

On shallow flats, a steady retrieve may work, especially if you think the fish are eating baitfish. But if you see wakes or tails or cruising fish, try imitating a small crustacean: cast well ahead of the fish's suspected path and let the fly sink to the bottom. When the fish gets within four or five feet of the fly, make it hop once by giving the line one short strip. Often, the fish will sweep over and inhale the fly without any further movement on your part, but if not, try a series of short hops along the bottom. You can even do this when fish aren't visible, although it takes a pretty good leap of faith. Cast out, let the fly sink, and use short strips punctuated by long pauses—five or ten seconds between strips.

Although the chartreuse-and-white variation of the Clouser shown here is the most popular, these flies are tied in a wide variety of colors, and you can use synthetic hair as well as other natural hairs such as squirrel or calf tail. Flies can be tailored to fishing conditions as well. For baitfish imitations in most waters, use very small amounts of hair and tie them long, about twice as long as the shank. Keep the eyes relatively small. For patterns used on the flats, where fish may be eating crustaceans, keep the flies sparse but shorten the hair to about one and one-half shank lengths. For surf fishing, particularly for striped bass, I like to follow the great surf guide Tony Stetzko and tie them very full, with big, heavy eyes.

A note of caution when using Clousers with heavy eyes in the windy surf: a gust of wind that blows your fly into the fragile tip of a graphite rod can fracture the graphite, and the only remedy for this is a new tip from the manufacturer. The same Clouser moving at 120 mph can make you see stars for a few minutes if it hits you in the back of your head.

Pattern Description

	MATERIAL	SUBSTITUTE
Hook	Pre-Sharpened Saltwater, Sizes 1/0 through 8.	Regular stainless hook.
Thread	White 3/0.	Black.
Eyes	Weighted dumbbell eyes, prepainted.	Machined brass eyes with recess on ends; painted or glued-on eyes.
Belly	White bucktail.	White Ultra Hair; or any other color Ultra hair or bucktail.
Lateral Line	Pearl Krystal Flash.	Any color Krystal Flash or Flashabou.
Back	Chartreuse bucktail.	Chartreuse Ultra Hair; or any other color Ultra Hair or bucktail.

1. Attach your thread to the shank near the front of the fly. Wind back and forth over the front one-third of the shank until you have about three layers of thread.

2. Hold a pair of dumbbell eyes across the shank, about one-quarter of the shank length behind the eye.

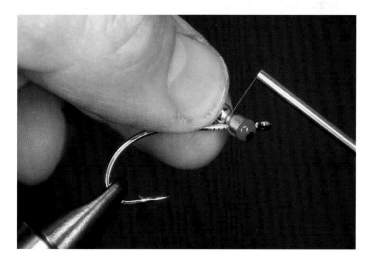

227

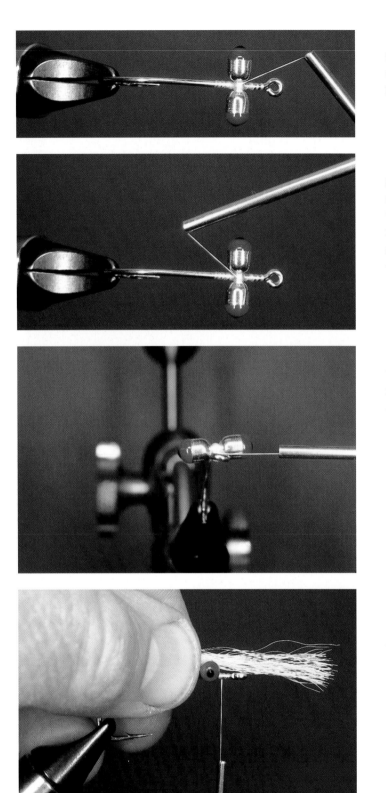

3. Wrap the thread diagonally between the eyes, from behind the eyes to the front and around the shank, with at least a dozen very firm wraps.

4. Straighten the eyes with your fingers until they are at a ninety-degree angle to the shank. Wrap another dozen turns in the opposite direction, from in front of the eyes to behind them and around the shank. Keep straightening the eyes with your finger.

5. Take about eight very tight turns of thread between the eyes and the shank in a circular fashion. This locks in the diagonal turns that you made previously.

6. Cut a bunch of white bucktail that is about half the hook gap in diameter when flattened into a fan. Measure the bucktail against the shank. It should be two to two-and-a-half shank lengths from the tie-in point. Make sure the thread is just in front of the eyes, and hold the bucktail right above the eyes.

7. Make about six firm wraps of thread over the bucktail. Because the eyes get in the way, you can't do a true Pinch Wrap, so if the bucktail rolls to the far side, straighten it with your fingers after tying it in.

8. Pull the bucktail toward the bend, from behind the eyes.

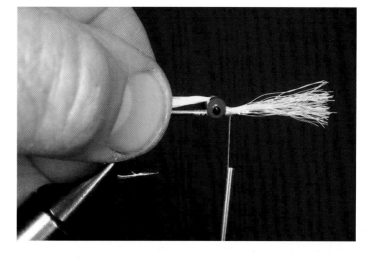

9. Bring the thread under the shank and behind the eyes and make another six firm wraps over the hair.

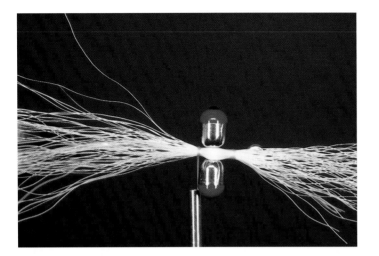

10. The bucktail should be in line with the shank as shown. If not, work it into place with your fingers.

11. Bring the thread back in front of the eyes and trim the butts of the bucktail close to the shank by lifting them up at about a forty-five-degree angle.

12. Make firm wraps over the butt ends of the bucktail, working toward the eye of the hook and then back to get a slight taper.

13. Turn the hook upside down in the vise or, if you have a rotary vise, rotate the jaws one hundred eighty degrees. Grab about a dozen strands of Krystal Flash and tie them in in front of the eyes with five or six turns of thread.

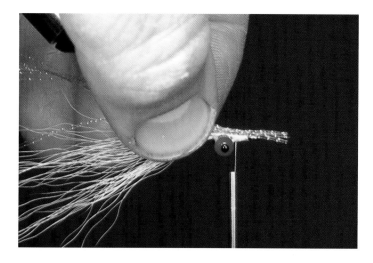

14. Trim the Krystal Flash the same way you did the bucktail.

15. Cut a bunch of chartreuse bucktail the same diameter as the white bucktail. Line it up with the white hair so that it is equal in length or slightly longer.

16. Tie in the bucktail with eight very tight wraps. Notice that it slipped to the far side because I couldn't get my fingers in there to make a proper Pinch Wrap.

17. Grasp the bucktail over the eyes with your left hand and use your right hand to roll it back on top of the shank. Make sure it is centered on top of the shank here in the front, but don't worry if the back end of the bucktail is not centered over the point of the hook at this stage. As long as it is lined up over the eyes, you can distribute it around the bend of the hook later.

18. Trim the chartreuse bucktail in the same manner.

19. Bind down the butts of the hair and form a tapered head by winding the thread back and forth from the hook eye to the dumbbell eyes. Whip finish and trim your thread.

20. I feel a Clouser is a better fly if the head is epoxied. The hair won't pull out and the eyes won't move off-center. Along with two-part, thirty-minute epoxy, you'll need a paper clip and a Post-It. You'll also need a battery-operated fly turner unless you want to baby-sit each fly by turning it in the vise every ten seconds for fifteen minutes. You can use five-minute epoxy and shorten the set-up time to about three minutes, but it's trickier to use.

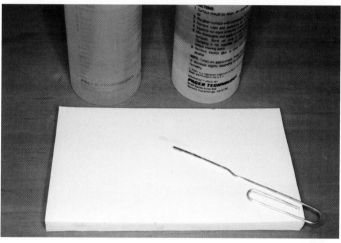

21. Place two equal globs of hardener and resin on the Post-It.

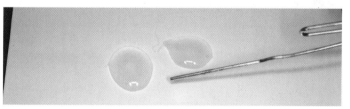

22. Mix the epoxy thoroughly until it is of a single consistency. Don't stir too hard or you'll introduce air bubbles. (I used to use toothpicks for mixing and applying epoxy until a young fly tier, 14-year-old Luca Adelphio of Washington, D.C., warned me that they would yellow the epoxy.)

23. Work some epoxy into the thread and hair between the eyes, and run just a bit onto the hair behind the eyes.

24. Carefully coat the head of the fly, making sure you get all sides. A rotary vise makes this easy. If you get any epoxy in the hook eye, remove it now with a toothpick or by drawing a feather through the eye. If it hardens there, you'll have to drill it out!

25. Place the hook in a rotating fly drier. The thirty-minute epoxy will set in fifteen minutes, but it will be tacky for a few hours. Heat speeds the process; humidity hinders it. If you are in a hurry or the weather is humid, place a desk lamp about six inches from the drier. Avoid touching the fly for six hours. When you're done, the head will be nearly indestructible and will look like this.

26. Now you can preen the hair and distribute it equally around the hook bend.

27. The completed Clouser Minnow.

28. A Clouser with eyes hand-painted on the ends of plain dumbbell eyes.

29. A Clouser with doll eyes attached to plain dumbbell eyes with head cement, then epoxied over the top for durability.

Lefty's Deceiver

I'll never forget my first attempt at bluefish on a fly, and Capt. Walter Ungermann's reaction to my meticulously tied Deceivers. Walter was, as far as I know, the first charterboat captain in the Northeast to specialize in fly fishing, and never one to mince words when you blew a cast or did something similarly stupid like strip a Skipping Bug too slowly. His lips curled into a sneer, then a grin, when he saw my delicate, sparse flies. "What do you think you're going to use those for, Atlantic *salmon?*"

The Deceiver is a rough-and-tumble fly that should be tied full, meaty, and rugged. Don't mince on materials. This fly has to survive the razor-sharp teeth of bluefish, mangling by big stripers, or the needle-studded jaws of Spanish mackerel. I have caught all of these species on Deceivers, plus sharks, bonefish, redfish, seatrout, trevally, jack crevalle, bonito, false albacore, weakfish, pike, trout, largemouth and smallmouth bass, and I'm

sure others I can't remember. If it eats baitfish, it will eat Deceivers.

The fly's success is probably due to its baitfish-like shape and slinky action in the water. Like a baitfish that has been corralled by predators, the Deceiver stays close to the surface and hangs there, pulsing with life even if you're barely moving the fly. For this reason, I feel it's a better fly when fish are actively feeding on bait or in shallow water, particularly at night. A weighted fly such as the Clouser Minnow will drop below the fish, and it is nearly impossible for a fish to see a fly at night when it's not silhouetted against the night sky. Experienced saltwater guides also feel the Deceiver looks like a fleeing squid, which is a meal most gamefish find about as hard to resist as I do a plate of fried calamari.

First developed by Lefty Kreh in the 1960s for Chesapeake Bay stripers, this fly is the most universal saltwater fly. In sales and popularity among saltwater fly rodders, the only other fly that comes close is the Clouser Minnow (which Lefty also worked on with Bob Clouser). It can be tied with any color feathers or bucktail, synthetic hair, flashy tinsel, or Icelandic sheep hair. The Deceiver has probably been tied and fished in any color you can imagine—and some you probably don't want to think about—but most anglers agree the three most useful colors are all white, all black, and chartreuse.

The all-white version is my favorite fly for open-water fishing during the day. If I'm blind-casting on the edge of a dropoff, in a channel, or to fish breaking in open water, my first choice will always be the albino variety with a topping of peacock herl. It's Lefty's original pattern and the one I've shown here. For night fishing, especially when fish are popping in the surf, the all-black one seems to produce, probably because it is most visible to the fish against the night sky. If the fish are deep and you need a sinking line to reach them, try the chartreuse version.

The Deceiver can be tied as small as an inch and a half and as large as almost a foot long for offshore fishing. You'll have trouble finding hackle long enough to tie them bigger than seven inches, though, and will have to substitute synthetic hair, Icelandic sheep, or an extended body to make them longer. For most saltwater fishing, three to five inches long is about right. It's important to think of saltwater flies in terms of total length rather than hook size. The size of a Deceiver is determined by the length of its saddle hackles, so use a hook as small as possible for better penetration and less damage to the fish. Tie these on hooks bigger than 1/0 only if you

think you will be fighting fish that will straighten a smaller hook—and many 120-pound tarpon have been taken on 1/0 hooks.

The most important consideration when tying Deceivers is hackle selection. You can't strip a big hackle down to make a smaller fly. You must tie in the thickest part of the stems, where the web starts; if you don't, the junction of the feather to the hook will hinge when cast and the feather will foul around the bend of the hook. A Deceiver that's fouled will not swim properly and will be ignored. Thus, you have to find feathers that match the length you intend to tie. Saddle hackles are long and wiggly and give a fly good action, but some are so flimsy that they foul often. Plus, in any given saddle patch or package of strung saddles, you will only get saddles of one length. I like big "saltwater" rooster necks for this purpose. A good one will offer perfect Deceiver feathers from two to six inches long, and the stems of neck hackles are much thicker and stiffer than those of saddles.

There are two other tricks to keep Deceivers from fouling. One is to make sure you tie in the hackles at the very end of the straight part of the shank, so they clear the bend if they happen to get wrapped around the hook. The other discipline is to make sure that the bucktail collar extends well beyond the bend and is substantial enough to keep the feathers in place when casting. On those original Deceivers that amused Walter Ungermann, my neat bucktail barely reached the bend of the hook and my thin saddle hackles were carefully stripped at the stem as you would prepare them for a trout streamer. Oh, the humiliation!

Pattern Description

	MATERIAL	SUBSTITUTE
Hook	Pre-Sharpened Saltwater, Sizes 6 through 3/0.	Standard stainless.
Thread	Black, Size 3/0.	White.
Hackles	Four to eight white hackles, flanked by silver or pearl tinsel on each side.	Grizzly, chartreuse, black, or yellow saddles. Tinsel flanking can contrast or match saddles.
Body	Silver Mylar tinsel.	Vinyl or nylon ribbing material in white or black.
Collar	White bucktail.	None.
Topping	Three to six peacock herls.	Strands of Flashabou or Krystal Flash.

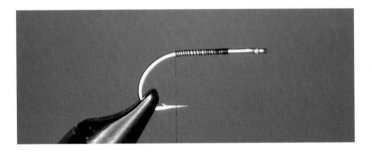

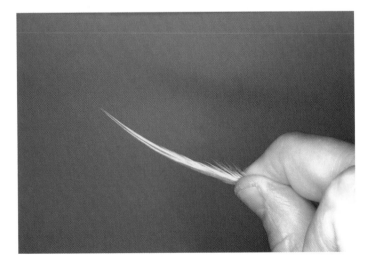

1. Place a saltwater hook in the vise. Make sure the hook is firmly set in the jaws, enough so that you can press down with your finger without moving it. You'll put more pressure on this fly than with other patterns. Attach your thread to the center of the shank and wind back to the spot just before it begins to bend below the horizontal.

2. Select four white hackles. The length of the feathers should be such that the distance from where the web starts to the tip of the hackles, plus the hook shank, will give you the desired length of your finished fly. You can tie in the hackles anywhere in the webby section, but if you tie them in beyond the web the stem may be too thin and the fly may foul. Pick the hackles from the same place on a neck or saddle or, if picking from loose hackles, make sure they are matched in length and curvature. Make two pairs, each with two hackles placed together so their curves go in the same direction, as shown with one pair here.

3. Bring the matched pairs together, concave sides inward. The easiest way to do this is to put one pair in each hand and bring them together, while you keep the heavy parts of the stems lined up. You should end by pinching the feathers together in your left hand, with your left fingertips just beyond where the web starts and the tips of the feathers facing in toward your palm. At this point, the feathers should form a single piece, like a pair of hands in prayer.

4. Hold the feathers on top of the shank, where the thread is hanging. The tips should point away from the bend, and the point where the web begins should be in line with the thread. Note that I could make a longer wing but not a shorter one with these feathers, because if I made the wing any shorter I would be tying the feathers down where the stem begins to thin. Pinch the hackles and the bend of the hook together with your left thumb and forefinger above the tie-in point. Try to keep the stems in line, on top of the shank.

5. Rock your fingertips back slightly and make a single wrap over the feathers. Pinch the thread, feathers, and sides of the hook bend all together and pull straight down with a very firm pull.

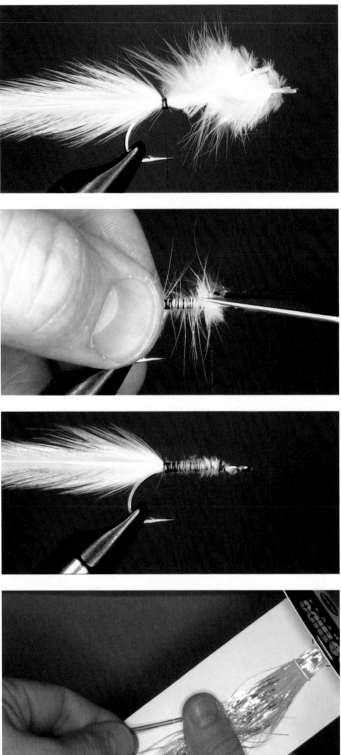

6. Repeat the process three or four times in the same place. Remove your fingers and make sure the feathers lie in a straight vertical line as if they were a single piece, and are not tilted to one side. If they are, unwind and try again.

7. Wind the thread forward toward the eye. Keep all four stems on top of the shank in a horizontal line. Try to keep them from crossing over each other, which will build up too much bulk in the body. Wind forward along two-thirds of the shank. Trim the butts of the feathers on a slight angle. Trim any fuzz sticking out along the shank.

8. Make sure your thread is flattened, and wind back to the bend.

9. Select two to four pieces of tinsel. They should be slightly longer than the feathers.

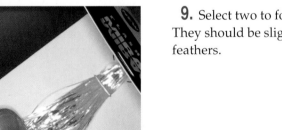

10. Place the tinsel along the centerline of the feathers and along the side of the shank. Tie in with light tension, tightening with a horizontal rather than the typical vertical pull.

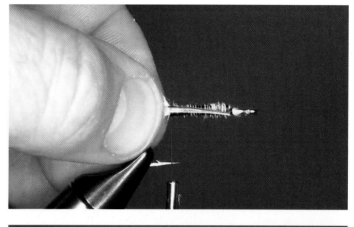

11. About three wraps should do it, with each one moving slightly forward. Trim the ends of the tinsel just short of the tip ends of the feathers.

12. Turn the hook over, either by removing it from the vise or by rotating the vise if you have a rotary model. Place the same number of tinsel pieces on the centerline of the other side of the feathers.

13. Make sure the thread is flattened. Wrap toward the eye, smoothing out any bumps and binding both sides of tinsel under. You may have to keep working the tinsel back into place as you wrap.

14. Stop about three-quarters of the way to the eye. Tie in an eight-inch piece of wide Mylar tinsel with the gold side facing you. A small part should be toward the eye, but most of the tinsel should trail back toward the bend.

15. Lift the tinsel straight up and twist it so the silver side now faces you. Crimp the first wrap of tinsel against the hook shank so it lies flat. Angle the tinsel back toward the bend just a bit.

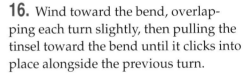

16. Wind toward the bend, overlapping each turn slightly, then pulling the tinsel toward the bend until it clicks into place alongside the previous turn.

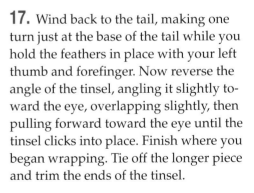

17. Wind back to the tail, making one turn just at the base of the tail while you hold the feathers in place with your left thumb and forefinger. Now reverse the angle of the tinsel, angling it slightly toward the eye, overlapping slightly, then pulling forward toward the eye until the tinsel clicks into place. Finish where you began wrapping. Tie off the longer piece and trim the ends of the tinsel.

18. Make a few smooth wraps to cover the ends of the tinsel. At this point you can apply a thin coat of head cement to the tinsel for durability, but wait until it dries completely before you tie in the bucktail. Some tiers make several flies up to this point, whip finish, cement, then finish them all later.

19. Select a bunch of white bucktail. It should be about one hook gap in diameter. If you gather the bucktail while it is still attached to the bone, then pull all the hair at right angles to the bone, you have a bunch with even ends. The best bucktail for Deceivers is in the middle of the tail. The stuff at the top is very fine, and great for the smallest Deceivers. The hair at the bottom is coarse and flares too much, unless you want a bulky fly that suspends in the water without sinking.

20. Hold the hair by its tips and clean the fuzz and short hairs from the heavy end.

21. Hold the hair by the heavy end and clean short hairs out of the tips. Hair for Deceivers should not be stacked. The ends should be somewhat even, but not perfectly, to imitate the natural taper of a baitfish's body.

22. Turn the fly upside down. Measure the bucktail so it extends to about half the length of the feather tail.

23. Tie the bucktail in place, just in front of the last turn of tinsel, with three very tight Pinch Wraps. Let it distribute along the sides of the shank a little as you tie it in.

24. While keeping the hair between your left thumb and forefinger, reach forward with them and grab about a quarter to a third of the bucktail. Pull it straight up and wind three tight turns of thread immediately in front of it, so the butt ends of the bucktail point almost straight up.

25. Repeat for the rest of the hair, working with a quarter to a third at a time, and making sure you secure the last bunch just short of the eye.

26. Trim the ends of the hair at an angle that matches the slope of the head.

27. Wind the thread back over the hair stubs to where you first tied in the bucktail. Turn the fly over and repeat the process with a bunch of hair the same size on the upper half of the fly. Trim at the same angle you did on the bottom bunch.

28. Flatten the thread, and wind back over the hair butts to the base of the collar.

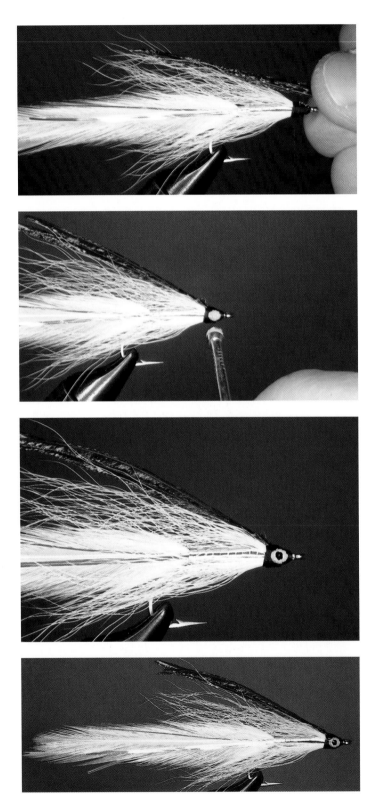

29. Select three to six long, straight peacock herls. Line them up so their curvature is all going in the same direction. Tie them in on top of the upper hair bunch with light tension, concave sides down so they flow along the top of the hair collar. Trim the excess herl.

30. Flatten the thread and wind back and forth over the head two or three times, until you have a smooth head with no white hairs sticking through. Whip finish in the middle of the head— too close to the eye and it may slip off the front, too close to the hair collar and it might knock the hair out of alignment. Dip a small nail or pin head into yellow hobby enamel, steady your hand, and touch the center of the head on each side.

31. When the yellow cement dries, touch the center of each eye with a smaller pin or nail dipped in black paint, to make the pupil.

32. Wait for the black paint to dry. Coat the head with a thin single layer of epoxy or two thin coats of head cement.

Part III

Pattern Index

The following pages offer pattern descriptions for all flies in the 2001 Orvis catalog, plus other patterns I felt were important, even though they may not be among today's hot sellers. Because fly-tying materials come and go, I have tried to be as generic as possible when specifying materials. Nothing is more frustrating to a tier than to try assembling materials for a fly, only to find that "Joe's Hot Pink Super Duper Scud Blend" is not made anymore. I have listed Orvis item numbers on all patterns because you may want to purchase samples of flies to see exactly how they are tied—you may even want to carefully slit the thread at the head of a fly and unwrap it to get hints on how to tie it.

The flies are grouped by broad groups and then by subgroups. For example, all terrestrial dry flies like ants and beetles and hoppers are in the same place. This should help you to decide which patterns you want to add to your fly box. One of the most useful aspects of this list is the "difficulty" number. It will help you to choose which patterns to attempt right away and which to save for later, when you are more experienced.

Pattern Name. This is the common name of the fly as it is known to fly fishers and tackle dealers.

Type. The broad group the fly belongs in; for example, dry flies, nymphs, or streamers.

Subtype. Further refining the use of the fly. For example, saltwater flies may be designed specifically for bonefish, redfish, or stripers. Please don't let this keep you from trying bonefish flies for stripers, or from fishing emergers deep, with weight on the leader. It's merely a way of organizing the flies and helping you find what you want to tie.

Item Number. This is the Orvis item number. By calling the company's 800 number or visiting its web site (www.orvis.com), you can order a sample of the pattern by asking for this number.

Most Popular Sizes. These are just the sizes most often asked for by fly fishers. Don't be afraid to tie some patterns smaller or larger than these sizes.

Color Options. Many flies are tied in a variety of color combinations. I have given the most popular ones.

Hook Type. I have given the generic version of a hook type here, unless one specific model is needed because of a special shape. For specific brand designations, see the hook chart in the "Hooks, Threads, and Cements" chapter.

Thread. The most common thread size and color. Don't be too worried if you don't have the exact color or size.

Tail. The material used for the tail of the fly.

Body. When the body is of one material and tied in as a single piece, the material will be listed here. When a fly has a distinct abdomen and thorax, these components will be listed here instead.

Rib. The material spiraled over the body of the fly. If the fly has an abdomen and thorax, the rib is usually tied over the abdomen only.

Wing. The material used for the wing of a fly. Whether the fly is an insect imitation or a baitfish imitation, the material that sticks straight up or extends along the back of the fly is known as the wing. "Wing case" means the material is pulled over the thorax of the fly and tied in at both ends.

Hackle. If the hackle is tied in around the wing or near the head of the fly, it is known as just "hackle." Palmered hackle is hackle used as a rib, spiraled through the body.

Abdomen. If the fly has a distinct abdomen, as do most nymphs, it is tied closest to the tails and is most often thinner than the thorax. On a well-tied nymph, the abdomen and thorax are of equal length.

Thorax. The heavier part of a fly's body, closest to the head. Usually a wing case is tied in over the top of the thorax.

Legs. If the legs of a fly are not made of hackle, the material will be listed here. Usually, where a material is specified for legs, it is tied in place as opposed to being wound around the hook.

Head. If the head of the fly is made from something other than thread, the material will be listed here. Typically, heads not made of thread are made from beads slid onto the hook or spun deer hair.

Other material. If a fly uses a material in an unusual way it is listed here. Special eyes, antennae, a shellback (a wing case tied over the entire body), and epoxy are some of the materials and techniques you'll find here.

Difficulty. This will guide you to the easier patterns and warn you of the more difficult ones. The designations are my opinions and are as follows:

1. You can tie this fly right away, knowing only the most basic techniques.
2. After you have a few patterns under your belt, move on to these patterns.
3. After a month or so of practice, these flies should not present too many problems.
4. This is a difficult pattern. Don't try it without considerable experience, as it requires some tricky thread handling.
5. One of the most difficult flies in this book. Don't worry if your attempts, even after a year or two of tying, don't look like the photos.

Notes. Any special tying instructions that don't fit in the other places are inserted here.

ADAMS

Type: Dry.   Subtype: Attractor.
Item Number: 0330. **Most Popular Sizes:** 10, 12, 14, 16, 18, 20, 22. **Hook Type:** Extra-fine dry; Bigeye dry in smaller sizes.
Thread: Black 8/0.
Tail: Brown and grizzly hackle fibers.
Body: Muskrat or medium gray dubbing.
Wing: Grizzly hackle tips, upright and divided.
Hackle: Brown and grizzly, mixed.
Difficulty: 3.

ADAMS HUMPY

Type: Dry.   Subtype: Attractor.
Item Number: 064T. **Most Popular Sizes:** 10, 12, 14, 16, 18.
Hook Type: Extra-fine dry. **Thread:** Gray 6/0.
Tail: Dark moose body hair.
Body: Dubbed natural muskrat.
Wing: Hen grizzly-hackle tips mixed with deer body hair tips.
Hackle: Brown and grizzly, mixed.
Thorax: Back: Same moose used for the tail pulled over the dubbed body.
Other Materials: Back: natural gray deer hair.
Difficulty: 4.

ADAMS PARACHUTE

Type: Dry.   Subtype: Attractor.
Item Number: 0356. **Most Popular Sizes:** 14, 16, 18, 20.
Hook Type: Extra-fine dry. **Thread:** Black 6/0 or 8/0.
Tail: Brown and grizzly hackle fibers, mixed.
Body: Muskrat fur or gray dubbing.
Wing: White calf tail, upright in a single clump.
Hackle: Brown and grizzly tied parachute style around wing base.
Difficulty: 3.

ADAMS TRUDE

Type: Dry.   Subtype: Attractor.
Item Number: 02RL. **Most Popular Sizes:** 10, 12, 14.
Hook Type: Extra-fine dry. **Thread:** Black 6/0.
Tail: Moose mane.
Body: Gray dubbing.
Wing: White calf tail, down-wing style.
Hackle: Mixed brown and grizzly.
Difficulty: 3.

ADAMS WULFF
Type: Dry. Subtype: Attractor.
Item Number: 0901. **Most Popular Sizes:** 10, 12, 14, 16.
Hook Type: Extra-fine dry fly. **Thread:** Gray 6/0.
Tail: Moose body hair.
Body: Gray fur.
Wing: White calf tail, upright and divided.
Hackle: Mixed brown and grizzly, heavy.
Difficulty: 3.

AUSABLE WULFF
Type: Dry. Subtype: Attractor.
Item Number: 0401. **Most Popular Sizes:** 10, 12, 14, 16, 18.
Hook Type: Extra-fine dry. **Thread:** Hot-orange 6/0.
Tail: Woodchuck tail fibers or moose body hair.
Body: Bleached Australian possum or other tan fur.
Wing: White calf tail, upright and divided.
Hackle: Brown and grizzly, mixed.
Difficulty: 4.

BIVISIBLE
Type: Dry. Subtype: Attractor.
Item Number: 0353. **Most Popular Sizes:** 12, 14.
Color Options: Brown, cream, black, blue dun.
Hook Type: Extra-fine dry. **Thread:** Black 6/0.
Tail: Brown hackle fibers.
Body: Three brown hackles of increasing size, tightly
palmered from tail to head.
Hackle: Cream, three turns.
Difficulty: 2.

BUGMEISTER
Type: Dry. Subtype: Attractor.
Item Number: 7239. **Most Popular Sizes:** 4, 6, 8, 10, 12, 14.
Color Options: Peacock, Golden, Royal.
Hook Type: 2×-long dry. **Thread:** Black 6/0.
Tail: Light elk body hair, stacked.
Body: Peacock herl or Antron/hare dubbing, picked out.
Rib: Fine copper or gold wire.
Wing: Light elk body hair over peacock herl and pearl
Krystal Flash.
Hackle: Grizzly or brown, tied parachute style.
Thorax: Wing post: white calf body hair, Z-Lon, or Antron.
Difficulty: 4.

CADDIS HUMPY

Type: Dry.   Subtype: Attractor.
Item Number: 12AA. **Most Popular Sizes:** 12, 14, 16, 18.
Color Options: Royal, yellow, orange.
Hook Type: Extra-fine dry. **Thread:** Black 6/0.
Tail: Bleached elk or bleached yearling elk (size 16 or smaller).
Body: Floss.
Wing: Overwing: bleached elk or yearling elk. Wing case:
   bleached elk or yearling elk pulled over the abdomen
   Humpy style.
Hackle: Grizzly or mixed grizzly and brown, thick.
Difficulty: 3.
Notes: This is a very productive pattern that can be designed to
   mimic both caddis and stoneflies.

CHARTREUSE TRUDE

Type: Dry.   Subtype: Attractor.
Item Number: 0988. **Most Popular Sizes:** 10, 12, 14, 16, 18.
Hook Type: Extra-fine dry. **Thread:** Black 6/0.
Tail: Golden pheasant tippets.
Body: In three sections: front and rear thirds peacock herl;
   middle third fluorescent chartreuse floss.
Wing: White calf tail tied down-wing style.
Hackle: Brown.
Difficulty: 4.

DENNIS PARA WULFF

Type: Dry.   Subtype: Attractor.
Item Number: 12CA. **Most Popular Sizes:** 12, 14, 16, 18.
Color Options: Ausable Wulff, Adams Wulff, Royal Wulff.
Hook Type: Extra-fine dry. **Thread:** 6/0 to match body color.
Tail: Spade hackle tips, Moose Mane.
Body: Antron dubbing.
Rib: Fine gold wire or tinsel (optional).
Wing: Calf body hair divided equally.
Hackle: Dry-fly hackle to match general pattern dressing,
   tied parachute style at the base of the wings.
Difficulty: 4.

DOUBLE HUMPY

Type: Dry.   Subtype: Attractor.
Item Number: 0599. **Most Popular Sizes:** 8, 10, 12, 14.
Hook Type: 2×-long dry. **Thread:** Yellow 6/0.
Tail: Natural deer body hair.
Body: Two equal sections of deer hair pulled over the top of
   tying-thread underbody and tied down.
Wing: Two pairs, one in the middle of body and one at head
   in standard position; upright and divided deer hair.
Hackle: Grizzly, in middle of body and at head.
Difficulty: 5.

DROPPER ROYAL WULFF

Type: Dry.   Subtype: Attractor.
Item Number: 937P. **Most Popular Sizes:** 10, 12, 14, 16.
Hook Type: Extra-fine dry. **Thread:** Black 6/0.
Tail: Brown bucktail.
Body: In three sections: front and rear thirds of peacock herl; middle third red floss.
Wing: White calf tail, upright and divided.
Hackle: Brown saddle, heavy.
Other Materials: A short loop of 3×tippet material is tied in first, under the tail.
Difficulty: 4.
Notes: The tippet loop is used to attach a piece of tippet material with a small dry fly or nymph dropper on the other end. The Royal Wulff doubles as a strike indicator.

H & L VARIANT

Type: Dry.   Subtype: Attractor.
Item Number: 0518. **Most Popular Sizes:** 10, 12, 14, 16, 18.
Hook Type: Extra-fine dry or Bigeye dry. **Thread:** Black 8/0.
Tail: White calf tail.
Body: Rear half stripped peacock; front half peacock herl.
Wing: White calf tail, upright and divided.
Hackle: Furnace.
Difficulty: 4.

HARE'S EAR PARACHUTE

Type: Dry.   Subtype: Attractor.
Item Number: 0792. **Most Popular Sizes:** 12, 14, 16.
Hook Type: Extra-fine dry. **Thread:** Tan 6/0.
Tail: Natural deer body hair tips.
Body: Rough and full, dubbed with dark hare's-ear dubbing.
Wing: White calf tail, tied as a single post.
Hackle: Grizzly, parachute style.
Difficulty: 3.

IRRESISTIBLE

Type: Dry.   Subtype: Attractor.
Item Number: 0409. **Most Popular Sizes:** 10, 12, 14, 16.
Hook Type: Extra-fine dry. **Thread:** Black 6/0.
Tail: Brown hackle fibers or mink-tail guard hairs.
Body: Spun gray deer hair clipped to shape.
Wing: Grizzly hackle tips, upright and divided.
Hackle: Brown and grizzly mixed.
Difficulty: 4.

KLINKHAMMER

Type: Dry.   Subtype: Attractor.
Item Number: 02BX. **Most Popular Sizes:** 10, 12, 14, 16.
Color Options: Gray, brown, olive, tan.
Hook Type: Extra-fine dry. **Thread:** Tan 6/0.
Wing: White Antron.
Hackle: Brown, parachute style.
Abdomen: Dubbed fur.
Thorax: Peacock herl.
Difficulty: 3.
Notes: The body should be started on the bend of the hook to get a curved shape.

MADAME X

Type: Dry.   Subtype: Attractor.
Item Number: 0077. **Most Popular Sizes:** 6, 8, 10, 12.
Hook Type: Extra-fine dry. **Thread:** Yellow 6/0.
Tail: Natural deer-hair tips.
Body: Yellow thread.
Wing: Natural light elk.
Legs: Living Rubber.
Head: Formed by pulling back the wing material.
Difficulty: 3.
Notes: The head takes up one fourth of hook shank; tied simple bullet-head style with rubber legs. Rear portion of legs should extend to tips of the tails.

PARACHUTE WULFF

Type: Dry.   Subtype: Attractor.
Item Number: 936B. **Most Popular Sizes:** 12, 14, 16, 18.
Color Options: Royal, Lime. **Hook Type:** Extra-fine dry.
Thread: Black 6/0.
Tail: Brown bucktail.
Body: In three sections: front and rear thirds peacock herl, middle third a band of red (Royal) or fluorescent chartreuse (Lime) floss.
Wing: White calf-tail post.
Hackle: Brown, tied parachute style post.
Difficulty: 4.

PATRIOT

Type: Dry.   Subtype: Attractor.
Item Number: 02B1. **Most Popular Sizes:** 12, 14, 16, 18.
Hook Type: Extra-fine dry. **Thread:** Brown 6/0.
Tail: Light deer-body hair.
Body: Three strands of smolt-blue Krystal Flash with a mid-band of two or three turns of red floss.
Wing: White Antron yarn, upright and divided.
Hackle: Brown neck hackle.
Difficulty: 3.

RENEGADE

Type: Dry. Subtype: Attractor.
Item Number: 0780. **Most Popular Sizes:** 8, 10, 12, 14, 16.
Hook Type: Extra-fine dry fly. **Thread:** Black 6/0.
Body: Peacock herl.
Hackle: Brown tied at hook bend, and white tied at head.
Other Materials: Tag: three turns of flat gold tinsel.
Difficulty: 2.

ROYAL COACHMAN

Type: Dry. Subtype: Attractor.
Item Number: 0332. **Most Popular Sizes:** 12, 14, 16.
Hook Type: Extra-fine dry. **Thread:** Black 6/0.
Tail: Golden pheasant tippets or brown hackle fibers.
Body: Peacock herl in two sections with a red floss center
band.
Wing: White duck-wing quill segments, upright and divided.
Hackle: Brown.
Difficulty: 4.

RUBBER-LEGGED DOUBLE HUMPY

Type: Dry. Subtype: Attractor.
Item Number: 02B9. **Most Popular Sizes:** 8, 10, 12, 14.
Hook Type: 2×-long dry. **Thread:** Yellow 3/0.
Tail: Elk hair.
Body: Yellow thread, with hair pulled over to make humps.
Wing: Elk hair, tied upright and divided in middle of body
and then again at head.
Hackle: Grizzly, tied around both sets of wings.
Legs: White rubber striped with black permanent marker, a
pair tied in at each wing.
Other Materials: Sections of elk hair are folded over the top
of the body behind each wing.
Difficulty: 4.
Notes: This is really two Humpy flies tied on a single hook.

SCHROEDER'S HI VIS HARE'S EAR

Type: Dry. Subtype: Attractor.
Item Number: 02LH.
Most Popular Sizes: 8, 10, 12, 14, 16.
Hook Type: Extra-fine dry.
Thread: Tan 6/0.
Tail: Brown bucktail.
Body: Hare's-ear dubbing, heavy.
Wing: Yellow strike-indicator yarn, short and very heavy.
Hackle: Grizzly saddle, tied very full, parachute style.
Difficulty: 3.

SUPER HUMPY DOUBLE

Type: Dry.   Subtype: Attractor.
Item Number: 942P. **Most Popular Sizes:** 8, 10, 12, 14.
Color Options: Yellow, red. **Hook Type:** 4×-long streamer.
Thread: Black 6/0.
Tail: Elk or moose mane.
Body: Green and yellow Flashabou, with elk hair pulled over
　　to make the hump.
Wing: Tips of the elk hair used for the hump, upright and
　　divided.
Hackle: Brown and grizzly, mixed.
Difficulty: 5.

SUPER HUMPY SINGLE

Type: Dry.   Subtype: Attractor.
Item Number: 941P. **Most Popular Sizes:** 10, 12, 14, 16.
Hook Type: 2×-long dry. **Thread:** Black 6/0.
Tail: Elk or moose mane.
Body: Green and yellow Flashabou, with elk-body hair
　　pulled over to make the hump.
Wing: Tips of the elk-body hair used as the hump, upright
　　and divided.
Hackle: Brown and grizzly, mixed.
Difficulty: 5.

TURK'S TARANTULA

Type: Dry.   Subtype: Attractor.
Item Number: 0235. **Most Popular Sizes:** 8, 10, 12.
Color Options: Green, tan, red. **Hook Type:** 2×-long dry.
Thread: Tan 3/0.
Tail: Golden pheasant tippets.
Body: Antron dubbing or floss.
Wing: White or tan calf body hair.
Hackle: Trimmed neck hackle palmered over body.
Thorax: Collar: deer body hair tips.
Legs: Round Living Rubber or Sili Legs tied in front of the collar.
Head: Spun deer body hair.
Difficulty: 4.

WHITE WULFF

Type: Dry.   Subtype: Attractor.
Item Number: 0402. **Most Popular Sizes:** 10, 12, 14.
Hook Type: Extra-fine dry. **Thread:** White 6/0.
Tail: White calf tail or mink-tail guard hairs.
Body: White dubbing.
Wing: White calf tail, upright and divided.
Hackle: Badger.
Difficulty: 3.

YELLOW HUMPY
Type: Dry. Subtype: Attractor.
Item Number: 0403. **Most Popular Sizes:** 10, 12, 14, 16, 18.
Hook Type: Extra-fine dry or Bigeye dry.
Thread: Bright yellow 6/0.
Tail: Light elk hair.
Body: Light elk hair pulled over thread underbody.
Wing: Formed from the tips of the elk hair used to make the body, upright and divided.
Hackle: Brown and grizzly mixed.
Difficulty: 4.

BLACK ELK WING CADDIS
Type: Dry. Subtype: Caddis.
Item Number: 0945. **Most Popular Sizes:** 14, 16, 18.
Hook Type: Extra-fine dry. **Thread:** Black 6/0.
Body: Black dubbing.
Rib: Copper wire.
Wing: Black elk hair.
Hackle: Black, palmered.
Head: Stubs of elk hair left after trimming wing.
Difficulty: 2.

CDC ADULT CADDIS
Type: Dry. Subtype: Caddis.
Item Number: 0388. **Most Popular Sizes:** 14, 16, 18, 20.
Color Options: Olive, peacock, tan, cream, gray, black.
Hook Type: Extra-fine dry. **Thread:** 6/0 to match body color.
Wing: One full CDC feather over sparse, light gray Z-Lon yarn.
Abdomen: Dubbed fur to match pattern.
Thorax: Same as abdomen, wrapped over butts of CDC feather.
Legs: The butt of the CDC feather is pulled upright and divided with a figure-eight so that half of the clump sticks out to each side.
Difficulty: 2.

CDC ELK WING CADDIS
Type: Dry. Subtype: Caddis.
Item Number: 0121. **Most Popular Sizes:** 12, 14, 16, 18, 20.
Color Options: Tan, gray, olive, or peacock.
Hook Type: Extra-fine dry. **Thread:** Tan 6/0.
Body: Dubbing or peacock herl.
Rib: Fine flat gold tinsel.
Wing: Underwing: gray CDC fibers. Overwing: bleached elk hair.
Other Materials: Antennae: a pair of stripped brown hackle stems almost as long as the body.
Difficulty: 3.

CDC Emerging Caddis

Type: Dry. Subtype: Caddis.
Item Number: 0389. **Most Popular Sizes:** 14, 16, 18, 20.
Color Options: Cream, olive, brown. **Hook Type:** Extra-fine
dry or Bigeye dry. **Thread:** 6/0 or 8/0 to match body color.
Tail: Sparse Z-Lon yarn to match body.
Body: Z-Lon or Antron yarn, twisted tightly before winding.
    Color to match pattern description.
Rib: Fine gold wire.
Wing: A few long wood-duck fibers for antennae, over which is
    tied sparse Z-Lon yarn, over which is tied a CDC feather.
Hackle: Cream, palmered through thorax area, trimmed on
    bottom.
Head: Dubbed Antron to match body.
Difficulty: 3.
Notes: Wing colors for cream variation is cream CDC over
    cream Z-Lon; olive is dark dun CDC over dark dun
    Z-Lon; brown is dun CDC over brown Z-Lon.

CDC Hare's Ear Caddis

Type: Dry. Subtype: Caddis.
Item Number: 0365. **Most Popular Sizes:** 14, 16, 18.
Color Options: Yellow, olive, tan. **Hook Type:** Extra-fine dry.
Thread: Tan 6/0.
Tail: Brown hackle fibers.
Body: Hare's-ear dubbing. The tan variation is tied with the
    natural color; olive and yellow are tied with dyed
    hare's-ear fur.
Rib: Flat fine gold tinsel.
Wing: One or two natural CDC feathers tied so they slant
    back over the body.
Difficulty: 1.

Davy's Caddis

Type: Dry. Subtype: Caddis.
Item Number: 7226. **Most Popular Sizes:** 12, 14, 16.
Color Options: Brown, black, hare's ear.
Hook Type: Extra-fine dry. **Thread:** 8/0 to match body color.
Wing: Yearling elk tied in by the tips and trimmed.
Hackle: Neck hackle wound figure-eight style over the thorax.
Body: Antron/Hare dubbing.
Head: Antennae: Two yearling elk tips from wing.
Difficulty: 3.

Dropper Caddis

Type: Dry. Subtype: Caddis.
Item Number: 938P. **Most Popular Sizes:** 10, 12, 14, 16.
Hook Type: Extra-fine dry. **Thread:** Olive 6/0.
Body: Olive dubbing.
Wing: Calf elk tied heavy and full.
Hackle: Brown hackle palmered over the body, heavy and full.
Other Materials: A short loop of 3 × tippet material is tied in
    at the bend of the hook.
Difficulty: 3.
Notes: The tippet loop is used to attach a piece of tippet
    material with a small dry fly or nymph at the other
    end. The caddis doubles as a strike indicator.

ELK WING CADDIS
Type: Dry. Subtype: Caddis.
Item Number: 0378. **Most Popular Sizes:** 10, 12, 14, 16, 18.
Color Options: Olive, tan, gray, black.
Hook Type: Extra-fine or Bigeye dry.
Thread: Brown 6/0 or 8/0.
Body: Dubbed fur to match color of pattern.
Rib: Copper wire.
Wing: Light elk hair tied on top of the hook, allowing some fibers to extend along sides. The wing butts should extend forward to form head.
Hackle: Brown, gray, or black, palmered over body.
Difficulty: 3.

EXTENDED BODY CADDIS
Type: Dry. Subtype: Caddis.
Item Number: 02BQ. **Most Popular Sizes:** 12, 14, 16.
Color Options: Burnt orange, olive, tan/brown.
Hook Type: Short-shank curved nymph. **Thread:** Olive 6/0.
Body: Micro chenille tied as extended body over bend of hook; the end is singed with butane lighter.
Wing: Deer hair over gray Z-Lon.
Hackle: Grizzly dyed dun.
Difficulty: 3.

GODDARD CADDIS
Type: Dry. Subtype: Caddis.
Item Number: 0902. **Most Popular Sizes:** 10, 12, 14, 16.
Hook Type: Extra-fine dry. **Thread:** Tan 6/0.
Body: Natural caribou or deer hair, spun and trimmed to shape, leaving longer hairs at bend.
Hackle: Brown.
Other Materials: Antennae: brown hackle stems.
Difficulty: 3.

HEMINGWAY CADDIS
Type: Dry. Subtype: Caddis.
Item Number: 08K8. **Most Popular Sizes:** 12, 14, 16, 18.
Hook Type: Extra-fine dry. **Thread:** Olive 6/0.
Rib: Medium dun hackle palmered through body.
Wing: Underwing: mallard dyed wood duck color.
Overwing: mallard-wing quill tied flat over the top.
Hackle: Medium dun palmered through thorax.
Abdomen: Olive fur.
Thorax: Peacock herl.
Difficulty: 4.

HENRYVILLE SPECIAL

Type: Dry. Subtype: Caddis.
Item Number: 0337. **Most Popular Sizes:** 12, 14, 16, 18.
Hook Type: Extra-fine dry. **Thread:** Olive 6/0 or 8/0.
Body: Olive floss.
Rib: Undersized grizzly hackle, palmered in an open spiral.
Wing: Underwing of wood-duck flank fibers with overwing
     of gray mallard-wing quill tied flat.
Hackle: Brown.
Difficulty: 4.

IRRESISTIBLE CADDIS

Type: Dry. Subtype: Caddis.
Item Number: 0711. **Most Popular Sizes:** 12, 14, 16.
Color Options: Olive, brown. **Hook Type:** Extra-fine dry.
Thread: Olive or brown 6/0.
Body: Spun and clipped deer hair, tight and small.
Rib: Grizzly dyed olive or brown, palmered through body.
Wing: Elk hair.
Head: Trimmed ends of elk-hair wing.
Other Materials: Antennae: stripped grizzly hackle stems.
Difficulty: 4.

JD'S SEDGE

Type: Dry. Subtype: Caddis.
Item Number: 08K7. **Most Popular Sizes:** 12, 14, 16.
Color Options: Tan, brown, black, olive.
Hook Type: Extra-fine dry. **Thread:** 8/0 to match body color.
Body: 1/16-inch-thick Fly Foam.
Rib: Tying thread.
Wing: Saddle-hackle tip or hen neck-hackle tip.
Hackle: Brown, black, or dun.
Other Materials: Antennae: Two stripped hackle stems.
Difficulty: 3.

KAUFMANN'S HOT BUTT CADDIS

Type: Dry. Subtype: Caddis.
Item Number: 12CC. **Most Popular Sizes:** 14, 16, 18.
Color Options: Tan, peacock, yellow, fluorescent green.
Hook Type: Extra-fine dry. **Thread:** 8/0 to match body color.
Tail: Fluorescent-orange Antron yarn.
Body: Antron dubbing.
Rib: Fine copper wire.
Wing: Dun or tan CDC topped with elk hair.
Hackle: Fine neck hackle palmered to match body color.
Head: Butts of elk hair clipped square.
Difficulty: 3.

259

MATHEWS X CADDIS

Type: Dry. **Subtype:** Caddis.
Item Number: 02B3. **Most Popular Sizes:** 14, 16, 18.
Color Options: Tan, olive. **Hook Type:** Extra-fine dry.
Thread: Tan 6/0.
Tail: Z-Lon or Antron.
Body: Dubbed fur.
Wing: Fine deer hair.
Head: Butts of wing hair, trimmed.
Difficulty: 2.

SCHROEDER'S HI VIS CADDIS

Type: Dry. **Subtype:** Caddis.
Item Number: 02LK. **Most Popular Sizes:** 12, 14, 16.
Hook Type: Extra-fine dry. **Thread:** Tan 6/0.
Body: Hare's-ear dubbing.
Wing: Yellow strike indicator yarn, short and very heavy.
   Second wing tied down over the body from dark
   mottled turkey quill.
Hackle: Grizzly saddle, tied very full, parachute style.
Difficulty: 3.

SLOW-WATER CADDIS

Type: Dry. **Subtype:** Caddis.
Item Number: 12A9. **Most Popular Sizes:** 14, 16, 18.
Color Options: Gray, ginger, olive, black, brown.
Hook Type: Extra-fine dry. **Thread:** 8/0 to match body color.
Body: Antron dubbing.
Wing: Two thin hen hackle tips coated with clear spray fixative.
Hackle: Dry-fly hackle to match body color.
Thorax: One or two wraps of the hackle over a dubbing base.
   Trim the hackle flat on the top and bottom.
Difficulty: 2.
Notes: Diluted cement can be used to coat the wings. It is
   important that any coating be put on the wings very
   sparingly.

STOCKING WING CADDIS

Type: Dry. **Subtype:** Caddis.
Item Number: 814E. **Most Popular Sizes:** 10, 12, 14, 16, 18.
Color Options: Tan, brown, gray, olive.
Hook Type: 2×-long dry. **Thread:** 6/0 to match body color.
Wing: Stocking wing (synthetic precut wing).
Abdomen: Loosely spun deer body hair.
Thorax: Deer hair spun in a loop.
Legs: Pick out the thorax for legs.
Other Materials: Wing case (optional): Short section of dark
   Antron yarn pulled over thorax as a wing
   case.
Difficulty: 3.

BRAIDED BUTT DAMSEL

Type: Dry. Subtype: Damsel.
Item Number: 02CF.
Most Popular Sizes: 10, 12, 14.
Color Options: Blue, tan.
Hook Type: Extra-fine dry.
Thread: 8/0 to match body color.
Tail: Dyed braided mono striped with black permanent marker.
Body: Fly Foam to match tail.
Wing: Upright post of white Antron.
Hackle: Grizzly, parachute style.
Other Materials: Overlay: white foam.
Difficulty: 4.

AIRE-FLOW CUTWING DUN

Type: Dry. Subtype: Mayfly.
Item Number: 036C. **Most Popular Sizes:** 12, 14, 16, 18.
Color Options: PMD, *Callibaetis*, BWO.
Hook Type: Extra-fine dry. **Thread:** Tan 8/0.
Tail: Microfibbets, split.
Body: PMD: yellowish-olive fur. *Callibaetis*: gray fur. BWO:
olive fur.
Wing: Premade Airflow or Poly Plus wings.
Hackle: PMD: light blue dun. *Callibaetis*: grizzly. BWO: dark
dun. Hackle is clipped on the bottom.
Abdomen: Fur dubbed tightly and sparsely.
Thorax: Fur dubbed heavier than abdomen; wings are tied
just ahead of it to raise them upright.
Difficulty: 3.

AK'S QUILLS

Type: Dry. Subtype: Mayfly.
Item Number: 03CA. **Most Popular Sizes:** 16, 18, 20, 22.
Color Options: Red Quill, BWO, Trico, PMD.
Hook Type: Extra-fine dry.
Thread: Brown, olive, or cream 8/0.
Tail: Spade hackle or Microfibbets to match body color.
Body: Stripped hackle quill.
Wing: Dun, brown, cream, or white hen-hackle tips.
Thorax: Antron dubbing to match body color.
Difficulty: 3.

BIG HORN SULFUR PARACHUTE

Type: Dry. Subtype: Mayfly.
Item Number: 0859. **Most Popular Sizes:** 16, 18.
Hook Type: Bigeye dry. **Thread:** Yellow 6/0.
Tail: Cream hackle fibers.
Body: Orange/yellow dubbing.
Wing: White calf tail, tied as a sparse post.
Hackle: Cream, four turns around parachute post.
Difficulty: 3.

BLACK GNAT

Type: Dry.   Subtype: Mayfly.
Item Number: 0335. **Most Popular Sizes:** 12, 14, 16, 18.
Hook Type: Extra-fine dry fly; Bigeye dry in smaller sizes.
Thread: Black 6/0.
Tail: Black hackle fibers.
Body: Black fur.
Wing: Natural mallard quill sections, upright and divided.
Hackle: Black.
Difficulty: 3.

BLUE DUN

Type: Dry.   Subtype: Mayfly.
Item Number: 0334. **Most Popular Sizes:** 12, 14, 16, 18, 20.
Hook Type: Extra-fine dry; Bigeye dry in smaller sizes.
Thread: Gray 6/0.
Tail: Medium-dun hackle fibers.
Body: Muskrat fur or gray dubbing.
Wing: Mallard-wing quill segments, upright and divided.
Hackle: Medium dun.
Difficulty: 3.

BLUE QUILL

Type: Dry.   Subtype: Mayfly.
Item Number: 766E. **Most Popular Sizes:** 14, 16, 18.
Hook Type: Extra-fine dry. **Thread:** White 6/0.
Tail: Blue-dun hackle fibers.
Body: Stripped peacock quill.
Wing: Matched pair of gray mallard primary wing-quill
        sections, upright and divided.
Hackle: Blue dun.
Difficulty: 4.

BLUE WING OLIVE PARACHUTE

Type: Dry.   Subtype: Mayfly.
Item Number: 0924. **Most Popular Sizes:** 14, 16, 18, 20.
Hook Type: Extra-fine dry. **Thread:** Olive 6/0.
Tail: Dark-dun hackle fibers.
Body: Olive-brown dubbing.
Wing: Dark-dun turkey-body feather clump.
Hackle: Dark dun, parachute style.
Difficulty: 3.

BLUE WINGED OLIVE

Type: Dry.   Subtype: Mayfly.
Item Number: 0338. **Most Popular Sizes:** 14, 16, 18, 20, 22.
Hook Type: Extra-fine dry. **Thread:** Olive 6/0 or 8/0.
Tail: Dark-dun hackle fibers.
Body: Medium olive fur.
Wing: Dark-dun hackle tips.
Hackle: Dark dun.
Difficulty: 3.

BLUE WINGED OLIVE THORAX

Type: Dry.   Subtype: Mayfly.
Item Number: 0368. **Most Popular Sizes:** 16, 18, 20, 22, 24.
Hook Type: Bigeye dry. **Thread:** Olive 6/0 or 8/0.
Tail: Medium-dun hackle fibers, split around small ball of
    dubbing.
Body: Medium olive dubbing.
Wing: Dark-dun turkey flat.
Hackle: Medium dun, clipped on bottom.
Difficulty: 3.

CANNON'S BUNNY DUN

Type: Dry.   Subtype: Mayfly.
Item Number: 761E. **Most Popular Sizes:** 20, 22, 24, 16, 18.
Color Options: Black, PMD, olive. **Hook Type:** Bigeye dry.
Thread: 6/0 to match body color.
Tail: Dun Microfibbets or hackle fibers, split around small
    ball of fur.
Body: Dubbed fur to match pattern description.
Wing: Clump of snowshoe-rabbit's-foot guard hairs and
    underfur.
Head: Body dubbing wound past wing to eye.
Difficulty: 3.

CDC COMPARADUN

Type: Dry.   Subtype: Mayfly.
Item Number: 733F. **Most Popular Sizes:** 16, 18, 20.
Color Options: Sulfur, Hendrickson, olive, brown.
Hook Type: Bigeye dry, down-eye. **Thread:** White 8/0.
Tail: Light-dun Microfibbets, split around small ball of fur,
    two per side.
Wing: Bunch of natural CDC fibers with a few fibers of
    wood-duck flank feather mixed in.
Abdomen: Biot quill to match pattern description.
Thorax: Fur dubbing to match pattern description.
Difficulty: 3.

CDC Mayfly Dun

Type: Dry. Subtype: Mayfly.
Item Number: 817E. **Most Popular Sizes:** 14, 16, 18.
Color Options: Sulfur, BWO, PMD, *Baetis*.
Hook Type: Extra-fine dry. **Thread:** 6/0 to match body color.
Tail: Dun or ginger Microfibbets, depending upon the pattern.
Body: Turkey biot.
Wing: Dun CDC topped with natural mallard.
Thorax: Superfine Antron dubbing.
Difficulty: 3.

CDC Mayfly Emerger

Type: Dry. Subtype: Mayfly.
Item Number: 801E. **Most Popular Sizes:** 14, 16, 18.
Color Options: Tan, yellow, olive.
Hook Type: Short-shank curved nymph.
Thread: To match body color.
Tail: Blue-dun hackle fibers.
Body: Dubbed fur to match pattern description.
Wing: Clump of natural CDC fibers tied slanting back over body.
Head: Body dubbing extended past wing.
Difficulty: 2.

Eastern Green Drake

Type: Dry. Subtype: Mayfly.
Item Number: 0150. **Most Popular Sizes:** 8, 10.
Hook Type: 2×-long dry. **Thread:** Olive 6/0.
Tail: Brown Microfibbets.
Body: Tannish olive fur.
Rib: Olive floss.
Hackle: Grizzly dyed olive.
Legs: Wood duck, divided style.
Difficulty: 3.

Extended Body Compara Dun

Type: Dry. Subtype: Mayfly.
Item Number: 0004. **Most Popular Sizes:** 12, 14, 16, 18.
Color Options: Tan, olive, gray, or Pale Evening Dun.
Hook Type: Extra-fine dry. **Thread:** Gray 8/0.
Tail: Light-dun Microfibbets, split.
Body: Antron dubbing.
Rib: Black Krystal Flash.
Wing: Coastal or fine white-tailed deer hair.
Difficulty: 3.
Notes: Body extensions are pre-tied. Place a thin-eyed sewing needle in the vise. Tie on the Microfibbetts, dub over the Microfibbett thread base until the extended section is complete. Slide the needle out, tie in the extended section, finish dubbing up to base.

EXTENDED BODY EASTERN GREEN DRAKE

Type: Dry.   Subtype: Mayfly.
Item Number: 11T5. **Most Popular Sizes:** 8, 10.
Hook Type: 2×-long dry. **Thread:** Tan 8/0.
Tail: Peacock sword surrounded by tips of dyed-brown elk
    from the body.
Rib: Tan 8/0 thread.
Wing: Brown hen hackle three fourths as long as the shank.
Hackle: Two brown hackles tied full, wrapped over half of
        the thorax.
Abdomen: Mixture of cream and golden tan Antron dubbing.
Thorax: Cream dubbing.
Difficulty: 4.
Notes: The tail is approximately one and a half times the
        length of the hook shank.

GRAY FOX

Type: Dry.   Subtype: Mayfly.
Item Number: 0345. **Most Popular Sizes:** 12, 14, 16.
Hook Type: Extra-fine dry. **Thread:** Yellow 6/0.
Tail: Ginger hackle fibers.
Body: Tan fur.
Wing: Gray mallard flank, upright and divided.
Hackle: Ginger and grizzly, mixed.
Difficulty: 3.

HAIRWING WESTERN GREEN DRAKE

Type: Dry.   Subtype: Mayfly.
Item Number: 02TF. **Most Popular Sizes:** 10, 12.
Hook Type: Extra-fine dry. **Thread:** Olive 6/0.
Tail: Moose mane.
Body: Light olive dubbing.
Rib: Brown monofilament or heavy thread.
Wing: Deer or elk hair.
Hackle: Olive-dyed grizzly.
Difficulty: 3.

HENDRICKSON, DARK

Type: Dry.   Subtype: Mayfly.
Item Number: 0341. **Most Popular Sizes:** 12, 14, 16.
Hook Type: Extra-fine dry. **Thread:** Gray 6/0.
Tail: Dark-dun hackle fibers.
Body: Dark muskrat or dark gray fur.
Wing: Wood-duck flank, upright and divided.
Hackle: Dark dun.
Difficulty: 3.

HENDRICKSON, LIGHT
Type: Dry.   Subtype: Mayfly.
Item Number: 0342. **Most Popular Sizes:** 12, 14, 16.
Hook Type: Extra-fine dry. **Thread:** Tan 6/0.
Tail: Medium-dun hackle fibers.
Body: Pinkish tan fox fur or dubbing.
Wing: Wood-duck flank, upright and divided.
Hackle: Medium dun.
Difficulty: 3.

HENDRICKSON THORAX
Type: Dry.   Subtype: Mayfly.
Item Number: 0362. **Most Popular Sizes:** 12, 14, 16.
Hook Type: Extra-fine dry. **Thread:** Olive 6/0.
Tail: Medium-dun hackle fibers, split around ball of dubbing.
Body: Fawn fox fur or pinkish-tan dubbing.
Wing: Medium-dun turkey flat.
Hackle: Medium dun, clipped on bottom.
Difficulty: 3.

INDICATOR PARACHUTE—ADAMS
Type: Dry.   Subtype: Mayfly.
Item Number: 11YC-09. **Most Popular Sizes:** 12, 14, 16, 18.
Hook Type: Extra-fine dry. **Thread:** Black 8/0.
Tail: Dark-dun Microfibbets, splayed.
Body: Adams Gray Antron dubbing blend.
Wing: Post: yellow and red Antron or Z-Lon (yellow forward).
Hackle: Mixed grizzly and brown dry-fly hackle, tied parachute style.
Difficulty: 4.

INDICATOR PARACHUTE—*BAETIS*
Type: Dry.   Subtype: Mayfly.
Item Number: 11YC-18. **Most Popular Sizes:** 14, 16, 18, 20.
Hook Type: Extra-fine dry. **Thread:** Brown 8/0.
Tail: Light-dun Microfibbets, splayed.
Body: *Baetis* Antron blend.
Wing: Post: yellow and red Antron or Z-Lon (yellow forward).
Hackle: Brown dry-fly hackle, tied parachute style.
Difficulty: 4.

INDICATOR PARACHUTE—BWO

Type: Dry.   Subtype: Mayfly.
Item Number: 11YC-21. **Most Popular Sizes:** 14, 16, 18, 20.
Hook Type: Extra-fine dry. **Thread:** Olive 8/0.
Tail: Light-dun Microfibbets, splayed.
Body: Blue-Winged Olive Antron blend.
Wing: Post: yellow and red Antron or Z-Lon (yellow
    forward).
Hackle: Light-dun dry-fly hackle, tied parachute style.
Difficulty: 4.

INDICATOR PARACHUTE—HARES EAR

Type: Dry.   Subtype: Mayfly.
Item Number: 11YC-11. **Most Popular Sizes:** 12, 14, 16, 18.
Hook Type: Extra-fine dry. **Thread:** Black 8/0.
Tail: Long fibers from hare's-ear mask, splayed (or brown
    Microfibbets).
Body: Hare's-ear dubbing blend.
Wing: Post: yellow and red Antron or Z-Lon (yellow
    forward).
Hackle: Grizzly dry-fly hackle, tied parachute style.
Difficulty: 4.

INDICATOR PARACHUTE—LT. CAHILL

Type: Dry.   Subtype: Mayfly.
Item Number: 11YC-33. **Most Popular Sizes:** 14, 16, 18.
Hook Type: Extra-fine dry. **Thread:** Cream 8/0.
Tail: Cream Microfibbets, splayed.
Body: Light Cahill Antron dubbing.
Wing: Post: yellow and red Antron or Z-lon (yellow forward).
Hackle: Cream, tied parachute style.
Difficulty: 4.

INDICATOR PARACHUTE—PHEASANT TAIL

Type: Dry.   Subtype: Mayfly.
Item Number: 11YC-02. **Most Popular Sizes:** 12, 14, 16, 18.
Hook Type: Extra-fine dry. **Thread:** Brown 8/0.
Tail: Brown Microfibbets, splayed.
Body: Pheasant tail fibers.
Wing: Yellow and red Antron or Z-lon (yellow forward).
Hackle: Brown, tied parachute style.
Thorax: Peacock herl.
Difficulty: 4.

INDICATOR PARACHUTE—PMD

Type: Dry.   Subtype: Mayfly.
Item Number: 11YC-00. **Most Popular Sizes:** 14, 16, 18.
Hook Type: Extra-fine dry. **Thread:** Cream 8/0.
Tail: Light Dun Microfibbets, splayed.
Body: PMD blend Antron dubbing.
Wing: Post: yellow and red Antron or Z-Lon (yellow forward).
Hackle: Light brown or ginger dry-fly hackle tied parachute style.
Difficulty: 4.

INDICATOR PARACHUTE—SULFUR

Type: Dry.   Subtype: Mayfly.
Item Number: 11YC-14. **Most Popular Sizes:** 14, 16, 18, 20.
Hook Type: Extra-fine dry. **Thread:** Cream 8/0.
Tail: Light dun Microfibbets, splayed.
Body: Sulphur Orange Antron blend.
Wing: Post: yellow and red Antron or Z-Lon (yellow forward).
Hackle: Light dun dry-fly hackle tied parachute style.
Difficulty: 4.
Notes: For sulfurs with a lighter body color, add cream dubbing to the blend and use white 8/0 thread.

INDICATOR SPINNER—MAHOGANY

Type: Dry.   Subtype: Mayfly.
Item Number: 11YK-23. **Most Popular Sizes:** 14, 16, 18.
Hook Type: Extra-fine dry. **Thread:** Brown 6/0.
Tail: Blue dun hackle fibers split in a V.
Wing: Post: yellow and red Antron or Z-Lon (yellow forward). Wing: white Evett's Spinner Wing.
Hackle: Brown dry-fly hackle tied parachute style.
Abdomen: Mahogany turkey biot.
Thorax: Dark brown Antron dubbing.
Difficulty: 4.

INDICATOR SPINNER—SULPHUR

Type: Dry.   Subtype: Mayfly.
Item Number: 11YK-14. **Most Popular Sizes:** 14, 16, 18.
Hook Type: Extra-fine dry. **Thread:** Yellow 6/0.
Tail: Blue dun hackle fibers split in a V.
Wing: Post: yellow and red Antron or Z-Lon (yellow forward). Wing: white Evett's Spinner Wing.
Hackle: Barred ginger dry-fly hackle tied parachute style.
Abdomen: Amber turkey biot.
Thorax: Amber Antron dubbing.
Difficulty: 4.

INDICATOR SPINNER—TAN

Type: Dry. Subtype: Mayfly.
Item Number: 11YK-10. **Most Popular Sizes:** 14, 16, 18.
Hook Type: Extra-fine dry. **Thread:** Tan 8/0.
Tail: Tan Microfibbets, splayed.
Wing: Post: yellow and red Antron or Z-Lon (yellow
  forward). Wing: white Evett's Spinner Wing.
Hackle: Tan dry-fly hackle tied parachute style.
Abdomen: Tan turkey biot.
Thorax: Tan Antron dubbing.
Difficulty: 4.

INDICATOR SPINNER—TRICO

Type: Dry. Subtype: Mayfly.
Item Number: 11YK-01. **Most Popular Sizes:** 20, 22, 24.
Hook Type: Extra-fine dry. **Thread:** Black 6/0 or 8/0.
Tail: Dun hackle fibers split in a V.
Wing: Post: yellow and red Antron or Z-Lon (yellow
  forward). Wing: white Evett's Spinner Wing.
Hackle: Grizzly dry-fly hackle tied parachute style.
Abdomen: Stripped grizzly hackle quill.
Thorax: Dark olive Antron dubbing.
Difficulty: 4.

LIGHT CAHILL

Type: Dry. Subtype: Mayfly.
Item Number: 0344.
Most Popular Sizes: 10, 12, 14, 16, 18, 20.
Hook Type: Extra-fine dry. **Thread:** Yellow 6/0 or 8/0.
Tail: Cream or light ginger hackle fibers.
Body: Red-fox belly or cream dubbing.
Wing: Wood-duck flank, upright and divided.
Hackle: Cream or light ginger.
Difficulty: 3.

LIGHT CAHILL THORAX

Type: Dry. Subtype: Mayfly.
Item Number: 0366. **Most Popular Sizes:** 12, 14, 16, 18, 20.
Hook Type: Extra-fine dry; Bigeye dry on smaller sizes.
Thread: Yellow 6/0.
Tail: Dark cream hackle fibers, split around small ball of fur.
Body: Cream dubbing.
Wing: Cream turkey flat.
Hackle: Dark cream or light ginger, clipped on bottom.
Difficulty: 3.

MARCH BROWN

Type: Dry.   Subtype: Mayfly.
Item Number: 0346. **Most Popular Sizes:** 12, 14.
Hook Type: Extra-fine dry. **Thread:** Yellow 6/0.
Tail: Brown hackle fibers.
Body: Fawn fox fur or tan dubbing.
Wing: Darkly speckled wood-duck flank, upright and
 divided.
Hackle: Brown and grizzly, mixed.
Difficulty: 3.

PALE EVENING DUN

Type: Dry.   Subtype: Mayfly.
Item Number: 0339. **Most Popular Sizes:** 14, 16, 18, 20.
Hook Type: Extra-fine dry fly. **Thread:** Cream 6/0 or 8/0.
Tail: Light dun hackle fibers.
Body: Pale yellow dubbing.
Wing: Light dun hackle tips, upright and divided.
Hackle: Light dun.
Difficulty: 3.

PALE MORNING DUN THORAX

Type: Dry.   Subtype: Mayfly.
Item Number: 0367. **Most Popular Sizes:** 16, 18, 20, 22.
Hook Type: Bigeye dry. **Thread:** Yellow 6/0 or 8/0.
Tail: Light dun hackle fibers, split around small ball of
 dubbing.
Body: Pale yellow dubbing with a touch of pale olive.
Wing: Light dun turkey flat.
Hackle: Light dun, clipped on bottom.
Difficulty: 3.

PALE OLIVE SPINNER

Type: Dry.   Subtype: Mayfly.
Item Number: 0374. **Most Popular Sizes:** 12, 16, 18, 20.
Hook Type: Extra-fine or Bigeye dry.
Thread: Olive 6/0 or 8/0.
Tail: Light dun hackle fibers, split.
Body: Pale olive dubbing.
Wing: Light gray poly-wing material or Z-Lon.
Hackle: Light dun, palmered through thorax area, trimmed
 on bottom.
Difficulty: 2.

PARACHUTE PHEASANT TAIL

Type: Dry.   Subtype: Mayfly.
Item Number: 937B. **Most Popular Sizes:** 12, 14, 16, 18.
Hook Type: Extra-fine dry. **Thread:** Orange 6/0.
Tail: Ring-necked pheasant tail fibers.
Rib: Fine copper wire.
Wing: White calf-tail post.
Hackle: Brown, tied parachute style around wing post.
Abdomen: Ring-necked pheasant tail fibers, twisted and
          wound.
Thorax: Brown dubbing around base of wing.
Difficulty: 4.

QUILL GORDON

Type: Dry.   Subtype: Mayfly.
Item Number: 0347. **Most Popular Sizes:** 12, 14, 16.
Hook Type: Extra-fine dry. **Thread:** Yellow 6/0.
Tail: Medium-dun hackle fibers.
Body: Stripped peacock quill.
Wing: Wood-duck flank, upright and divided.
Hackle: Medium dun.
Difficulty: 3.

RED QUILL

Type: Dry.   Subtype: Mayfly.
Item Number: 0343. **Most Popular Sizes:** 12, 14, 16.
Hook Type: Extra-fine dry. **Thread:** Olive 6/0.
Tail: Medium-dun hackle fibers.
Body: Stripped Coachman-brown hackle quill.
Wing: Wood-duck flank, upright and divided.
Hackle: Medium dun.
Difficulty: 3.
Notes: Strip and soak hackle stems in water prior to using.

RS 2

Type: Dry.   Subtype: Mayfly.
Item Number: 067T.
Most Popular Sizes: 14, 16, 18, 20, 22, 24.
Color Options: Trico (black), gray, olive, PMD (yellowish
          olive).
Hook Type: Bigeye dry. **Thread:** 8/0 to match body color.
Tail: Clear Microfibbets, splayed.
Body: Fine synthetic dubbing to match pattern color.
Wing: White or natural gray CDC.
Difficulty: 2.

SPARKLE DUN

Type: Dry.   Subtype: Mayfly.
Item Number: 749F. **Most Popular Sizes:** 14, 16, 18, 20.
Color Options: Tan, olive, black, *Baetis* (olive/brown).
Hook Type: Extra-fine dry or Bigeye dry. **Thread:** Tan 8/0.
Tail: Brown Z-Lon tied as trailing shuck.
Body: Dubbed fur the color of pattern description.
Wing: Coastal deer hair tied in single clump and splayed
across top 180 degrees of hook.
Head: Body dubbing, continued past wing.
Difficulty: 3.

SULPHUR PARACHUTE

Type: Dry.   Subtype: Mayfly.
Item Number: 0923. **Most Popular Sizes:** 14, 16, 18, 20.
Hook Type: Extra-fine dry. **Thread:** Pale yellow 6/0.
Tail: Light-dun hackle fibers.
Body: Pale yellow dubbing.
Wing: Light-dun turkey-body feather clump.
Hackle: Cream, parachute style.
Difficulty: 3.

TASHIRO' BUBBLE FLY

Type: Dry.   Subtype: Mayfly.
Item Number: 02CE. **Most Popular Sizes:** 14, 16, 18.
Color Options: PMD, BWO. **Hook Type:** Extra-fine dry.
Thread: 8/0 to match body color.
Tail: Natural mallard or wood duck.
Body: Superfine Antron dubbing, or thread on smallest flies.
Wing: Post: small piece of Styrofoam packing material.
Hackle: Dun or ginger.
Difficulty: 3.

TRAVIS EXTENDED BODY GREEN DRAKE

Type: Dry.   Subtype: Mayfly.
Item Number: 0154. **Most Popular Sizes:** 10, 12, 14.
Hook Type: Extra-fine dry. **Thread:** Black 6/0.
Tail: Four dark moose-body hairs.
Body: Dark olive camel fur.
Rib: Yellow Krystal Flash.
Wing: Black Antron yarn (single upright post).
Hackle: Yellow grizzly, tied parachute style.
Difficulty: 3.

TRICO SPINNER

Type: Dry.   Subtype: Mayfly.
Item Number: 0372. **Most Popular Sizes:** 20, 22, 24.
Hook Type: Bigeye dry. **Thread:** Black 6/0 or 8/0.
Tail: Light-dun hackle fibers.
Wing: Light-dun hackle fibers.
Abdomen: Tying thread.
Thorax: Fine black dubbing.
Difficulty: 3.
Notes: The hackle is wound and flattened with your fingers, then held in place with a figure-eight of dubbing around the wing.

TRICO THORAX

Type: Dry.   Subtype: Mayfly.
Item Number: 0363. **Most Popular Sizes:** 18, 20, 22, 24.
Hook Type: Bigeye dry. **Thread:** Black 8/0.
Tail: Black hackle fibers, split.
Wing: White turkey-flat fibers.
Hackle: Black, clipped on bottom.
Abdomen: Tying thread.
Thorax: Black fur.
Difficulty: 3.

WESTERN CDC SULPHUR

Type: Dry.   Subtype: Mayfly.
Item Number: 02B5. **Most Popular Sizes:** 16, 18.
Hook Type: Extra-fine dry. **Thread:** Yellow 8/0.
Tail: Light dun or sulfur Microfibbets.
Body: Presoaked quill dyed sulfur orange.
Wing: Yellow CDC plumes.
Thorax: Antron dubbing in cream or sulfur.
Difficulty: 3.
Notes: This fly is effective tied with either a traditional sulfur orange body color, or when mixed with cream to lighten the color.

WHITE FLY SPINNER

Type: Dry.   Subtype: Mayfly.
Item Number: 11Y5. **Most Popular Sizes:** 12, 14.
Hook Type: Extra-fine dry. **Thread:** White 8/0.
Tail: Four white Microfibbets, splayed two per side.
Body: Stripped white hackle stem.
Hackle: Grizzly hackle mixed with white hackle, clipped top and bottom.
Difficulty: 2.
Notes: Cream hackle is also appropriate.

CDC CRIPPLED MIDGE EMERGER
Type: Dry. Subtype: Midge.
Item Number: 746F. **Most Popular Sizes:** 18, 20, 22.
Hook Type: Bigeye dry, down-eye. **Tail:** Black CDC fibers.
Rib: Pearl blue Krystal Flash.
Wing: Wing case: black CDC, tied down over thorax. Ends
are left long, sticking out over eye.
Hackle: Grizzly wound through thorax.
Abdomen: Black thread.
Thorax: Peacock herl.
Difficulty: 3.

CRANE FLY
Type: Dry. Subtype: Midge.
Item Number: 11Y6. **Most Popular Sizes:** 14, 16, 18.
Color Options: Orange, cream. **Hook Type:** Extra-fine dry.
Thread: Cream 8/0.
Body: Antron dubbing to match pattern color.
Wing: Two white neck-hackle tips, splayed over back.
Hackle: Cream, wound parachute style.
Thorax: Post: orange Antron or Z-Lon.
Legs: Six fine pheasant fibers, three on each side, knotted.
Difficulty: 3.
Notes: This fly is very effective when skittered.

GRIFFITH'S GNAT
Type: Dry. Subtype: Midge.
Item Number: 0922. **Most Popular Sizes:** 16, 18, 20.
Hook Type: Bigeye dry. **Thread:** Black 8/0.
Body: Peacock herl from base of stem.
Rib: Fine silver wire.
Hackle: Grizzly with fibers the length of hook gap, palmered
through body.
Difficulty: 1.

HERTER'S BASTARD MIDGE
Type: Dry. Subtype: Midge.
Item Number: 047C. **Most Popular Sizes:** 18, 20, 22.
Hook Type: Bigeye dry. **Thread:** Red 8/0 or 10/0.
Tail: Three mallard-flank fibers.
Body: Tying thread with shellback of about six fibers of
coastal deer hair pulled over the top.
Wing: Fine natural ends of deer-hair shellback left sticking
forward of the eye.
Hackle: Grizzly.
Difficulty: 2.

I.C.S.I. MIDGE FLY

Type: Dry. Subtype: Midge.
Item Number: 02RP. **Most Popular Sizes:** 18, 20, 22.
Hook Type: Bigeye dry. Thread: Olive 8/0.
Body: Gray, olive, or black dubbing.
Wing: High-visibility orange yarn.
Hackle: Grizzly, tied parachute style.
Difficulty: 3.

MATT'S MIDGE

Type: Dry. Subtype: Midge.
Item Number: 12AR. **Most Popular Sizes:** 18, 20, 22, 24.
Color Options: Cream, olive, black, gray, red.
Hook Type: Extra-fine dry.
Thread: 8/0 to match pattern color.
Body: 8/0 thread.
Wing: White Antron or Z-Lon splayed to a V shape.
Hackle: Grizzly.
Difficulty: 2.
Notes: The proper length of the wing is to a point opposite
the hook barb.

MIDGE

Type: Dry. Subtype: Midge.
Item Number: 0836. **Most Popular Sizes:** 20, 22, 24, 26.
Color Options: Gray, black, cream, olive.
Hook Type: Bigeye dry. **Thread:** 8/0, to match body color.
Tail: Hackle fibers to match pattern color.
Body: Dubbing to match pattern color.
Hackle: Sparse, to match pattern color.
Difficulty: 2.

MIDGE CLUSTER

Type: Dry. Subtype: Midge.
Item Number: 712F. **Most Popular Sizes:** 16, 18, 20, 22.
Hook Type: Bigeye dry. **Thread:** Black 8/0.
Wing: Black poly yarn post, tied short and stubby.
Hackle: Black, tied sparse parachute style around base of
wing post.
Difficulty: 2.

PALOMINO MIDGE

Type: Dry. Subtype: Midge.
Item Number: 724F. **Most Popular Sizes:** 18, 20, 22.
Color Options: Red, olive.
Hook Type: Short-shank curved nymph. **Thread:** White 8/0.
Wing: Wing case: white Z-Lon.
Abdomen: Red or olive Microchenille, tied in at bend and extended one shank length beyond hook, singed at end.
Thorax: Smoky-beige synthetic dubbing.
Other Materials: Antennae: section of wing case left sticking out over hook eye.
Difficulty: 3.

TRAVIS PARA MIDGE

Type: Dry. Subtype: Midge.
Item Number: 0289. **Most Popular Sizes:** 16, 18, 20, 22.
Color Options: Olive/black, black, gray.
Hook Type: Short-shank curved nymph. **Thread:** Black 8/0.
Wing: Olive Easy Dubbing.
Hackle: Black or grizzly, parachute style.
Abdomen: Section of Microchenille tied over bend of hook and singed at the end.
Thorax: Fur dubbing.
Difficulty: 3.

AK'S SPINNER

Type: Dry. Subtype: Spinner.
Item Number: 06B1. **Most Popular Sizes:** 14, 16.
Color Options: BOW, *Callibaetis*, PMD, Trico, *Baetis.*
Hook Type: Extra-fine dry. **Thread:** 8/0 to match body color.
Tail: Spade hackle or Microfibbets.
Wing: Clear Antron or hen-hackle tips.
Abdomen: Stripped hackle quill to match pattern color.
Thorax: Superfine Antron dubbing.
Difficulty: 3.
Notes: A Pantone marking pen can be used to mark the wings (*Callibaetis*).

COFFINFLY

Type: Dry. Subtype: Spinner.
Item Number: 812E. **Most Popular Sizes:** 10.
Hook Type: 2×-long dry. **Thread:** Black 6/0.
Tail: Dun Microfibbets.
Body: White deer hair, extended.
Rib: Black thread, cross-ribbed.
Wing: White poly, spent.
Thorax: Black beaver dubbing.
Difficulty: 3.
Notes: Tail is one and a half times the length of the hook shank. Body and wing are each twice the shank length. Thorax is one half shank length.

EXTENDED BODY GREEN DRAKE SPINNER
Type: Dry.   Subtype: Spinner.
Item Number: 11T6. **Most Popular Sizes:** 8, 10.
Hook Type: 2×-long dry. **Thread:** Cream 6/0.
Tail: Dark-dun Microfibbets or moose mane.
Hackle: Dyed-cream badger neck hackle trimmed top and
        bottom.
Abdomen: Bleached deer-body hair tied extended over hook
        shank.
Thorax: Cream Antron.
Difficulty: 3.
Notes: Tail and wing are each as long as shank.

SPARKLE WING TRICO
Type: Dry.   Subtype: Spinner.
Item Number: 0259. **Most Popular Sizes:** 16, 18, 20, 22, 24.
Hook Type: Bigeye dry. **Thread:** Black 8/0.
Tail: Two white Microfibbets, split.
Body: Black dubbing.
Wing: Pearl Krystal Flash, tied spent.
Difficulty: 2.

CABE STONE FLY
Type: Dry.   Subtype: Stonefly.
Item Number: 02TG. **Most Popular Sizes:** 4, 6, 8, 10, 12.
Hook Type: 2×-long dry. **Thread:** Black 6/0.
Tail: Red Antron.
Body: Brown Leech Yarn.
Wing: Natural calf tail.
Hackle: Mixed brown and grizzly.
Difficulty: 2.

DROPPER STONE
Type: Dry.   Subtype: Stonefly.
Item Number: 939P. **Most Popular Sizes:** 4, 6, 8, 10.
Color Options: Black/orange, yellow/cream.
Hook Type: 2×-long dry. **Thread:** Black 6/0.
Body: Round Fly Foam cylinder.
Wing: Flat piece of packing foam trimmed to wing shape.
Thorax: Collar: tips of deer-body hair used to form the
        head.
Legs: Round black Living Rubber.
Head: Head formed by pulling deer-body hair back to
        form a collar.
Difficulty: 3.
Notes: The segmentation for the body is formed on a
        needed prior to tying the fly.

GREEN STONE FLY

Type: Dry. Subtype: Stonefly.
Item Number: 02B8. **Most Popular Sizes:** 16, 18.
Hook Type: Extra-fine dry. **Thread:** Brown 8/0.
Wing: Snowshoe hare tied in by the tips.
Hackle: Grizzly, trimmed flat underneath the shank.
Abdomen: Bright green, yellow, or chartreuse Fly Foam.
Thorax: Uni-Stretch in color to match the abdomen.
Legs: Fine black Living Rubber.
Head: Small thread head.
Difficulty: 3.
Notes: Cut the foam in the shape of a square strip
approximately ⅟₁₆ by ⅟₁₆ of an inch.

ROGUE FOAM STONE GIANT

Type: Dry. Subtype: Stonefly.
Item Number: 02BR. **Most Popular Sizes:** 4, 6, 8.
Color Options: Golden, brown, black.
Hook Type: 2×-long dry. **Thread:** 6/0 to match body color.
Body: Round Foam Body.
Rib: Same as thread.
Wing: Black bucktail over a flat trimmed sheet of packing
foam over ten to fifteen strands of pearl Krystal Flash.
Legs: Round Living Rubber or Sili Legs tied on each side of
the head.
Head: Deer body hair pulled back so that tips form a collar.
Difficulty: 3.
Notes: The segmentation to the foam body is done on a
needle prior to tying the fly.

ROYAL STIMULATOR

Type: Dry. Subtype: Stonefly.
Item Number: 0935. **Most Popular Sizes:** 8, 10, 12, 14.
Hook Type: Curved nymph. **Thread:** Fluorescent fire-orange
6/0.
Tail: Light elk hair.
Rib: Fine copper wire.
Wing: Natural bull-elk hair.
Hackle: Grizzly, palmered through thorax.
Abdomen: In three bands; front and rear third are peacock
herl, middle third is fluorescent red floss. Entire
abdomen ribbed with brown hackle.
Thorax: Fluorescent fire-orange Antron dubbing.
Difficulty: 4.

SCHROEDER'S HI-VIS YELLOW STONE

Type: Dry. Subtype: Stonefly.
Item Number: 02LJ. **Most Popular Sizes:** 10, 12, 14, 16.
Hook Type: Extra-fine dry. **Thread:** Yellow 6/0.
Body: Pale yellow dubbing.
Wing: Yellow strike-indicator yarn, short and very heavy.
Second wing tied down over the body from yellow-
dyed turkey quill.
Hackle: Grizzly saddle, tied very full, parachute style.
Difficulty: 3.

STIMULATOR

Type: Dry.   Subtype: Stonefly.
Item Number: 0927. **Most Popular Sizes:** 8, 10, 12, 14, 16.
Color Options: Olive, yellow, orange.
Hook Type: Curved nymph.
Thread: Fluorescent fire-orange 6/0.
Tail: Natural elk hair.
Rib: Fine gold wire.
Wing: Bull elk hair.
Hackle: Grizzly, palmered over the thorax.
Abdomen: Dubbing the color of the pattern description, palmered with brown saddle hackle.
Thorax: Dubbing the color of the pattern description.
Difficulty: 2.

STONEFLY ADULT

Type: Dry.   Subtype: Stonefly.
Item Number: 071T. **Most Popular Sizes:** 6.
Hook Type: 3×-long nymph/streamer. **Thread:** Black 6/0.
Tail: Natural moose body hair tips.
Body: Natural elk mane, or orange elk mane.
Rib: Black thread bands, three throughout length of body.
Wing: Underwing: mallard flank feather. Overwing: natural gray moose mane.
Legs: A pair of black, round-rubber legs tied in at each side of the head.
Head: Black elk hair, bullet style.
Other Materials: Collar: elk hair dyed black.
Difficulty: 3.

YELLOW SALLY

Type: Dry.   Subtype: Stonefly.
Item Number: 02CA. **Most Popular Sizes:** 14, 16, 18.
Hook Type: Extra-fine dry. **Thread:** Yellow 6/0.
Tail: Red floss.
Body: Yellow dubbing.
Wing: Elk hair.
Hackle: Cream or yellow.
Difficulty: 2.

CDC ANT

Type: Dry.   Subtype: Terrestrial.
Item Number: 0523. **Most Popular Sizes:** 14, 16, 18.
Color Options: Cinnamon, black. **Hook Type:** Bigeye dry.
Thread: Black 8/0.
Body: Rear: black fur. Center: tying thread. Front: black fur.
Wing: Light CDC, tied in middle and extending back over the rear half of the body.
Difficulty: 1.

DAVE'S CRICKET

Type: Dry. Subtype: Terrestrial.
Item Number: 0795. **Most Popular Sizes:** 8, 10, 12.
Hook Type: 2×-long dry. **Thread:** Black 6/0.
Tail: Black deer hair and dark brown yarn loop.
Body: Dark brown yarn.
Rib: Black hackle palmered through body, trimmed short.
Wing: Black turkey wing quill segment, tied flat over body.
Legs: Pair of black turkey-wing quill fibers, trimmed and
knotted.
Head: Spun and clipped black deer hair, formed into a square
shape with some fibers left trailing over the wing as a
collar.
Difficulty: 4.

DAVE'S HOPPER

Type: Dry. Subtype: Terrestrial.
Item Number: 0414. **Most Popular Sizes:** 8, 10, 12.
Hook Type: 3×-long nymph/streamer. **Thread:** Yellow 6/0.
Tail: Red deer hair with cream yarn folded over the top.
Body: Cream yarn.
Rib: Brown hackle palmered through body, trimmed short.
Wing: Underwing of yellow deer hair, overwing of mottled
turkey quill.
Legs: Trimmed and knotted stems from yellow grizzly
hackle.
Head: Deer hair spun and trimmed into square shape. Tips
are left untrimmed on top of the back of the head to
form a collar.
Difficulty: 4.

DROPPER HOPPER

Type: Dry. Subtype: Terrestrial.
Item Number: 242P. **Most Popular Sizes:** 4, 6, 8.
Color Options: Tan, yellow, green. **Hook Type:** 2×-long dry.
Thread: Red 6/0.
Tail: Tiny loop of 3× tippet material.
Body: Round Fly Foam cylinder.
Wing: Mottled turkey tail, tied tent style.
Hackle: Grizzly or ginger, tied parachute style.
Legs: Dyed grizzly hackle stems, trimmed and bent to shape.
Head: Same foam as the body, separated by red thread.
Difficulty: 3.
Notes: Prior to tying the fly, thread the foam cylinder onto the
hook shank.

FIRE BEETLE

Type: Dry. Subtype: Terrestrial.
Item Number: 08LA. **Most Popular Sizes:** 10, 14.
Color Options: Black, olive, red. **Hook Type:** 2×-long dry.
Thread: Black or green 8/0.
Body: Loop-dubbed Lite Brite.
Wing: Wing case: Foam pulled over the back.
Legs: Black or white Living Rubber or Sili Legs.
Head: Eyes: plastic Damsel Eyes.
Difficulty: 3.
Notes: For added visibility, tie in a short piece of white foam
atop the fly.

GREEN LEAF HOPPER
Type: Dry.   Subtype: Terrestrial.
Item Number: 11TX. **Most Popular Sizes:** 20.
Hook Type: Bigeye dry. **Thread:** Green 8/0.
Body: Green thread.
Wing: Shellback: green Fly Foam.
Legs: Microfibbets trimmed, or paintbrush bristles.
Other Materials: Feelers: Microfibbet tips, splayed.
Difficulty: 1.
Notes: This fly can also be effective when tied with red foam
as a ladybug imitation.

HARD BODY ANT
Type: Dry.   Subtype: Terrestrial.
Item Number: 710F. **Most Popular Sizes:** 10, 12, 14, 16, 18.
Color Options: Brown, black.
Hook Type: Big Eye dry, straight eye. **Thread:** Black 6/0.
Body: Balls of brown or black epoxy at front and rear of hook
shank.
Hackle: Black, in middle of shank.
Difficulty: 2.
Notes: The balls are formed by adding paint to the epoxy
when it is being mixed and are then applied to the
hook. The hook should be rotated until the epoxy balls
are dry, then the hackle is applied.

MONSTER HOPPER FLY
Type: Dry.   Subtype: Terrestrial.
Item Number: 02B4. **Most Popular Sizes:** 6, 8.
Hook Type: 2×-long dry. **Thread:** Brown 3/0.
Body: Brown foam, tied in at bend and head.
Legs: Knotted pheasant-tail fibers.
Head: Section of body foam extending over eye.
Other Materials: Section of orange foam tied in at head to
improve visibility.
Difficulty: 2.

QUICK SIGHT BEETLE
Type: Dry.   Subtype: Terrestrial.
Item Number: 0410. **Most Popular Sizes:** 12, 14, 16.
Hook Type: Extra-fine dry. **Thread:** Black 6/0 or 8/0.
Body: Wide piece of black foam tied over back.
Legs: Three pieces of black, varnished thread straddling the
shank to form six legs.
Head: Small piece of foam left untrimmed at head.
Other Materials: A dot formed with bright orange fabric glue
is painted on top of the foam for visibility.
Difficulty: 2.

281

SCHROEDER'S HI-VIS ANT FLY

Type: Dry. Subtype: Terrestrial.
Item Number: 03CB. **Most Popular Sizes:** 10, 12, 14, 16.
Hook Type: Extra-fine dry. **Thread:** Black 6/0.
Body: Two large, distinct clumps of black fur.
Wing: Yellow strike-indicator yarn, heavy.
Hackle: Grizzly, parachute style, very full.
Difficulty: 2.
Notes: The front ball of fur is dubbed around the base of the
wing.

SCHROEDER'S HI-VIS HOPPER

Type: Dry. Subtype: Terrestrial.
Item Number: 02B6. **Most Popular Sizes:** 8, 10, 12, 14.
Hook Type: 2×-long dry. **Thread:** Yellow 6/0.
Body: Tan fur.
Wing: Mottled turkey quill tied flat over body.
Hackle: Grizzly, tied parachute style and very full.
Legs: Knotted pheasant-tail fibers.
Other Materials: Parachute post: bright yellow calf tail.
Difficulty: 3.

SCHROEDER'S PARACHUTE HOPPER

Type: Dry. Subtype: Terrestrial.
Item Number: 017K. **Most Popular Sizes:** 8, 10, 12, 14.
Color Options: Yellow or olive. **Hook Type:** 2×-long dry.
Thread: Cream 6/0.
Body: Yellow or olive dubbing.
Wing: Mottled turkey quill.
Hackle: Grizzly, parachute style.
Legs: Knotted pheasant-tail fibers.
Other Materials: Post: white calf tail.
Difficulty: 3.

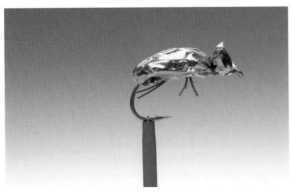

SKILTON'S CRYSTAL BEETLE

Type: Dry. Subtype: Terrestrial.
Item Number: 012C. **Most Popular Sizes:** 12, 14, 16.
Hook Type: Extra-fine dry. **Thread:** Black 6/0.
Body: ¼-inch strip of thin black Fly Foam wrapped in
cellophane or Swiss Straw.
Legs: Six Beetle Legs or paintbrush bristles.
Difficulty: 3.
Notes: Prior to tying in the foam strip, wrap a layer of
cellophane around the strip. Tie the fly as you would
any foam beetle from this point forward.

STEEVE'S FIREFLY

Type: Dry.   Subtype: Terrestrial.
Item Number: 0099. **Most Popular Sizes:** 12, 14, 16, 18.
Hook Type: Extra-fine dry. **Thread:** Black or orange 6/0.
Tail: Butt: yellow Metallic Glow in the Dark Braid, ⅛-inch
size.
Body: Peacock herl.
Wing: Back: Black closed-cell foam ⅛-inch thick. Wing case:
⅛-inch black Metallic Flat Ribbon. Wing: mixture of
pearl Krystal Flash and unraveled black Metallic Ribbon.
Difficulty: 2.

TRAVIS PARA-ANT

Type: Dry.   Subtype: Terrestrial.
Item Number: 936P. **Most Popular Sizes:** 12, 14, 16, 18.
Color Options: Black cinnamon. **Hook Type:** Extra-fine dry.
Thread: 8/0 to match body color.
Hackle: To match body, or dyed grizzly to match body color.
Abdomen: Antron dubbing in desired color.
Thorax: To match abdomen.
Other Materials: Post: white or fluorescent-orange Antron.
Difficulty: 3.

X HOPPER FLY

Type: Dry.   Subtype: Terrestrial.
Item Number: 02B7. **Most Popular Sizes:** 10, 12, 14.
Color Options: Yellow, yellow/brown.
Hook Type: 2×-long dry. **Thread:** Yellow 6/0.
Body: Yellow closed-cell foam.
Rib: Pearl Mylar
Wing: Bleached yearling elk tied bullet-head style.
Underwing: pheasant-tail fibers.
Head: The butt ends of the elk-hair wing are tied forward and
then folded back and tied down to form a bullet head.
Difficulty: 3.

GOODMAN'S CDC EMERGER

Type: Emerger.   Subtype: Mayfly.
Item Number: 02QT.
Most Popular Sizes: 12, 14, 16, 18, 20, 22.
Color Options: March Brown, BWO, PMD.
Hook Type: Short-shank curved nymph.
Thread: Brown, gray, or yellow 8/0.
Tail: Wood-duck flank.
Wing: Dun or tan CDC.
Abdomen: Turkey biot or stripped quill to match pattern
color.
Thorax: March Brown Antron dubbing.
Difficulty: 3.

HATCHING NYMPH

Type: Emerger.   Subtype: Mayfly.
Item Number: 02TJ. **Most Popular Sizes:** 12, 14, 16.
Color Options: Olive, brown, cream, black.
Hook Type: Extra-fine dry. **Thread:** 6/0 to match body color.
Tail: Pheasant-tail fibers.
Rib: Fine copper or gold wire.
Wing: Bronze Flashabou.
Abdomen: Hare's-ear dubbing.
Thorax: Hare's-ear dubbing, picked out to simulate legs.
Head: Spun deer hair clipped to shape.
Difficulty: 3.

SULFUR EMERGER

Type: Emerger.   Subtype: Mayfly.
Item Number: 12AK. **Most Popular Sizes:** 14, 16, 18, 20.
Hook Type: 2×-long nymph. **Thread:** Cream 6/0.
Tail: Pheasant-tail fibers.
Rib: Fine gold wire.
Wing: Light dun CDC.
Abdomen: Claret dubbing.
Hackle: Light blue dun, parachute.
Thorax: Yellow-orange dubbing.
Difficulty: 3.

TRAVIS HI-VIS *BAETIS* PARA EMERGER

Type: Emerger.   Subtype: Mayfly.
Item Number: 11Y8-21. **Most Popular Sizes:** 16, 18, 20, 22.
Hook Type: Short-shank curved nymph.
Thread: Dark olive 8/0.
Tail: Natural wood-duck flank fibers.
Rib: Two strands of Gray Ghost Krystal flash, twisted and
    spiraled.
Wing: Post: strip of yellow dry-cell Fly Foam.
Hackle: Light blue dun, undersize, tied parachute style.
Abdomen: Dark olive/brown Antron dubbing.
Thorax: Mixed pale olive and pale dun Antron dubbing.
Difficulty: 3.

TRAVIS HI-VIS BWO PARA EMERGER

Type: Emerger.   Subtype: Mayfly.
Item Number: 11Y8-02.
Most Popular Sizes: 12, 14, 16, 18, 20, 22.
Hook Type: Short-shank curved nymph. **Thread:** Black 8/0.
Tail: Dyed olive pheasant tail.
Rib: Two strands of peacock Krystal Flash, twisted and
    spiraled.
Wing: Post: strip of yellow dry-cell Fly Foam.
Hackle: Medium blue dun, undersize, tied parachute style.
Abdomen: Peacock Antron dubbing.
Thorax: Mix of dark olive and reddish brown Antron
       dubbing.
Difficulty: 3.

TRAVIS HI-VIS *CALLIBAETIS* PARA EMERGER

Type: Emerger.   Subtype: Mayfly.
Item Number: 11Y8-09. **Most Popular Sizes:** 14, 16, 18.
Hook Type: Short-shank curved nymph. **Thread:** Gray 8/0.
Tail: Mallard-flank fibers.
Rib: Two strands of Gray Ghost Krystal Flash, twisted and
   spiraled.
Wing: Post: strip of yellow dry-cell Fly Foam.
Hackle: Grizzly, undersize, tied parachute style.
Abdomen: Gray Antron dubbing.
Thorax: Pale dun Antron dubbing.
Difficulty: 3.

TRAVIS HI-VIS GREEN DRAKE PARA EMERGER

Type: Emerger.   Subtype: Mayfly.
Item Number: 11Y8-08. **Most Popular Sizes:** 10, 12, 14.
Hook Type: Short-shank curved nymph. **Thread:** Olive 8/0.
Tail: Natural wood-duck flank fibers.
Rib: Two strands of yellow Krystal Flash, twisted and spiraled.
Wing: Post: strip of yellow dry-cell Fly Foam.
Hackle: Grizzly dyed yellow, undersize, tied parachute style.
Abdomen: Dark olive/brown Antron dubbing.
Thorax: Green Drake Antron dubbing.
Difficulty: 3.

TRAVIS HI-VIS PMD PARA EMERGER

Type: Emerger.   Subtype: Mayfly.
Item Number: 11Y8-00. **Most Popular Sizes:** 14, 16, 18, 20.
Hook Type: Short-shank curved nymph. **Thread:** Rust 8/0.
Tail: Dyed olive pheasant tail.
Rib: Dark Ultra Translucent thread.
Wing: Post: strip of yellow dry-cell Fly Foam.
Hackle: Light blue dun, undersize, tied parachute style.
Abdomen: Medium olive/brown Antron dubbing.
Thorax: Pale olive/yellow mixed Antron dubbing.
Difficulty: 3.

TRAVIS HI-VIS SULFUR PARA EMERGER

Type: Emerger.   Subtype: Mayfly.
Item Number: 11Y8-14.
Most Popular Sizes: 14, 16, 18, 20, 22.
Hook Type: Short-shank curved nymph. **Thread:** Cream 8/0.
Tail: Natural wood-duck flank fibers.
Rib: Two strands of root-beer Krystal Flash, twisted and
   spiraled.
Wing: Post: strip of yellow dry-cell Fly Foam.
Hackle: Grizzly dyed ginger, undersize, tied parachute style.
Abdomen: Pale olive dubbing.
Thorax: Dark amber Antron dubbing.
Difficulty: 3.

TRAVIS HI-VIS TRICO PARA EMERGER

Type: Emerger.   Subtype: Mayfly.
Item Number: 11Y8- **Most Popular Sizes:** 18, 20, 22, 24.
Hook Type: Short-shank curved nymph. **Thread:** Brown 8/0.
Tail: Natural pheasant-tail fibers.
Rib: Two strands of peacock Krystal Flash, twisted and
    spiraled.
Post: strip of yellow dry-cell Fly Foam.
Hackle: White, undersize, tied parachute style.
Abdomen: Medium olive/brown Antron dubbing.
Thorax: Black Antron dubbing.
Difficulty: 3.

NYMPH—ATTRACTOR

BEAD HEAD RAINBOW PRINCE

Type: Nymph.   Subtype: Attractor.
Item Number: 944P. **Most Popular Sizes:** 10, 12, 14, 16.
Hook Type: 2×-long nymph. **Thread:** Brown 6/0.
Tail: Two brown goose biots, splayed.
Body: Lite Brite dubbing applied in a loop.
Rib: Fine copper or gold wire (optional).
Wing: Two strands white Living Rubber three-quarters the
    length of the hook shank.
Hackle: Brown hen or partridge, tied collar style.
Head: Copper, gold, or brass bead.
Difficulty: 3.

BEAD HEAD RUBBER-LEG CDC

PHEASANT TAIL

Type: Nymph.   Subtype: Attractor.
Item Number: 08LB. **Most Popular Sizes:** 12, 14, 16, 18.
Hook Type: Short-shank curved nymph. **Thread:** Brown 6/0.
Tail: Pheasant-tail fibers.
Wing: Wing case: dun CDC.
Abdomen: Pheasant-tail fibers, twisted.
Thorax: Peacock herl.
Legs: Black Living Rubber.
Head: Gold bead.
Difficulty: 3.

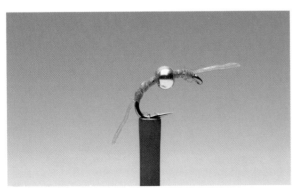

BEADED MICRO WORM

Type: Nymph.   Subtype: Attractor.
Item Number: 12C5. **Most Popular Sizes:** 18.
Color Options: Red, olive, tan.
Hook Type: Short-shank curved nymph.
Thread: Red or olive 8/0.
Body: Micro vernille or Flexi-Floss, leaving an extension over
    the front and back of the hook.
Other Materials: Brass or gold bead mounted at mid-shank.
Difficulty: 1.
Notes: The micro vernille and bead can be mounted at the
    same time by threading the bead onto the vernille
    prior to mounting it on the hook shank.

GREEN WEENIE

Type: Nymph.   Subtype: Attractor.
Item Number: 02H8. **Most Popular Sizes:** 12, 14, 16.
Hook Type: 2×-long nymph. **Thread:** Chartreuse 6/0.
Body: Chartreuse vernille looped at bend and then wound over shank.
Head: Tying thread built up and epoxied.
Difficulty: 1.

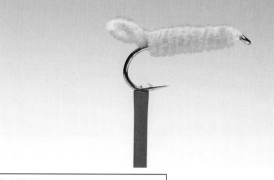

NYMPH—BEAD HEAD

B.H. *CALLIBAETIS*

Type: Nymph.   Subtype: Bead head.
Item Number: 02H7. **Most Popular Sizes:** 14, 16.
Hook Type: 2×-long nymph. **Thread:** Tan 6/0.
Tail: Partridge fibers.
Body: Tan ostrich.
Rib: Gray Larva Lace.
Hackle: Tan hen hackle.
Thorax: Hare's-ear dubbing.
Head: 3/32 brass bead.
Difficulty: 3.

BARR'S EMERGER FLY

Type: Nymph.   Subtype: Bead head.
Item Number: 02H9. **Most Popular Sizes:** 18, 20, 22.
Color Options: PMD, BWO.
Hook Type: Short-shank curved nymph.
Thread: Gray or olive 8/0.
Tail: Brown stiff hackle fibers.
Wing: Wing case: dun or pale olive hackle fibers.
Abdomen: Olive/brown Superfine Antron dubbing.
Thorax: Blue-dun or pale olive Superfine Antron dubbing.
Difficulty: 2.

BEAD HEAD BRASSIE

Type: Nymph.   Subtype: Bead head.
Item Number: 0957. **Most Popular Sizes:** 12, 14, 16, 18.
Hook Type: Short-shank curved nymph.
Thread: Black 6/0.
Body: Copper wire.
Head: Peacock herl.
Other Materials: Copper bead between eye of hook and peacock herl.
Difficulty: 1.

BEAD HEAD BREADCRUST

Type: Nymph.   Subtype: Bead head.
Item Number: 11X5. **Most Popular Sizes:** 12, 14, 16, 18.
Hook Type: 2×-long nymph. **Thread:** Black 6/0.
Body: Orange wool or fur.
Rib: Stripped tail quill from ruffed or sharptail grouse.
Hackle: Grizzly hen saddle, tied collar style.
Head: Brass, gold, or copper bead.
Difficulty: 3.
Notes: To get the rough appearance of the body, leave some stubble on the stripped tail quill.

BEAD HEAD CADDIS LARVA

Type: Nymph.   Subtype: Bead head.
Item Number: 0456. **Most Popular Sizes:** 10, 12, 14, 16, 18.
Color Options: Olive, hare's ear.
Hook Type: 2×-long nymph. **Thread:** Olive 6/0.
Body: Olive or natural hare's-ear dubbing.
Rib: Fine oval silver tinsel.
Head: Brass bead.
Difficulty: 1.

BEAD HEAD CADDIS PUPA

Type: Nymph.   Subtype: Bead head.
Item Number: 02H5. **Most Popular Sizes:** 12, 14, 16.
Hook Type: Bead head. **Thread:** Olive 6/0.
Body: Caddis-green Lite Brite dubbing.
Hackle: Partridge.
Head: ⅛-inch gold bead.
Difficulty: 3.

BEAD HEAD EMERGING SPARKLE CADDIS

Type: Nymph.   Subtype: Bead head.
Item Number: 012T. **Most Popular Sizes:** 12, 14, 16.
Hook Type: 2×-long nymph. **Thread:** Olive 6/0.
Tail: Section of Antron shuck left hanging over rear.
Abdomen: Olive dubbing with cream Antron-yarn shuck.
Thorax: Peacock herl.
Legs: Brown partridge fibers.
Head: Brass bead.
Difficulty: 4.

BEAD HEAD FLASHBACK HARE'S EAR

Type: Nymph.   Subtype: Bead head.
Item Number: 803E. **Most Popular Sizes:** 12, 14, 16.
Color Options: Hare's ear, black, olive.
Hook Type: 2×-long nymph. **Thread:** Black 6/0.
Tail: Hare's guard hairs the color of body.
Rib: Oval gold tinsel tied over abdomen.
Wing: Wing case: pearlescent tinsel tied over top of abdomen.
Abdomen: Natural hare's-ear dubbing, or dyed hare's ear in black or olive. Pearlescent tinsel tied over top.
Thorax: Same as abdomen.
Legs: Dubbing picked out at sides of thorax.
Head: Brass bead between thorax and eye of hook.
Other Materials:
Difficulty: 3.

BEAD HEAD HARE'S EAR NYMPH

Type: Nymph.   Subtype: Bead head.
Item Number: 0251. **Most Popular Sizes:** 12, 14, 16, 18.
Hook Type: 2×-long nymph. **Thread:** Tan 6/0.
Body: Rough-dubbed hare's ear.
Rib: Gold wire.
Wing: Wing pads: black hackle, tied in by the tips and tied down along half of body.
Head: Gold bead.
Difficulty: 2.

BEAD HEAD PHEASANT TAIL

Type: Nymph.   Subtype: Bead head.
Item Number: 0459. **Most Popular Sizes:** 14, 16, 18.
Hook Type: Short-shank curved nymph.
Thread: Brown 6/0 or 8/0.
Tail: Four to eight pheasant-tail fibers.
Body: Pheasant-tail fibers.
Rib: Copper wire.
Head: Copper bead.
Difficulty: 2.

BEAD HEAD PRINCE

Type: Nymph.   Subtype: Bead head.
Item Number: 0009. **Most Popular Sizes:** 12, 14, 16, 18.
Hook Type: 2×-long nymph. **Thread:** Black 6/0.
Tail: Brown goose-quill fibers.
Body: Peacock herl.
Rib: Flat gold tinsel.
Legs: Brown hackle fibers, collar style.
Head: Brass bead.
Other Materials: Horns: white goose-quill fibers (biots).
Difficulty: 2.

BEAD HEAD SERENDIPITY

Type: Nymph. Subtype: Bead head.
Item Number: 0958. **Most Popular Sizes:** 12, 14, 16, 18.
Color Options: Green, red.
Hook Type: Short-shank curved nymph. **Thread:** Tan 6/0.
Body: Red or green Antron, twisted and wound like yarn.
Wing: About a dozen strands of deer hair left over top of body after deer-hair head is trimmed.
Head: Spun and clipped deer hair.
Other Materials: Brass bead between eye of hook and deer-hair head.
Difficulty: 2.

BEAD HEAD SOFT-HACKLE HARE'S EAR

Type: Nymph. Subtype: Bead head.
Item Number: 940B. **Most Popular Sizes:** 10, 12, 14, 16.
Hook Type: 2×-long nymph. **Thread:** Tan 6/0.
Tail: Mottled brown partridge fibers.
Body: Hare's-ear dubbing or Dubbing Brush.
Rib: Oval gold tinsel if body is dubbed; none if Dubbing Brush is used.
Hackle: Brown partridge, wound as a sparse collar.
Other Materials: Brass bead between body and hackle.
Difficulty: 2.

BEAD HEAD SOFT-HACKLE PHEASANT TAIL

Type: Nymph. Subtype: Bead head.
Item Number: 164J. **Most Popular Sizes:** 12, 14, 16.
Hook Type: 2×-long nymph. **Thread:** Orange 6/0.
Tail: Pheasant-tail fibers.
Rib: Copper wire.
Hackle: Brown partridge hackle wound as a collar.
Abdomen: Pheasant-tail fibers, twisted and wound.
Thorax: Short section of peacock herl.
Head: Copper bead between hackle and eye of hook.
Difficulty: 3.

BEAD HEAD STONEFLY

Type: Nymph. Subtype: Bead head.
Item Number: 0027. **Most Popular Sizes:** 4, 6, 8, 10.
Color Options: Brown, yellow.
Hook Type: 4×-long streamer. **Thread:** Yellow 6/0.
Tail: Yellow goose biot.
Rib: Light brown Flexi Floss.
Wing: Light mottled turkey, folded twice.
Abdomen: Brown or pale amber dubbing.
Thorax: Same dubbing as abdomen.
Legs: Yellow grizzly hackle.
Head: Two brass beads.
Difficulty: 3.

BEAD HEAD STONEFLY PRINCE

Type: Nymph.   Subtype: Bead head.
Item Number: 4374. **Most Popular Sizes:** 6, 8, 10, 12, 14.
Hook Type: Short-shank curved nymph. **Thread:** Black 6/0.
Tail: Two brown goose biots tied short in a V.
Rib: Fine gold wire over abdomen.
Wing: White goose biots, tied between abdomen and thorax
    in a V over the top of the abdomen.
Hackle: Brown, tied collar style between abdomen and thorax.
Abdomen: Peacock herl.
Thorax: Peacock herl.
Other Materials: Brass bead between thorax and eye of hook.
Difficulty: 2.

CREEPY HARE'S EAR

Type: Nymph.   Subtype: Bead head.
Item Number: 02CR. **Most Popular Sizes:** 2, 4, 6, 8.
Color Options: Black, golden, copper.
Hook Type: 2×-long nymph hook. **Thread:** Brown 6/0.
Tail: Pair of goose biots.
Rib: Gold wire.
Wing: Mottled turkey quill over abdomen, folded in two
    sections.
Abdomen: Dubbed fur to match pattern description.
Thorax: Hare's-ear fur.
Legs: Three pairs of goose biots: one behind first quill section,
    one between them, and one in front.
Head: Copper tungsten bead.
Difficulty: 3.

LEPAGE'S BEAD HEAD HARE'S EAR NATURAL

Type: Nymph.   Subtype: Bead head.
Item Number: 015T. **Most Popular Sizes:** 12, 14, 16, 18.
Hook Type: 2×-long nymph. **Thread:** Tan 6/0.
Tail: Hare's-ear guard hairs.
Body: Natural hare's-ear fur.
Rib: Flat gold tinsel.
Wing: Mottled turkey pulled over thorax bead.
Thorax: Copper bead.
Difficulty: 2.

LEPAGE'S BEAD HEAD MAYFLY

Type: Nymph.   Subtype: Bead head.
Item Number: 0293. **Most Popular Sizes:** 12, 14, 16, 18.
Color Options: Brown or olive.
Hook Type: 2×-long nymph. **Thread:** Brown 6/0.
Tail: Natural wood-duck, six to twelve fibers.
Rib: Copper wire.
Wing: Goose wing-quill segment tied over thorax bead.
Abdomen: Dubbed fur.
Thorax: Brass bead.
Legs: Brown partridge tied at sides.
Difficulty: 3.

LEPAGE'S TUNGHEAD HARE'S EAR

Type: Nymph.   Subtype: Bead head.
Item Number: 129J. **Most Popular Sizes:** 10, 12, 14, 16.
Hook Type: 2X-long nymph. **Thread:** Black 6/0.
Tail: Hare's-ear guard hairs.
Rib: Oval gold tinsel.
Wing: Wing case: section of gray mallard primary wing
feather pulled over bead and tied down at both ends.
Abdomen: Rough dubbed hare's ear.
Thorax: Gold-colored tungsten bead.
Difficulty: 3.

LEPAGE'S TUNGHEAD MAYFLY

Type: Nymph.   Subtype: Bead head.
Item Number: 167J. **Most Popular Sizes:** 12, 14, 16.
Hook Type: 2×-long nymph. **Thread:** Olive 6/0.
Tail: Wood-duck flank fibers.
Rib: Gold wire.
Wing: Wing case: mottled turkey secondary wing-quill
section.
Abdomen: Brown dubbing.
Thorax: Gold-colored tungsten bead.
Legs: Brown partridge fibers tied in ahead of bead and split
when wing case is pulled forward.
Difficulty: 4.

SCHROEDER'S OSTRICH NYMPH

Type: Nymph.   Subtype: Bead head.
Item Number: 02H3. **Most Popular Sizes:** 12, 14, 16.
Hook Type: Bead head. **Thread:** Brown 6/0.
Body: Olive ostrich herl palmered heavily.
Rib: Fine gold wire.
Hackle: Collar: One or two turns of partridge hackle.
Difficulty: 3.

SCHROEDER'S T.H. CARROT NYMPH

Type: Nymph.   Subtype: Bead head.
Item Number: 02HZ. **Most Popular Sizes:** 10, 12, 14.
Hook Type: 2×-long nymph. **Thread:** Orange 3/0.
Tail: Pheasant-tail fibers.
Rib: Fine gold wire.
Wing: Pearl Flashabou as a wing case over the thorax.
Peacock herl as an overlay over the abdomen.
Hackle: Brown soft hackle.
Abdomen: 3/0 orange thread.
Thorax: Two peacock-herl fibers twisted and wrapped.
Difficulty: 3.

SCHROEDER'S T.H. OSTRICH STONE
Type: Nymph.   Subtype: Bead head.
Item Number: 02H2. **Most Popular Sizes:** 8, 10, 12.
Hook Type: Bead head. **Thread:** Brown 3/0.
Tail: Brown goose biots.
Body: Natural brown ostrich.
Rib: Fine gold wire.
Legs: Pheasant-tail fibers.
Head: Tungsten bead.
Difficulty: 2.

SCHROEDER'S TUNGHEAD GREEN WEENIE
Type: Nymph.   Subtype: Bead head.
Item Number: 02CH. **Most Popular Sizes:** 10, 12, 14, 16.
Hook Type: 2×-long nymph. **Thread:** Brown 6/0.
Body: Chartreuse Antron dubbing or yarn.
Rib: Black ostrich.
Head: Tungsten bead.
Difficulty: 1.

SCHROEDER'S TUNGHEAD LIME CADDIS
Type: Nymph.   Subtype: Bead head.
Item Number: 02H1. **Most Popular Sizes:** 10, 12, 14, 16.
Hook Type: 2×-long nymph. **Thread:** Brown 6/0.
Body: Lime-green Antron yarn or dubbing.
Rib: Fine gold wire.
Wing: Peacock herl pulled over the back of the abdomen.
Legs: Two turns of Partridge.
Other Materials: Collar: peacock herl.
Difficulty: 2.

T.H. GOLDEN STONE FLY
Type: Nymph.   Subtype: Bead head.
Item Number: 02CP. **Most Popular Sizes:** 6, 8, 10, 12, 14.
Hook Type: 3×-long nymph/streamer. **Thread:** Brown 3/0.
Tail: Imitation wood duck.
Rib: Fine gold wire.
Wing: Wing case: full overlay of peacock herl.
Abdomen: Golden-tan Antron dubbing.
Thorax: Same as abdomen, except picked out to simulate legs.
Head: Tungsten bead.
Difficulty: 3.

T.H. Soft Hackle Caddis Pupa
Type: Nymph. Subtype: Bead head.
Item Number: 02CQ. **Most Popular Sizes:** 12, 14, 16.
Color Options: Olive, cream, black, tan, brown.
Hook Type: Bead head. **Thread:** 6/0 to match body color.
Body: Medium olive Antron dubbing.
Rib: Fine gold wire.
Hackle: Sharptail grouse or natural partridge.
Head: ⅛-inch black tungsten bead.
Difficulty: 2.

The Fly Formerly Known As Prince
Type: Nymph. Subtype: Bead head.
Item Number: 02CT. **Most Popular Sizes:** 12, 14, 16, 18.
Hook Type: 2×-long nymph. **Thread:** Red 8/0.
Tail: Two brown goose biots, splayed using ball of red thread.
Body: Two to four fibers of peacock herl.
Rib: Flat gold tinsel.
Wing: Two pieces of holographic film cut in the shape of biots.
Hackle: Brown rooster.
Head: Tungsten bead.
Difficulty: 2.

Travis Glass Bead Caddis Emerger
Type: Nymph. Subtype: Bead head.
Item Number: 773F. **Most Popular Sizes:** 12, 14, 16, 18, 20.
Color Options: Gray, olive, tan.
Hook Type: Short-shank curved nymph. **Thread:** Tan 8/0.
Body: Tan Antron dubbing.
Rib: Root-beer Krystal Flash.
Legs: Natural hungarian partridge.
Head: Glass bead.
Other Materials: Collar: brown Philo Tube. Shuck: tan Z-Lon.
    Antennae: root-beer Krystal Flash.
Difficulty: 3.

Tunghead Bitch Creek
Type: Nymph. Subtype: Bead head.
Item Number: 02CK. **Most Popular Sizes:** 6, 8, 10, 12.
Hook Type: 2×-long nymph. **Thread:** Black 6/0.
Tail: White Living Rubber.
Hackle: Church-window pheasant feather.
Abdomen: Black chenille.
Thorax: Orange chenille.
Head: Black tungsten bead.
Difficulty: 3.

TUNGHEAD BLACK SOFT-HACKLE CADDIS PUPA

Type: Nymph.　Subtype: Bead head.
Item Number: 02CL. **Most Popular Sizes:** 16, 18.
Color Options: Olive, tan, cream.
Hook Type: 2×-long nymph. **Thread:** Black 8/0.
Body: Medium olive dubbing.
Hackle: Grouse or speckled partridge.
Head: Black tungsten bead.
Difficulty: 3.
Notes: Any soft hackle is appropriate for the hackle, as long
as it is darker than the body.

TUNGHEAD BREADCRUST

Type: Nymph.　Subtype: Bead head.
Item Number: 11X7-00. **Most Popular Sizes:** 12, 14, 16, 18
Hook Type: 2×-long nymph. **Thread:** Black 6/0.
Body: Orange wool or fur.
Rib: Stripped tail quill from ruffed or sharptail grouse.
Hackle: Grizzly hen saddle tied collar style.
Head: Faceted tungsten bead.
Difficulty: 3.
Notes: To get the rough appearance of the body, leave some
stubble on the stripped tail quill.

TUNGHEAD EGG FLY

Type: Nymph.　Subtype: Bead head.
Item Number: 02CZ. **Most Popular Sizes:** 12, 14.
Hook Type: Short-shank curved nymph. **Thread:** White 6/0.
Body: Pink egg yarn pulled over tungsten bead and secured.
Difficulty: 1.

TUNGHEAD HALFBACK, COPPER

Type: Nymph.　Subtype: Bead head.
Item Number: 02CJ. **Most Popular Sizes:** 8, 10, 12, 14.
Hook Type: Bead-head. **Thread:** Brown 6/0.
Tail: Two pieces of brown Flexi-Floss and pheasant-tail fibers.
Body: Peacock Dubbing Brush.
Hackle: Brown or black hen hackle.
Legs: One piece of brown Flexi-Floss on each side.
Head: Copper-plated tungsten bead.
Other Materials: Remainder of pheasant tail used for tail is
pulled over top of body to form a shellback.
Difficulty: 2.

TUNGHEAD HARE'S EAR
Type: Nymph.   Subtype: Bead head.
Item Number: 154J. **Most Popular Sizes:** 12, 14, 16.
Hook Type: Short-shank curved nymph. **Thread:** Black 6/0.
Body: Rough hare's-ear dubbing.
Head: Gold-colored tungsten bead.
Difficulty: 2.

TUNGHEAD HARE'S EAR CADDIS
Type: Nymph.   Subtype: Bead head.
Item Number: 003C. **Most Popular Sizes:** 10, 12, 14, 16.
Hook Type: Short-shanked curved nymph.
Thread: Black 6/0.
Hackle: Brown partridge between abdomen and thorax.
Abdomen: Rough hare's-ear dubbing.
Thorax: Peacock herl.
Head: Tungsten bead.
Difficulty: 2.

TUNGHEAD OSTRICH CADDIS
Type: Nymph.   Subtype: Bead head.
Item Number: 004C. **Most Popular Sizes:** 10, 12, 14, 16.
Hook Type: 2×-long nymph. **Body:** Olive ostrich herl.
Rib: Fine gold wire.
Legs: Two turns of partridge hackle, split.
Head: Tungsten bead.
Difficulty: 2.

TUNGHEAD PHEASANT TAIL
Type: Nymph.   Subtype: Bead head.
Item Number: 144J. **Most Popular Sizes:** 10, 12, 14, 16.
Hook Type: Short-shank curved nymph. **Thread:** Orange 6/0.
Tail: Ring-necked pheasant tail fibers.
Body: Ring-necked pheasant tail fibers, twisted and wound.
Rib: Copper wire.
Head: Copper-colored tungsten bead.
Difficulty: 2.

Tunghead Prince

Type: Nymph.   Subtype: Bead head.
Item Number: 121J. **Most Popular Sizes:** 10, 12, 14, 16.
Hook Type: 2×-long nymph. **Thread:** Black 6/0.
Tail: Two brown biots, split.
Body: Peacock herl.
Rib: Flat gold tinsel.
Wing: Two wide white biots, tied flat over body in a narrow
     V shape.
Hackle: Brown, tied as a collar and pulled under.
Head: Gold-colored tungsten bead.
Difficulty: 3.

Tunghead Soft Hackle Hare's Ear

Type: Nymph.   Subtype: Bead head.
Item Number: 941B.
Most Popular Sizes: 10, 12, 14, 16.
Hook Type: 2×-long nymph.
Thread: Tan 6/0.
Tail: Brown hackle fibers.
Body: Hare's ear dubbing.
Rib: Oval gold tinsel.
Hackle: Mottled brown partridge wound as a collar.
Head: Tungsten bead tied between hackle and eye of hook.
Difficulty: 2.

Tunghead Squirrel Tail

Type: Nymph.   Subtype: Bead head.
Item Number: 02H4. **Most Popular Sizes:** 10, 12, 14, 16.
Hook Type: Bead head. **Thread:** Brown 6/0.
Tail: Red squirrel tail.
Body: Squirrel Bright Dubbing.
Rib: Fine gold wire.
Hackle: Hoffman hen saddle.
Head: ⅛ or ³⁄₃₂ tungsten bead.
Difficulty: 2.

Tunghead Stonefly

Type: Nymph.   Subtype: Bead head.
Item Number: 139J. **Most Popular Sizes:** 4, 6, 8, 10, 12, 14.
Color Options: Peacock, black, yellow. **Hook Type:** 3×-long
nymph/streamer. **Thread:** 6/0 to match body color.
Tail: Two goose biots, splayed.
Rib: Fine copper wire.
Wing: Wing case: mottled turkey, folded twice.
Hackle: Sparse saddle or hen hackle to match body, clipped
     short on the bottom.
Abdomen: Antron/Hare dubbing.
Thorax: Two faceted tungsten beads.
Difficulty: 3.
Notes: Dub lightly between the two beads in the thorax with
     the same dubbing used for the abdomen.

TUNGHEAD ZUG BUG
Type: Nymph.   Subtype: Bead head.
Item Number: 142J. **Most Popular Sizes:** 10, 12, 14, 16.
Hook Type: 2×-long nymph. **Thread:** Red 6/0.
Tail: A few peacock-sword fibers.
Body: Peacock herl.
Rib: Oval silver tinsel.
Wing: Wing case: wood duck (or dyed mallard imitation) tied
flat over the body and clipped short.
Hackle: Brown, wound and pulled under.
Head: Gold-colored tungsten bead.
Difficulty: 3.

NYMPH—CADDIS

BEAD HEAD BARR'S NET BUILDER
Type: Nymph.   Subtype: Caddis.
Item Number: 08C5. **Most Popular Sizes:** 12, 14.
Color Options: Olive, cream.
Hook Type: Short-shank curved nymph. **Thread:** Brown 6/0.
Tail: Gray ostrich herl.
Body: Back: plastic from Zip-Loc bag or Scud Back.
Rib: 4×mono.
Abdomen: Scintilla dubbing in desired color.
Thorax: Dark dun or brown ostrich herl.
Head: ⅛-inch brass bead.
Other Materials: Markings on the thorax with a brown
Pantone marking pen.
Difficulty: 3.

BEAD HEAD CADDIS PUPA
Type: Nymph.   Subtype: Caddis.
Item Number: 0416. **Most Popular Sizes:** 12, 14, 16, 18.
Color Options: Brown, cream, olive.
Hook Type: Short-shank curved nymph.
Thread: Olive 6/0 or 8/0.
Body: Dubbed fur to match pattern color.
Wing: Pads: Black hackle, tied in by the tips, pulled down,
and trimmed.
Head: Brass bead.
Difficulty: 2.

BEAD HEAD KRYSTAL CADDIS LARVA
Type: Nymph.   Subtype: Caddis.
Item Number: 725F. **Most Popular Sizes:** 10, 12, 14, 16.
Color Options: Olive, cream.
Hook Type: Short-shank curved nymph. **Thread:** Black 8/0.
Rib: Olive or pearl Krystal Flash.
Abdomen: Cream or olive Antron dubbing.
Thorax: Black fur dubbing, short.
Head: Brass bead.
Difficulty: 1.

BEAD HEAD OVIPOSITING CADDIS

Type: Nymph.   Subtype: Caddis.
Item Number: 08LC. **Most Popular Sizes:** 14, 16, 18.
Color Options: Tan, black, olive.
Hook Type: 2×-long nymph.
Thread: 6/0 to match body color.
Body: Antron/Hare dubbing.
Wing: Swiss Straw cut into tent shape.
Hackle: Two or three turns of hen saddle hackle.
Thorax: Brass or gold bead.
Difficulty: 3.
Notes: The bead used for the thorax is covered by the wing and the hen hackle.

BREADCRUST

Type: Nymph.   Subtype: Caddis.
Item Number: 0415. **Most Popular Sizes:** 10, 12, 14, 16.
Hook Type: 2×-long nymph or standard wet.
Thread: Black 6/0.
Body: Orange wool or fur.
Rib: Stripped ruffed-grouse tail quill doubled and wrapped with gold wire. A stripped brown hackle stem is often substituted.
Hackle: Grizzly hen hackle, collar style.
Difficulty: 2.

CZECH MATE NYMPH

Type: Nymph.   Subtype: Caddis.
Item Number: 946P. **Most Popular Sizes:** 12, 14, 16.
Color Options: Olive, cream.
Hook Type: Short-shank curved nymph.
Thread: Olive or cream 6/0.
Rib: Gold wire or oval tinsel.
Wing: Wing case: latex strip.
Abdomen: Antron/Hare dubbing.
Thorax: Antron/Hare dubbing, picked out.
Difficulty: 3.

DOUBLE BEAD HEAD CADDIS

Type: Nymph.   Subtype: Caddis.
Item Number: 810E. **Most Popular Sizes:** 12, 14, 16.
Hook Type: 3×-long nymph/streamer. **Thread:** Brown 6/0.
Body: Peacock herl with gold bead at mid-shank.
Hackle: Two or three turns of partridge.
Head: Brass or gold bead.
Difficulty: 1.

GLASS AND OSTRICH FLY

Type: Nymph.   Subtype: Caddis.
Item Number: 02RJ. **Most Popular Sizes:** 12, 14, 16.
Color Options: Olive, cream, black, brown.
Hook Type: Short-shank curved nymph. **Thread:** Olive 6/0.
Wing: Mallard or natural wood duck.
Hackle: Beard: dun CDC.
Abdomen: Superfine dubbing, sparse, over which three to
           five clear glass or plastic craft beads are placed.
Thorax: Dark Antron/Hare dubbing.
Difficulty: 3.

LaFontaine Sparkle Pupa

Type: Nymph.   Subtype: Caddis.
Item Number: 0442. **Most Popular Sizes:** 12, 14, 16.
Color Options: Brown/green, brown/yellow.
Hook Type: Extra-fine dry fly. **Thread:** Brown 6/0.
Tail: Brown or tan Antron or Z-Lon yarn, sparse and scraggly.
Body: Brown, yellow, or green dubbing, with Antron or Z-
         Lon yarn pulled over top and bottom to encase the
         body in a "bubble."
Leg: Mallard flank.
Head: Brown fur.
Difficulty: 4.

MUSTANG CADDIS

Type: Nymph.   Subtype: Caddis.
Item Number: 02RA. **Most Popular Sizes:** 12, 14, 16.
Hook Type: 2×-long nymph. **Thread:** Black 6/0.
Tail: Two pheasant-tail fibers.
Body: Peacock herl.
Rib: Fine gold wire.
Head: Chartreuse Ultra Chenille with two small glass beads.
Difficulty: 3.
Notes: Tied in reverse so the tails point over the eye.

OLIVER EDWARDS *RHYCOPHILA* LARVA

Type: Nymph.   Subtype: Caddis.
Item Number: 12CR. **Most Popular Sizes:** 10, 12, 14, 16.
Hook Type: Short-shank curved nymph. **Thread:** Olive 6/0.
Body: Four-ply Antron yarn.
Rib: Pale green Flashabou or 6× tippet material.
Legs: Partridge dyed yellow/olive.
Difficulty: 4.
Notes: Use only three of the four strands of Antron for the
         body. Twist the yarn and wrap forward to the legs.
         After you have tied in the legs, pull the last piece of
         Antron over for the back. Finish the fly by adding
         marking to the first three segments on the body above
         the legs with a black felt marker.

POLISH NYMPH FLY

Type: Nymph. Subtype: Caddis.
Item Number: 02JC. **Most Popular Sizes:** 12, 14, 16.
Color Options: Brown/green, olive/cream.
Hook Type: Short-shank curved nymph. **Thread:** Black 6/0.
Tail: Short bunch of brown or olive saddle or hen-hackle fibers.
Body: Woven floss body with darker color for the back.
Wing case: Darker floss color, doubled and tied over thorax.
Legs: Stripped hackle tips or stripped peacock herl, crumpled
             and bent to shape.
Head: Built-up tying thread.
Difficulty: 3.

TRAVIS SOFT-HACKLE CADDIS PUPA

Type: Nymph. Subtype: Caddis.
Item Number: 776F. **Most Popular Sizes:** 12, 14, 16, 18, 20.
Hook Type: Curved nymph. **Thread:** Olive 8/0.
Abdomen: Olive turkey blot.
Thorax: Dark olive-brown Scintilla.
Legs: Olive Hungarian partridge feathers.
Head: Dark olive-brown Scintilla.
Other Materials: Collar: olive aftershaft feather.
Difficulty: 3.

CRAYFISH

Type: Nymph. Subtype: Crayfish.
Item Number: 811E. **Most Popular Sizes:** 4, 8.
Color Options: Olive, brown.
Hook Type: 3×-long nymph/streamer. **Thread:** Brown 6/0.
Tail: Antennae: two stripped brown hackle quills. Tail: short
             section of red squirrel tail tips. Eyes: melted mono tied
             in at the bend.
Rib: Fine wire, red.
Wing: Wing case: double thickness of Ultra Suede.
Hackle: Light brown saddle hackle wrapped three turns over
             the thorax.
Abdomen: Brown Antron/Hare dubbing.
Thorax: Brown Antron/Hare dubbing.
Legs: Claws: Ultra Suede strip cut into pincher shape.
Other Materials: .030 wire at mid-shank.
Difficulty: 4.
Notes: Prior to trimming the Ultra Suede, glue one Ultra
             Suede piece to another to make a double thickness.

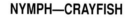

TRAVIS BEAD HEAD SWIMMING DAMSEL

Type: Nymph. Subtype: Damsel.
Item Number: 032T. **Most Popular Sizes:** 10, 12, 14.
Color Options: Olive, brown.
Hook Type: Swimming nymph. **Thread:** Olive 8/0.
Tail: Olive hackle fluff.
Rib: Fine copper wire.
Abdomen: Olive pheasant-tail fibers.
Hackle: Collar of olive hackle fluff.
Thorax: Olive dubbed fur with olive pheasant-tail wing case.
Head: Black monofilament eyes.
Difficulty: 3.

ALASKAN EGG CRITTER

Type: Nymph. Subtype: Egg.
Item Number: 12C4. **Most Popular Sizes:** 4, 6.
Color Options: Chartreuse, white, pink, orange, or a combination of these colors.
Hook Type: Heavy wet/nymph hook.
Thread: 6/0 to match body color.
Tail: One marabou blood feather (shank length) mixed with ten to fifteen strands of Pearl Krystal Flash.
Body: Large Ice Chenille, Krystal Chenille, or Estaz.
Legs: Living Rubber to match body color, tied two on each side.
Head: Dumbbell eyes.
Difficulty: 3.
Notes: Tie in the tail at mid-shank. The Chenille/Estaz body should wrap around the eyes to encase the dumbbell.

COMET POM

Type: Nymph. Subtype: Egg.
Item Number: 12A5. **Most Popular Sizes:** 4.
Color Options: Pink, orange.
Hook Type: Heavy wet/nymph hook. **Thread:** Red 6/0.
Tail: 4mm craft pom-pom secured to the shank on a ½-inch section of .009 monofilament.
Wing: Six to eight strands of pearl Flashabou and white FisHair.
Thorax: Egg yarn.
Head: Plume of egg yarn from the thorax pulled forward over the eye.
Difficulty: 2.

MEG-A-EGG

Type: Nymph. Subtype: Egg.
Item Number: 0933. **Most Popular Sizes:** 4, 6, 8.
Color Options: Chartreuse, orange, pink, peach.
Hook Type: Short-shank curved nymph.
Body: Manufactured sparkle pom-pom threaded onto hook over the point and glued to the shank with superglue.
Difficulty: 1.
Notes: Tiers often try to duplicate the sparkle egg by tying this Glo-Bug style with yarn, but this fly is best tied with pre-made pom-poms.

MICRO EGG

Type: Nymph. Subtype: Egg.
Item Number: 12A6. **Most Popular Sizes:** 20.
Color Options: Peach, flame, chartreuse.
Hook Type: Heavy wet/nymph hook.
Thread: 8/0 to match body color.
Body: Egg yarn or poly yarn.
Difficulty: 2.
Notes: This fly is tied using standard egg-tying techniques, however only one to two strands of yarn are needed to complete the fly. Another option is to loop-dub the egg and trim to shape.

TRAVIS TROUT EGG CLUSTER

Type: Nymph. Subtype: Egg.
Item Number: 727F. **Most Popular Sizes:** 12.
Hook Type: Short-shank curved nymph.
Thread: Orange 6/0.
Body: Three 5mm orange pom-poms strung on
4×monofilament and secured with superglue. Secured
to front of hook with thread.
Wing: Three pearl Krystal Flash fibers, tied in behind egg
ball, twice hook length.
Difficulty: 2.

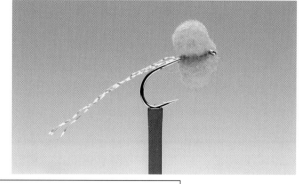

NYMPH—GENERAL

HARE'S EAR

Type: Nymph. Subtype: General.
Item Number: 0485. **Most Popular Sizes:** 10, 12, 14, 16.
Color Options: Black, olive, natural.
Hook Type: 2×-long nymph. **Thread:** Black 6/0.
Tail: Hare's-mask guard hairs, same color as body.
Body: Hare's-mask dubbing.
Rib: Oval gold tinsel.
Wing: Mallard wing-quill segment tied over thorax.
Abdomen: Hare's-mask dubbing.
Thorax: Hare's-mask dubbing.
Legs: Thorax dubbing picked out at sides.
Difficulty: 2.

COPPER JOHN

Type: Nymph. Subtype: General.
Item Number: 12CY. **Most Popular Sizes:** 10, 12, 14, 16, 18.
Color Options: Red, copper, green.
Hook Type: 2×-long nymph.
Thread: 6/0 to match body color.
Tail: Two goose biots tied splayed, to match body color.
Abdomen: Colored copper wire over a tapered base of
dubbing.
Thorax: Peacock herl with epoxied Flashabou or tinsel
shellback.
Legs: Partridge.
Head: Brass, copper, or gold bead.
Difficulty: 2.

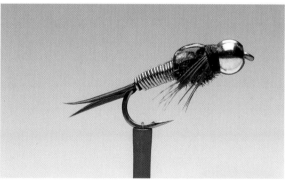

HAREY PRINCE

Type: Nymph. Subtype: General
Item Number: 7238. **Most Popular Sizes:** 12, 14, 16.
Hook Type: 2×-long nymph. **Thread:** Black 6/0.
Tail: Two brown or rust goose biots.
Body: Hare's-ear dubbing.
Rib: Oval gold tinsel.
Wing: Two white goose biots.
Hackle: Sparse brown hen, divided.
Difficulty: 3.

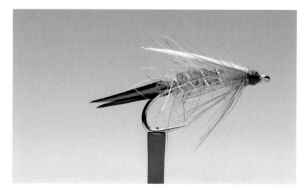

HOLY GRAIL
Type: Nymph. Subtype: General.
Item Number: 722H. **Most Popular Sizes:** 12, 14, 16.
Color Options: Black, hare's ear, olive.
Hook Type: Short-shank curved nymph.
Thread: Black, brown, or olive 6/0.
Body: Antron/Hare dubbing.
Rib: Strand of pearl flashabou.
Wing: Wing case: peacock herl.
Legs: Partridge tied as beard.
Difficulty: 3.

SERENDIPITY
Type: Nymph. Subtype: General.
Item Number: 0254. **Most Popular Sizes:** 14, 16, 18.
Color Options: Gray, olive, red.
Hook Type: Short-shank curved nymph. **Thread:** Gray 6/0.
Body: Twisted Antron yarn.
Head: Spun and trimmed deer hair.
Difficulty: 2.

TELLICO
Type: Nymph. Subtype: General.
Item Number: 0484. **Most Popular Sizes:** 10, 12, 14.
Hook Type: 2×-long nymph. **Thread:** Black 6/0.
Tail: Guinea-hackle fibers.
Body: Yellow floss.
Rib: Peacock herl.
Wing: Pheasant-tail segment tied over body as shellback.
Hackle: Furnace or brown tied as collar.
Difficulty: 2.

YUK BUG NYMPH
Type: Nymph. Subtype: General.
Item Number: 0250. **Most Popular Sizes:** 4, 6, 8, 10.
Hook Type: 3×-long nymph/streamer. **Thread:** Brown 6/0.
Body: Black chenille.
Rib: Grizzly hackle, palmered through body.
Legs: Three white rubber legs sticking out each side,
distributed evenly through body.
Difficulty: 1.

FRANKE HELLGRAMMITE

Type: Nymph.   Subtype: Hellgrammite.
Item Number: 02JB. **Most Popular Sizes:** 4, 6.
Hook Type: 4×-long streamer. **Thread:** Black 6/0.
Tail: Two strands Black Living rubber.
Abdomen: Medium peacock-colored chenille with palmered black or dark brown hen feather.
Thorax: Same as abdomen, but topped with black closed-cell Fly Foam.
Legs: Black Living Rubber.
Head: Pinchers: black Living Rubber.
Difficulty: 4.

AMERICAN PHEASANT TAIL

Type: Nymph.   Subtype: Mayfly.
Item Number: 0458. **Most Popular Sizes:** 12, 14, 16, 18.
Hook Type: 2×-long nymph. **Thread:** Orange 6/0.
Tail: Pheasant-tail fibers.
Rib: Copper wire.
Wing: Pheasant-tail fibers tied over thorax as wing case.
Abdomen: Pheasant-tail fibers.
Thorax: Peacock herl.
Legs: Ends of wing-case fibers tied back on each side and clipped.
Difficulty: 3.

BEAD HEAD AMERICAN PHEASANT TAIL

Type: Nymph.   Subtype: Mayfly.
Item Number: 942B. **Most Popular Sizes:** 12, 14, 16, 18, 20.
Hook Type: 2×-long nymph. **Thread:** Orange 6/0.
Tail: Pheasant-tail fibers.
Rib: Fine copper wire.
Wing: Wing case: pheasant-tail fibers.
Abdomen: Twisted and wound pheasant-tail fibers.
Thorax: Peacock herl.
Legs: Ends of wing case pulled to each side after wing case is tied in at head.
Difficulty: 3.
Notes: This fly is tied thicker and fuller than the traditional English Pheasant Tail.

BEAD HEAD BARR EMERGER

Type: Nymph.   Subtype: Mayfly.
Item Number: 02Q0. **Most Popular Sizes:** 18, 20, 22.
Color Options: PMD, BWO.
Hook Type: Short-shank curved nymph.
Thread: Gray or olive 8/0.
Tail: Stiff brown hackle fibers.
Wing: Wing case: Dun or pale olive hackle fibers.
Abdomen: Olive/brown Superfine Antron dubbing.
Thorax: Blue dun or pale olive Superfine Antron dubbing.
Head: Brass or gold bead.
Difficulty: 3.

BEAD HEAD HENDRICKSON

Type: Nymph.   Subtype: Mayfly.
Item Number: 943P. **Most Popular Sizes:** 14.
Hook Type: 2×-long nymph. **Thread:** Brown 6/0.
Tail: Wood-duck flank.
Wing: Wing case: dark mottled turkey tail.
Abdomen: Amber/reddish brown dubbing picked out
      lightly on the sides.
Thorax: Same as abdomen.
Legs: Partridge, divided on both sides.
Difficulty: 3.

BEAD HEAD SWIMMING HARE'S EAR

Type: Nymph.   Subtype: Mayfly.
Item Number: 12C2. **Most Popular Sizes:** 12, 14, 16, 18, 20.
Hook Type: Heavy wet/nymph hook.
Thread: Brown or black 8/0.
Tail: Pheasant-tail fibers.
Body: Hare's-ear dubbing.
Rib: Fine gold wire or tinsel.
Hackle: One or two turns of partridge.
Legs: Six strands (three on each side) Living Rubber tied in
      one-quarter of the shank length behind the hook eye.
Head: Brass or tungsten bead.
Difficulty: 3.

BEAD HEAD ZUG BUG

Type: Nymph.   Subtype: Mayfly.
Item Number: 0422. **Most Popular Sizes:** 12, 14, 16, 18.
Hook Type: 2×-long nymph. **Thread:** Red 6/0.
Tail: Peacock-sword fibers.
Body: Peacock herl.
Rib: Flat silver tinsel.
Wing: Natural wood duck side feather, tied flat and trimmed
      to half of body length.
Hackle: Brown, collar style.
Head: Brass bead.
Difficulty: 2.

CDC EMERGER

Type: Nymph.   Subtype: Mayfly.
Item Number: 08C1. **Most Popular Sizes:** 16, 18, 20.
Color Options: Rust brown, Trico, Sulfur, olive, slate olive.
Hook Type: Short-shank curved nymph.
Thread: 8/0 to match body color.
Tail: Short bunch of hen-hackle fibers.
Rib: Fine tinsel (optional).
Wing: Dun or white CDC.
Abdomen: Superfine Antron dubbing or turkey biot.
Thorax: Superfine Antron dubbing.
Legs: Trim out a few fibers of CDC from the wingcase.
Head: Superfine Antron dubbing.
Difficulty: 2.

EASTERN GREEN DRAKE NYMPH

Type: Nymph.   Subtype: Mayfly.
Item Number: 12AG. **Most Popular Sizes:** 8, 10.
Hook Type: 3×-long nymph/streamer.
Thread: Cream or tan 8/0.
Tail: Light-dun goose biots, splayed.
Wing: Wing case: bleached badger hackle tips. Extension: medium-dun CDC plume.
Hackle: Cream saddle.
Abdomen: Cream or light tan dubbing.
Thorax: To match abdomen.
Difficulty: 3.
Notes: Often this nymph will have a grayish or tannish/olive appearance.

FLASHBACK HARE'S EAR NYMPH

Type: Nymph.   Subtype: Mayfly.
Item Number: 0891. **Most Popular Sizes:** 10, 12, 14, 16, 18.
Hook Type: 2×-long nymph. **Thread:** Brown 6/0 or 8/0.
Tail: Natural hare's-mask guard hairs.
Rib: 6×monofilament, over abdomen only.
Wing: Wing case: continue overlay of pearlescent tinsel over thorax.
Abdomen: Hare's-mask dubbing with an overlay of pearlescent tinsel.
Thorax: Rough, loose hare's-mask fur dubbed on a loop.
Legs: Thorax dubbing picked out at sides.
Difficulty: 2.

MERCER'S POXYBACK *BAETIS*

Type: Nymph.   Subtype: Mayfly.
Item Number: 08LF.21 **Most Popular Sizes:** 18, 20.
Hook Type: 2×-long nymph. **Thread:** Chartreuse 6/0.
Tail: Three pheasant-tail fibers.
Rib: Chartreuse 6/0 thread.
Wing: Wing case: dark turkey-tail segment, epoxied.
Hackle: Gills: light tan marabou.
Abdomen: Rusty-olive Antron.
Thorax: Same as abdomen.
Difficulty: 4.

MERCER'S POXYBACK *CALLIBAETIS*

Type: Nymph.   Subtype: Mayfly.
Item Number: 08LF.09 **Most Popular Sizes:** 16, 18.
Hook Type: 2×-long nymph. **Thread:** Chartreuse 6/0.
Tail: Three gray ostrich-herl fibers.
Rib: One strand pearl Flashabou.
Wing: Wing case: dark turkey-tail segment, epoxied.
Hackle: Gills: light gray marabou.
Abdomen: Light tan-olive Antron.
Thorax: Same as abdomen.
Difficulty: 4.

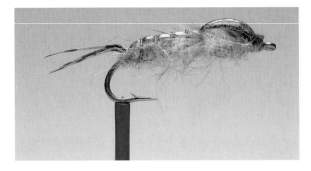

MERCER'S POXYBACK GREEN DRAKE
Type: Nymph. Subtype: Mayfly.
Item Number: 08LF.08 **Most Popular Sizes:** 8, 10, 12.
Hook Type: 2×-long nymph. **Thread:** Olive 6/0.
Tail: Grouse or hen partridge saddle fibers.
Rib: Fine copper wire.
Wing: Wing case: dark turkey-tail segment, epoxied.
Hackle: Dark olive aftershaft feather.
Abdomen: Dark olive/brown Antron.
Thorax: Same as abdomen.
Difficulty: 4.

MERCER'S POXYBACK *ISONYCHIA*
Type: Nymph. Subtype: Mayfly.
Item Number: 08LF.67 **Most Popular Sizes:** 12, 14, 16.
Hook Type: 2×-long nymph. **Thread:** Black 6/0.
Tail: Three dark charcoal-dyed ostrich herl fibers.
Rib: Fine copper wire.
Wing: Wing case: dark turkey tail segment, epoxied.
   Shellback: mixture red squirrel and Krystal Flash
   pulled over abdomen and thorax, epoxied.
Hackle: Gills: dark-dun ostrich herl tips, four to eight per side.
Abdomen: Dark slate gray Antron dubbing.
Thorax: Dark slate gray Antron dubbing, picked out on sides.
Legs: Grouse or partridge divided to the side and tied in at
   the front of the wing case.
Head: Short section of dark slate gray Antron.
Difficulty: 4.
Notes: Several variations of this dressing are used to
   represent the *Isonychia*.

MERCER'S POXYBACK PMD
Type: Nymph. Subtype: Mayfly.
Item Number: 08LF-14. **Most Popular Sizes:** 16, 18.
Hook Type: Curved nymph. **Thread:** Orange 8/0.
Tail: Pheasant-tail fibers.
Rib: One strand of pearl Flashabou.
Abdomen: Rusty orange/brown Antron dubbing, overlay of
   dark mottled turkey tail.
Thorax: Rusty orange/brown Antron dubbing, wing case of
   dark mottled turkey tail. The wing case is epoxied.
Legs: Dark brown mottled grouse tied at sides of wing case.
Other Materials: Gills: tufts of light tan marabou at each side
   between abdomen and thorax.
Difficulty: 4.

MERCER'S POXYBACK TRICO
Type: Nymph. Subtype: Mayfly.
Item Number: 08LF.10 **Most Popular Sizes:** 20, 22, 24.
Hook Type: 2×-long nymph. **Thread:** Black 6/0.
Tail: Three dark partridge fibers.
Rib: Fine copper wire.
Wing: Wing case: dark turkey tail segment, epoxied.
Abdomen: Dark chocolate-brown ostrich.
Thorax: Same as abdomen.
Difficulty: 4.

Olive Flashback

Type: Nymph. Subtype: Mayfly.
Item Number: 0908. **Most Popular Sizes:** 10, 12, 14, 16, 18.
Hook Type: 2×-long nymph. **Thread:** Brown 6/0.
Tail: Olive hackle fibers.
Rib: Copper wire.
Abdomen: Olive fur with overlay of pearlescent Mylar.
Thorax: Olive fur with overlay of pearlescent Mylar to form
 wing case.
Legs: Thorax fur picked out at sides.
Difficulty: 2.

Oliver Edwards' Heptagenid Nymph

Type: Nymph. Subtype: Mayfly.
Item Number: 12CK. **Most Popular Sizes:** 12, 14, 16.
Color Options: This style fly can be tied in any color to
 represent a variety of flat, clinging nymphs.
Hook Type: 2×-long nymph. **Thread:** Brown 6/0.
Tail: Three pheasant-tail fibers.
Rib: Fine copper wire.
Wing: Wing case: grouse tail feather coated with flexible cement.
Abdomen: Tan ostrich herl or grouse aftershaft feather.
Thorax: Same as abdomen.
Head: Brown Swiss Straw pulled over base of tan ostrich herl
 and mono eyes.
Other Materials: Eyes: burnt mono eyes.
Difficulty: 5.
Notes: Dark partridge is an appropriate substitute for grouse.

Pheasant Tail

Type: Nymph. Subtype: Mayfly.
Item Number: 0434.
Most Popular Sizes: 10, 12, 14, 16, 18, 20.
Color Options: Flashback, natural, olive.
Hook Type: 2×-long nymph.
Thread: Rusty brown or orange 6/0.
Tail: Natural pheasant-tail fibers.
Rib: Copper wire.
Wing: Pheasant-tail fibers tied over thorax as wing case.
Abdomen: Pheasant-tail fibers.
Thorax: Pheasant-tail fibers.
Difficulty: 2.
Notes: In the Flashback version, the wing case is made from
 pearl Flashabou or similar iridescent material instead
 of pheasant-tail fibers.

Red Quill Emerger

Type: Nymph. Subtype: Mayfly.
Item Number: 02CB. **Most Popular Sizes:** 12, 14, 16.
Hook Type: 2×-long nymph. **Thread:** Orange 6/0.
Tail: Three wood-duck flank fibers.
Hackle: Medium or dark dun hen.
Abdomen: Stripped and soaked red/brown hackle stem,
 wound over a thin layer of monofilament and
 coated with head cement.
Thorax: Rust Antron, thinly dubbed.
Difficulty: 2.

SULFUR NYMPH
Type: Nymph.   Subtype: Mayfly.
Item Number: 12AL. **Most Popular Sizes:** 14, 16, 18, 20.
Hook Type: Swimming nymph. **Thread:** Brown 6/0.
Tail: Pheasant-tail fibers.
Body: Claret dubbing.
Rib: Fine gold wire.
Wing: Pheasant tail pulled over as a wing case.
Abdomen: Claret dubbing.
Thorax: Claret dubbing.
Legs: Pheasant-tail fibers splayed to the side.
Head: Brown 6/0 thread.
Difficulty: 3.

TRAVIS FLOATING NYMPH
Type: Nymph.   Subtype: Mayfly.
Item Number: 029T. **Most Popular Sizes:** 16, 18, 20, 22.
Color Options: Sulfur, olive, PMD (yellow/olive).
Hook Type: 2×-long dry. **Thread:** Yellow 8/0.
Tail: Wood-duck flank.
Rib: Fine monofilament.
Wing case: Yellow foam.
Abdomen: Pheasant-tail fibers.
Thorax: Dubbed fur.
Legs: Wood-duck flank.
Head: Same as thorax.
Difficulty: 2.

TRAVIS GREEN DRAKE NYMPH
Type: Nymph.   Subtype: Mayfly.
Item Number: 12AP. **Most Popular Sizes:** 8, 10, 12, 14.
Hook Type: 3×-long nymph/streamer. **Thread:** Olive 8/0.
Tail: Natural Wood-duck flank.
Body: Olive and rust-brown dubbing.
Rib: Dark Ultra Thread.
Hackle: Two wraps of black hen.
Head: Mix of olive and dark brown dubbing.
Other Materials: Collar: Olive-dyed grizzly aftershaft
                    feather.
Difficulty: 3.

TUNGHEAD HARE'S EAR FLASHBACK
Type: Nymph.   Subtype: Mayfly.
Item Number: 956P. **Most Popular Sizes:** 10, 12, 14, 16.
Color Options: Natural, olive. **Hook Type:** 2×-long nymph.
Thread: Black 6/0.
Tail: Guard hairs from a hare's mask, stacked.
Body: Dark hare's-ear dubbing.
Rib: Fine gold wire or tinsel.
Wing: Wing case: pearl Flashabou.
Head: Faceted tungsten bead.
Difficulty: 3.

TUNGHEAD SOFT-HACKLE PHEASANT TAIL

Type: Nymph.   Subtype: Mayfly.
Item Number: 957P. **Most Popular Sizes:** 12, 14, 16.
Hook Type: 2×-long nymph. **Thread:** Black 6/0.
Tail: Pheasant-tail fibers.
Hackle: One or two wraps of pheasant or partridge hen
      feather.
Abdomen: Three pheasant-tail feathers twisted with a short
      section of fine copper wire.
Thorax: Peacock herl.
Head: Faceted tungsten bead.
Difficulty: 2.

ZUG BUG

Type: Nymph.   Subtype: Mayfly.
Item Number: 0487. **Most Popular Sizes:** 10, 12, 14, 16, 18.
Hook Type: 2×-long nymph. **Thread:** Black 6/0.
Tail: Peacock-sword fibers.
Body: Peacock herl.
Rib: Flat silver tinsel.
Wing: Wood-duck side feather, tied flat over body and
      trimmed to half of body length.
Hackle: Brown.
Difficulty: 2.

B.H. MIDGE

Type: Nymph.   Subtype: Midge.
Item Number: 02TK. **Most Popular Sizes:** 16, 18.
Hook Type: Bigeye dry. **Thread:** 10/0 red.
Body: Red Larva Lace.
Head: 2mm brass bead.
Difficulty: 1.

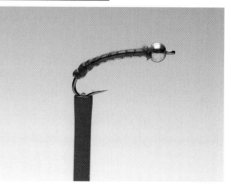

BIRCHELL'S HATCHING MIDGE

Type: Nymph.   Subtype: Midge.
Item Number: 12A1. **Most Popular Sizes:** 16, 18, 20, 22, 24.
Color Options: Cream, olive, black, gray, red.
Hook Type: Curved nymph hook.
Thread: 8/0 to match body color.
Tail: Six to eight fibers of Z-Lon or Antron.
Wing: Post: white turkey-flat fibers tied short.
Hackle: Grizzly, tied parachute style around the post.
Abdomen: Dyed goose or turkey biot.
Thorax: Peacock herl or ostrich herl.
Difficulty: 3.
Notes: In larger sizes this is an effective emerging mayfly
      nymph pattern.

311

BLACK BEAUTY

Type: Nymph.   Subtype: Midge.
Item Number: 02JF. **Most Popular Sizes:** 18, 20, 22.
Hook Type: Swimming nymph. **Thread:** Black 8/0.
Tail: White Antron, CDC, or hen-hackle fibers.
Rib: White floss.
Wing: Wing case: same white floss used for the rib.
Abdomen: Black tying thread or floss.
Thorax: Peacock or ostrich herl.
Head: Gills: continuation of floss wing case, white CDC, or
white Antron yarn.
Difficulty: 2.

BRASSIE

Type: Nymph.   Subtype: Midge.
Item Number: 0413. **Most Popular Sizes:** 14, 16, 18, 20.
Hook Type: 2×-long nymph. **Thread:** Black 8/0.
Abdomen: Fine copper wire.
Thorax: Peacock herl.
Difficulty: 1.

CANNON'S SNOWSHOE EMERGER

Type: Nymph.   Subtype: Midge.
Item Number: 12A2. **Most Popular Sizes:** 16, 18, 20, 22, 24.
Color Options: Cream, olive, black, gray, red.
Hook Type: Swimming nymph.
Thread: 8/0 to match body color.
Tail: White marabou, aftershaft feather, CDC, or Antron tied
very short.
Abdomen: Micro Larva Lace or stripped dyed-grizzly quill.
Thorax: Antron Dubbing to match body color.
Head: A tuft of snowshoe rabbit tied in under thorax and
extending beyond the hook eye.
Difficulty: 3.
Notes: On the smallest sizes use the stripped grizzly quill,
because it makes better segmentation.

CDC MIDGE PUPA

Type: Nymph.   Subtype: Midge.
Item Number: 12A4. **Most Popular Sizes:** 16, 18, 20, 22, 24.
Color Options: Cream, olive, black, gray, red.
Hook Type: Heavy wet/nymph hook.
Thread: 8/0 to match body color.
Wing: Extension: white or light-dun CDC plume extending
over hook eye.
Abdomen: Turkey or goose biot to match pattern color.
Thorax: Peacock herl or dubbing.
Difficulty: 3.
Notes: In the smallest sizes a thread body can be substituted
for the biot and the herl or dubbing.

CRYSTAL MIDGE

Type: Nymph.   Subtype: Midge.
Item Number: 947B. **Most Popular Sizes:** 16, 18.
Color Options: Gray, black, olive.
Hook Type: Short-shank curved nymph.
Thread: 6/0 to match body color.
Rib: Fine gold or silver wire.
Wing: Pearl Krystal Flash fibers, clipped short.
Abdomen: Two twisted Antron-yarn fibers, or buildup of 6/0 thread.
Thorax: Antron dubbing or ostrich herl to match abdomen color.
Head: Clear glass craft bead.
Difficulty: 2.

DISCO MIDGE

Type: Nymph.   Subtype: Midge.
Item Number: 0297. **Most Popular Sizes:** 16, 18, 20, 22.
Color Options: Olive, pearl, red, pink.
Hook Type: Bigeye dry.
Thread: Cream 8/0 to match pattern color, forms body.
Rib: Pearlescent Krystal Flash.
Thorax: Peacock herl or fur.
Difficulty: 1.

M & M MIDGE PUPA

Type: Nymph. Subtype: Midge.
Item Number: 12AY. **Most Popular Sizes:** 16, 18, 20, 22, 24.
Color Options: Cream, olive, black, gray, red.
Hook Type: Curved nymph.
Thread: 8/0 to match body color.
Wing: Wing case: white Antron or Z-Lon tied under thorax and pulled back from the eye.
Abdomen: Turkey or goose biot to match pattern color.
Thorax: Peacock or ostrich herl.
Difficulty: 3.

MIDGE PUPA

Type: Nymph.   Subtype: Midge.
Item Number: 0495. **Most Popular Sizes:** 16, 18, 20.
Color Options: Gray, black, cream.
Hook Type: Bigeye dry. **Thread:** Gray, black, or cream 8/0.
Abdomen: Tying thread.
Thorax: Gray, black, or cream dubbing.
Difficulty: 1.

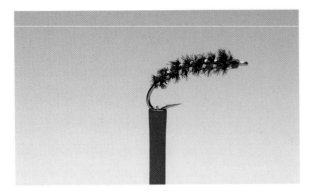

PEACOCK MIDGE FLY
Type: Nymph. Subtype: Midge.
Item Number: 02JH. **Most Popular Sizes:** 16, 18.
Hook Type: Curved nymph. **Thread:** Red 8/0.
Body: Peacock herl.
Rib: Pearl Krystal Flash.
Difficulty: 1.

WD-40
Type: Nymph. Subtype: Midge.
Item Number: 02CX. **Most Popular Sizes:** 18, 20, 22.
Color Options: Tan, gray, olive. **Hook Type:** Bigeye dry.
Thread: Olive 8/0.
Tail: Mallard-flank fibers.
Wing: Mallard flank pulled over thorax.
Abdomen: Tying thread.
Thorax: Gray fur.
Difficulty: 1.

NYMPH—SCUD

BEAD BODY SCUD
Type: Nymph. Subtype: Scud.
Item Number: 019T. **Most Popular Sizes:** 10, 12, 14.
Color Options: Olive, pink, orange.
Hook Type: Short-shank curved nymph. **Thread:** Olive 6/0.
Tail: Mallard dyed olive.
Body: Antron dubbing.
Rib: Copper wire.
Other Materials: Gold bead in middle of body. Shellback:
　　　　　　　　　clear Scud Back.
Difficulty: 3.

BIGHORN SCUD
Type: Nymph. Subtype: Scud.
Item Number: 0932. **Most Popular Sizes:** 10, 12, 14, 16.
Hook Type: Short-shank curved nymph.
Thread: Orange 6/0.
Tail: Pheasant-tail fibers.
Body: Orange Antron picked out on the underside.
Rib: Fine copper wire.
Other Materials: Back: clear plastic or Scudback.
Difficulty: 2.
Notes: This fly is often tied weighted.

FLASHBACK SCUD

Type: Nymph.   Subtype: Scud.
Item Number: 0472. **Most Popular Sizes:** 12, 14, 16.
Hook Type: Daiichi 1150 short-shank curved nymph.
Thread: Olive 6/0.
Body: Mixed gray/olive synthetic dubbing, rough.
Pearlescent Mylar pulled over the top and bound in
place with the ribbing.
Rib: Fine monofilament (6×).
Difficulty: 2.
Notes: Pick out dubbing under shank to imitate legs.

OSTRICH SOW BUG

Type: Nymph.   Subtype: Scud.
Item Number: 02CY. **Most Popular Sizes:** 14, 16.
Color Options: Gray, pink. **Hook Type:** Heavy wet/nymph.
Thread: Red 6/0.
Body: Ostrich herl to match pattern.
Other Materials: Pearlescent tinsel strand pulled over body
to form shellback.
Difficulty: 1.

SCUDD

Type: Nymph.   Subtype: Scud.
Item Number: 02RB. **Most Popular Sizes:** 14, 16, 18.
Color Options: Orange, pink, olive.
Hook Type: Heavy wet/nymph. **Thread:** 8/0 to match body.
Tail: Partridge dyed to match body color.
Body: Four strands of twisted orange ostrich herl.
Wing: Shellback: Scud Back to match body color.
Hackle: Light-dun hen hackle.
Difficulty: 3.
Notes: The fly is commonly weighted with 10 turns of .028 or
.030 non-toxic wire.

SOFT-HACKLE SOW

Type: Nymph.   Subtype: Scud.
Item Number: 02TB. **Most Popular Sizes:** 14, 16.
Color Options: Gray, pink, orange.
Hook Type: Short-shank curved nymph.
Thread: 8/0 to match body.
Body: Ostrich herl to match pattern.
Wing: Shellback: pearl Mylar.
Hackle: Light-blue dun.
Difficulty: 2.

BEAD HEAD GIANT STONE
Type: Nymph.   Subtype: Stonefly.
Item Number: 713F. **Most Popular Sizes:** 6, 8, 10.
Color Options: Brown, black. **Hook Type:** 3×-long
nymph/streamer. **Thread:** Black 6/0.
Tail: Black or brown goose biots, tied short in a V.
Rib: Black or brown Body Glass.
Wing: Wing case: black or brown Swiss Straw or feather
   section, folded twice over thorax.
Abdomen: Black or brown Antron dubbing.
Thorax: Black or brown Antron dubbing, tied rough and
   picked out.
Other Materials: Antennae: black or brown goose biots tied
   forward over eye.
Difficulty: 4.

BITCH CREEK
Type: Nymph.   Subtype: Stonefly.
Item Number: 0614. **Most Popular Sizes:** 4, 6, 8.
Hook Type: 3×-long nymph/streamer.
Thread: Black 6/0.
Tail: Two white rubber legs.
Body: Woven black and orange chenille.
Hackle: Brown palmered over thorax.
Thorax: Black chenille.
Other Materials: Antennae: two white rubber legs.
Difficulty: 3.

CHARTREUSE MONTANA NYMPH
Type: Nymph.   Subtype: Stonefly.
Item Number: 0920. **Most Popular Sizes:** 10, 12, 14.
Hook Type: 3×-long nymph/streamer.
Thread: 6/0 black.
Tail: Black hackle fibers.
Hackle: Black, palmered through thorax.
Abdomen: Black chenille.
Thorax: Chartreuse chenille with overlay of two strands of
   black chenille to form wing case.
Difficulty: 2.

EARLY BLACK STONE
Type: Nymph.   Subtype: Stonefly.
Item Number: 0604. **Most Popular Sizes:** 10, 12.
Hook Type: 2×-long nymph. **Thread:** Black 6/0.
Tail: Two Canada goose quill fibers tied in a V.
Rib: Black Body Glass or V-Rib.
Wing: Two black goose-quill segments, folded and pulled
   over thorax.
Hackle: Black.
Abdomen: Dark brownish black fur.
Thorax: Amber fur.
Difficulty: 3.

EARLY BROWN STONE

Type: Nymph.   Subtype: Stonefly.
Item Number: 0603. **Most Popular Sizes:** 10, 12.
Hook Type: 2×-long nymph. **Thread:** Tan 6/0.
Tail: Two white-tip turkey-tail fibers tied in a V.
Rib: Dark brown Body Glass or V-Rib.
Wing: Two white-tip turkey-tail segments, folded and pulled
over the thorax.
Hackle: Webby tan grizzly hackle.
Abdomen: Medium, brown fur.
Thorax: Medium brown fur.
Difficulty: 3.

GIANT BLACK STONE

Type: Nymph.   Subtype: Stonefly.
Item Number: 0600. **Most Popular Sizes:** 4, 6, 8.
Hook Type: 3×-long nymph/streamer. **Thread:** Black 6/0.
Tail: Two dark Canada goose quill fibers tied in a V.
Rib: Dark brown Body Glass or V-Rib.
Wing: Two white-tip turkey-tail segments, folded and pulled
over the thorax.
Hackle: Black.
Abdomen: Brownish black fur.
Thorax: Brownish black fur.
Difficulty: 3.

GOLDEN STONE

Type: Nymph.   Subtype: Stonefly.
Item Number: 0500. **Most Popular Sizes:** 6, 8.
Hook Type: 3×-long nymph/streamer. **Thread:** Yellow 6/0.
Tail: Two tan goose biots tied in a V.
Wing: Two folded sections of mottled turkey-wing quill.
Hackle: Light ginger.
Abdomen: Golden yellow dubbing, ribbed with cream V-Rib
or Larva Lace.
Thorax: Golden yellow dubbing.
Difficulty: 3.

HALFBACK NYMPH

Type: Nymph.   Subtype: Stonefly.
Item Number: 0437. **Most Popular Sizes:** 8, 10, 12, 14, 16.
Hook Type: Curved nymph. **Thread:** Black 6/0.
Tail: Pheasant-tail fibers.
Rib: Brown saddle hackle palmered through both abdomen
and thorax.
Abdomen: Peacock herl, with a shellback of pheasant-tail
fibers over the top.
Thorax: Peacock herl.
Difficulty: 3.

INNIS STONE

Type: Nymph. Subtype: Stonefly.
Item Number: 029C. **Most Popular Sizes:** 6, 8, 10, 12, 14.
Color Options: Amber, brown, black.
Hook Type: Curved nymph. **Thread:** Tan 6/0.
Tail: Pair of goose biots to match body color.
Body: Dubbed fur.
Rib: Gray ostrich herl.
Legs: Pair of goose biots to match tail, tied along sides.
Difficulty: 2.

KAUFFMAN'S STONE

Type: Nymph. Subtype: Stonefly.
Item Number: 0613. **Most Popular Sizes:** 2, 4, 6, 8, 10.
Color Options: Brown, black. **Hook Type:** Curved nymph.
Thread: Brown 6/0.
Tail: Black or reddish brown goose biots.
Rib: Black or brown transparent Body Glass, V-Rib, or
     Swannundaze.
Wing: Three segments or dark turkey tail, cut or burned to
     notched shape.
Abdomen: Black or brown dubbing, rough, with translucent
     synthetic or natural fibers.
Thorax: Same as body.
Legs: Dubbing picked out at thorax. **Head:** Same as body.
Other Materials: Antennae: reddish brown or black goose biots.
Difficulty: 4.

KAUFMAN'S MINI STONE FLY

Type: Nymph. Subtype: Stonefly.
Item Number: 02TH. **Most Popular Sizes:** 8, 10, 12.
Color Options: Brown, black.
Hook Type: 3×-long nymph/streamer.
Thread: Brown or black 6/0.
Tail: One pair turkey biots, splayed.
Body: Antron/Hare dubbing.
Rib: Swannundaze.
Wing: Wing case: dark turkey-tail segment.
Legs: Black Living Rubber.
Head: Antennae: same as tail.
Other Materials: Gold bead.
Difficulty: 4.

MICRO STONE

Type: Nymph. Subtype: Stonefly.
Item Number: 939B. **Most Popular Sizes:** 14, 16, 18.
Hook Type: Heavy wet/nymph. **Thread:** Brown 6/0.
Tail: Two goose biots, splayed.
Wing: Wing case: brown hen.
Abdomen: Golden Antron overwrapped with golden turkey
     biot, marked with black or brown Pantone pen.
Thorax: Golden Antron.
Legs: Brown hen divided under the wing case.
Head: Copper or gold bead.
Other Materials: Antennae: goose biots to match tail (optional).
Difficulty: 4.

MONTANA NYMPH

Type: Nymph. Subtype: Stonefly.
Item Number: 0481. **Most Popular Sizes:** 8, 10, 12, 14.
Hook Type: 3×-long nymph/streamer.
Thread: Black 6/0 or 8/0.
Tail: Black hackle fibers.
Wing: Two strands of black chenille pulled over the thorax as
    wing case.
Abdomen: Black chenille.
Thorax: Yellow chenille, with black saddle hackle palmered
    through.
Difficulty: 1.

PRINCE NYMPH

Type: Nymph. Subtype: Stonefly.
Item Number: 0483. **Most Popular Sizes:** 8, 10, 12, 14, 16.
Hook Type: 2×-long nymph. **Thread:** Brown 6/0.
Tail: Two goose biots, brown, tied in a V.
Body: Peacock herl.
Rib: Oval gold tinsel.
Wing: Two broad white goose biots, tied flat in a V over body.
Hackle: Brown.
Difficulty: 2.

STONEFLY BUGGER

Type: Nymph. Subtype: Stonefly.
Item Number: 0268. **Most Popular Sizes:** 6, 8, 10.
Hook Type: 3×-long nymph/streamer. **Thread:** Brown 6/0.
Tail: Dark brown marabou.
Body: Dark brown leech yarn.
Legs: Brown partridge tied in at each segment.
Other Materials: Back: dark mottled turkey tail, folded with
    seven equally spaced sections.
Difficulty: 4.

SWIMMING MONTANA

Type: Nymph. Subtype: Stonefly.
Item Number: 955P. **Most Popular Sizes:** 10, 12, 14.
Hook Type: Swimming nymph. **Thread:** Black 6/0.
Tail: Black marabou with two strands of Pearl Krystal Flash
    on each side.
Wing: Wing case: black chenille pulled over thorax.
Abdomen: Black chenille or Leech yarn.
Thorax: Orange or yellow chenille.
Difficulty: 3.

TED'S GOLDEN STONE

Type: Nymph.   Subtype: Stonefly.
Item Number: 938B. **Most Popular Sizes:** 8, 10.
Hook Type: 3×-long nymph/streamer. **Thread:** Black 6/0.
Tail: Two pieces of O×mono, mottled with a black Sharpie marker.
Body: Golden Stone Antron/Hare dubbing over flattened plastic form.
Rib: Medium-dun size A Monocord or Kevlar.
Wing: Wing case: Fifteen to twenty stripped peacock herl strands highlighted with Sharpie marker.
Legs: Six yellow knotted turkey biots highlighted with Sharpie marker.
Head: Eyes: melted mono dumbbell.
Other Materials: Weight: Medium nontoxic wire wrapped around or beside the plastic underbody.
Difficulty: 4.

TUNGHEAD RUBBER LEGGED STONE

Type: Nymph.   Subtype: Stonefly.
Item Number: 02C0.
Most Popular Sizes: 6, 8, 10, 12.
Hook Type: 3×-long nymph/streamer.
Thread: Black 6/0.
Tail: White Living Rubber.
Rib: Fine gold wire.
Hackle: Church-window pheasant feather.
Abdomen: Six strands of peacock herl, twisted.
Thorax: Peacock Lite Brite dubbing.
Head: Black tungsten bead.
Difficulty: 3.

FIRE ANT

Type: Nymph.   Subtype: Terrestrial.
Item Number: 12C3. **Most Popular Sizes:** 14, 16.
Color Options: Black, cinnamon, or a combination of the two.
Hook Type: Heavy wet/nymph.
Thread: 8/0 to match body color.
Body: Waist: thread wrapped just enough to color hook shank.
Abdomen: Lite Brite dubbing dubbed in a tapered shape.
Thorax: Lite Brite dubbing dubbed in a ball to form a short thorax.
Legs: Black living rubber tied in an X shape.
Head: Brass or tungsten bead.
Difficulty: 3.

JR CRANEFLY

Type: Nymph.   Subtype: Terrestrial.
Item Number: 12AC. **Most Popular Sizes:** 6, 8.
Hook Type: Swimming nymph. **Thread:** Black 8/0.
Wing: Wing case: peacock herl.
Hackle: Very pale dun palmered heavily to the thorax.
Abdomen: Very pale dun or dirty cream Antron/Hare dubbing.
Thorax: Peacock herl.
Head: Black brass or tungsten bead.
Difficulty: 3.

VERNILLE SAN JUAN WORM

Type: Nymph. Subtype: Worm.
Item Number: 0290. **Most Popular Sizes:** 8, 10, 12, 14, 16.
Color Options: Tan or red.
Hook Type: Short-shank curved nymph. **Thread:** Red 6/0.
Body: Vernille tied in at bend and head, singed at both ends
with butane lighter.
Difficulty: 1.

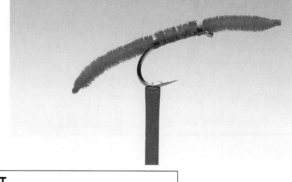

WET

HORNBERG

Type: Wet.
Item Number: 0443. **Most Popular Sizes:** 8, 10, 12.
Hook Type: 3×-long nymph. **Thread:** Black 6/0.
Body: Flat silver tinsel.
Wing: Two yellow hackle tips inside two mallard-flank
feathers.
Hackle: Brown and grizzly, mixed.
Difficulty: 2.
Notes: The wing is wide and tied on the side of the shank so
that it covers the body.

MARCH BROWN WET

Type: Wet.
Item Number: 0449. **Most Popular Sizes:** 12, 14.
Hook Type: Heavy wet/nymph. **Thread:** Black 6/0.
Tail: Brown partridge.
Body: Fawn fox fur or other tan dubbing.
Rib: Yellow thread or floss.
Wing: Mottled turkey or speckled hen wing-quill segments.
Hackle: Brown partridge, collar style.
Difficulty: 3.

PARTRIDGE SOFT HACKLES

Type: Wet.
Item Number: 765F. **Most Popular Sizes:** 12, 14, 16.
Color Options: Partridge and Yellow, Partridge and Orange.
Hook Type: Heavy wet fly/nymph. **Thread:** Black 8/0.
Body: Orange or yellow floss, thin.
Hackle: Brown Hungarian partridge wound collar style,
sparse.
Difficulty: 2.

WOOLLY WORM

Type: Wet.
Item Number: 0440. **Most Popular Sizes:** 6, 8, 10, 12.
Color Options: Black, brown, olive.
Hook Type: 3×-long nymph. **Thread:** Black 6/0.
Tail: Red hackle fibers.
Body: Black, olive, or brown chenille.
Hackle: Badger or grizzly, palmered over body.
Difficulty: 1.

STREAMER

BARNES SPECIAL

Type: Streamer.
Item Number: 11T9. **Most Popular Sizes:** 6, 8.
Hook Type: 4×-long streamer. **Thread:** Red 6/0.
Body: Medium flat silver tinsel, double wrapped.
Rib: Oval silver tinsel.
Wing: Lower wing: white bucktail with sparse topping of red bucktail. Upper wing: two yellow saddle hackles inside two grizzly saddles.
Head: Red thread.
Difficulty: 3.

BEAD HEAD LEECH

Type: Streamer.
Item Number: 086T. **Most Popular Sizes:** 4, 6, 8.
Color Options: Black, yellow, rust.
Hook Type: 3×-long nymph/streamer. **Thread:** Black 6/0.
Tail: Marabou to match pattern color.
Body: Fuzzy Leech Yarn to match pattern color.
Head: Gold bead.
Difficulty: 1.

BEAD HEAD LITE BRITE BUGGER

Type: Streamer.
Item Number: 931E. **Most Popular Sizes:** 4, 6, 8.
Color Options: Brown, black, olive.
Hook Type: 4×-long streamer.
Thread: 6/0 to match body color.
Tail: Marabou to match pattern description.
Body: Lite Brite dubbing to match pattern description.
Rib: Grizzly saddle hackle.
Head: Black brass bead.
Difficulty: 2.

BEAD HEAD LITE BRITE ZONKER

Type: Streamer.
Item Number: 930E. **Most Popular Sizes:** 4, 6, 8.
Color Options: White, olive, black.
Hook Type: 4×-long streamer.
Thread: 6/0 to match pattern color.
Tail: Zonker strip cut so that it tapers to a point.
Rib: Fine gold wire or copper wire (optional).
Wing: Same Zonker strip used for the tail, continued to the hook eye.
Abdomen: Lite Brite dubbing twisted in a dubbing loop.
Thorax: Red Lite Brite dubbing twisted in a dubbing loop; picked out to simulate gills.
Head: Brass or tungsten bead.
Difficulty: 4.

BEAD HEAD MINNOW

Type: Streamer.
Item Number: 0133. **Most Popular Sizes:** 6, 8, 10.
Hook Type: 4×-long streamer. **Thread:** Red 6/0.
Wing: White Lite Brite tied under the shank, olive/gold Lite Brite tied on top of the shank.
Head: Brass bead.
Difficulty: 2.
Notes: Should be tied very sparse.

BEAD HEAD WOOLLY BUGGER

Type: Streamer.
Item Number: 0311. **Most Popular Sizes:** 4, 6, 8, 10.
Color Options: Olive/brown, black.
Hook Type: 4×-long streamer. **Thread:** Black 6/0.
Tail: Black or olive marabou.
Body: Olive or black chenille.
Hackle: Medium olive or black saddle, palmered through body.
Head: Brass bead.
Difficulty: 1.

BLACK GHOST

Type Streamer.
Item Number: 949B. **Most Popular Sizes:** 6, 8, 10, 12.
Hook Type: 6×-long streamer. **Thread:** Black 3/0 or 6/0.
Tail: Yellow hackle fibers.
Body: Black floss.
Rib: Flat silver tinsel.
Wing: White saddle hackle or marabou.
Hackle: Beard: yellow hackle fibers.
Difficulty: 3.

BLACK NOSE DACE

Type: Streamer.
Item Number: 0647. **Most Popular Sizes:** 6, 8, 10.
Hook Type: 4×-long streamer. **Thread:** Black 6/0.
Tail: Short, stubby red wool (if using flat silver tinsel for body).
Body: Flat silver tinsel or fine silver Mylar piping.
Rib: Oval silver tinsel (if body is flat silver tinsel).
Wing: Brown bucktail over dyed-black squirrel tail or bucktail over sparse white bucktail.
Other Materials: Tag: red 3/0 thread to secure end of Mylar-piping body.
Difficulty: 3.

CONE HEAD MARABOU MUDDLER

Type: Streamer.
Item Number: 083T. **Most Popular Sizes:** 2, 4, 6, 8.
Color Options: Black, white, yellow.
Hook Type: 4×-long streamer. **Thread:** Gray 6/0.
Tail: Red hackle fibers.
Body: Flat silver tinsel.
Wing: Marabou, to match pattern color, topped with several strands of peacock herl.
Head: Natural deer, clipped to shape with unclipped natural ends left pointing back toward the bend as a collar. Gold cone ahead of the deer-hair head.
Difficulty: 4.

CONE HEAD MUDDLER MINNOW

Type: Streamer.
Item Number: 084T. **Most Popular Sizes:** 2, 4, 6, 8.
Hook Type: 4×-long streamer. **Thread:** Gray 3/0.
Tail: Mottled turkey wing-quill segment.
Body: Flat gold tinsel.
Rib: Medium gold wire.
Wing: Mottled turkey quill paired segments with underwing of gray squirrel tail.
Head: Natural deer, clipped to shape with unclipped natural ends left pointing back toward the bend as a collar. Gold cone ahead of the deer-hair head.
Difficulty: 4.

CONE HEAD WOOLLY BUGGER

Type: Streamer.
Item Number: 085T. **Most Popular Sizes:** 2, 4, 6, 8, 10.
Color Options: Olive, black. **Hook Type:** 4×-long streamer.
Thread: Black 6/0.
Tail: Black or olive marabou and pearl Krystal Flash.
Body: Black or olive vernille.
Rib: Dark monofilament thread.
Hackle: Black, palmered.
Head: Brass cone.
Difficulty: 2.

CONEHEAD DOUBLE BUNNY

Type: Streamer.
Item Number: 959P. **Most Popular Sizes:** 4, 6, 8, 10.
Hook Type: 4×-long streamer. **Thread:** White 3/0.
Rib: Fine silver or gold wire.
Wing: Belly: gray Zonker strip. Back: olive Zonker strip. Pearl
     Krystal flash tied in along the hook shank on each side.
     Vein: 10–15 strands of Krystal Flash tied in along each
     side of the fly.
Head: Brass or gold Conehead.
Other Materials: Stick-on prismatic eyes coated with epoxy.
Difficulty: 4.
Notes: For durability, wrap the rib around both the belly and
     back Zonker strips.

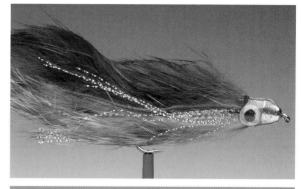

CONE HEAD ZUDDLER

Type: Streamer.
Item Number: 12C0. **Most Popular Sizes:** 2, 4, 6, 8.
Color Options: Purple, black, brown, olive, white.
Hook Type: 3×-long nymph/streamer.
Thread: 6/0 to match body color.
Tail: Zonker strip cut so that it tapers to a point. On the
     outside of the tail lay six strands of pearl Krystal Flash
     on each side for accent.
Body: Lite Brite dubbing to match pattern color.
Rib: Fine gold or copper wire to secure the rabbit strip along
     the back of the fly (optional).
Wing: Continuation of the Zonker strip used for the tail.
Hackle: Collar: spun deer-body hair to match pattern color.
Legs: Six strands (three on each side) Living Rubber tied in
     just behind the deer hair collar.
Head: Brass or gold Conehead.
Difficulty: 4.

FRANKE SHINER

Type: Streamer.
Item Number: 02JL.
Most Popular Sizes: 4, 6, 8, 10.
Hook Type: 4×-long streamer.
Thread: Olive 6/0.
Body: Fluorescent white floss and pearlescent Mylar.
Wing: Six to eight strands of olive Krystal Flash, light olive
     arctic fox or deer hair, and dark olive arctic fox or deer
     hair.
Head: Olive 6/0 thread with an eye painted on each side.
Difficulty: 3.

GIRDLE BUGGER

Type: Streamer.
Item Number: 0291. **Most Popular Sizes:** 4, 6, 8.
Hook Type: 4×-long streamer. **Thread:** Black 6/0.
Tail: Black marabou.
Body: Orange vernille.
Rib: Fine monofilament.
Wing: Black marabou.
Hackle: Collar: black saddle.
Legs: Three pairs of white Living Rubber.
Difficulty: 3.

GRAY GHOST

Type: Streamer.
Item Number: 0640. **Most Popular Sizes:** 6, 8, 10, 12.
Hook Type: 6×-long streamer. **Thread:** Black 6/0.
Body: Orange floss with a tag of flat silver tinsel.
Rib: Flat silver tinsel.
Wing: Four gray saddle hackles over golden pheasant crest curving downward.
Other Materials: Throat: three or four strands of peacock herl over sparse bunch of white bucktail over golden pheasant crest curving upward. Shoulders: silver-pheasant body feathers. Cheeks: jungle cock.
Difficulty: 5.
Notes: Most tiers leave off the expensive jungle cock.

JOE'S SMELT

Type: Streamer.
Item Number: 11T7. **Most Popular Sizes:** 6, 8.
Hook Type: 4×-long streamer. **Thread:** Black 6/0.

Tail: Red floss. Tag: red 6/0 thread.
Body: Small silver Mylar piping.
Wing: Lower wing: six to eight strands of pearl Flashabou. Upper wing: two mallard-flank feathers tied flat on top of the hook shank.
Head: Black thread.
Other Materials: Eyes: painted white with black pupils.
Difficulty: 2.

KRYSTAL BUGGER

Type: Streamer.
Item Number: 0314. **Most Popular Sizes:** 4, 6, 8, 10, 12.
Color Options: Black, olive. **Hook Type:** 4×-long streamer.
Thread: Black 6/0.
Tail: Olive or black marabou with a few strands of pearl Krystal Flash.
Body: Silver or pearl Ice Chenille or Sparkle Chenille.
Hackle: Black or olive, palmered through body.
Difficulty: 1.

MARABOU MUDDLER

Type: Streamer.
Item Number: 0658. **Most Popular Sizes:** 4, 6, 8.
Color Options: Gray/white, gray/black, gray/yellow.
Hook Type: 4×-long streamer. **Thread:** Gray 3/0.
Tail: Two red duck-quill sections.
Body: Silver or gold (on yellow version) tinsel chenille or flat tinsel.
Wing: White, black, or yellow marabou topped with several strands of peacock herl.
Head: Spun natural gray deer hair, clipped to shape leaving untrimmed natural ends extending toward bend as a collar.
Difficulty: 3.

MATUKA

Type: Streamer.
Item Number: 0641. **Most Popular Sizes:** 6, 8.
Color Options: Black, olive. **Hook Type:** 4×-long streamer.
Thread: Black 6/0.
Body: Medium chenille in desired color.
Rib: Fine copper wire, or oval gold or silver tinsel.
Wing: Four dyed hen grizzly saddles.
Hackle: Dyed grizzly saddle.
Head: Eyes (optional): painted yellow with black pupils.
Difficulty: 3.

MEG-A-EGG-SUCKING LEECH

Type: Streamer.
Item Number: 059T. **Most Popular Sizes:** 2, 4, 6.
Color Options: Black/chartreuse, purple/pink.
Hook Type: Salmon wet fly. **Thread:** Black 6/0.
Tail: Purple or black marabou with pearl Krystal Flash.
Body: Purple or black chenille.
Hackle: Purple or black, palmered through body.
Head: Pink or chartreuse Crystal Egg, slipped over point and
glued to shank before tying fly.
Difficulty: 2.

MICKEY FINN

Type: Streamer.
Item Number: 0648. **Most Popular Sizes:** 6, 8, 10, 12.
Hook Type: 4×-long streamer. **Thread:** Black 6/0.
Body: Flat silver tinsel or fine silver Mylar piping.
Rib: Oval silver tinsel (if body is flat silver tinsel).
Wing: Yellow bucktail over red bucktail over sparse yellow
bucktail.
Other Materials: Tag: red 3/0 thread to secure end of Mylar-
piping body.
Difficulty: 3.

MINI MUDDLER

Type: Streamer.
Item Number: 0900. **Most Popular Sizes:** 10, 12.
Color Options: Natural, black.
Hook Type: Heavy wet/nymph. **Thread:** Brown 6/0.
Tail: Section of mottled turkey quill (natural) or black goose
quill (black).
Body: Flat gold tinsel.
Wing: Paired sections of mottled turkey quill (natural) or
black goose quill (black).
Head: Spun deer hair, fine ends left pointing back toward
bend as collar.
Difficulty: 3.

327

Moto's Minnow

Type: Streamer.
Item Number: 960P. **Most Popular Sizes:** 6, 8, 10.
Color Options: Tan, brown.
Hook Type: 3×-long nymph/streamer.
Thread: Tan or brown 6/0.
Tail: Gray marabou.
Body: Mottled hen hackle palmered the full length of the body.
Hackle: Collar: three to four turns of white hen hackle or a soft, webby saddle hackle.
Head: Brass or tungsten Conehead.
Difficulty: 4.

Mudd Bugger Fly

Type: Streamer.
Item Number: 02RX. **Most Popular Sizes:** 4, 6, 8, 10.
Color Options: White, black/olive, gold.
Hook Type: 4×-long streamer.
Thread: 3/0 to match pattern color.
Tail: White marabou with two strands of pearlescent Flashabou on each side.
Body: Pearlescent Chenille, Ice Chenille, or Estaz.
Hackle: Brown, ginger, or cree saddle, tied palmer style through body.
Head: Deer hair spun and clipped.
Difficulty: 2.

Muddler Minnow

Type: Streamer.
Item Number: 0655. **Most Popular Sizes:** 2, 4, 6, 8, 10, 12.
Hook Type: 4×-long streamer. **Thread:** Black 6/0.
Tail: Mottled turkey-quill segment.
Body: Flat gold tinsel.
Wing: Underwing: gray squirrel tail. Overwing: Mottled turkey-quill segments.
Head: Spun natural gray deer hair, clipped to shape leaving untrimmed natural ends extending toward bend as a collar.
Difficulty: 4.

Orange Blossom Special

Type: Streamer.
Item Number: 02JK. **Most Popular Sizes:** 4, 6, 8.
Hook Type: 4×-long streamer. **Thread:** Brown 6/0.
Body: Olive brown Crystal Chenille.
Rib: Gold wire.
Wing: One orange, one yellow, and two brown webby neck hackles.
Hackle: One yellow and one brown hackle tied as collar.
Head: Brass cone with brown dubbed fur behind to hold it in place.
Difficulty: 3.

ROYAL COACHMAN BUCKTAIL

Type: Streamer.
Item Number: 0649. **Most Popular Sizes:** 6, 8, 10, 12.
Hook Type: 4×-long streamer. **Thread:** Black 6/0.
Tail: Golden pheasant tippet.
Body: Peacock herl with a red floss center band.
Wing: White bucktail.
Hackle: Dark brown.
Difficulty: 3.

STRIP TEASE

Type: Streamer.
Item Number: 12C1. **Most Popular Sizes:** 2, 4, 6, 8.
Color Options: Purple, black, brown, olive, white.
Hook Type: 3×-long nymph/streamer.
Thread: 6/0 to match body.
Tail: Zonker strip cut so that it tapers to a point. On the
outside of the tail lay six strands of Pearl Krystal Flash
on each side for accent.
Body: Zonker strip used for the tail wrapped forward around
the hook shank.
Legs: Six strands (three on each side) Living Rubber tied in
one fourth of the shank length behind the eye.
Head: Hot Cone or Hot Bead.
Difficulty: 3.

TEQUEELY STREAMER

Type: Streamer.
Item Number: 002C. **Most Popular Sizes:** 2, 4, 6.
Hook Type: 4×-long streamer. **Thread:** Black 6/0.
Tail: Yellow and black marabou, mixed.
Body: Brown Estaz or sparkle chenille.
Legs: Three pairs of yellow rubber legs sticking out each side.
Head: Gold bead.
Difficulty: 3.

TRAVIS BEAD-A-BUGGER

Type: Streamer.
Item Number: 082T. **Most Popular Sizes:** 4, 6, 8, 10, 12.
Color Options: Olive, black. **Hook Type:** Orvis 0167.
Thread: Black 6/0.
Tail: Black or olive marabou with pearl Krystal Flash.
Body: Black or olive chenille.
Rib: Fine dark monofilament thread.
Hackle: Black, palmered.
Legs: White and black Flexi-Floss.
Head: Silver bead.
Difficulty: 2.

TUNGHEAD & MARABOU MUDDLER

Type: Streamer.
Item Number: 963P. **Most Popular Sizes:** 4, 6, 8, 10.
Color Options: Black/gray, white/gray, gray/yellow.
Hook Type: 4×-long streamer. **Thread:** White 3/0.
Tail: Red hackle tips.
Body: Flat Gold or Silver Mylar Tinsel.
Wing: Underwing: Marabou to match pattern description.
Topping: 2–6 Peacock swords.
Hackle: Collar: Deer Body Hair tips.
Head: Spun Deer Body Hair behind a brass or tungsten conehead.
Difficulty: 4.

TUNGHEAD WOOLLY BUGGER

Type: Streamer.
Item Number: 962P. **Most Popular Sizes:** 2, 4, 6, 8, 10.
Hook Type: 4×-long streamer. **Thread:** Black 3/0.
Tail: Marabou with four strands of Krystal Flash on each side.
Body: Chenille.
Wing: Black marabou.
Hackle: Saddle, grizzly or same color as body.
Head: Tungsten bead.
Difficulty: 1.

WOOLHEAD SCULPIN

Type: Streamer.
Item Number: 0895. **Most Popular Sizes:** 4, 6, 8.
Color Options: Brown, olive. **Hook Type:** 4×-long streamer.
Thread: 6/0 to match body color.
Tail: Pair of matched hen pheasant feathers.
Body: Wool.
Rib: Oval gold tinsel.
Wing: Pair of pheasant-flank feathers or mottled turkey quill segments.
Legs: Fins: pair of pheasant-flank feathers tied splayed, one on each side of the fly.
Head: Spun wool, clipped to shape.
Difficulty: 4.
Notes: If pheasant flank is used for the wing, the gold tinsel can be wrapped through the wing for extra durability.

WOOLLY BOMBER

Type: Streamer.
Item Number: 0424. **Most Popular Sizes:** 4, 6, 8, 10.
Hook Type: 4×-long streamer. **Thread:** Black 6/0.
Tail: Black marabou, as long as the hook shank.
Body: Black chenille.
Rib: Grizzly hackle palmered through body.
Head: Weighted dumbbell eyes painted yellow at ends.
Difficulty: 1.

STREAMER

WOOLLY BUGGER
Type: Streamer.
Item Number: 0878. **Most Popular Sizes:** 4, 6, 8, 10, 12, 14.
Color Options: Black, tan, white, olive.
Hook Type: 4×-long streamer. **Thread:** Black or white 6/0.
Tail: Marabou to match pattern description.
Body: Chenille to match pattern color.
Rib: Grizzly hackle palmered through body; or a hackle to
    match pattern color.
Difficulty: 1.

ZONKER
Type: Streamer.
Item Number: 0616. **Most Popular Sizes:** 4, 6, 8.
Color Options: Pearl, black, olive, Black Ghost.
Hook Type: 4×-long streamer.
Thread: 6/0 to match body color.
Tail: Frayed ends of Mylar piping used for the body.
Body: Mylar piping over cut plastic form.
Wing: Zonker strip.
Difficulty: 3.

STEELHEAD

BRAD'S BRAT
Type: Steelhead.
Item Number: 0590. **Most Popular Sizes:** 4, 6.
Hook Type: Salmon wet fly. **Thread:** White 6/0.
Tail: White bucktail over orange bucktail.
Body: Rear half orange yarn; front half red yarn.
Rib: Flat gold tinsel.
Wing: Orange bucktail over white bucktail.
Hackle: Dark brown, collar style.
Difficulty: 3.

BURLAP
Type: Steelhead.
Item Number: 0370. **Most Popular Sizes:** 4, 6, 8.
Hook Type: Salmon wet fly. **Thread:** Black 6/0.
Tail: Coastal deer hair, tied full.
Body: Burlap jute fibers wrapped like yarn.
Hackle: Grizzly, tied as a collar.
Difficulty: 2.

FLESH FLY
Type: Steelhead.
Item Number: 975B. **Most Popular Sizes:** 4, 6.
Color Options: Pink, tan.
Hook Type: 3×-long nymph/streamer. **Thread:** Tan 3/0.
Tail: Guard hairs from a cross-cut rabbit strip.
Body: Cross-cut rabbit wrapped from hook bend to eye.
Difficulty: 1.

GLO-BUG
Type: Steelhead.
Item Number: 02RE. **Most Popular Sizes:** 8, 10, 12, 14.
Color Options: Chartreuse, pink, orange, white, blue, red, black.
Hook Type: Short-shank curved nymph.
Thread: To match yarn color.
Body: Glo-Bug or egg yarn.
Difficulty: 2.
Notes: Tie about a hook-gap width of yarn firmly to the top of the hook in the center of the shank. Raise the yarn straight up and take several circular turns of thread around its base. Then trim the yarn quickly with a sharp pair of serrated scissors while pulling the yarn straight up.

GREEN BUTT SKUNK
Type: Steelhead.
Item Number: 0530. **Most Popular Sizes:** 4, 6, 8.
Hook Type: Salmon wet fly. **Thread:** Black 6/0.
Tail: Red hackle fibers.
Body: Rear quarter: fluorescent green chenille. Front three quarters: black chenille.
Rib: Oval silver tinsel.
Wing: White calf tail.
Hackle: Black, tied as collar.
Difficulty: 2.

MACK'S CANYON
Type: Steelhead.
Item Number: 0266. **Most Popular Sizes:** 4, 6.
Hook Type: Salmon wet fly. **Thread:** Black 6/0.
Tail: Orange and white calf tail fibers, mixed.
Body: Rear one third: hot-orange yarn. Front two thirds: black yarn.
Rib: Oval silver tinsel.
Wing: White over orange calf tail.
Hackle: Black.
Difficulty: 3.

POLAR SHRIMP

Type: Steelhead.
Item Number: 0234. **Most Popular Sizes:** 4, 6, 8.
Hook Type: Salmon wet fly. **Thread:** Black 6/0.
Tail: Red hackle fibers.
Body: Fluorescent orange chenille.
Wing: White calf tail.
Hackle: Fluorescent orange.
Difficulty: 2.
Notes: The hackle fibers are one and a half to two times as long as the hook gap is wide.

PURPLE PERIL

Type: Steelhead.
Item Number: 0448. **Most Popular Sizes:** 4, 6, 8.
Hook Type: Salmon wet fly. **Thread:** Black 6/0.
Tail: Purple hackle fibers.
Body: Purple chenille.
Rib: Oval silver tinsel.
Wing: Natural brown bucktail.
Hackle: Purple, collar style.
Difficulty: 2.

RUSHER'S STEELHEAD FLIES

Type: Steelhead.
Item Number: 973B. **Most Popular Sizes:** 6, 8, 10.
Color Options: Black/blue, black/red, chartreuse, green, purple.
Hook Type: 1×-long nymph. **Thread:** 6/0 to match pattern color.
Tail: Goose biots, splayed.
Wing: Wing case: flat-black or peacock metallic braid.
Abdomen: Chenille in desired color.
Thorax: Ice Chenille, Estaz, or Crystal Chenille.
Difficulty: 2.

SILVER HILTON

Type: Steelhead.
Item Number: 0067. **Most Popular Sizes:** 4, 6.
Hook Type: Salmon wet fly. **Thread:** Black 6/0.
Tail: Mallard-flank fibers.
Body: Black chenille.
Rib: Oval silver tinsel.
Wing: Two grizzly hackles.
Hackle: Grizzly.
Difficulty: 2.

SKUNK

Type: Steelhead.
Item Number: 0477. **Most Popular Sizes:** 4, 6.
Hook Type: Salmon wet fly. **Thread:** Black 6/0.
Tail: Red hackle fibers.
Body: Black chenille.
Rib: Flat silver tinsel.
Wing: White bucktail or calf tail.
Hackle: Black, wound as collar.
Difficulty: 2.

SPRING WIGGLER

Type: Steelhead.
Item Number: 0763. **Most Popular Sizes:** 4, 6, 8.
Hook Type: Salmon wet fly. **Thread:** Tan 3/0.
Tail: Tips of match-thick clump of red squirrel tail used for the wing case.
Body: Cream/tan Antron dubbed full at mid-shank.
Wing: Match-thick clump of red squirrel tail tied as a full back, with butts extending over the hook eye and tips extending as a tail.
Hackle: Brown saddle hackle, palmered.
Head: Trim the butts of the wing case to form a flat head ¼ inch beyond hook eye.
Difficulty: 2.

STARLITE LEECH FLY

Type: Steelhead.
Item Number: 02JT. **Most Popular Sizes:** 2, 4.
Color Options: Red/black, orange/black, chartreuse/black, black, pink, purple, red/white.
Hook Type: Salmon wet fly. **Thread:** Black 3/0.
Tail: Zonker strip.
Body: Large Estaz or Ice Chenille.
Hackle: Saddle hackle to match body color.
Head: Chenille, vernille, or Crystal Chenille wrapped around the dumbbell eyes.
Other Materials: Stainless Deepwater eyes.
Difficulty: 2.

TWO EGG SPERM

Type: Steelhead.
Item Number: 0723. **Most Popular Sizes:** 4, 6, 8.
Color Options: Pink, red, chartreuse.
Hook Type: Salmon wet fly. **Thread:** Red 3/0.
Body: Two bands of chenille of pattern color with thinner band of oval silver tinsel in between.
Wing: White marabou, to bed of hook.
Difficulty: 2.

BOMBER

Type: Salmon. Subtype: Dry.
Item Number: 0375. **Most Popular Sizes:** 2, 4, 6.
Color Options: Brown, green, white.
Hook Type: Salmon dry fly. **Thread:** White 3/0.
Tail: White calf tail.
Body: Spun tightly from deer-belly hair to match the color of
    the pattern.
Rib: Brown hackle, palmered.
Wing: White calftail.
Hackle: Brown.
Difficulty: 4.
Notes: The tips of the hackle should be even with point of hook.

SALMON—WET

BLACK BEAR GREEN BUTT

Type: Salmon   Subtype: Wet.
Item Number: 0683. **Most Popular Sizes:** 4, 6, 8, 10, 12.
Hook Type: Salmon wet fly. **Thread:** Black 6/0.
Tail: Black hackle fibers.
Body: Rear third fluorescent green floss; from two thirds
    black floss.
Rib: Oval silver tinsel.
Wing: Black bear hair or gray squirrel tail dyed black.
Hackle: Black, tied as a sparse beard.
Other Materials: Tag: flat silver tinsel.
Difficulty: 3.

BLACK DOSE

Type: Salmon.   Subtype: Wet.
Item Number: 0746. **Most Popular Sizes:** 4–10.
Hook Type: Single or double salmon wet fly.
Thread: Black 6/0.
Tail: Golden pheasant tippet.
Body: Black floss.
Rib: Flat silver tinsel.
Wing: Black bear or squirrel tail over peacock-sword fibers.
Hackle: Black, tied collar style.
Difficulty: 3.

BLUE CHARM

Type: Salmon.   Subtype: Wet.
Item Number: 0734. **Most Popular Sizes:** 4, 6, 8, 10, 12.
Hook Type: Single or double salmon wet fly.
Thread: Black 6/0.
Tail: Golden pheasant crest.
Body: Black floss.
Rib: Flat silver tinsel.
Wing: Turkey-tail sections, veiled with overwing of teal along
    upper edge.
Hackle: Deep blue hackle, beard style.
Other Materials: Tip: flat silver tinsel or mylar. Tag: yellow
        floss. Topping: golden pheasant crest.
Difficulty: 3.

COSSEBOOM
Type: Salmon.   Subtype: Wet.
Item Number: 0684. **Most Popular Sizes:** 4, 6, 8, 10, 12.
Hook Type: Single or double salmon wet fly.
Thread: Bright red 6/0.
Tail: Olive green floss, cut short.
Body: Olive green floss.
Rib: Flat silver embossed tinsel.
Wing: Gray squirrel tail.
Hackle: Bright yellow tied as collar.
Other Materials: Tag: flat silver tinsel.
Difficulty: 3.

GREEN HIGHLANDER
Type: Salmon.   Subtype: Wet.
Item Number: 0738. **Most Popular Sizes:** 4, 6, 8, 10, 12.
Hook Type: Single or double salmon wet fly.
Thread: Black 6/0.
Tail: Golden pheasant crest fibers with Lady Amherst tippets
     laid on top.
Body: Rear third light tan floss; front two-thirds bright green
     floss or spiky dubbing.
Rib: Oval silver tinsel.
Wing: Fox-squirrel tail fibers, over which are small bunches
     of yellow and green bucktail hairs, mixed.
Hackle: Bright green hackle wound over the green part of the
     body. Bright yellow tied as a collar in front of the wing.
Other Materials: Tag: three turns of flat silver tinsel. Butt:
     three turns of black ostrich herl.
Difficulty: 5.

HAIRY MARY
Type: Salmon.   Subtype: Wet.
Item Number: 0681. **Most Popular Sizes:** 4, 6, 8.
Hook Type: Salmon wet fly. **Thread:** Black 6/0.
Tail: Golden pheasant crest or yellow hackle fibers.
Body: Black floss.
Rib: Flat gold tinsel.
Wing: Fox-squirrel tail fibers.
Hackle: Bright blue tied as a collar.
Other Materials: Tag: flat gold tinsel.
Difficulty: 3.

LAXA BLUE
Type: Salmon.   Subtype: Wet.
Item Number: 0880. **Most Popular Sizes:** 4, 6, 8, 10, 12.
Hook Type: Salmon wet fly. **Thread:** Black 6/0.
Tail: Yellow hackle fibers.
Body: Medium blue floss.
Rib: Fine oval silver tinsel.
Wing: Gray squirrel tail dyed pale blue.
Hackle: Pale blue, as a beard.
Other Materials: Tip: oval silver tinsel. Tag: hot-orange floss.
Difficulty: 3.

RUSTY RAT

Type: Salmon. Subtype: Wet.
Item Number: 0676. **Most Popular Sizes:** 4, 6, 8.
Hook Type: Single or double salmon wet.
Thread: Red 3/0 or 6/0.
Tail: Peacock-sword fibers, tied short.
Body: Rear half yellowish orange floss; front half peacock herl. A strand of floss extends over rear half of body on the top of fly as a veil.
Rib: Oval gold tinsel.
Wing: Gray-fox guard hairs.
Hackle: Soft grizzly hackle tied as a collar.
Other Materials: Tag: fine oval gold tinsel.
Difficulty: 3.

SILVER RAT

Type: Salmon. Subtype: Wet.
Item Number: 0678. **Most Popular Sizes:** 2, 4, 6, 8, 10.
Hook Type: Single or double salmon wet.
Thread: Red 3/0 or 6/0.
Tail: Yellow hackle fibers or golden pheasant crest.
Body: Flat silver tinsel.
Rib: Oval gold tinsel.
Wing: Gray-fox guard hairs.
Hackle: Soft grizzly tied as collar.
Other Materials: Tag: fine oval gold tinsel.
Difficulty: 3.

UNDERTAKER

Type: Salmon. Subtype: Wet.
Item Number: 0881. **Most Popular Sizes:** 4, 6, 8, 10, 12.
Hook Type: Single or double salmon wet. **Thread:** Black 6/0.
Body: Peacock herl.
Rib: Oval gold tinsel.
Wing: Black bear hair or black bucktail.
Hackle: Black, tied as a beard.
Other Materials: Tag: oval gold tinsel. Butt: fluorescent green floss next to tag, then fluorescent fire orange floss next to body.
Difficulty: 2.

BEADEYE CHARLIE

Type: Saltwater. Subtype: Bonefish.
Item Number: 0869. **Most Popular Sizes:** 4, 6, 8.
Color Options: White, tan, yellow, pink.
Hook Type: Pre-sharpened saltwater. **Thread:** White 6/0.
Body: Pearlescent Mylar tinsel overwrapped with clear V-Rib.
Wing: White, tan, yellow, or pink calf tail.
Head: Silver bead chain.
Difficulty: 1.

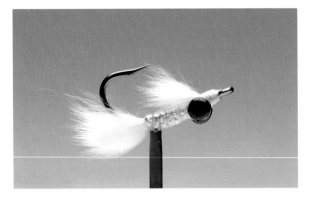

BEARDED CHARLEY
Type: Saltwater.   Subtype: Bonefish.
Item Number: 0550. **Most Popular Sizes:** 4, 6, 8.
Color Options: Tan, white, pink.
Hook Type: Pre-sharpened stainless. **Thread:** Tan 3/0 or 6/0.
Tail: Tan rabbit guard hairs.
Body: Twisted Krystal Flash, metallic braid, or Mylar.
Head: Beard: tan rabbit guard hairs, tied short.
Other Materials: Eyes: bead-chain or lead dumbbell.
Difficulty: 2.

BELIZE BOMBER FLY
Type: Saltwater.   Subtype: Bonefish.
Item Number: 02KA. **Most Popular Sizes:** 4, 6.
Hook Type: Pre-sharpened stainless.
Thread: Fluorescent orange 6/0.
Tail: Two small melted monofilament eyes.
Body: Burnt-orange dubbing.
Wing: Krystal Flash over fine synthetic hair.
Legs: Orange Sili Legs or orange mottled Living Rubber.
Difficulty: 3.
Notes: The eyes tied on as a tail are two short sections of
heavy mono that have been singed by a match flame.
Singe the mono to form the eyes before the pieces are
tied in at the tail.

BONE CRUSHER
Type: Saltwater.   Subtype: Bonefish.
Item Number: 964P. **Most Popular Sizes:** 4, 6.
Hook Type: Pre-sharpened stainless. **Thread:** White 3/0.
Body: Twisted gold Krystal Flash, floss, or Flashabou.
Rib: Optional: the body can be overwrapped with clear mono.
Wing: Tan calf tail.
Legs: Mottled Living Rubber or Sili Legs.
Head: Bead-chain eyes with pearl Ice Chenille, Estaz, or
Krystal Chenille.
Difficulty: 3.

BONEFISH BITTERS FLY
Type: Saltwater.   Subtype: Bonefish.
Item Number: 02KB. **Most Popular Sizes:** 6, 8.
Color Options: Olive, amber, orange.
Hook Type: Pre-sharpened saltwater.
Thread: 6/0 to match body color.
Wing: Sparse deer hair over Z-Lon underwing, same color as
body.
Legs: About eight legs made from Grizzly Rubber Legs or Sili
Legs, tied in middle of body.
Head: Gold bead-chain eyes covered with colored epoxy or
hot glue.
Difficulty: 3.

Borski's Bonefish Slider

Type: Saltwater.   Subtype: Bonefish.
Item Number: 018Y. **Most Popular Sizes:** 4, 6, 8.
Hook Type: Pre-sharpened stainless. **Thread:** White 3/0.
Tail: Tan Fly Fur, striped medium brown with permanent
        marker.
Body: Thread.
Hackle: Grizzly, clipped on top and sides.
Head: Tan deer hair, clipped to shape.
Other Materials: Sides: yellow Krystal Flash. Collar: tan
                deer-hair tips, clipped on top and sides.
                Eyes: yellow with black pupil.
Difficulty: 2.

Borski's Fur Shrimp

Type: Saltwater.   Subtype: Bonefish.
Item Number: 029Y. **Most Popular Sizes:** 2, 4.
Hook Type: Pre-sharpened saltwater. **Thread:** White 3/0.
Tail: Orange Krystal Flash over tan Fly Fur, with black stripes
        made with permanent marker.
Body: White floss.
Hackle: Grizzly hackle wound over entire hook shank,
        clipped top and sides.
Head: White thread, epoxy.
Other Materials: Eyes: yellow lead dumbbell with black
                pupil. Weed guard: stiff mono.
Difficulty: 2.

Deep Water Gotcha

Type: Saltwater.   Subtype: Bonefish.
Item Number: 804E. **Most Popular Sizes:** 2, 4, 6, 8.
Hook Type: Pre-sharpened stainless. **Thread:** Pink 3/0.
Tail: Pearl Mylar tubing, picked out.
Body: Pearl Mylar tubing or Pearl Glimmer twisted over
        underbody of pink thread.
Wing: Blond Fly Fur with pearl Krystal Flash topping.
Head: Stainless-steel dumbbell eyes.
Difficulty: 2.

Gotcha

Type: Saltwater.   Subtype: Bonefish.
Item Number: 041T. **Most Popular Sizes:** 2, 4, 6, 8.
Color Options: Pink, chartreuse.
Hook Type: Standard stainless hook.
Thread: Pink or chartreuse 3/0.
Tail: Frayed pearl Mylar tubing.
Body: Clear V-Rib, Larva Lace, or pearl Diamond Braid over
        tapered tying thread.
Wing: Fine beige synthetic hair with a half-dozen fibers of
        pearl Krystal Flash.
Head: Bead chain.
Difficulty: 2.

M.O.E. Bonefish

Type: Saltwater. Subtype: Bonefish.
Item Number: 0323. **Most Popular Sizes:** 4, 6.
Color Options: Amber, pearl, pink.
Hook Type: Pre-sharpened saltwater. **Thread:** Brown 6/0.
Wing: Sparkle yarn with two grizzly hackles dyed color of
yarn.
Hackle: Grizzly, dyed color of yarn.
Head: Bead chain eyes with head of epoxy or hot glue over
the eyes.
Difficulty: 4.

Ruoff's Absolute Flea

Type: Saltwater. Subtype: Bonefish.
Item Number: 030T. **Most Popular Sizes:** 4, 6.
Hook Type: Pre-sharpened saltwater. **Thread:** Tan 3/0.
Tail: Grizzly saddle hackles, splayed.
Body: Light tan Fuzzy Leech Yarn with butt of white chenille
at bend.
Hackle: White and grizzly hackle tied just forward of the
butt, clipped on top of the hook.
Head: Pre-painted saltwater eyes.
Other Materials: Weed guard made from two posts of stiff
nylon tied in front of the eyes.
Difficulty: 2.

Ruoff's Deep-Flea

Type: Saltwater. Subtype: Bonefish.
Item Number: 034T. **Most Popular Sizes:** 4, 6.
Hook Type: Pre-sharpened saltwater. **Thread:** White 3/0.
Body: Light ran Fuzzy Leech Yarn.
Wing: White calf tail with cree hackle on each side, pearl
Krystal Flash.
Head: Silver dumbbell eyes.
Other Materials: Two pieces of stiff monofilament in front of
eyes for weed guard.
Difficulty: 2.
Notes: The wing is tied in the middle of the shank, upright
and slanted back toward the point.

Simram

Type: Saltwater. Subtype: Bonefish.
Item Number: 764F. **Most Popular Sizes:** 2, 4.
Hook Type: Pre-sharpened stainless. **Thread:** Hot-pink 3/0.
Tail: Light gold synthetic Fly Fur, yellow Krystal Flash, twice
shank length.
Body: Rear half: pearl Krystal Flash. Front half: tan crosscut
rabbit strip, clipped top and sides.
Head: Tied bigger than normal with tying thread.
Other Materials: Shellback: pearl Mylar piping tied flat over
top of rabbit strip. Eyes: silver dumbbell eyes
tied on top of hook in the middle of the body.
Difficulty: 3.
Notes: This fly rides upside down, so what is referred to as the
top here is actually the bottom of the fly when fished.

SPAWNING GOTCHA
Type: Saltwater.   Subtype: Bonefish.
Item Number: 805E. **Most Popular Sizes:** 2, 4, 6, 8.
Hook Type: Pre-sharpened stainless.
Thread: Fluorescent-pink 3/0.
Tail: Hot-orange hackle tips.
Body: Pearl Poly Flash or wrapped Krystal Flash.
Wing: Light gold Fly Fur, with Pearl Krystal Flash on top.
Head: Thread head.
Difficulty: 2.

SALTWATER—CRAB

FLEXO CRAB
Type: Saltwater.   Subtype: Crab.
Item Number: 966P. **Most Popular Sizes:** 2.
Color Options: Light blue, pearl. **Hook Type:** Pre-sharpened
stainless. **Thread:** 3/0 to match body color.
Body: ¼-inch or ⅜-inch Flexo tubing.
Legs: Mottled Living Rubber or Sili Legs threaded through
        Flexo body, knotted to keep them in place.
Head: Eyes: melted mono inserted into Flexo body and
        epoxied in place.
Other Materials: Pinchers: two pheasant-flank feathers,
        epoxied, trimmed to shape. Coat tips with
        red or orange paint for accent.
Difficulty: 4.
Notes: A rattle chamber can easily be added to the interior of
the Flexo body.

GIBB'S CRAB
Type: Saltwater.   Subtype: Crab.
Item Number: 11YA.
Most Popular Sizes: 2/0, 2, 4, 6.
Hook Type: Pre-sharpened stainless.
Thread: Pink or tan 3/0.
Tail: Tan marabou mixed with holographic tinsel, overlaid
        with two light-brown saddle hackles tied splayed.
Body: Gray and dark cream Antron rug yarn.
Legs: Mottled orange Sili Legs or round Living Rubber.
Difficulty: 3.
Notes: The rug yarn is tied onto the hook perpendicular to
        the shank and alternates in color from band to band.
        The legs are tied in at mid-shank.

JACK'S FIGHTING CRAB
Type: Saltwater.   Subtype: Crab.
Item Number: 807E. **Most Popular Sizes:** 2, 4, 8, 10.
Hook Type: Pre-sharpened stainless. **Thread:** Tan 3/0.
Tail: Claws: mallard-flank feathers with five to ten fibers at
        the tip trimmed out, extending past bend and hook eye.
Body: Two tan Velcro adhesive strips trimmed to oval crab
        shape.
Legs: Knotted rubber bands or Living Rubber.
Head: Eyes: wide melted-mono dumbbell eyes.
Difficulty: 2.

KELLIHER'S CRAB-EEL FLY
Type: Saltwater. Subtype: Crab.
Item Number: 03HT. **Most Popular Sizes:** 1/0.
Hook Type: Pre-sharpened stainless. **Thread:** Black 3/0.
Tail: Four dyed-olive grizzly saddle hackles, splayed.
Body: Olive cross-cut rabbit strip wrapped from bend to the dumbbell eyes.
Head: Stainless steel dumbbell eyes.
Difficulty: 2.

LATHAM'S CRAB
Type: Saltwater. Subtype: Crab.
Item Number: 11YL. **Most Popular Sizes:** 2, 4, 6.
Hook Type: Pre-sharpened stainless.
Thread: 6/0 to match body.
Tail: Tan Fly Fur, over which two grizzly saddles are splayed.
Body: Medium tan Crystal Chenille, Ice Chenille, or Estaz.
Hackle: Dyed-orange grizzly saddle hackle that is palmered over the body.
Head: Bead-chain or Lead Dumbbell.
Other Materials: Weed guard: heavy mono tied in a V.
Difficulty: 3.

PETERSON'S SPAWNING CRAB
Type: Saltwater. Subtype: Crab.
Item Number: 808E. **Most Popular Sizes:** 1, 2, 4, 6.
Hook Type: Pre-sharpened stainless. **Thread:** Clear mono.
Tail: Egg sac: bright orange Antron yarn.
Body: Underbody: light tan Antron yarn.
Wing: Shellback: natural deer-hair tips.
Legs: Six brown Sili Legs or Round Living rubber mottled with a black marking pen.
Head: Eyes: black glass beads glued on mono posts.
Difficulty: 3.
Notes: The eyes and egg sac are half as long as the hook shank. The legs are one and three-quarters times as long as the shank. Underbody and shellback are flattened to give the body a wide shape.

RATTLIN FLEXO CRAB FLY
Type: Saltwater. Subtype: Crab.
Item Number: 02J4. **Most Popular Sizes:** 1/0, 1, 2.
Hook Type: Pre-sharpened saltwater. **Thread:** White 3/0.
Body: Clear Flexo tubing, tied at bend of hook, pushed in to form flat shape; rattle is inserted into the braid, then it is secured at head.
Legs: Four pairs of Sili Legs drawn through braid with bobbin threader, knotted, and secured with epoxy.
Head: Dull colored dumbbell eyes.
Other Materials: Eyes: plastic nylon eyes glued into braid.
Claws: Pheasant-breast feathers with center snipped out, stiffened with flexible cement, tips painted orange, then glued into place.
Difficulty: 5.

342

SimCrab

Type: Saltwater.   Subtype: Crab.
Item Number: 11X8. **Most Popular Sizes:** 2/0, 2, 6.
Hook Type: Pre-sharpened stainless. **Thread:** Light pink 3/0.
Tail: Light tan saddle hackle, tied splayed.
Body: Light tan and pink rug yarn.
Legs: Orange/black barred Sili Legs or round Living Rubber.
Head: Deep Water Eyes.
Difficulty: 3.
Notes: The rug yarn is tied in perpendicular to the hook
shank in alternating bands of color. The legs are tied in
by overhand knots.

Turneffe Crab

Type: Saltwater.   Subtype: Crab.
Item Number: 982P. **Most Popular Sizes:** 2, 4, 6.
Color Options: Cream, olive.
Hook Type: Pre-sharpened stainless. **Thread:** White 3/0.
Body: Furry Foam cut in an oval shape with V cut in one end
for attachment.
Wing: Deer body hair, stacked.
Legs: Living Rubber or mottled Sili Legs.
Head: Lead dumbbell.
Other Materials: A brown Pantone marking pen can be used
to add markings to the Living Rubber legs.
Difficulty: 3.

Whisper Crab

Type: Saltwater.   Subtype: Crab.
Item Number: 03G7. **Most Popular Sizes:** 2, 4, 6.
Color Options: Sand, olive.
Hook Type: Pre-sharpened stainless. **Thread:** Tan 6/0.
Tail: Two thin saddle hackles, splayed.
Body: Two to four saddle hackles wrapped full, trimmed top
and bottom.
Abdomen: Bottom: bleached saddle hackle tied flat over the
trimmed hackle on the bottom; coated with
penetrating cement.
Thorax: Weed guard: 20-pound Mason tied in a V.
Legs: Four thin saddle; one pair tied at mid-shank, the other
pair just behind the eyes.
Head: Dumbbell eyes painted white on their bottom half.
Other Materials: Secondary eyes: burnt-mono dumbbell eyes
mounted just behind the lead eyes.
Difficulty: 5.

Del Brown's Permit Fly

Type: Saltwater.   Subtype: Permit.
Item Number: 0673. **Most Popular Sizes:** 2/0, 2, 4, 6.
Hook Type: Standard stainless.
Thread: Fluorescent green 3/0.
Tail: Pearl Flashabou with two splayed cree hackles on each side.
Body: Alternating bands of tan and brown yarn, tied across
the shank and brushed out.
Legs: Three pairs of white rubber legs, distributed through
the body. Tips of the legs are painted red.
Head: Nickel-plated dumbbell.
Difficulty: 3.

343

FLEXO POPPER

Type: Saltwater.   Subtype: Popper.
Item Number: 967P. **Most Popular Sizes:** 2/0, 2.
Hook Type: Mustad 90233S bent at slight angle.
Tail: Extension: partial hook shank with four white hen saddles covering ten to fifteen strands of pearl Krystal Flash.
Body: ⅜- or ½-inch Flexo tubing.
Head: Eyes: stick-on prismatic eyes covered with a thin coat of epoxy.
Other Materials: Waterproof markers are used to color the fly.
Difficulty: 3.
Notes: The Flexo body is filled with a coiled 2mm-thick sheet of closed-cell foam.

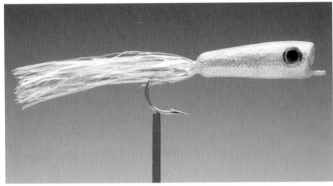

MYLAR POPPER

Type: Saltwater.   Subtype: Popper.
Item Number: 02J3. **Most Popular Sizes:** 2/0.
Color Options: Chartreuse, pearl.
Hook Type: 4×-long popper hook. **Thread:** White 3/0.
Tail: Picked-out ends of large pearl Mylar tubing.
Body: Preformed popper body covered by large pearl Mylar tubing, epoxied.
Head: Eyes: prismatic stick-on eye, epoxied.
Difficulty: 2.
Notes: Whip-finish the tubing both behind the eye and opposite the point of the barb.

RUOFF'S BACKCOUNTRY POPPER

Type: Saltwater.   Subtype: Popper.
Item Number: 0559. **Most Popular Sizes:** 1.
Hook Type: Mustad 33903. **Thread:** White 3/0.
Tail: White saddle hackles splayed two per side.
Body: Preformed and painted popper head.
Hackle: Black neck hackle tied full behind popper head.
Difficulty: 2.

SKIPPING BUG

Type: Saltwater.   Subtype: Popper.
Item Number: 0815. **Most Popular Sizes:** 2/0, 2.
Color Options: Red/white, blue/white.
Hook Type: 3×-long stainless. **Thread:** White 3/0.
Tail: White bucktail.
Body: 3-inch perch float cut in half and painted.
Difficulty: 2.
Notes: Forward face of cork is cut at a slight angle. Slit bottom of cork with hacksaw blade and epoxy to hook shank.

ULTIMATE OFFSHORE POPPER

Type: Saltwater.   Subtype: Popper.
Item Number: 15HP. **Most Popular Sizes:** 6/0.
Color Options: Pink/white, blue/white, pink/red,
blue/pink.
Hook Type: Two rigged 6/0 Gamakatsu. The fly itself is tied
on a ⅛-inch ID plastic tube.
Thread: White size A Monocord or Kevlar.
Tail: Twelve to sixteen Cocktail saddle hackles tied on a
plastic tube.
Hackle: Six to ten marabou blood feathers tied around the
tube just ahead of the saddles.
Head: Preshaped foam head painted white on the bottom and
darker on its back.
Other Materials: 2-Ton epoxy for securing the head to the tube.
Difficulty: 4.

CURT'S LINESLIDER

Type: Saltwater.   Subtype: Redfish.
Item Number: 03C3. **Most Popular Sizes:** 1/0.
Color Options: Natural deer hair, white, chartreuse.
Hook Type: Pre-sharpened stainless.
Thread: 3/0 to match pattern color.
Tail: Match-stick-size clump of Polar Hair, same color as head.
Wing: Grizzly neck hackles, one on each side, curving
inward, accented by pearl or chartreuse Wing-and-
Flash (shredded Flashabou).
Hackle: Collar: very webby grizzly saddle dyed to match
pattern color.
Head: Spun and clipped deer or elk hair.
Other Materials: V-shaped mono weed guard.
Difficulty: 4.
Notes: To form the weed guard, tie in a 3-inch piece of heavy
mono as a loop extending to the hook point. Trim the
loop into two distinct prongs and flatten the end of the
prongs with pliers. Trim to the desired length.

CURT'S MANGROVE MUDDLER

Type: Saltwater.   Subtype: Redfish.
Item Number: 03HZ. **Most Popular Sizes:** 1/0.
Hook Type: 3✕-long pre-sharpened stainless.
Thread: White 3/0.
Tail: Black Krystal Flash 1-inch in length underneath ⅞-inch
silver or gold Krystal Flash.
Body: Sparkle Braid double wrapped the full length of the
hook, then epoxied.
Wing: Underwing: match-stick-size clump of rust or white
craft fur striped with black marker. Overwing: copper
or pearl Wing-and-Flash (shredded Flashabou).
Topping: eight strands of peacock herl.
Hackle: Collar: red Krystal Flash tied in as gills.
Head: Spun and clipped deer or elk hair.
Other Materials: V-shape mono weed guard.
Difficulty: 4.
Notes: To form the weedguard, tie in a 3-inch piece of heavy
mono as a loop extending to the hook point. Trim the
loop into two distinct prongs and flatten the end of the
prongs with pliers. Trim to the desired length.

DR. MILLER'S REDBONE FLY

Type: Saltwater.   **Subtype:** Redfish.
Item Number: 02TL. **Most Popular Sizes:** 2, 4.
Color Options: Brown, chartreuse.
Hook Type: Pre-sharpened stainless.
Thread: 3/0 to match pattern color.
Tail: FisHair and pearl Krystal Flash.
Wing: White or tan marabou.
Hackle: Grizzly.
Head: Lead dumbbell.
Other Materials: Five-minute epoxy.
Difficulty: 3.
Notes: Once the fly is complete, coat the head and the eyes
with a thin coat of five-minute epoxy. Turn on a rotary
vise or with forceps until the epoxy hardens.

SALTWATER—SHRIMP

AC'S REDFISH HORS D'OUVRE

Type: Saltwater.   **Subtype:** Shrimp.
Item Number: 11YY. **Most Popular Sizes:** 2, 4, 6.
Color Options: White, chartreuse, tan, pink, gray.
Hook Type: Pre-sharpened stainless.
Thread: 6/0 to match body.
Tail: Melted mono eyes with marabou to match body color.
Body: Crystal Chenille, Ice Chenille, or Estaz.
Wing: FisHair or Fluoro Fibre with Krystal Flash the same
color as the body folded over the body as a shellback.
Epoxy over shellback.
Other Materials: Weed guard: 12-pound Mason hard nylon.
Difficulty: 3.

JACK'S MANTIS SHRIMP

Type: Saltwater.   **Subtype:** Shrimp.
Item Number: 962B. **Most Popular Sizes:** 2, 4.
Hook Type: 3×-long stainless.
Thread: White or light green 3/0.
Tail: Two green saddle hackle plumes mixed with six clear
Microfibbets.
Body: Olive chenille.
Wing: Back: green Shimmmer Skin.
Thorax: Pinchers: extra small black lead eyes.
Head: Eyes: plastic ³⁄₁₆-inch silver hologram eyes. Antennae:
Four or five clear Microfibbets.
Other Materials: Six to eight wraps of .030 lead wire near
bend in the hook shank.
Difficulty: 3.
Notes: The lead eyes should be put on the hook shank
directly behind the .030 lead wire.

JOE'S GRASS SHRIMP

Type: Saltwater.   **Subtype:** Shrimp.
Item Number: 969P. **Most Popular Sizes:** 2, 4, 6.
Hook Type: Pre-sharpened stainless. **Thread:** White 6/0.
Tail: White marabou and frayed ends of pearl Mylar tubing.
Body: Pearl Mylar tubing.
Legs: Frayed ends of pearl Mylar piping.
Head: Bead-chain eyes.
Other Materials: Five-minute epoxy is used to coat the Mylar
piping body.
Difficulty: 3.
Notes: Mount the bead-chain eyes atop the hook shank so the
fly will ride hook point up.

LATHAM'S SHRIMP

Type: Saltwater.   Subtype: Shrimp.
Item Number: 11YP. **Most Popular Sizes:** 2, 4, 6.
Color Options: Olive/gold, red/white, chartreuse/white,
chartreuse/gold, tan/gold.
Hook Type: 3×-long pre-sharpened stainless.
Thread: 6/0 to match body color. **Tail:** Root-beer Fly Fur.
Body: Medium root-beer Crystal Chenille, Ice Chenille, or Estaz.
Wing: Chartreuse grizzly hackle.
Hackle: Chartreuse grizzly hackle. **Head:** Dumbbell eyes.
Other Materials: Topping: sixteen strands of Krystal Flash in
the dominant body color, fourteen strands
in another color to accent.
Difficulty: 3.
Notes: A weed guard of hard nylon is usually added to the
pattern, and can be tied in at the bend or as a V.

MOUSAM SHRIMP

Type: Saltwater.   Subtype: Shrimp.
Item Number: 961B. **Most Popular Sizes:** 1, 2, 4, 6, 10.
Color Options: White, gray. **Hook Type:** Pre-sharpened
stainless. **Thread:** 3/0 to match body color.
Tail: Pearl or silver Krystal Flash mixed with calf tail and
marabou, tied short.
Body: Antron leech yarn, picked out.
Wing: Silver Mylar piping pulled flat over the back.
Head: Eyes: burnt-mono dumbbell, brass bead chain, or
plastic bead chain tied in at atop bend of hook shank
opposite the barb.
Difficulty: 3.

PETERSON SPAWNING SHRIMP

Type: Saltwater.   Subtype: Shrimp.
Item Number: 809E. **Most Popular Sizes:** 1, 2, 4, 6.
Hook Type: Pre-sharpened stainless.
Thread: Fluorescent pink 3/0.
Tail: Light tan Antron. Antennae: two long strands of pearl
Krystal Flash under four short strands of pearl Krystal
Flash.
Body: Flat pearl ribbon, wrapped over rear one-third only.
Rib: Shellback: flat pearl ribbon, pulled over back and weight.
Wing: Tan rabbit, tied in four segments.
Abdomen: Egg sac: bright orange rug yarn.
Legs: Clear and black Sili Legs.
Head: Pink thread. Eyes: black glass beads glued onto mono
posts.
Other Materials: Silver dumbbell eyes.
Difficulty: 4.
Notes: Antennae: twice shank length. Eye stalks: gap width.
Egg sac: gap width. Body: one third of shank.
Shellback: one third of shank. Wing: twice shank
length. Head: one sixth of shank.

RHETT'S CINNAMON SHRIMP
Type: Saltwater. Subtype: Shrimp.
Item Number: 12EK. **Most Popular Sizes:** 2, 4.
Hook Type: Pre-sharpened stainless. **Thread:** Rust 3/0.
Tail: Cinnamon Fly Fur.
Body: Gold tinsel.
Wing: Root-beer Krystal Flash.
Hackle: Furnace.
Head: Lead eyes.
Difficulty: 2.

RHETT'S MANGROVE GHOST SHRIMP
Type: Saltwater. Subtype: Shrimp.
Item Number: 12EH. **Most Popular Sizes:** 2, 4, 6.
Hook Type: Standard saltwater. **Thread:** White 3/0.
Body: Pearl Krystal Flash twisted into a rope and wound forward.
Wing: White Fly Fur or FisHair over rainbow Krystal Flash.
Head: Black bead-chain eyes.
Other Materials: EZ-Sparkle Epoxy added to the head.
Difficulty: 3.

T. BAIRD HULA SHRIMP
Type: Saltwater. Subtype: Shrimp.
Item Number: 963B. **Most Popular Sizes:** 6, 8.
Color Options: Pearl, chartreuse.
Hook Type: 3×-long pre-sharpened stainless.
Thread: White 3/0.
Tail: Short sparse bunch of arctic fox hair with guard hairs removed, mixed with twelve strands of pearl Krystal Flash.
Body: Flat pearlescent Mylar tinsel wrapped over and around five pairs of pearlescent plastic eyes.
Head: Bead-chain eyes.
Other Materials: Dot the bead-chain eyes with black paint and coat the body with epoxy.
Difficulty: 4.

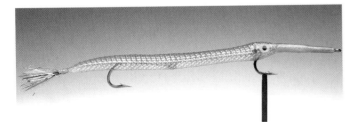

BARRACUDA FLY
Type: Saltwater. Subtype: Streamer.
Item Number: 03YT. **Most Popular Sizes:** 1/0, 2/0.
Color Options: Blue/white, chartreuse/white, orange/white.
Hook Type: Pre-sharpened stainless.
Thread: Size A yellow Monocord or Kevlar.
Tail: Tie off Flexo tubing used for the body and pick out the ends of the tubing.
Body: ¼- to ⅜-inch pearl Flexo tubing tied in at the bend.
Head: Stick-on Prismatic eyes, covered with epoxy. Continue tapering the thread head to the hook eye and coat with epoxy.
Difficulty: 2.

BEAD EYE CLOUSER

Type: Saltwater. Subtype: Streamer.
Item Number: 12A8. **Most Popular Sizes:** 2/0, 2, 4, 6.
Color Options: Chartreuse/white, gray/white, olive/white, tan/white.
Hook Type: Pre-sharpened stainless. **Thread:** White 3/0.
Wing: Belly: white bucktail. Midwing: pearl, silver, or Gold Krystal Flash. Topping: Bucktail of a darker color than the belly.
Head: Bead-chain eyes.
Difficulty: 1.
Notes: This fly is tied just like the popular Clouser Minnow. The only difference is that the fly has bead-chain eyes rather than lead eyes.

BENDBACK

Type: Saltwater. Subtype: Streamer.
Item Number: 0896. **Most Popular Sizes:** 2/0.
Color Options: Blue/yellow, blue/white, purple/white.
Hook Type: 3×-long stainless. **Thread:** White 3/0.
Body: White chenille.
Wing: A layer white bucktail (or yellow on blue/yellow version), then pearl and silver Flashabou, a grizzly saddle hackle on each side, then blue or purple bucktail and eight strands of peacock herl over the top.
Head: Painted eyes: white with black pupil and red band at rear of head.
Difficulty: 2.
Notes: The front third of the hook is bent up about 30 degrees.

BIG-EYED SKIPJACK

Type: Saltwater. Subtype: Streamer.
Item Number: 03X8-05. **Most Popular Sizes:** 6/0.
Hook Type: Gamakatsu SC15-2H.
Thread: White size A Monocord.
Tail: 2-inch loop of Berkley Sea Strand wire.
Wing: Lower wing: white bucktail mixed with pearl Krystal Flash, pearl Flashabou, and pearl holographic tinsel, four to six strands each. Upper wing: mixture dark blue FisHair and bucktail mixed with blue and rainbow holographic tinsel.
Hackle: Topping: six to eight strands of peacock herl.
Head: Built up of tying thread to a tapered shape. Coated with Blue Glitter EZ Sparkle Body (top) and Pearl EZ Sparkle Body (bottom). A final coat of epoxy is added to the head for durability.
Other Materials: Prismatic eyes, yellow with black pupils.
Difficulty: 3.
Notes: Clear Glitter EZ Sparkle Body can be used, but it will let the thread wraps underneath the head show.

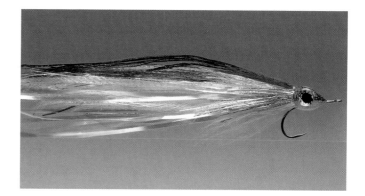

BONEFISH CLOUSER FOXY RED

Type: Saltwater.   Subtype: Streamer.
Item Number: 02J0. **Most Popular Sizes:** 4, 6.
Hook Type: 3×-long stainless. **Thread:** Tan 6/0.
Wing: Underwing: Tan guard hairs from red-fox tail.
  Midwing: gold and rust Flashabou. Topping: black-
  tipped red-fox tail guard hairs.
Head: Lead dumbbell eyes painted red with black pupils.
Difficulty: 2.

CAPE COD SAND EEL

Type: Saltwater.   Subtype: Streamer.
Item Number: 02J6. **Most Popular Sizes:** 2/0, 1/0, 2.
Color Options: Chartreuse, olive.
Hook Type: Pre-sharpened saltwater. **Thread:** White 3/0.
Tail: One long, thin saddle hackle tied flat, either chartreuse
  or olive.
Body: Silver Mylar tinsel.
Wing: White bucktail long enough to extend beyond the bend
  of the hook, over which is shorter bucktail the same
  color as the tail. Two strands of silver tinsel between
  the layers of bucktail.
Difficulty: 2.

CLOUSER MINNOW

Type: Saltwater.   Subtype: Streamer.
Item Number: 0506. **Most Popular Sizes:** 2/0, 2, 6.
Color Options: Olive/white, black/orange, chartreuse/white.
Hook Type: Pre-sharpened saltwater. **Thread:** White 3/0.
Wing: Bottom: white or orange (on black/orange pattern)
  bucktail tied down in front of eyes, pulled over them and
  tied down behind. Top: rainbow Krystal Flash and olive,
  black, or chartreuse bucktail, tied down in front of eyes.
Head: Dumbbell eyes.
Difficulty: 1.
Notes: Eyes are set back one fourth the length of hook shank,
  on top of shank. Fly rides upside down.

CONEHEAD DECEIVER

Type: Saltwater.   Subtype: Streamer.
Item Number: 981P. **Most Popular Sizes:** 2/0, 2.
Hook Type: Pre-sharpened stainless. **Thread:** White 3/0.
Tail: Four white saddles tied atop hook shank at the bend,
  concave sides in.
Wing: Lower: white bucktail tied along the sides of the hook
  shank. Upper: contrasting-color bucktail tied atop the
  white bucktail lower wing. Topping: peacock herl
  mixed with peacock Krystal Flash, mounted directly
  on top of the hook shank.
Head: Brass or tungsten Conehead.
Other Materials: Prismatic stick-on eyes, covered with epoxy.
Difficulty: 3.

COWEN'S ALBIE ANCHOVIE

Type: Saltwater.   Subtype: Streamer.
Item Number: 11Y2. **Most Popular Sizes:** 4, 6.
Hook Type: 3×-long pre-sharpened stainless.
Thread: White 3/0.
Body: Just behind the eye, tie in two equal bunches of fine
   pink synthetic hair on the top and bottom of the hook
   shank.
Abdomen: Belly: Pearl Krystal Flash.
Thorax: EZ Body braid tubing placed from the hook eye back
   to three-quarters the length of the fly.
Head: Prismatic 2mm or 3mm eyes applied to the EZ Body
   Braid. A layer of clear epoxy is then applied to the
   braid, covering the eyes.
Other Materials: Five-minute epoxy.
Difficulty: 4.
Notes: When preparing the EZ Body braid, remove only the
   inner strings from one side of the tubing. When
   sliding the tubing in place, place the portion with the
   string so that it straddles the Gliss and Glow flash
   material on the belly.

COWEN'S BAITFISH

Type: Saltwater.   Subtype: Streamer.
Item Number: 11X4. **Most Popular Sizes:** 2/0, 2.
Color Options: Chartreuse/white, olive/white, gray/white.
Hook Type: Pre-sharpened stainless. **Thread:** White 3/0.
Tail: White Polar Fibre.
Wing: Bottom: white Slinky Fibre. Top: chartreuse, olive, or
   gray Slinky Fibre.
Hackle: Throat: pink Slinky Fibre, tied sparse.
Head: 4mm or 6mm prismatic eyes.
Difficulty: 3.

COWEN'S MAGNUM HERRING

Type: Saltwater.   Subtype: Streamer
Item Number: 957B.
Color Options: Royal, blue/white (herring), olive/white
   (Bunker).
Hook Type: Pre-sharpened stainless. **Thread:** White 3/0.
Body: Underwing: white Icelandic sheep. Midwing: white
   bucktail tied at hook bend. Overwing: olive or blue
   Icelandic sheep. Topping: mixture of peacock
   Flashabou and peacock herl.
Head: 6mm or 7mm prismatic eyes.
Other Materials: A quick-drying epoxy is used to secure the
   eyes in place.
Difficulty: 4.
Notes: This fly is tied using the Brooks Hi-Tie method.

CURLY TAILED BUNNY

Type: Saltwater.   Subtype: Streamer.
Item Number: 11XA. **Most Popular Sizes:** 1/0.
Color Options: Black, purple, brown, chartreuse, white.
Hook Type: Pre-sharpened stainless. **Thread:** Black 3/0.
Tail: Latex glitter strip cut to a twin curly-tail shape; color to match or contrast with the body.
Body: Cross-cut rabbit, palmered.
Legs: Mottled Sili Legs or round Living Rubber to match body or tail.
Head: Prepainted yellow/black dumbbell eyes.
Other Materials: .020 or larger mono weed guard.
Difficulty: 3.
Notes: Prior to finishing the head, tie in a V-style mono weed guard.

DAHLBERG DEEP WIGGLER

Type: Saltwater.   Subtype: Streamer.
Item Number: 983P. **Most Popular Sizes:** 4, 6, 8.
Color Options: Pink, bronze.
Hook Type: Pre-sharpened stainless. **Thread:** White 3/0.
Abdomen: Lite Brite dubbed on extension made of a cut hook shank.
Thorax: Lite Brite dubbing.
Legs: Three pairs of Sili Legs: two on the extended abdomen, one on the thorax.
Head: Prepainted Dumbbell eyes, red with black pupils.
Difficulty: 4.
Notes: The extension is attached via a mono or wire loop tied in at the bend of the hook.

DARK DAY FLY

Type: Saltwater.   Subtype: Streamer.
Item Number: 03X8-61. **Most Popular Sizes:** 6/0.
Hook Type: Gamakatsu SC15-2H.
Thread: Black size A Monocord.
Tail: 2-inch loop of Berkley Sea Strand wire.
Wing: Lower wing: 3-inch black bucktail over 8-inch black Ultra Hair mixed with dark blue Krystal Flash, blue Flashabou, and blue holographic tinsel, six to eight strands each. Midwing: ten to twelve 8-inch strands of wide pearl Flashabou. Upper wing: 3-inch dark blue bucktail.
Hackle: Topping: eight to ten strands of peacock herl.
Head: Built up of tying thread to a tapered shape. Coated with Clear Glitter EZ Sparkle Body (top) and Pearl EZ Sparkle Body (bottom). A final coat of epoxy is added to the head for durability.
Other Materials: Prismatic eyes, yellow with black pupil.
Difficulty: 4.

DR. MILLER'S FLEX-TAIL BUNNY
Type: Saltwater.   Subtype: Streamer.
Item Number: 11X1. **Most Popular Sizes:** 1/0, 2, 6.
Color Options: Chartreuse, white, pink, tan, brown.
Hook Type: Pre-sharpened stainless.
Thread: 3/0 to match body color.
Tail: Latex glitter strip cut to curly tail shape. In color to
    match or contrast with the body.
Body: Cross-cut rabbit, palmered.
Legs: Mottled Sili Legs or Round Living Rubber to match
    body or tail.
Head: Bead-chain or Deepwater eyes.
Other Materials: .020 or larger mono weed guard.
Difficulty: 3.
Notes: Prior to finishing the head, tie in a V-style mono weed
    guard.

FLATS CANDY
Type: Saltwater.   Subtype: Streamer.
Item Number: 11YT. **Most Popular Sizes:** 2, 4, 6.
Color Options: Chartreuse/white, olive/white, gray/white,
    brown/tan.
Hook Type: Pre-sharpened stainless.
Thread: 6/0 to match body.
Tail: Two to four splayed saddle hackles to match body color.
Body: Rear two thirds: light cross-cut rabbit wrapped tightly
    up hook shank. Front one-third: darker cross-cut rabbit
    wrapped to hook eye.
Head: Thread head covered with prismatic epoxy.
Other Materials: Heavy mono weed guard.
Difficulty: 3.
Notes: The weed guard can be tied in as a V or as a loop from
    the bend of the hook. Tie in the weed guard prior to
    finishing the head.

FLOATING VINEYARD EEL
Type: Saltwater.   Subtype: Streamer.
Item Number: 978P. **Most Popular Sizes:** 2, 6.
Hook Type: Pre-sharpened stainless. **Thread:** White 3/0.
Tail: Frayed end of pearl Flexo tubing used for the body.
Body: Pearl Flexo tubing covering thin interior of a rolled
    2mm sheet of Fly Foam.
Head: Stick-on prismatic eyes covered with a thin coat of
    epoxy.
Difficulty: 3.
Notes: The Flexo tubing is whip-finished on one end so that
    the foam insert doesn't come out of the body during
    casting.

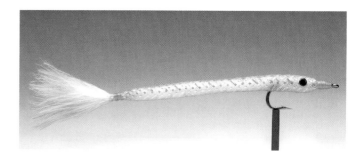

GLASS MINNOW
Type: Saltwater.   Subtype: Streamer.
Item Number: 958B. **Most Popular Sizes:** 1/0, 1.
Hook Type: Pre-sharpened stainless. **Thread:** White 6/0.
Tail: Black hen hackle with the tip clipped off to form a V.
Body: Belly: silver mylar tubing. Back: black FisHair.
Head: Stick-on eyes.
Other Materials: Five-minute epoxy.
Difficulty: 3.
Notes: Epoxy the tail into the thin Mylar tubing. Secure the
    tubing at the bend of the hook with the black FisHair
    and pull them forward to the hook eye. Do not pull
    them too tight. Fill the area between and around the
    FisHair and the mylar with epoxy. Rotate until dry.
    Add eyes and apply a thin coat of epoxy over the eye.

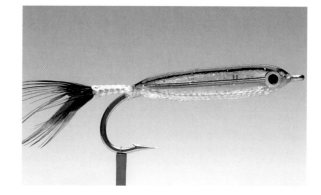

GLENN'S ROOT BEER FLY

Type: Saltwater.   **Subtype:** Streamer.
Item Number: 03CP-02. **Most Popular Sizes:** 6/0, 4/0, 2/0.
Hook Type: Gamakatsu SC15.
Thread: White size A Monocord.
Wing: Bottom: Gray bucktail mixed with twenty to twenty-five strands of pearl Krystal Flash. Top: Brown bucktail mixed with fifteen to twenty strands of holographic tinsel.
Hackle: Topping: six to eight strands of peacock herl.
Abdomen: Sides: holographic tinsel and rainbow Krystal Flash.
Head: Built up of tying thread to a tapered shape. Coated with Gold Glitter EZ Sparkle Body (top) and Pearl Glitter EZ Sparkle Body (bottom). A final coat of epoxy is added to the head for durability.
Other Materials: Silver prismatic eyes.
Difficulty: 3.
Notes: Clear Glitter EZ Sparkle Body can be used, but it will let the thread wraps underneath the head show.

HALF AND HALF

Type: Saltwater.   **Subtype:** Streamer.
Item Number: 953B. **Most Popular Sizes:** 2/0, 1/0, 1.
Color Options: Tan/white, black, olive/white, chartreuse/white.
Hook Type: Pre-sharpened stainless. **Thread:** White 3/0.
Tail: Four saddle hackles tied concave sides in at hook bend. Add Krystal Flash or Flashabou for accent.
Wing: Lower wing: white bucktail tied on each side of the hook shank. Upper wing: contrasting-color bucktail tied directly atop the lower wing on each side. Topping: mixture of peacock herl and peacock Krystal Flash for accent.
Head: Painted dumbbell eyes covered with epoxy.
Other Materials: Gills: red Krystal Flash, tied short.
Difficulty: 3.

JOHNNY'S ANGEL

Type: Saltwater.   **Subtype:** Streamer.
Item Number: 034C. **Most Popular Sizes:** 1, 2.
Color Options: White, olive/white, olive.
Hook Type: Pre-sharpened stainless. **Thread:** White 3/0.
Body: Bottom: Light Ultra Hair or Long Brite. Top: Contrasting color Ultra Hair or Long Brite.
Rib: Vein: wide pearlescent Mylar tinsel or holographic tinsel, one on each side.
Head: SofTex or clear five-minute epoxy coating the fly from just behind the eye to the bend of the hook.
Difficulty: 3.
Notes: Several materials can be used for the body, including bucktail.

KELLIHER'S HERRING

Type: Saltwater.   Subtype: Streamer.
Item Number: 03HY. **Most Popular Sizes:** 3/0.
Color Options: Olive/white, blue/white, yellow.
Hook Type: Pre-sharpened stainless.
Thread: Size A yellow Monocord or Kevlar.
Tail: Four to six schlappem feathers tied concave sides in at bend.
Body: In Hi-Tie fashion: tie in light bucktail topped with thicker portion of darker bucktail, filling the upper hook shank. Between clumps tie in 3 long strands of Saltwater Flashabou on each side.
Head: Eyes: 5mm doll eyes or prismatic eyes, covered with epoxy, ⅜ of an inch behind the hook eye.
Difficulty: 3.

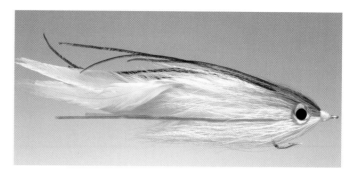

KELLIHER'S JUVIE FLY

Type: Saltwater.   Subtype: Streamer.
Item Number: 03HX. **Most Popular Sizes:** 1/0.
Color Options: Light blue, chartreuse/white, olive/white, lavender/white.
Hook Type: Pre-sharpened stainless. **Thread:** White 6/0.
Tail: Thirty to forty strands of pearl Krystal Flash.
Body: The Krystal Flash tied in for the tail, twisted and wrapped forward.
Wing: Bottom: fine, white synthetic hair. Topping: Dark synthetic hair.
Difficulty: 3.

KIRK'S HOT TAIL BENDBACK

Type: Saltwater.   Subtype: Streamer.
Item Number: 02J9. **Most Popular Sizes:** 1.
Color Options: Root beer, black, purple.
Hook Type: Pre-sharpened saltwater bent upward at the eye for Bendback shape. **Thread:** Black 3/0.
Tail: 2-inch piece of heavy mono tie in under the wing, to which a hot-orange piece of Zonker strip or marabou is attached.
Body: Estaz or Ice Chenille.
Wing: Fly Fur, FisHair, or Long Brite half again as long as the hook shank.
Head: Built-up tying thread with painted yellow eyes with black pupils.
Difficulty: 3.

KIRK'S RATTLE ROUSER

Type: Saltwater.   Subtype: Streamer.
Item Number: 0093. **Color Options:** Pink, chartreuse, olive.
Hook Type: Pre-sharpened saltwater.
Thread: Hot-red 3/0.
Tail: Pearlescent tubing, frayed (formed from body).
Body: Pearlescent tubing with rattle inside, epoxied.
Wing: Metallic Krystal Flash and bucktail.
Other Materials: Underbody: hot-red thread.
Difficulty: 4.
Notes: Tie in tubing above point of barb. When forming the body, take a piece of Mylar tubing, slide in the rattle, and fray out the proper amount of tubing to form tail.

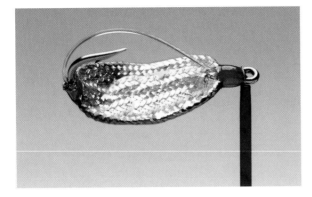

KIRK'S SPOON FLY

Type: Saltwater.   Subtype: Streamer.
Item Number: 970P. **Most Popular Sizes:** 2, 4, 6.
Color Options: Silver/blue, gold/red, pearl/chartreuse.
Hook Type: 3×-long pre-sharpened stainless.
Thread: Black 3/0.
Body: Extra-large Mylar tubing.
Other Materials: Epoxy is used to coat the Mylar-tubing body and is painted with Pantone marking pens.
Difficulty: 3.
Notes: Underneath the Mylar tubing, put a precut flexible piece of metal such as aluminum foil. Bend it to shape prior to epoxying the body.

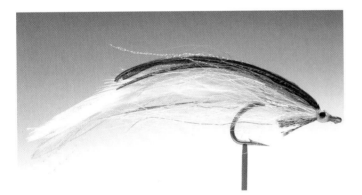

LEFTY'S DECEIVER

Type: Saltwater.   Subtype: Streamer.
Item Number: 0826. **Most Popular Sizes:** 2/0, 1.
Color Options: Black, white, yellow, olive/white, chartreuse, red/white, red/yellow, green/white.
Hook Type: Pre-sharpened saltwater. **Thread:** White 3/0.
Tail: Four to six saddle hackles, not splayed.
Body: Silver Mylar tinsel.
Hackle: Bucktail tied in equal bunches on top of and below the shank; must extend beyond the bend of the hook.
Other Materials: Topping of peacock herl or Flashabou over the top bunch of bucktail.
Difficulty: 3.
Notes: If the fly is two-toned (e.g., olive/white), the darker color is tied on top of the shank and the lighter color goes underneath.

LIME AIDE FLY

Type: Saltwater.   Subtype: Streamer.
Item Number: 03CP-14. **Most Popular Sizes:** 2/0, 4/0, 6/0.
Hook Type: Gamakatsu SC15.
Thread: White size A Monocord.
Wing: Bottom: white bucktail mixed with pearl Krystal Flash. Top: chartreuse bucktail over pearl Krystal Flash and Pearl holographic tinsel (ten to fifteen strands).
Hackle: Topping: six to eight strands of peacock herl.
Abdomen: Sides: silver holographic tinsel for accent.
Head: Built up of tying thread for tapered shape. Coated with Chartreuse Glitter EZ Sparkle Body (top) and Pearl EZ Sparkle Body (bottom). A final coat of epoxy is then added to the head for durability.
Other Materials: Prismatic eyes, yellow with black pupil.
Difficulty: 3.
Notes: Clear Glitter EZ Sparkle Body can be used, though it will allow the thread wraps underneath the head to show.

MAGIC MACKEREL

Type: Saltwater.   Subtype: Streamer.
Item Number: 03X8-21. **Most Popular Sizes:** 6/0.
Hook Type: Gamakatsu SC15-2H.
Thread: White size A Monocord.
Tail: 2-inch loop of Berkley Sea Strand wire.
Wing: Bottom: 3-inch white bucktail over 8-inch white Ultra
   Hair mixed with pearl Krystal Flash, pearl Flashabou,
   and pearl holographic tinsel, six to eight strands each.
   Middle: ten to twelve 8-inch strands of wide Pearl
   Flashabou. Top: 3-inch olive Bucktail over 8-inch blue
   Ultra Hair, mixed with pearl Krystal Flash, pearl
   Flashabou and pearl holographic tinsel.
Hackle: Topping: eight to ten strands of peacock herl.
Head: Built up of tying thread to a tapered shape. Coated
   with Olive Glitter EZ Sparkle Body (top) and Pearl EZ
   Sparkle Body (bottom). A final coat of epoxy is added
   to the head for durability.
Other Materials: Prismatic eyes, yellow with black pupils.
Difficulty: 4.

MAGNA HERRING

Type: Saltwater.   Subtype: Streamer.
Item Number: 968P. **Most Popular Sizes:** 2/0, 4/0.
Color Options: Blue/white, gold.
Hook Type: Plastic-worm hook such as the Gamakatsu 5110
   Offset AK1 Worm hook.
Thread: White size A monocord.
Body: ⅜- or ½-inch Flexo tubing.
Difficulty: 3.
Notes: The hook is threaded "Texas style" into the tubing
   much like rigging a plastic worm.

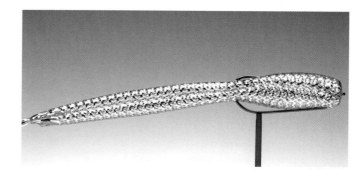

MATT'S 40

Type: Saltwater.   Subtype: Streamer.
Item Number: 03H1. **Most Popular Sizes:** 1.0, 1.
Color Options: Green/white, black/chartreuse, white.
Hook Type: Pre-sharpened stainless. **Thread:** Black 3/0.
Tail: Two light-colored marabou blood feathers tied on each
   side of the hook opposite the barb, and a darker blood
   feather atop the hook shank.
Body: Back: Six to ten strands of peacock herl.
Wing: Two neck hackles to match the body color tied concave
   sides in and alongside the marabou tail. Extend the
   neck hackles beyond the length of the marabou.
Head: Tying thread built up and epoxied.
Other Materials: Eyes: adhesive Prismatic eyes, epoxied around
   their bases. Weed guard: wire keel guard.
Difficulty: 3.
Notes: Do not epoxy over the eyes because it will cloud them.
   A loop or V-style mono weed guard is also
   appropriate.

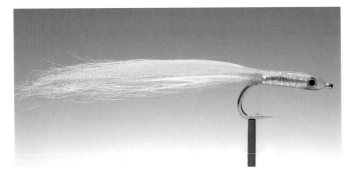

MIKKLESON'S BARRACUDA FLY

Type: Saltwater.   Subtype: Streamer.
Item Number: 971P. **Most Popular Sizes:** 2.
Color Options: Chartreuse/white, dark olive/white,
olive/silver, white.
Hook Type: Pre-sharpened stainless.
Thread: White 3/0 or size A Monocord.
Tail: White bucktail and silver Krystal Flash.
Rib: Pearl Krystal Flash.
Wing: Dark olive bucktail and olive Krystal Flash.
Hackle: Two strands of red Flashabou, trimmed short.
Difficulty: 3.

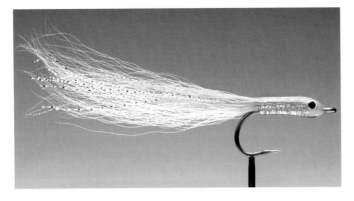

MIKKLESON'S EPOXY BAITFISH

Type: Saltwater.   Subtype: Streamer.
Item Number: 716F. **Most Popular Sizes:** 2.
Color Options: Chartreuse/white, dark olive/white,
olive/silver, white.
Hook Type: Pre-sharpened stainless.
Thread: White 3/0 or size A Monocord.
Tail: White bucktail and silver Krystal Flash.
Rib: Pearl Krystal Flash.
Wing: Darker bucktail mixed with matching color Krystal Flash.
Head: Five-minute epoxy coating the entire body to the eye.
Difficulty: 3.

MUD MINNOW SLIDER

Type: Saltwater.   Subtype: Streamer.
Item Number: 11XY. **Most Popular Sizes:** 4, 6.
Color Options: Pink, gray, tan.
Hook Type: Pre-sharpened stainless.
Thread: 6/0 to match pattern color.
Tail: Pearl, silver, or gold Krystal Flash between two splayed
saddle hackles.
Thorax: Collar: Aqua Fibre or Slinky Fibre spun and clipped
to shape.
Head: Aqua Fibre or Slinky Fibre spun and clipped to shape.
Other Materials: Prismatic eyes.
Difficulty: 3.

NIHO SQUID

Type: Saltwater.   Subtype: Streamer.
Item Number: 11Y3. **Most Popular Sizes:** 1, 4.
Color Options: White, pink.
Hook Type: 3×-long pre-sharpened stainless.
Thread: 6/0 to match body color.
Tail: Rabbit hair and Lite Brite of the same color with a
mixture of pearl and green Krystal Flash and bleached
mallard-flank tips.
Body: Underbody dubbed with rabbit to match body color.
Overbody is natural pearl, medium EZ-Body braid.
Legs: Sili Legs or round Living Rubber to match body color,
tied in at the bend of the hook with the tail.
Other Materials: Eyes: two stemmed glass eyes tied in at the tail.
Difficulty: 3.

PETERSON'S BABY BUNKER

Type: Saltwater.   Subtype: Streamer.
Item Number: 0993. **Most Popular Sizes:** 2/0.
Hook Type: Pre-sharpened stainless.
Thread: Clear mono or white size A Monocord.
Body: Two white marabou blood feathers.
Rib: Sides: six to ten strands of pearl glimmer.
Wing: Cheeks: golden pheasant tippets tied on each side.
Hackle: Topping: olive Flashabou with ten to twelve strands of peacock herl on top.
Head: Eyes: silver prismatic stick-on eyes placed on forward portion of cheeks.
Other Materials: Clear silicone: Apply from hook eye back twice the length of the hook shank.
Difficulty: 4.
Notes: Body and sides are 4 inches long. Cheeks are three fourths as long as hook shank. Topping is 4 ½ inches long.

PETERSON'S TINKER MACKEREL

Type: Saltwater.   Subtype: Streamer.
Item Number: 0992. **Most Popular Sizes:** 1/0.
Hook Type: Pre-sharpened stainless. **Thread:** Clear mono.
Body: Twenty to twenty-five fibers of white ostrich herl surrounded by white bucktail.
Wing: Overlay the body with pearl Glimmer for accent.
Hackle: Topping: six strands of peacock herl, blue bucktail, and dyed-green grizzly saddles tied flat atop the hook.
Head: Eyes: silver prismatic stick-on eyes.
Other Materials: Clear silicone: apply from the hook eye back one and three quarters times the length of the hook shank.
Difficulty: 4.
Notes: Ostrich is 5 inches in length. Bucktail overlay is 2 ½ inches long. Glimmer is three-quarters length of the ostrich. Topping: blue is one-half length of ostrich, saddle hackles and peacock herl are 5 ½ inches long.

PINK FINK

Type: Saltwater.   Subtype: Streamer.
Item Number: 03X8-17. **Most Popular Sizes:** 6/0.
Hook Type: Gamakatsu SC15-2H.
Thread: White size A Monocord.
Tail: 2-inch loop of Berkley Sea Strand wire over which four thin white saddle hackles are placed concave sides in.
Wing: Bottom: 3-inch white bucktail over 8-inch white Ultra Hair mixed with pearl Krystal Flash, pearl Flashabou, and pearl holographic tinsel, six to eight strands each. Midwing: ten to twelve 8-inch strands of wide pearl Flashabou. Upper wing: Mixture 3-inch Pink Bucktail over 8-inch white Ultra Hair.
Hackle: Topping: eight to ten strands of peacock herl.
Head: Built up of tying thread for tapered shape. Coated with Pink Glitter EZ Sparkle Body (top) and Pearl EZ Sparkle Body (bottom). A final coat of epoxy is then added to the head for durability.
Other Materials: Eyes: Prismatic eyes, yellow with black.
Difficulty: 3.

SARDINA FLY

Type: Saltwater.   Subtype: Streamer.
Item Number: 03CP-69. **Most Popular Sizes:** 2/0, 4/0, 6/0.
Hook Type: Gamakatsu SC15.
Thread: White size A Monocord.
Wing: Bottom: white bucktail mixed with pearl Krystal Flash. Top: light blue bucktail over rainbow Krystal Flash and holographic tinsel (ten to fifteen strands).
Hackle: Topping: six to eight strands of peacock herl.
Abdomen: Sides: holographic tinsel and rainbow Krystal Flash mixed for accent.
Head: Built up of tying thread for tapered shape. Coated with Blue Glitter EZ Sparkle Body (top) and Pearl Glitter EZ Sparkle Body (bottom). A final coat of epoxy is then added to the head for durability.
Other Materials: Eyes: Prismatic eyes, yellow with black pupil.
Difficulty: 3.
Notes: Clear Glitter EX Sparkle Body can be used, though it will allow the thread wraps underneath the head to show.

SARDINA LIL' TUNNEY

Type: Saltwater.   Subtype: Streamer.
Item Number: 03CP-10. **Most Popular Sizes:** 2/0, 4/0, 6/0.
Color Options: Blue, chartreuse, white.
Hook Type: Gamakatsu SC15.
Thread: White size A Monocord.
Wing: Bottom: white Bucktail mixed with pearl Krystal Flash. Top: bright chartreuse bucktail over pearl Krystal Flash and pearl holographic tinsel (ten to fifteen strands).
Hackle: Topping: six to eight strands of peacock herl.
Abdomen: Sides: silver Flashabou for accent.
Head: Built up of tying thread for tapered shape. Coated with Chartreuse Glitter EZ Sparkle Body (top) and Pearl EZ Sparkle Body (bottom). A final coat of epoxy is then added to the head for durability.
Other Materials: Eyes: Prismatic eyes, yellow with black.
Difficulty: 3.
Notes: Clear Glitter EZ Sparkle Body can be used, though it will allow the thread wraps underneath the head to show.

SARDINA MACKEREL

Type: Saltwater.   Subtype: Streamer.
Item Number: 03CP-05. **Most Popular Sizes:** 2/0, 4/0, 6/0.
Hook Type: Gamakatsu SC15.
Thread: White size A Monocord.
Wing: Bottom: White bucktail mixed with pearl Krystal Flash. Top: Olive bucktail over rainbow Krystal Flash and holographic tinsel (ten to fifteen strands).
Hackle: Topping: six to eight strands of peacock herl.
Abdomen: Sides: holographic tinsel and rainbow Krystal Flash mixed for accent.
Head: Built up of tying thread for tapered shape. Coated with Olive Glitter EX Sparkle Body (top) and Pearl Glitter EZ Sparkle Body (bottom). A final coat of epoxy is then added to the head for durability.
Other Materials: Eyes: prismatic eyes, silver with black pupil.
Difficulty: 3.
Notes: Clear Glitter EZ Sparkle Body can be used, though it will allow the thread wraps underneath the head to show.

SNOOKZIT

Type: Saltwater.   Subtype: Streamer.
Item Number: 970B. **Most Popular Sizes:** 1/0.
Color Options: White, red/white, red/yellow, black.
Hook Type: Pre-sharpened stainless.
Thread: 3/0 to match body.
Tail: Zonker strip with pearl Krystal Flash and red Flashabou.
Body: Wool or Antron leech yarn, wrapped heavy.
Head: Eyes: glass eyes on stems.
Difficulty: 3.

SQUID FLY

Type: Saltwater.   Subtype: Streamer.
Item Number: 02J7. **Most Popular Sizes:** 1/0, 2/0.
Color Options: White, pink.
Hook Type: Pre-sharpened stainless. **Thread:** White 3/0.
Tail: Two or four long, thin saddles, splayed.
Body: Estaz or Ice Chenille.
Hackle: Collar: short, webby hen saddle, one half shank length.
Abdomen: Eyes: 5mm or 6mm prismatic or doll eyes epoxied in place.
Difficulty: 3.

SUPER CLOUSER

Type: Saltwater.   Subtype: Streamer.
Item Number: 977P. **Most Popular Sizes:** 2/0, 2, 6.
Color Options: Tan/white, brown, chartreuse/white, gray/white, chartreuse/white, olive/white.
Hook Type: Pre-sharpened stainless. **Thread:** White 3/0.
Body: Underwing: white Ultra Hair. Midwing: rainbow, pearl, or gold Krystal Flash.
Head: Eyes: Prepainted dumbbell eyes covered with epoxy.
Difficulty: 2.
Notes: This is essentially a standard Clouser Minnow tied with synthetic materials. The addition of epoxy over the head and around the dumbbell eyes makes for an extremely durable pattern.

TABORY'S AL-BONE-TUNA RABBIT

Type: Saltwater.   Subtype: Streamer.
Item Number: 11Y1. **Most Popular Sizes:** 4.
Hook Type: Pre-sharpened stainless. **Thread:** White 6/0.
Body: Pearlescent flat tinsel, double wrapped.
Wing: White rabbit-hair fibers one and a half times the length of the shank, mixed with fine Flashabou.
Head: Prismatic or stick-on eyes.
Other Materials: Five-minute epoxy.
Difficulty: 2.
Notes: Twisted Krystal Flash or a similar material can be used on the body.

TABORY'S GLITTER SQUID

Type: Saltwater. Subtype: Streamer.
Item Number: 11X3. **Most Popular Sizes:** 2/0, 2.
Color Options: Tan/pink, light gray/pink.
Hook Type: Pre-sharpened stainless.
Thread: 3/0 to match pattern color.
Tail: Pink Fluoro Fibre tied in as a vein surrounded by white
      or shrimp-colored Slinky Fibre.
Body: Clear or white Ice Chenille or Estaz.
Head: Eyes: 6mm or 10mm prismatic eyes.
Difficulty: 2.
Notes: The eyes are epoxied on the Fluoro Fibre just behind
      the body of the fly.

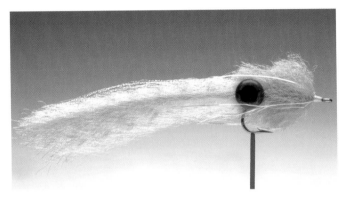

TABORY'S GLOW SQUID

Type: Saltwater. Subtype: Streamer.
Item Number: 11X2. **Most Popular Sizes:** 2/0, 2.
Color Options: Light gray/white, tan/shrimp.
Hook Type: Pre-sharpened stainless.
Thread: 3/0 to match body color.
Tail: Hot-pink Fluoro Fibre tied in as a vein surrounded by
      white or shrimp Slinky Fibre on the bottom and light
      gray or tan Slinky Fibre on top.
Body: White or shrimp Slinky Fibre spun and trimmed to shape.
Hackle: Veil: Mother of Pearl Gliss n' Glow.
Head: Eye: 8mm or 10mm prismatic eyes.
Difficulty: 3.
Notes: For the veil, tie in no more than four fibers atop the
      hook shank at the eye. Trim them to shank length.

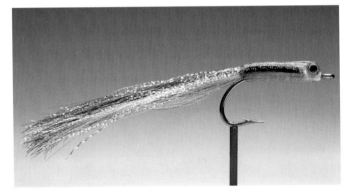

TABORY'S NOSE DOWN SAND FLY

Type: Saltwater. Subtype: Streamer.
Item Number: 11Y0. **Most Popular Sizes:** 2/0, 2.
Hook Type: 3×-long pre-sharpened stainless.
Thread: White or light tan 6/0.
Body: Thread base.
Rib: Fine gold tinsel or twisted Krystal Flash.
Wing: Lower wing: shrimp or white fine synthetic hair.
      Midwing: Blue fine synthetic hair. Topping: pearl or
      rainbow Krystal Flash.
Head: Deepwater Eyes.
Other Materials: Five-minute epoxy.
Difficulty: 3.
Notes: A variety of eyes can be used on this pattern, making
      for a variety of sink rates.

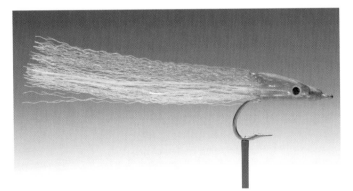

TABORY'S SAND LANCE

Type: Saltwater. Subtype: Streamer.
Item Number: 0281. **Most Popular Sizes:** 2.
Hook Type: Pre-sharpened stainless hook.
Thread: Green 3/0.
Body: Epoxy.
Wing: Olive, lavender, and white Super Hair.
Other Materials: Sides: pearl Flashabou. Eyes: painted
                  yellow with black pupils.
Difficulty: 2.

TABORY'S SEA RAT

Type: Saltwater. Subtype: Streamer.
Item Number: 0282. **Most Popular Sizes:** 2/0.
Color Options: Black, red/white, white.
Hook Type: Pre-sharpened stainless.
Thread: Black, white, or red 3/0.
Tail: Six to eight saddle hackles.
Wing: Marabou.
Hackle: Spun deer hair.
Head: White vernille.
Other Materials: Eyes: Yellow dumbbell with black pupils,
epoxied.
Difficulty: 3.
Notes: The deer hair also forms a collar.

TABORY'S SLAB FLY

Type: Saltwater. Subtype: Streamer.
Item Number: 0580. **Most Popular Sizes:** 2/0, 4/0.
Hook Type: Pre-sharpened saltwater. **Thread:** White 3/0.
Wing: Peacock herl; gray, pink, and white bucktail; pearl
Krystal Flash mixed in.
Head: White deer hair, clipped flat on sides.
Other Materials: Collar: white deer hair. Eyes: yellow
prismatic eyes glued to side of head.
Difficulty: 4.

TABORY'S SNAKE FLY

Type: Saltwater. Subtype: Streamer.
Item Number: 0583. **Most Popular Sizes:** 01.
Color Options: White, chartreuse, black, orange.
Hook Type: Pre-sharpened saltwater.
Thread: 3/0 to match pattern color.
Tail: Ostrich herl, two times shank length.
Wing: Marabou, very full.
Hackle: Collar of deer-hair head.
Head: Deer hair clipped to bullet shape.
Difficulty: 3.

THE OLIVE & BROWN

Type: Saltwater. Subtype: Streamer.
Item Number: 03CP-21. **Most Popular Sizes:** 2/0, 4/0, 6/0.
Hook Type: Gamakatsu SC15.
Thread: White size A Monocord.
Wing: Bottom: white bucktail mixed with rainbow Krystal
Flash. Top: dark olive and brown bucktail over gold
holographic tinsel and pearl Flashabou (ten to fifteen
strands).
Hackle: Topping: six to eight strands of peacock herl.
Abdomen: Sides: silver and gold holographic tinsel for accent.
Head: Built up of tying thread for tapered shape. Coated with
Olive Glitter EZ Sparkle Body (top) and Pearl EZ
Sparkle Body (bottom). A final coat of epoxy is added
to the head for durability.
Other Materials: Prismatic eyes, silver with black pupils.
Difficulty: 3.
Notes: Clear Glittzer EZ Sparkle Body can be used, but it will
let the thread warps underneath the head show.

THE SHADY LADY

Type: Saltwater. Subtype: Streamer.
Item Number: 03CP-60. **Most Popular Sizes:** 2/0, 4/0, 6/0.
Hook Type: Gamakatsu SC15.
Thread: Black size A Monocord.
Wing: Bottom: black bucktail mixed with rainbow
    holographic tinsel. Top: black bucktail over smolt-blue
    holographic tinsel (ten to fifteen strands).
Hackle: Topping: six to eight strands of peacock herl.
Abdomen: Sides: red holographic tinsel for accent.
Head: Built up of tying thread for tapered shape. Coated with
    Dark Gray Glitter EZ Sparkle Body. A final coat of
    epoxy is added to the head for durability.
Other Materials: Prismatic eyes, yellow with black pupils.
Difficulty: 3.
Notes: Clear Glittzer EZ Sparkle Body can be used, but it will
    let the thread warps underneath the head show.

THE SPRITE FLY

Type: Saltwater. Subtype: Streamer.
Item Number: 03CP-08. **Most Popular Sizes:** 2/0, 4/0, 6/0.
Hook Type: Gamakatsu SC15.
Thread: White size A Monocord.
Wing: Bottom: bright yellow/chartreuse bucktail mixed with
    pearl holographic tinsel and pearl Krystal Flash.
Hackle: Topping: four to six strands of peacock herl.
Abdomen: Sides: pearl holographic tinsel for accent.
Head: Built up of tying thread for tapered shape. Coated with
    Chartreuse Glitter EZ Sparkle Body (top) and Pearl EZ
    Sparkle Body (bottom). A final coat of epoxy is added
    to the head for durability.
Other Materials: Prismatic eyes, red with black pupils.
Difficulty: 3.
Notes: Clear Glittzer EZ Sparkle Body can be used, but it will
    let the thread warps underneath the head show.

VELVET EEL FLY

Type: Saltwater. Subtype: Streamer.
Item Number: 02J2. **Most Popular Sizes:** 1/0.
Hook Type: Pre-sharpened stainless. **Thread:** White 3/0.
Tail: Burn the end of the tubing and trim at an angle.
Body: Velvet tubing colored with Pantone pens on the back.
Head: Prepainted dumbbell eyes.
Difficulty: 1.
Notes: Thread the tubing onto the hook after the lead eyes are
    added to the hook shank.

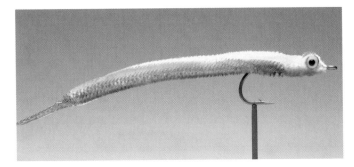

WEJEBE SPANISH FLY

Type: Saltwater. Subtype: Streamer.
Item Number: 02JY. **Most Popular Sizes:** 2/0.
Hook Type: Pre-sharpened stainless. **Thread:** White 3/0.
Tail: Six white saddles tied concave sides facing, overlaid
    with white Ultra Hair.
Wing: Bottom: pearl/white Lite Brite dubbing. Top: blue Lite
    Brite dubbing.
Legs: Accent: three to four strands of holographic tinsel on
    each side of the fly.
Head: 6mm doll eyes, epoxied.
Difficulty: 4.
Notes: This fly is tied so that the head is three quarters of the
    way back on the hook shank.

WINSLOW'S AFTERNOON DELIGHT

Type: Saltwater.　Subtype: Streamer.
Item Number: 047T. **Most Popular Sizes:** 3/0.
Color Options: Black, white. **Hook Type:** 3×-long stainless.
Thread: Black 3/0.
Tail: Six wide black or white saddle hackles.
Hackle: Red, tied as a collar.
Head: Black or white closed-cell foam, tied slider or bullet-
　　　head style, glued to the hook and taking up about
　　　three-quarters of the shank.
Difficulty: 2.

MALZONE'S BLACK DEATH

Type: Saltwater.　Subtype: Tarpon.
Item Number: 11XC. **Most Popular Sizes:** 4/0, 3/0, 2/0, 1/0.
Hook Type: Owner AK1 Cutting Point.
Thread: Black size A Monocord.
Tail: Four black saddle hackles splayed over eight to ten
　　　strands of black Flashabou.
Wing: Gray squirrel dyed red.
Head: Black size A Monocord, tapered.
Difficulty: 2.

MALZONE'S BLONDE

Type: Saltwater.　Subtype: Tarpon.
Item Number: 11XC-02.
Most Popular Sizes: 4/0, 3/0, 2/0, 1/0.
Color Options: Light Blonde, Medium Blonde.
Hook Type: Owner AK1 Cutting Point.
Thread: Light tan size A Monocord or Flat Waxed Nylon.
Tail: Four honey cree or light badger saddles tied splayed at
　　　the bend, two on each side.
Body: Bleached red squirrel.
Head: Tan thread.
Difficulty: 2.
Notes: Matching the color of this pattern can be very difficult.
　　　The originator has found basic tan also to be effective.

MALZONE'S GREENIE WEENIE

Type: Saltwater.　Subtype: Tarpon.
Item Number: 11XC. **Most Popular Sizes:** 4/0, 3/0, 2/0, 1/0.
Hook Type: Owner AK1 Cutting Point.
Thread: Fluorescent chartreuse size A Monocord or Flat
　　　Waxed Nylon.
Tail: Four fluorescent chartreuse saddle hackles, between
　　　which are two grizzly saddle hackles. Tail is tied
　　　splayed, with two chartreuse saddles and one grizzly
　　　saddle on each side.
Body: Collar: dyed-chartreuse gray or red squirrel.
Head: Built up of tying thread wrapped to a bullet shape.
Difficulty: 2.

365

MALZONE'S PURPLE DEMON
Type: Saltwater. Subtype: Tarpon.
Item Number: 11XC. **Most Popular Sizes:** 4/0, 3/0, 2/0, 1/0.
Hook Type: Owner AK1 Cutting Point.
Thread: Black size A Monocord.
Tail: Four badger saddles dyed purple, splayed over eight to
ten strands of black Flashabou.
Wing: Gray squirrel dyed black.
Head: Black size A Monocord, tapered.
Difficulty: 2.

RUOFF LAY-UP TARPON FLY
Type: Saltwater. Subtype: Tarpon.
Item Number: 0514. **Most Popular Sizes:** 1/0, 2/0.
Color Options: Yellow, chartreuse, brown, pink.
Hook Type: Pre-sharpened saltwater. **Thread:** White 3/0.
Tail: Chartreuse, yellow, pink, or tan cree saddle hackles, tied
splayed. Center tail of red Krystal Flash and synthetic
fur the color of saddles.
Body: Fuzzy Leech Yarn, color of tail.
Hackle: Saddle hackle the color of tail, wrapped just in front
of tail.
Head: Body yarn wrapped in front of black plastic eyes.
Other Materials: Weed guard: wire filament.
Difficulty: 2.

TARPON BUNNY
Type: Saltwater. Subtype: Tarpon.
Item Number: 975P. **Most Popular Sizes:** 4/0, 2/0.
Color Options: Tan, purple.
Hook Type: Pre-sharpened stainless.
Thread: Size A Monocord to match body color.
Tail: Zonker strip.
Body: Same Zonker strip as the tail, palmered to the hook eye.
Difficulty: 2.

FOAM SPIDER
Type: Warmwater. Subtype: Bluegill.
Item Number: 11TT. **Most Popular Sizes:** 10, 12.
Color Options: Black/white, green/white, yellow/white.
Hook Type: Extra-fine dry. **Thread:** 6/0 to match body.
Body: Preformed foam spider/beetle body.
Legs: Living Rubber tied splayed in an X shape.
Head: Foam from the body.
Difficulty: 1.
Notes: It is not necessary to thread the hook through the foam
body, though doing so will make for a more durable
fly with better hooking properties.

MINI POP

Type: Warmwater. Subtype: Bluegill.
Item Number: 11TK. **Most Popular Sizes:** 10.
Color Options: Chartreuse, white scale.
Hook Type: Mustad popper hook. **Thread:** White 6/0.
Tail: A combination of floss, Living Rubber, and saddle
hackles tied splayed; tail color to match body color.
Body: Preformed popper body.
Head: Painted on the preformed body.
Difficulty: 2.

GULLEY'S CRAYFISH

Type: Warmwater. Subtype: Crayfish.
Item Number: 03CL. **Most Popular Sizes:** 4, 1/0.
Color Options: Brown, olive. **Hook Type:** Bass bug.
Thread: Orange 3/0.
Tail: Claws: two Zonker strips splayed out at the bend of the
hook.
Body: Four or five brown schlappen feathers.
Hackle: Schlappen to match the body color.
Legs: Feelers: Orange Living Rubber.
Head: One or two sets of dumbbell eyes.
Other Materials: Claws: Brown rabbit strips with orange
rabbit-strip sections glued onto the tips.
Weedguard: .020 or larger mono.
Difficulty: 3.
Notes: Weedguard is best tied in as a loop from the bend of
the hook to the eye.

CHUG BUG

Type: Warmwater. Subtype: Foam.
Item Number: 0136. **Most Popular Sizes:** 2, 6, 10.
Color Options: Red/white, yellow. **Hook Type:** Bass bug.
Thread: Red 3/0.
Tail: Four white saddle hackles, splayed two per side.
Body: Yellow or red/white striped foam material cut to shape.
Hackle: Hackle fluff and hackle fibers tied just ahead of tail.
Legs: Four white rubber legs drawn through body with
sewing needle.
Difficulty: 2.
Notes: Weed guard: Doubled length of heavy mono sticks out
and down from front of fly, set just behind eye of hook;
should be long enough to loop over point of hook.
Bodies can be bought pre-cut and glued to hooks.

WIGGLE ONE
Type: Warmwater.   Subtype: Foam.
Item Number: 0319.
Most Popular Sizes: 2, 6.
Hook Type: 3×-long nymph.
Thread: Green 3/0.
Tail: Chartreuse marabou with six strands of pearl Krystal Flash.
Body: Chartreuse Ice Chenille.
Head: Glued-on glass eyes.
Other Materials: A shaped piece of foam is tied down at tail after poking hook eye through it at head.
Difficulty: 3.

DAHLBERG DIVER
Type: Warmwater.   Subtype: Hair bug.
Item Number: 0854-10. **Most Popular Sizes:** 2.
Color Options: Black, light blue/purple, yellow, white.
Hook Type: Bass bug. **Thread:** Black 3/0.
Tail: Black marabou with pearl Flashabou; black and grizzly saddle hackle along each side. Light blue marabou with peacock herl and gold Flashabou; purple grizzly and blue grizzly saddle hackle along each side. Pale yellow marabou with gold Flashabou; yellow grizzly and olive grizzly saddle hackle along each side.
Hackle: Black deer-hair collar.
Head: Black deer hair. Purple deer hair. Pale yellow deer hair.
Other Materials: 20-pound monofilament weed guard bound in at eye and bend of hook.
Difficulty: 4.
Notes: The head is trimmed to a cone shape with a large collar of blunt trimmed ends on top so the fly dives when pulled through the water.

DRY RIND FROG
Type: Warmwater.   Subtype: Hair bug.
Item Number: 0107. **Most Popular Sizes:** 2, 6.
Hook Type: Bass bug. **Thread:** Olive 3/0.
Tail: Rawhide, cut to shape and colored with magic marker.
Body: Yellow and olive spun and clipped deer hair in alternating segments. Flat on top and bottom; rounded on sides.
Other Materials: Glued-on doll eyes. White rubber legs made from three pieces knotted together are tied on before last few segments of deer hair. V-shaped monofilament weed guard.
Difficulty: 5.

MINI FROG
Type: Warmwater.   Subtype: Hair bug.
Item Number: 0312. **Most Popular Sizes:** 8.
Color Options: Green/white, green/yellow.
Hook Type: 2×-long nymph. **Thread:** Olive 3/0.
Tail: Four olive hackles, splayed two per side.
Body: Spun deer-body hair stacked green on top and white or
　　yellow on the belly.
Hackle: Olive saddle hackle.
Head: Painted eyes (optional).
Difficulty: 4.

MINI HAIR BUG BLACK & YELLOW
Type: Warmwater.   Subtype: Hair bug.
Item Number: 0318. **Most Popular Sizes:** 8.
Hook Type: 2×-long nymph. **Thread:** Yellow 3/0.
Tail: Two black and one yellow hackle per side, splayed.
　　Yellow is on the outside.
Body: Alternating bands of yellow and black deer hair, spun
　　and trimmed.
Hackle: Black saddle.
Head: Trimmed to shape; see Dahlberg Diver.
Difficulty: 2.

SWIMMING FROG
Type: Warmwater.   Subtype: Hair bug.
Item Number: 0419. **Most Popular Sizes:** 2, 6.
Color Options: White belly or yellow belly.
Hook Type: Bass bug. **Thread:** Size A Monocord or Kevlar.
Tail: Pearl Krystal Flash mixed with six saddle hackles (two
　　each grizzly, light yellow or olive-dyed grizzly, and dark
　　yellow or olive-dyed grizzly) tied splayed with lightest
　　color saddle hackle sandwiched between the grizzly and
　　dyed-grizzly saddles.
Body: Mix of white or yellow deer-body hair (belly), with
　　black, olive, green, or fluorescent yellow deer-body
　　hair (back).
Hackle: Collar: stacked deer hair of the same color as the
　　spun body.
Legs: White or mottled Living Rubber or Sili Legs.
Head: The top of the head is brown bucktail dyed yellow
　　with black bands; and the bottom of the head is white
　　bucktail dyed yellow.
Other Materials: Glass eyes glues to side of head. Weedguard
　　　　is monofilament loop.
Difficulty: 5.

WHITLOCK MOUSERAT

Type: Warmwater.   Subtype: Hair bug.
Item Number: 0889. **Most Popular Sizes:** 6.
Hook Type: Bass bug. **Thread:** Black 3/0.
Tail: Tan chamois.
Body: Natural deer hair tied so natural ends are left long on top.
Head: Deer hair trimmed into cone shape.
Other Materials: Ears: tan chamois. Eyes: black paint or marker. Whiskers: moose-mane fibers. Weed guard: 20-pound monofilament.
Difficulty: 5.

BASS POPPER

Type: Warmwater.   Subtype: Popper.
Item Number: 12A7. **Most Popular Sizes:** 1/0, 6.
Color Options: Frog, chartreuse/white, black/red.
Hook Type: Bass bug. **Thread:** White 3/0.
Tail: Grizzly saddle dyed to match head color.
Hackle: Same as tail, wrapped tight to the back of the head.
Legs: Living Rubber pulled through the head with a needle. Often epoxied in place.
Head: Preformed balsa, foam, or plastic popper head. Often painted by the manufacturer.
Other Materials: Weed guard: heavy mono tied in a loop from the bend of the hook to the eye.
Difficulty: 2.

BLUEGILL BUG

Type: Warmwater.   Subtype: Popper.
Item Number: 0759. **Most Popular Sizes:** 12.
Color Options: Yellow, black, white.
Hook Type: 2×-long nymph. **Thread:** Black or white 3/0.
Tail: Two wide saddle hackles, splayed apart.
Body: Cork popper head with painted eyes.
Hackle: Saddle hackle, same color as tail.
Difficulty: 2.
Notes: This kind of fly is easier if you buy pre-made bodies and paint and dress them yourself.

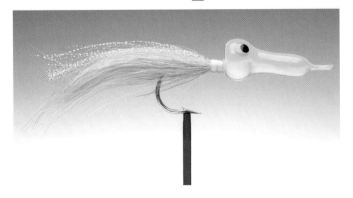

BOTTLE POPPER

Type: Warmwater.   Subtype: Popper.
Item Number: 11TL. **Most Popular Sizes:** 2/0, 2.
Color Options: Chartreuse/white, blue/white, gray/white, olive/white.
Hook Type: Kinked-shank popper hook.
Thread: White 3/0.
Tail: Bucktail clump equal to the length of the popper body.
Body: Preformed popper body.
Head: Painted on the body.
Difficulty: 2.

GATOR BUG

Type: Warmwater.   Subtype: Popper.
Item Number: 11TG. **Most Popular Sizes:** 4, 8.
Color Options: Chartreuse, green/yellow.
Hook Type: Mustad popper hook. **Thread:** White 6/0.
Tail: Floss, Living Rubber, and splayed saddle hackles; tail color to match body color.
Body: Preformed popper body.
Head: Painted on preformed body.
Difficulty: 2.

GULLEY'S CHUG A SHAD

Type: Warmwater.   Subtype: Popper.
Item Number: 03HR. **Most Popular Sizes:** 5/0.
Color Options: Red/white, chartreuse.
Hook Type: 5/0 Gamakatsu plastic-worm hook.
Thread: Red 3/0.
Tail: Long, taper-cut Zonker strip.
Body: Silver Ice Chenille or Estaz with Red Ice Chenille or Estaz.
Hackle: White schlappen.
Head: Preformed hard foam popper head.
Other Materials: Rattle chamber: pearlescent Mylar tubing with a Zorro spinnerbait rattler inserted.
Difficulty: 3.
Notes: The rattle chamber is tied onto the hook at the hook bend and is finished on both ends by thread wraps.

HARD BODY POPPER

Type: Warmwater.   Subtype: Popper.
Item Number: 934P. **Most Popular Sizes:** 4, 8.
Color Options: Black, frog, yellow, red/white.
Hook Type: Bass bug. **Thread:** 6/0 to match body color.
Tail: Krystal Flash mixed with bucktail, overlaid by four splayed saddle hackles.
Body: Preformed popper head.
Hackle: Collar: deer-hair tips.
Legs: Living Rubber or Sili Legs tied in splayed behind the body (optional).
Other Materials: Weed guard: Mason 20-pound mono.
Difficulty: 2.

HARD BODY SNEAKY SLIDER

Type: Warmwater.   Subtype: Popper.
Item Number: 935P. **Most Popular Sizes:** 4, 8.
Color Options: Black, frog, yellow, red/white.
Hook Type: Bass bug. **Thread:** 6/0 to match body color.
Tail: Krystal Flash mixed with bucktail, overlaid by four splayed saddle hackles.
Body: Preformed popper head.
Hackle: Collar: Deer-hair tips.
Legs: Living Rubber or Sili Legs tied in splayed behind the body (optional).
Other Materials: Weed guard: Mason 20-pound mono.
Difficulty: 2.

PEEPER POPPER

Type: Warmwater.   Subtype: Popper.
Item Number: 0764. **Most Popular Sizes:** 2, 4, 6, 8, 10.
Hook Type: Kinked popper hook. **Thread:** Yellow 3/0.
Tail: A pair of green and yellow hackle tips on each side.
Body: Cork sanded to shape and painted yellow on bottom
   with green dots on top.
Hackle: Green and yellow mixed.
Legs: Living Rubber drawn through cork body.
Difficulty: 2.
Notes: Rubber legs may be pulled through cork body with a
   sewing needle.

REVERSED BOTTLE POPPER

Type: Warmwater.   Subtype: Popper.
Item Number: 11TP. **Most Popular Sizes:** 2/0, 2.
Color Options: Chartreuse/white, blue/white, gray/white,
   olive/white.
Hook Type: Kinked-shank popper hook. **Thread:** White 3/0.
Tail: Bucktail clump equal to the length of the popper body.
Body: Preformed popper body.
Head: Painted on the body.
Difficulty: 2.

SNEAKY PETE

Type: Warmwater.   Subtype: Popper.
Item Number: 0762. **Most Popular Sizes:** 4, 8.
Hook Type: Bass bug. **Thread:** Black 3/0.
Tail: Fluorescent green floss and white rubber legs.
Body: Slider-type popper body painted chartreuse with black
   and white eyes.
Hackle: Black.
Difficulty: 2.
Notes: This kind of fly is easier if you buy pre-made bodies
   and paint and dress them yourself.

SOFT BODY POPPER

Type: Warmwater.   Subtype: Popper.
Item Number: 950B. **Most Popular Sizes:** 6, 1/0.
Color Options: Chartreuse, black, frog.
Hook Type: Bass bug. **Thread:** 3/0 to match body color.
Tail: White Ultra Hair mixed with Krystal Flash, overlaid
   with four grizzly saddles (two splayed on each side).
Body: Soft foam preformed popper head.
Legs: White Living Rubber.
Head: Eyes: 5mm or 6mm glue-on doll eyes.
Other Materials: Weed guard: heavy mono in either a V style
   or in a double loop from the bend of the
   hook to the hook eye.
Difficulty: 3.
Notes: The Living Rubber is pulled through the foam head
   with a needle and epoxied in place.

CONE HEAD BUNNY WORM

Type: Warmwater.   Subtype: Streamer.
Item Number: 951B. **Most Popular Sizes:** 1/0, 2.
Color Options: Black, olive, purple. **Hook Type:** Bass bug.
Thread: 3/0 to match body color.
Tail: Zonker strip.
Body: Ice Chenille, Krystal Chenille, or Estaz.
Rib: Fine copper or gold wire (optional).
Wing: More of the Zonker strip used for the tail.
Head: Black conehead.
Other Materials: Weed guard: heavy mono in either a V style
                    or in a double loop from the bend of the
                    hook to the hook eye.
Difficulty: 3.
Notes: The wire rib can be wrapped through the Zonker strip
          for durability.

CRAYFISH

Type: Warmwater.   Subtype: Streamer.
Item Number: 014K. **Most Popular Sizes:** 2/0, 2.
Color Options: Olive or rust. **Hook Type:** Bass bug.
Thread: Olive 3/0.
Tail: Olive and chartreuse bucktail, mixed, and two strands of
        brown Living Rubber tied in a V.
Body: Light brown Crystal Chenille or Estaz.
Hackle: Brown, palmered through body.
Other Materials: Flat strip of foam tied over back of fly and
        colored with permanent marker. Black plastic eyes tied
        over foam at rear of fly.
Difficulty: 3.

GULLEY'S PERCH

Type: Warmwater.   Subtype: Streamer.
Item Number: 03HP. **Most Popular Sizes:** 3/0, 1/0, 2.
Color Options: Orange, olive. **Hook Type:** Bass bug.
Thread: Red 3/0.
Tail: Zonker strip cut so that it tapers to a point.
Wing: Underwing: gold Flashabou. Overwing: Streamer Hair
        to match Zonker strip. Topping: peacock herl.
Hackle: Schlappen to match the Zonker strip.
Head: Bead-chain eyes.
Difficulty: 3.
Notes: The originator of this pattern uses a hook designed for
        bass fishing, but a standard saltwater tarpon-style
        hook is also appropriate.

GULLEY'S THREADFIN SHAD

Type: Warmwater.   Subtype: Streamer.
Item Number: 03HQ. **Most Popular Sizes:** 3/0, 1/0, 2.
Hook Type: Bass bug. **Thread:** Red 3/0.
Tail: White Zonker strip cut so that it tapers to a point.
Body: Two to four white schlappen feathers tied along the
        hook shank.
Wing: Underwing: silver Flashabou. Overwing: light blue
        Streamer Hair. Topping: peacock herl.
Hackle: White schlappen.
Head: Bead-chain eyes.
Difficulty: 3.
Notes: The originator of this pattern uses a hook designed for
        bass fishing, but a standard saltwater tarpon style -
        hook is also appropriate.

Index

Page numbers in *italics* refer to pages with illustrations.